# REASON, COMMUNITY AND RELIGIOUS TRADITION

*Reason, Community and Religious Tradition* examines key questions about the relationship of rationality to its contexts by tracing the early history of the so-called 'ontological' argument. The book follows Anselm's *Proslogion* from its origins in the private, devotional context of an eleventh-century monastery to its reception in the public and adversarial contexts of the friars' schools in the thirteenth century.

Using unpublished manuscript evidence from the Dominican and Franciscan schools at Oxford, Paris and Bologna in the thirteenth century, Matthews argues that the debate over Anselm's argument embodied the broader religious differences between the Franciscan and Dominican communities. By comparing the most famous figures of the period with their lesser-known contemporaries, Matthews argues that the Friars thought as communities and developed as traditions as they developed their arguments.

This book will interest anyone concerned with the nature of rationality, and its relationship to communities and traditions, and what this entails for rational debate across cultural divides. In particular, it offers a fresh perspective on traditional approaches to the rationality of religion and religious belief.

# ASHGATE NEW CRITICAL THINKING IN RELIGIOUS STUDIES

The *Ashgate New Critical Thinking in Religious Studies* series aims to bring high quality research monograph publishing back into focus for authors, the international library market, and student, academic and research readers. Headed by an international editorial advisory board of acclaimed scholars spanning the breadth of religious studies, this new, open-ended monograph series presents cutting-edge, international research from established as well as exciting new authors in the field. With specialist focus, yet clear contextual presentation of contemporary research, this series aims to take research into important new directions and open the field to new critical debate within the discipline, into areas of related study, and in key topics for contemporary society.

# Reason, Community and Religious Tradition

## Anselm's argument and the Friars

SCOTT MATTHEWS
*University of Stirling, UK*

Routledge
Taylor & Francis Group
LONDON AND NEW YORK

First published 2001 by Ashgate Publishing

Reissued 2018 by Routledge
2 Park Square, Milton Park, Abingdon, Oxon OX14 4RN
711 Third Avenue, New York, NY 10017, USA

*Routledge is an imprint of the Taylor & Francis Group, an informa business*



A Library of Congress record exists under LC control number: 2001016116

ISBN 13: 978-1-138-70256-1 (hbk)
ISBN 13: 978-1-315-20954-8 (ebk)

# Contents

# Preface

For Alasdair MacIntyre, the variety and heterogeneity of moral practices, beliefs and conceptual schemes, defeats any attempt by the philosopher to 'study *the* concepts of morality merely by reflecting, Oxford armchair style, on what he or she and those around him or her say and do' (*After Virtue*). We need to understand the contexts and the traditions of enquiry from which those concepts have become disconnected. Similarly, for Charles Taylor, understanding our moral predicament involves an act of historical 'retrieval' to understand the 'richer background languages in which we set the basis and point of the moral obligations we acknowledge'. The point of such an act is that it allows us to explore the 'background picture of our spiritual nature and predicament which lies behind some of the moral and spiritual intuitions of our contemporaries' (*Sources of the Self*).

It has long seemed to me that what MacIntyre, Taylor and others have been saying in the context of moral philosophy about the importance of looking at the relationship of philosophy to its history, is equally pertinent for the philosophy of religion. In religion the variety of background pictures, practices, beliefs and conceptual schemes is even more obvious than it is in contemporary morality. Yet philosophers 'of religion' concern themselves with a narrow range of abstractly-defined and culturally-specific concepts which are regularly identified as representing 'religion'. At the very least, traditional philosophy of religion has tended to preclude enquiry into the rationalities that are internal to religious traditions themselves. Moreover, implicit within the questions addressed by philosophers of religion is the assumption that philosophical issues are primarily a matter for the individual – despite the fact that neither religious life nor rational discourse normally occur outside the context of a community.

The following book attempts to do two things. In the first place, it attempts to illustrate an approach to the rationality of religion that looks at the operations of reason *within* religious traditions. It does so by focusing upon a text that has been important within philosophy of religion in the twentieth century when read as the so-called 'ontological' argument for the existence of God. There it has become an example of the attempt to justify belief in 'God' by reason, from outside of faith, on 'non-religious grounds'. That this represents an entirely anachronistic reading of a medieval text has been pointed out on innumerable occasions, and is the least of the concerns of this book. The point of the following chapters is to illustrate what happens to our ideas of 'reason' and 'rationality' as well as traditional concepts such as 'God' and 'religion' when we look at this argument within contexts very different from our own.

This book follows the journey of Anselm's argument from its origins within the private, devotional context of an eleventh-century monastery to its reception within the public and adversarial atmosphere of the universities of the thirteenth century. What Anselm's argument was being used to do, and how the argument was validated in those various contexts, are issues that can only be understood by looking at the religious assumptions, beliefs and practices of the individuals and communities involved. What is significant about looking at Anselm's argument in those contexts, however, is that it tells us something about the ways in which rationality is constructed within religious communities, and how it functions within such communities. Anselm's argument, for example, was used in the schools of the Franciscan and Dominican Friars to articulate and contest the competing assumptions embedded in their rival forms of religious life and practice. Philosophical argument served not to provide rational foundations for religious belief, but rather to open up the space within shared religious doctrines where competing assumptions could receive articulation. In sum, the philosophical arguments of the Friars represented the metaphysical counterparts to their respective ways of life.

It is critical to stress that the point of this kind of historical exercise is not merely historical. The second aim of this book, intertwined with the first, is to illustrate something about rationality itself: that it is constituted in and through the contexts in which it is used. The difficulty of defining terms like 'reason' and 'rationality' is that they are themselves the product of a discourse that is itself historical. The merest acquaintance with the role of Anselm's argument within the devotional context of Anselm's monastery already indicates that what reason is being used to do there is very different from what it is being used to do when the same argument is employed in contemporary analytic philosophy. Without reference to the context of interests, background pictures, beliefs and commitments within which an argument like Anselm's is used, it becomes impossible to understand what it means and how it is being assessed in that context. Yet the significance of this point does not end there. By comparing the uses of an argument across contexts, we get some idea of how reason can function in ways other than those prescribed by traditional academic philosophy; and in fact, we get an idea of how reason often functions in practice.

The historical retrieval enacted here suggests that reason has something more to offer religious communities than the attempt to justify belief in the generic 'god' of 'theism' on foundations that are separate from religious commitments themselves. In the thirteenth century the very survival of the Franciscan and Dominican Friars depended upon their making their specific interests rationally, and therefore, publicly accountable. The reception of Anselm's argument within the Friars' schools illustrates the ways in which they made those interests so accountable, not by seeking a rational justification separate from their commitments, relationships and beliefs, but by expressing their commitments and assumptions in rational and therefore publicly contestable ways. Reason did not replace the religious sources of their traditions; it served to make those sources available for dialogical encounter. Through such encounter, reason was constructed and so too were the Friars' religious traditions. Indeed, without the process of rational articulation and defence, the Friars would have atrophied.

The significance of this story lies precisely in what it tells us about the way reason functions. In sum, rational enquiry proceeds not through separation from our commitments, but by expressing those commitments in publicly contestable terms. In other words, what is valuable about reason for religious communities is precisely that which seems to be precluded by traditional academic philosophy. Rational accountability demands not that commitments be given rational foundations wholly external and separate from those commitments. It demands rather that such commitments be expressed in terms not only recognisable within a community defined by those commitments, but beyond that community. The history of the Franciscan and Dominican orders in the thirteenth century provides an example not only of the ways in which reason provides a language of public accountability, but also of the ways in which the survival and growth of religious traditions depend upon their utilising that language.

The claims I am making, therefore, are at once historical *and* philosophical. In making them, however, I am already conscious of the need for more argument and of some of the deficiencies of the arguments here presented. In historical terms, I particularly regret not being able to say more about Franciscan and Dominican masters toward the end of the thirteenth century, as well as about some of their secular counterparts at the University of Paris. Among the omissions, I was especially disappointed not to have been able to include a discussion of Bonaventure's mostly unpublished, immediate successors, Gilbert of Tournai, and Eustachius of Arras, as well as of certain published works of William de la Mare and Peter John Olivi. Despite such absences, the Franciscan and Dominican schools emerge with sufficient clarity from the group portraits painted here to illustrate the ways in which the Friars' arguments expressed competing religious interests. The broader case about the relationship of context and rationality, illustrated and supported by those group portraits, will, I hope, be criticised by philosophers committed to stressing the independence and autonomy of reason. It could, for example, be argued that the importance of context for arguments would have to be demonstrated in every individual case. The broader thesis to which this book points, therefore, would only ever be capable of partial justification. Despite its weaknesses, however, I hope that this book contributes to a wider debate about the relationship of philosophy and history, particularly in its significance for the philosophy of religion.

# Acknowledgements

My indebtedness to MacIntyre and Taylor is already obvious. In the course of writing this book I have incurred many others. In institutional terms, I would like to thank the British Academy for grants allowing me to consult manuscripts in Paris, Rome, Assisi and Bologna. I would also like to thank the library staff at Lancaster and at Stirling who were of particular help in acquiring rare materials for this project. I am also very grateful to St Deiniol's library in North Wales, which granted me a residential scholarship allowing me to consult a collection of Franciscan texts bequeathed by the late Franciscan scholar, J. R. H. Moorman. Finally, I would like to thank my publisher and the staff at Ashgate Publishing for bringing the book to press. In individual terms, I would like to thank Prof. David Luscombe at Sheffield for his advice and help at earlier stages of the project. Prof. John Hinnell's assistance at the early stages of the publication process was also very much appreciated. At Stirling, I would especially like to thank Dr. Matthew Elton in the Philosophy Department and Dr. Stephen Penn in the English Department for their many invaluable suggestions regarding the main text and the transcriptions in the footnotes. For their advice and encouragement during the writing process, I would also like to thank Michael Brady in Philosophy, and my colleague in Religious Studies, Clare Palmer. The list of acknowledgements would be radically incomplete, however, were it not to mention Prof. John Clayton of the Department of Religion at Boston University. To his inspiration, generosity and encouragement I owe a great deal. Most of all, however, I would like to thank Dee Mitchell for conserving my sanity while I struggled to complete the last draft!

*For*
*Eddie and Janette*

## Introduction

# Arguments, Texts and Contexts

Anselm of Bec composed the *Proslogion* as a prayer while a monk in the monastery of Bec about the year 1078. Composed for a devotional audience of monks and (mainly) female patrons of the monastery, the argument emerged over a hundred years later in the public and adversarial context of the universities at the beginning of the thirteenth century. In particular it was read by representatives of the new religious orders, the Franciscan and Dominican Friars, the best known of whom were Bonaventure (d. 1274) and Thomas Aquinas (d. 1274), exact contemporaries at the University of Paris.

Anselm's argument is more familiar to philosophers of religion as the most famous example of the so-called 'ontological argument'. In the context of their discussions about proofs for the existence of God, Bonaventure and Thomas Aquinas are considered early examples of the ways in which the ontological argument has served to divide philosophers. What philosophers of religion tend to be less familiar with, however, are the reasons for which Anselm composed the argument and what precisely was at stake in the debate over the argument at the University of Paris in the thirteenth century.

The following chapters trace the journey of the *Proslogion* from its origins in the private, devotional context of the monastery of Bec in the eleventh century to its reception in the public and adversarial atmosphere of the thirteenth-century universities. The point of doing this is not merely to point out that philosophers of religion read their assumptions into the texts of Anselm, Thomas and Bonaventure, though that they certainly do. The point is rather to explore the ways in which reason is constituted in and through the contexts in which it is used, and in particular, to promote an awareness of the ways in which reason operates *within* religious communities and traditions. In this case, it was used within Anselm's monastery for devotional ends, and in the schools of the Friars in the training of their preachers, but ultimately in giving publicly accountable expressions of their own experience of God.

### Modern and Medieval Contexts

Philosophy of religion generally claims to examine the rationality of religion, but whilst the religious traditions or the religious claims it examines may vary (though not much), rationality itself as a concept is rarely questioned. More precisely, philosophers of religion generally test religious claims according to the external or independent criteria of 'reason', and it is the very 'independent' character of reason that makes it a worthy measure of religious claims, or our beliefs and assumptions more generally. Perhaps for that reason, philosophers of religion have generally been uninterested in the attempt to understand the ways in which reason functions *within* religious contexts. It is assumed that rationality is everywhere the same, and that the issues discussed by philosophers are 'eternal questions' – a 'fact' that is supported by the persistence of philosophy's central questions throughout history. Not the least of those questions of course, is the question of the existence of God.

The view of philosophy as a 'timeless' discourse, separable from, and 'independent' of its contexts, finds general expression in philosophical anthologies and even in the writing of the history of philosophy itself. Most anthologies in the philosophy of religion assume that there is an obvious distinction between the context in which arguments are presented and the philosophical issues raised by the arguments themselves. This distinction allows for texts to be drawn together from diverse periods and places apparently without prejudice to their philosophical meaning. What anthologies tend not to do is alert their readers to the ways in which the presentation of texts carries implications for the ways in which they are read. Nor for that matter do they note that the very context of the reader shapes the reading of the text. These points are rarely explored in the history of ideas more generally, not just because of the difficulties which they imply for the writing of such history, but also because of assumptions embedded within the modern idea of philosophy itself.

What Roger Scruton announces, as a new approach to philosophical history, is in fact a classic expression of usually unwritten assumptions:

> A new style of philosophical history has emerged, which attempts to discover arguments which might be put forward and accepted, not just at the time when they were first announced, but at any time. ... It becomes necessary to translate the thought of previous philosophers from the jargon that might obscure its meaning, to remove from it all that is parochial and time-bound, and to present it in the idiom which modern people would use in the expression of their own most serious beliefs.[1]

The justification for this re-creation of the philosophical past lies in a modern image of philosophy as the disinterested pursuit of truth separable from context and from other kinds of enquiry. Reason, as Scruton's description of the history of philosophy makes clear, is only superficially tied to time and place. In Scruton's terms, and the tradition of which he is representative, Anselm, Thomas and Bonaventure have equal access to essentially the same rational conversation as everyone else. To read the history of philosophy in the way suggested by Scruton, however, is to impose a particular understanding of philosophy and reason upon that history.[2]

Perhaps ironically, the history of arguments for God's existence in general and the history of Anselm's *Proslogion* in particular help bring out the significance of context for understanding arguments and philosophical issues. Nicholas Wolterstorff for one has already drawn attention to the shift in roles played by theistic arguments between the Middle Ages and the Enlightenment.[3] According to Wolterstorff, who takes both Thomas Aquinas (13th century) and Anselm (11th century) as his medieval examples, theistic arguments had three roles in the Middle Ages under the broader project of natural theology. The first of these did not require faith, the second and third, did. The first of these was the project of attaining scientific knowledge of the cosmos: this was shared by both Christian and non-Christian communities in the Middle Ages and did not depend upon faith. The second role of theistic argument was apologetic: this involved believers persuading unbelievers of the validity of at least part of their scriptures. Finally, and most importantly, the role of theistic arguments lay within the project of 'faith seeking understanding': that is, of turning what is believed through faith into something understood through reason. In this case, theistic arguments provided a foretaste of, and a step on the road to, beatitude.

In the seventeenth century, by contrast with the medievals, after the work of John Locke, theistic arguments came to be used as a means of defending the rational dignity of the individual committed to theistic beliefs. From this time onward, the believer is faced with the 'evidentialist' challenge: that is, the challenge to show that his or her beliefs are well founded and not merely the product of passion. Wolterstorff draws our attention to the underlying assumptions:

> To follow the way of reason rather than the way of passion and impulse is to guard one's dignity as a human being and to act freely rather than being put upon. Hence the believer is obliged to meet the evidentialist challenge on pain of violating his dignity and freedom. Belief, unlike unbelief, constitutes a threat to our dignity and freedom. The threat can be met only by believing on evidence. There is a presumption in favour of atheism.[4]

It is this Enlightenment project that continues to inform modern ideas of the individual and modern ideas about the relationship between reason and religious belief:

> Scarcely anything has been more characteristic of the modern Western intellectual than the conviction that *unless one has good reasons for one's theistic beliefs, one ought to give them up.*[5]

The important point to note here, however, is that the very arguments that were at work in the medieval project of 'faith seeking understanding' were now put to work in this, quite different project:

> Some of the very proofs that the believer once used to attain his felicity [beatitude] are now used to fend off the charge that he is violating his dignity [as a rational, and free, agent].[6]

Although the texts and the arguments were the same, therefore, their meaning was quite different. Wolterstorff illustrates the ways in which the same arguments can be used for very different ends: an indication that reason cannot be understood apart from its contexts.

The following chapters broaden Wolterstorff's exploration of the role of theistic arguments in the medieval world, by focusing on the history of a particular argument from its origins in the eleventh to its reception in the thirteenth century. The point of doing this, however, is not merely to revise Wolterstorff's account of theistic argument in this period – although the following chapters do so. Rather, it is to say something about the operations of reason *within* religious contexts, and to illustrate something about the nature of rationality more generally. In this sense, the historical case presented here offers a means of opening up broader questions about the ways in which rationality is constructed in and through its operations.

To contextualise philosophy is not just a question of using contextual information to interpret arguments, however: it is also about remembering that people in other contexts do not necessarily share our cultural preconceptions. Recovering medieval preconceptions is in part a process of identifying the key modern assumptions that the medievals do not share with us.

In the case of theistic arguments, the key modern assumptions concern the very question of the existence of God. The Middle Ages was a culture for which the existence of God had not been problematised in the way that it has come to be for us. The role of theistic arguments during the seventeenth century was both a cause, and an expression, of a profound shift in consciousness. During the Enlightenment, public atheism emerged for the first time, because only then were the preconditions for the rejection of religion in place. Those pre-conditions included the emergence of the concepts 'religion' and 'the religions' to designate systems of salvation essentially in competition with each other.[7] The emergence of those concepts in the course of the seventeenth century was itself a mark of alienation from the Christian traditions that had been involved both in the so-called 'Wars of Religion' as well as in domestic political struggles of the period. It was in the context of cultural alienation from religion *per se* that the project of justifying belief in God from outside every and any religious standpoint first emerged as a concern not merely of individual thinkers, but of Northern European culture as a whole.[8]

The immediate product of cultural alienation from 'religion' was 'deism', a movement that sharply distinguished between what it considered the common core within all religions, and the historical or 'positive' traditions that had grown up around the core and were the cause of religious division. The common core of religions – and all that was good within them – could be established by reason alone, and could therefore be freely accessed by the individual as a rational agent. The common elements in all religions – common, in fact, mainly to seventeenth-century European traditions – were belief in God and the immortality of the soul.[9] It was only in the wake of this project that radical Enlightenment intellectuals took the fateful step of rejecting belief in God altogether. Even the culture of the radical Enlightenment is someway distant from our own, but it was critical in the formation of modern secularism and for the emergence of the question of 'whether God exists' in the form that we know it today.

Although not all historians accept Lucien Febvre's claim that there could be no 'atheism' in the Middle Ages, it can at least be said that atheism never formed or formed part of a philosophically-defensible public phenomenon in that period as it was to do by the eighteenth century.[10] Whatever arguments for God's existence were doing in the Middle Ages, they were being used neither to promote a religion based upon rational argument, nor to convince atheists that God exists. Whatever the role of proofs for God's existence in this period, therefore, it would be fair to say that in the religious cultures of the Middle Ages, Jewish, Islamic and Christian alike, no one required proof of the *fact* of God's existence. This was simply because belief in God was the inescapable framework for understanding human life.

It is *that* framework, therefore, that provides the perspective for any enquiry into the role and meaning of Anselm's argument among his medieval readers. The enquiry can only begin, however, after we have identified another key modern preconception, one which underpinned the emergence of both Deism and Atheism, and of which both movements represented key expressions. That preconception is the idea of reason itself as 'independent', and the source of human freedom and responsibility. The significance of this idea is explained at length in Alasdair MacIntyre's *Three Rival Versions of Moral Enquiry*.[11] In MacInytre's terms the birth of modern philosophy in the Enlightenment is characterised by its rejection of the classical and medieval vision of philosophy as a *techne*, an art or 'craft' in the service of tradition within a community.[12] In the Enlightenment, 'independent reason' became itself the source of authority and of guidance, independently of other, non-rational, sources. Whereas the significance of reason in the pre-modern world lay in its service of tradition, therefore, its significance in the modern period came to reside precisely in its rejection of, and independence from, 'irrational' tradition.

To understand reason in the pre-modern world, therefore, it is necessary to look at context not merely because rationality operates against specific cultural 'backgrounds'. It is necessary also because the very nature of philosophical discourse in this period was communal, and tradition-constituted. MacIntyre himself has devoted substantial portions of his work to tracing the role of philosophy in the service of moral communities and traditions that happen also to be religious. What MacIntyre has not done, however, is explore the role of rational enquiry within communities in terms of their specifically religious concerns, despite the importance of such concerns in pre-modern Europe.[13] The history of Anselm's argument and its reception among the Franciscan and Dominican Friars provides an opportunity for doing so.

By attempting to recover the ends for which Anselm, Bonaventure and Thomas employed reason we may come to understand the role of argument or the *techne* or 'craft' of philosophy within each of their communities. The exercise involves looking beyond isolated textual expressions of Anselm's argument to the broader projects within which it was used and then reading those citations in the light of those projects. More importantly, however, the exercise also involves looking beyond the isolated cases of Bonaventure and Thomas Aquinas, toward their lesser-known predecessors and contemporaries. In many cases, it is the very obscurity of their fellow Franciscans and Dominicans that will make them important for this study, precisely because they might be identified as what might be called 'ordinary' Franciscan and Dominican teachers. Instead of looking at Bonaventure and Thomas only in terms of their personal philosophical development, therefore, the following chapters attempt to determine how far their thinking was representative of their broader communities. For those reasons, Anselm's argument provides the connecting theme of the following story, not its solitary focus.

It is part of the contention of the following chapters that the supposedly 'time-bound' and 'parochial' concerns of religious life were the very issues that concerned Anselm, Thomas and Bonaventure along with their contemporaries even when they treated the 'timeless' issue of God's existence. Instead of providing an account of the rational foundations of religion, the Franciscans and Dominicans employed theistic arguments for the purpose of expressing the idea of God to which their communities were committed. This was because even within the context of shared Christian doctrines, different assumptions about the nature of God were already being lived out in practice. Philosophical arguments expressed the assumptions embedded in the practices of the Friars' communities and put them in a form capable of being defended and contested. It was for this reason, above all else, that Bonaventure and Thomas disagreed about the natural route to the knowledge of God. Their differences were religious, and not merely 'intellectual'. Hence, when they used reason they were not separating themselves from their commitments, background languages, doctrinal schemes and relationships. Rather, they were using reason to express the assumptions involved in those commitments.

The story about the reception of Anselm's argument should not, therefore, be taken as an illustration merely of the ways in which the *expression* of reason is influenced by contextual considerations. That, after all, is the very thing that Scruton contends when he suggests that the particularities of time and place can be stripped away, leaving pure reason behind, unencumbered. Rather, the following story should be taken as an illustration of the ways reason is constituted in and through its contexts, in the course of its operations. Without looking at the contexts of an argument, the rational issues themselves cannot be fully retrieved. What Anselm's argument was being used to do in the private, devotional context of an eleventh-century monastery, was quite different from what it was used to do in the public and adversarial context of the thirteenth-century universities. To the extent that arguments always embody historically-specific assumptions, however, the case of Anselm's argument may illustrate a point about rationality more generally.

## Previous Interpretations

In presenting an account of the reception of Anselm in the thirteenth century, the following chapters attempt to weave the philosophical threads within the fabric of the broader culture. In doing so, however, they have nonetheless drawn heavily upon the work of previous commentators on the history of Anselm's argument. To understand the argument presented here, it is helpful to look at some of those preceding accounts and the issues that were central to debate on the subject. In doing so, the next few pages outline the philosophical theses that developed over the course of the thirteenth century and that are explored over the course of the following chapters.

In the first chapter of the *Proslogion*, usually omitted by anthologists, Anselm declares that he does not seek understanding in order that he might believe, but that he believes in order that he might understand. Moreover, he declares his conviction that if he does not believe he cannot understand. In response to those words, and in reaction to the interpretation that has dominated Anselm's argument since the Enlightenment, Karl Barth argued that philosophers reversed the priority of faith and reason in treating Anselm's argument as an 'ontological proof' for God's existence. In making this case, Barth not only influenced interpretations of the argument itself, but also interpretations of Anselm's later medieval receptors and critics.

According to Barth, it is a mistake to read the *Proslogion* – which Anselm originally entitled 'Faith Seeking Understanding' – as an argument justifying belief in God from outside of faith. Instead, it should be read as its author intended, as an argument *within* faith. As far as Barth is concerned the argument did not move from a definition of God to God's existence, but rather from a name of God 'received in faith' to an understanding of what that name entailed for thought 'within faith'. The believer already believes that God exists: this is in no need of demonstration. However, the believer also believes that God is something than which no greater can be thought. How is this to be understood? *That*, for Barth, is the question addressed by the *Proslogion*. Rather than representing an 'ontological' argument, therefore, Barth argued (no less inaccurately) that the *Proslogion* represented a 'theological' argument.[14] By treating Anselm's argument as an argument from the definition to the existence of

God, said Barth, scholars as diverse as Aquinas and Kant had totally misunderstood it.[15]

Far from suggesting that Anselm's argument should be located in its religious contexts, however, Barth's interpretation tended to promote an unhelpful question: if the whole point and movement of the argument takes place within faith, can it even be considered a 'rational' argument at all? Jean Châttillon drew the conclusion that if the argument *was* used rationally, it could not longer be understood as an argument *within* faith. Châttillon argued that what distinguished Anselm from his thirteenth-century readers was precisely that. The scholastics of the latter period inserted intellectual assumptions into the argument that finally made it viable as a 'purely rational proof'. For that reason, Aquinas's rejection of Anselm's argument was not so much a rejection of the argument that Anselm composed, but of the rational proof it became in the hands of his thirteenth-century contemporaries.[16]

What were the intellectual assumptions loaded into Anselm's argument by his thirteenth-century readers? According to Châttillon, Bonaventure made Anselm's argument admissible as a proof by setting it in the context of arguments for divine illumination. According to these, broadly speaking, the mind depends for its knowledge of truth on its contact with the eternal and immutable Truth Itself. In that context the conclusion of Anselm's argument 'that God cannot be thought not to be' makes sense, for God's existence is presupposed in the very operations of the mind.

It was in the context of a broader account of the workings of the mind that Anselm's argument therefore made sense. Indeed, one earlier historian of theistic arguments in the thirteenth century had already argued that the doctrine of divine illumination was in fact the intellectual 'prerequisite' for the acceptance of Anselm's argument.[17] A more recent commentator has even gone so far as to argue that by supplying the metaphysical framework of divine illumination, Bonaventure not only completed the 'ontological' argument, but rendered it invulnerable to Aquinas's criticisms.[18] According to Châtillon, however, it was precisely because Aquinas did not accept the Augustinian doctrine of divine illumination, as taught by Bonaventure, that he could not accept Anselm's argument:

> In the idea of something than which no greater can be thought, where St Bonaventure believed he could see a reflection of the divine light, St Thomas Aquinas could see only a concept.[19]

However, another aspect of Thomas Aquinas's criticism that continued to trouble Châttillon was the rubric under which Thomas had dealt with Anselm's argument: 'Whether God's existence is self-evident (*per se notum*)?' Neither Anselm nor Bonaventure nor any thirteenth-century defender of Anselm's argument before Aquinas used the argument to defend such a view, so why did Aquinas criticise it for having done so? Again, according to Châtillon, the answer lies in the omission of 'we believe' (*credimus*) from the formula 'we believe God is that than which no greater can be conceived'. According to Châttillon, what had begun as a statement of belief became, in the work of the thirteenth-century scholastics William of Auxerre, Richard Fishacre and Bonaventure, a first principle of human understanding, an innate truth that was the reflection of the divine light. Moreover, Aquinas would have regarded the statement that God's existence was an indubitable truth and the thesis that God's existence was self-evident as two different ways of expressing an identical thesis.[20] Hence, Aquinas rejected the Anselmian argument as an argument moving from an idea to existence.

Disagreeing with Barth's 'theological' interpretation of Anslem's argument, Anton Pegis also disagreed with Châtillon's account of its reception in the thirteenth century. According to Pegis, Anselm's argument was certainly a work of 'Faith seeking understanding' – the title Anselm originally gave the *Proslogion* – but it was also and at the same time, a 'rational' quest. What was key to the argument in the first place was not its statement of faith but the rational assumptions it had always depended upon. According to Pegis, the reasons for Aquinas's rejection of Anselm's argument in the terms he did had nothing to do with the omission of the statement of faith and everything to do with his rejection of those assumptions. Pegis's objective, in the first of a series of articles on theistic arguments in the Middle Ages, was to show that neither Anselm nor Bonaventure derived the existence of God from the idea of God. Pegis therefore agreed with the conclusion of Barth and Châtillon that Thomas Aquinas's reading of Anselm's argument was a 'total misinterpretation'; but he did so for very different reasons.[21]

Pegis put forward the view that Anselm's 'concept' of 'that than which no greater can be conceived' was in fact derived from experience, and did not depend upon faith. In that case, Anselm, Bonaventure and Aquinas all agreed that the existence of God is derived from experience. For none of them, therefore, was God's existence self-evident. Where they disagreed was in how experience led to a knowledge of God.[22]

To read the *Proslogion* in isolation from his earlier meditation, the *Monologion*, according to Pegis, is a 'worse than useless exercise'.[23] For Anselm, 'that than which no greater can be conceived' derives, not from an inspection of what God is, but from looking at the nature of things in the world which ultimately lead us back to their source.[24] This is the way Anselm began seeking the supreme nature in the early chapters of the *Monologion*. In this work Anselm arrived at a knowledge of the supreme being by looking at the existence of various goods in the world. None of these can exist by themselves alone, nor do they derive their goodness from themselves. They must therefore exist and have their goodness by virtue of participation in some self-existent being that is good through itself. God is thereby presupposed in the world, and without God nothing could be:

> God is present in the community of things as the transcendent source of the perfection they have and cannot explain except by reduction to him. Given the universe of things such as they are, God is the highest thinkable reality in the sense that He is that absolute and maximum source of being without which things would not be intelligible. Anselm did not artificially make up such a maximal object of thought: the universe and its perfections required it, since it was the condition of their existence.[25]

What Anselm presented in the *Proslogion* as 'that than which no greater can be conceived' was a way of conceptualising the participational dialectic of the *Monologion* in a form that was internal to thought. It was thus a single argument, sufficient by itself, to show all that had been shown by the many arguments of the *Monologion*. 'That than which no greater can be thought' expresses in one phrase what all things presuppose.

Pegis writes that Bonaventure shared Anselm's participational outlook and partly for that reason adopted the argument of the *Proslogion*. The only difference was that it had become richer in Bonaventure's thought, partly as a response to the natural philosophy of Aristotle. Aristotle's empiricism raised new questions about epistemology that had not occurred to Anselm. While Bonaventure adapts the Aristotelian doctrine of abstraction into his account of the mind's knowledge of the natural world, it serves in Bonaventure's system to lead the mind beyond the world of sense.[26] In Bonaventure's teaching it was not just the case that nothing could be understood without reference to the maximal term, but even the very workings of the intellect itself required the presence of God. Whenever the mind has certain knowledge – that is, when it recognises the certain truth as certain – it does so in the light of the immutable divine being that is the source of truth in created things and in the created intellect.

For Bonaventure, the mind is dependent upon the senses for its knowledge of God, but in the act of knowing it knows God. Hence it does not arrive at a knowledge of God by virtue of inference from what it knows, but rather knows God in the very act of knowing itself. For as it judges it judges in the light of the eternal truth; as it defines it defines in more general terms until it arrives at the most general term of all: that which is being through itself. Thus in Bonaventure, the knowledge of God's existence begins in the senses, but as soon as the mind knows something, it knows God, for God is presupposed not just in the existence of things, but also in the workings of the mind itself. Without God the mind could not know truth, and it is for that reason that Anselm's argument caps the Bonaventurean approach to a God that 'cannot be thought not to be'.[27]

According to Pegis, Thomas Aquinas used the rubric of 'whether God's existence is self evident?' deliberately. Thomas was rejecting the participational and illuminative account presented by St Augustine, and in his own time, by St Bonaventure. He was adopting instead a thoroughly Aristotelian account of knowledge which eschewed the doctrine of ideas, and entailed the rejection of divine illumination:[28]

> From the time of St Augustine, nature, intelligence and creation had been explained by Christian thinkers in Platonic terms, and the point of that explanation was the unique presence of an absolute and immutable God within the created universe, indeed within the truth that was visible in the world of time. Participation was the Platonic cornerstone of that explanation.[29]

Thomas rejected Bonaventure's position, according to Pegis, because although he accepted that God was present to the soul, and God was the unique teacher of the human intellect, he did not locate God's uniqueness within creation or within its structure as Bonaventure did. For Aquinas, the existence of God was not proclaimed in and through the imperfections of the world, but rather in the order and self-sufficiency of nature. It was as an inference from nature that God was found by Aquinas. Aquinas's treatment of Anselm's argument was therefore a key move in his 'translation of Platonism to Aristotelianism'. In Aristotelian terms, something which underpins all knowledge is a first principle or self-evident truth. To reject the notion of God as a self-evident truth was therefore to reject Platonic participation and Augustinian illumination for Aristotelian reasons, and to state that rejection in Aristotelian terms.[30]

Pegis did not suggest that the argument of Anselm's *Proslogion* was used as an external justification for religious belief, but neither was it employed 'theologically' in the Barthian sense. Rather, it was used as a means of formulating a particular approach to God within 'a context of conflicting intellectual possibilities'. As far as Pegis was concerned, all three thinkers – Anselm, Bonaventure and Thomas – could be seen 'in their individual religious adventures', as engaged in the project of 'faith seeking understanding'.[31]

## Reasons, Contexts and Communities

The following chapters owe a great deal to Pegis's illuminating analyses. Where they differ from Pegis, is in presenting the thoughts of Anselm, Thomas and Bonaventure in the contexts of historical change, of religious interests, and above all, in the contexts of wider communities of interpretation. It is the contention of the following chapters that Bonaventure and Thomas were representative of wider communities that thought as communities, and that to think of them as the heroes of 'individual religious adventures' is to misunderstand the point of their arguments. The context of 'competing intellectual possibilities' described so well by Pegis was in fact the context of competing religious interests. What reason was doing, and how arguments were validated in this context, are matters that can only be fully appreciated by understanding the background pictures, commitments and relationships against which competing claims were measured. Moreover, the process of 'faith seeking understanding' could be a far more competitive and 'public' enterprise than scholars like Wolterstorff, Barth, Châttillon or Pegis might lead us to imagine. Besides illustrating something about the competing perspectives that lay within the heart of medieval Christianity, the following chapters attempt to reveal something about the nature and function of reason as those perspectives were contested in the universities of the thirteenth century.

## Notes

1. Roger Scruton, *A Short History of Modern Philosophy*, 2nd ed. (London, 1995), p. viii.
2. An illustration of the fact that Scruton's approach dominates the study of medieval philosophy no less than that of the modern period is provided by *The Cambridge History of Later Medieval Philosophy*, ed. by N. Kretzmann, et al. (Cambridge, 1982): 'Because the areas of concentration in contemporary philosophical scholarship on medieval thought naturally reflect the emphases in contemporary philosophy, our editorial strategy has led to a concentration on those parts of later medieval philosophy that are most readily recognisable as philosophical to a student of twentieth-century philosophy... It is one of our aims to help make the activity of contemporary philosophy intellectually continuous with medieval philosophy...' (p. 3). Notwithstanding the exceptional standards of the contributions to *The Cambridge History*, it is nonetheless a work that reflects and reinforces particular assumptions about the history of philosophy and about the content and nature of philosophical enquiry.
3. Nicholas Wolterstorff, 'The Migration of the Theistic Arguments: From Natural Theology to Evidentialist Apologetics', in R. Audi, and W. J. Wainwright, *Rationality, Religious Belief and Moral Commitment: New Essays in the Philosophy of Religion* (Cornell UP, 1986), pp. 38-81.
4. Ibid., p. 79.
5. Ibid., p. 38.
6. Ibid., p. 79.
7. On the concept of religion, see T. Asad, *Genealogies of Religion: Discipline and Reasons of Power in Christianity and Islam* (Baltimore; London, 1993), esp. pp. 40-43. On the emergence of atheism, see Michael J. Buckley, *At The Origins of Modern Atheism* (New Haven, 1987), and Alan Charles Kors, *Atheism in France, 1650-1729* (Princeton, 1990).
8. This claim parallels that made by Alasdair MacIntyre in relation to the justification of morality in the Enlightenment. See Alasdair MacIntyre, *After Virtue: a Study in Moral Theory* (London, 1981), p. 39.
9. For a brief account of the culture of European Deism and its reception in America, see J. Clayton, *Thomas Jefferson and the Study of Religion* (Lancaster, 1992).
10. Lucien Febvre, *Le Problème de L'Incroyance au XVI Siècle* (Paris, 1949), p. 6. Febvre thought that it was anachronistic to talk of 'atheism' in the Middle Ages. His

position has been contested by, among others, Jonathan Edwards, 'Religious Faith and Doubt in Late Medieval Spain: Soria c. 1450-1500', *Past and Present*, vol. 120 (1988), 3-25; and Susan Reynolds, 'Social Mentalities and the Case of Medieval Scepticism', *Transactions of the Royal Historical Society*, 6th series, vol. 1 (1991), 21-41.

11. See especially Charles Taylor, *Sources of the Self: The Making of the Modern Identity* (Harvard, 1989). See also Alasdair MacIntyre, *After Virtue*; Idem, *Whose Justice? Which Rationality?* (London, 1988); and Idem, *Three Rival Versions of Moral Inquiry: Encyclopaedia, Genealogy, and Tradition* (London, 1990).
12. MacIntyre, *Three Rival Versions*, pp. 60-66.
13. See, especially MacIntyre, *Three Rival Versions*, pp. 82-148. MacIntyre's account of pre-modern philosophy as a craft has been closely followed by C. J. F. Martin, *An Introduction to Medieval Philosophy* (Edinburgh, 1996). Following MacIntyre, Martin considers the craft of philosophy but with little reference to its operations among the Franciscans and Dominicans as religious communities.
14. For an illuminating discussion of Barth's anachronistic appropriation of Anselm to his own project, see J. P. Clayton, 'The Otherness of Anselm', in *Neue Zeitschrift Für Systematische Theologie und Religionsphilosophie*, 37 (1995), 125-143.
15. K. Barth, *Anselm: Fides Quarens Intellectum*, trans. by I. W. Robertson (Cleveland and New York, 1962; 1st pub. in 1931).
16. J. Châtillon, 'De Guillaume d'Auxerre à Saint Thomas d'Aquin: L'Argument de Saint Anselme chez les Premiers Scolastiques du xiiie Siècle', in *Spicilegium Beçcense*, vol. 1 (1959), 209-231 (p. 228).
17. P. A. Daniels, *Quellenbeiträge und Untersuchungen zur Geschicte der Gottesbeweise im Dreizehnten Jahrhundert* (Münster, 1909), p. 156: 'What was the prerequisite which led Bonaventure and his school, and Duns Scotus to accept the proof of God in his *Proslogion*? The answer seems to be: in this argument there was a perceptible use of the causality principle, not of *causalitas efficiens*, but of causalitas exemplaris.' Exemplar causality refers to the mind's apprehension of the idea of a thing in the divine light.
18. H. R. Klocker, 'Bonaventure's refinement of the ontological argument', in *Mediaevalia*, vol. 4 (1978), 209-223.
19. Châtillon, 'De Guillaume d'Auxerre...', p. 230: 'En cette idée de quelque chose dont on ne peut rien concevoir de plus grand où saint Bonaventure avait cru percevoir un reflect de la lumière divine, saint Thomas d'Aquin ne veut reconnaitre qu'un concept.'
20. Ibid., p. 228.
21. A. C. Pegis, 'St Anselm and the Argument of the *Proslogion*', in *Medieval Studies*, vol. 28 (1966), 228-267 (p. 261).
22. Pegis, 'Four medieval ways to God', in *The Monist*, vol. 54 (1970), 317-358, (p. 355): 'St Thomas Aquinas certainly agrees that the world designates God: this is why for all three God's existence can be proved. But St Thomas disagrees as to the structure of the world, the character of the designation and therefore the way to God.'
23. Ibid., p. 322.

24. Pegis, 'St Anselm...', pp. 259-260.
25. Ibid., pp. 260-261.
26. Pegis, 'Four medieval ways...', pp. 332-333.
27. A. C. Pegis, 'The Bonaventurean Way to God', in *Medieval Studies*, vol. 29 (1967), 206-242 (p. 240).
28. Pegis, 'St Anselm...', p. 265.
29. Ibid.
30. Ibid.
31. Pegis, 'Four medieval ways to God...', p. 317.

# Chapter 1

# Anselm and Tradition

That Anselm (c. 1033-1109) was living as a monk when he composed the *Proslogion* often goes unmentioned by commentators on the argument. To understand the role of argument in his monastery at Bec in Normandy in the eleventh century it is necessary to realise that 'reason', when it was considered at all in this period, was considered in terms supplied by Scripture and by the broader Christian tradition. Reason was not an autonomous instrument of the individual regarded as solely or even chiefly competent for leading the mind/soul to the apprehension of truth. Rather, if reason were to be defined at all, it would be in terms of the soul's very inadequacy for attaining a vision of truth by itself. God is Reason in the truest sense, and human beings are rational to the extent that they were created in God's image. The Fall, however, ensured that God was cut off from human vision, and that the image of God within the soul was deformed. Henceforth, human beings would have some apprehension of God through the divine self-revelation in Scripture.

Monastic life, according to the *Rule of St Benedict* was conceived as a journey of obedience that effected the return of the soul to the state that it had lost through disobedience. Integral to this process was the life of the gospel, and in particular, the reading and comprehension of God's self-revelation. Christ was the *logos*, the Word made flesh. To be Christ-like involved not so much an imitation of the life of Christ as depicted in the gospels, as an internalisation of the divine Word through meditation on Scripture. In a context where all reading was oral, meditation was truly a 'rumination' on the words of the sacred text:

> To meditate is to attach oneself closely to the sentence being recited and weigh all its words in order to sound the depths of their full meaning. It means assimilating the content of a text by means of a kind of mastication which releases its full flavour. It means, as St Augustine, St Gregory, John of Fécamp and others say… to taste it with the *palatum cordis* (palate of the heart) or in the *ore cordis* (mouth of the heart).[1]

Moreover, meditation involved memorisation. Being effected by oral repetition, memorisation was 'muscular' and 'aural' as well as visual. The sacred text, says Leclercq, was 'inscribed in the body and in the soul'.[2] In the life of the monk, the Word is made flesh once more. The monk became a living text, an embodied revelation and to that extent, a restored image of God.

## Memory, Understanding and Will

It is in the context of divine reading and the restoration of the image of God within the soul that Anselm's meditation and prayer, the *Monologion* (1077) and the *Proslogion* (1078) are to be understood. To an extent, Anselm is going beyond traditional forms of monastic meditation, where repetition and non-rational internalisation of the Scripture was as important as any rational understanding of its words. However, just as human beings are rational to the extent that they are made in the image of God, so the restoration of this image may itself be effected through an exercise of the soul through the understanding. The process of 'faith seeking understanding' is an extension of devotional meditation, for it involves the attempt to apprehend the face of God within Scripture – to regain the rational apprehension of God lost at the fall.

Anselm presented the arguments of the *Monologion* in the guise of a mind thinking from scratch about that which it had formerly no knowledge.[3] That Anselm attempted to reach the truths which 'Christians necessarily believe', by reason without the aid of authorities is sometimes read as an attempt to provide convincing proofs for belief directed to an unbeliever. The 'practical use' for which Anselm's brethren requested the work has to be seen in terms of the enclosed life of the monastic community, however, and not in terms of an anachronistic evangelical mission. Nor is it the case that Anselm was seeking to provide or to find the 'rational basis for faith' which the faith of the individual somehow depended upon or even could depend upon.[4] Rather, if Anselm was concerned with finding the 'reason of faith', it was the reason inherent in the reality apprehended by faith. The 'reason of faith', is the reason that is internal to the divine truth revealed in Scripture, to which our minds have only limited access. The point of the *Monologion* is the edification of the soul through the apprehension of the 'reason' of faith: the structure of reality itself.

The ignorance of the person seeking truth in the *Monologion* is not a device to secure the autonomy of reason. Anselm rejects categorically any suggestion that he is working independently of the sacred authorities, by invoking Augustine's *On the Trinity* as a precedent for the rational exercise he presents before us. Also, in the prologue, Anselm challenges the reader to find anything in the *Monologion* that is not already found in the works of the Fathers. Not only is his understanding of reason shaped by tradition, therefore, but his reason is validated in and through tradition. In a context where all truth is found in God, novelty, originality (even independence), are not desirable attributes of the inquirer. In such a context, it is in terms of sacred tradition – the self-revelation of God – that any statement, opinion or argument must be validated. Anything worth saying must already be found within tradition at some level. When the inquirer strays from the authority, he or she will not only be led astray, but he or she will soon cease to be properly rational. For all medieval Christians, the boundaries of the rational were provided by the teachings of the faith.

Anselm's adoption of ignorance in the *Monologion* should also be understood in the context of the humility that is the key to obedience within the *Rule of St Benedict*. The ignorance of the person thinking 'within himself' in the *Monologion* is a form of humility rather than an attempt to usurp independence. It is also, in fact, a kind of heuristic device. The point of the exercise, as in divine reading generally, lay not in the effect that it might have on an unbeliever, but rather the effect that the arguments have on the believer. Anselm's adoption of the standpoint of ignorance is a device that is analogous to the scepticism of Descartes' *Meditations*. Indeed, such devices may be an integral part of the genre. In Anselm's case, however, the ignorance is used for a project that draws the individual further within tradition, not as a kind of scepticism that would free him or her from it. Since the text involves a transformation of the understanding, however, there is a sense in which the point of the exercise of the *Monologion* only becomes apparent to someone already well-advanced along its chain of arguments.

The arguments from which the meditation begins reflect Anselm's two central, platonic assumptions about the nature of existence: participation and hierarchy. Beginning from the senses, Anselm writes, the easiest way for a mind to arrive at a knowledge of the supreme being is by consideration of those goods that it knows in the world. There must be some one good through which all other things are good. The good through itself is the supreme good, since all other things are good through it (c. 1). Anselm applies the same principles to greatness and to existence. All things that are great must be great through some other which is great through itself, and the greatest among all great things, since it is the source of all greatness (c. 2). All existing things exist through one thing that exists through itself (c. 3). Thus, all things exist by means of participation in some other.

In this participational account, the axiological and the ontological are one: the source of existence is also the source of value and esteem. That which exists through itself exists most greatly, and is the source of all great and good things. It is therefore supreme among all existing things (c. 3). Anselm consolidates this participational account of being and goodness, by reference to degrees of value between beings: a horse has more dignity than a tree, a human being more dignity than a horse. There must be an end to that hierarchy of beings and the supreme being is also that through which all other things exist and have their dignity (c. 4). This is the thing through which all others have being and existence, and from which they have being and existence (c. 5). Without this supreme nature, nothing at all would exist; and this thing exists from itself and is inferior to none. Whatever it is, it exists through itself and from itself alone (c. 6).

Hence, when the mind reflects on the source of being and goodness in things, it arrives at a being that is unique, that is the highest in the hierarchy of things, and which alone owes its existence to itself. All things are made from nothing by this supreme essence (cc. 7-9). Moreover, just as all things owe their origin to the creative presence of the supreme being, they also remain in existence through the creative presence of the supreme being (c. 13). It follows that wherever this being does not exist, nothing exists. Therefore, this being exists everywhere, in all things and through all things, transcending, encompassing and penetrating all things:

> Therefore, if these things are joined to the things we found earlier: it is the same thing that exists in all things and through all things, and from whom, through whom and in whom all things exist (c. 14).

Anselm goes on to consider what can be said about this supreme being. He argues that the supreme being (which he does not call 'God' until the final, 80th chapter), can be said to be whatever it is better to be than not to be. The supreme being must therefore be something that has no superior (c. 15). Since the supreme being is not what it is by participation it cannot be composed of attributes. When the supreme being is said to be just, it is not some property of its being that is described – since the supreme being is not composed – but the essence of the supreme being itself (c. 16). It is possible to say what that supreme being is, but not how great or what kind of thing this being is, since all of its attributes are one and the same and only designate the supreme being itself (c. 17).

This being exists always and everywhere, is eternal and omnipresent, and yet is contained in no time or place and is not subject to change (cc. 18-25). Since the supreme being exists in such a unique way, it follows that the supreme being is uniquely whatever it is. In consequence, if any word is applied to the supreme being that is also applied to other beings, it must have a very different meaning when applied to the supreme being (c. 26). Thus, even if in one sense the supreme being has been 'found' there is another, deeper sense, in which the supreme being remains hidden.

The sense of the 'otherness' of the supreme being – which is present in all things, and is yet absent from, and wholly other than, all things – permeates the remainder of the *Monologion*. When the mind later tries to understand the nature of the supreme being as a trinity, it looks to itself since the supreme being may only be approached and expressed through some likeness and cannot be understood in itself (cc. 64-65). That which most nearly approaches the supreme being is that which is greater than all other created things: the human mind or soul (*mens*). It is in trying to understand the supreme being through itself, that the mind discovers its true self as a trinity of remembering, thinking and loving. It cannot think without remembering and willing, nor can it remember without thinking and willing, nor can it will anything without remembering and thinking of that which it wills. It is in this way that the soul is an image of God as trinity: at the same time, one and three. In knowing this, the soul approaches the image of the supreme being:

> The more the rational mind tries to know itself, the more efficaciously it ascends to a knowledge of the supreme being;

> and the more that it neglects to study itself, the more it descends from its reflection (c. 66).

In finding what it is, the soul discovers its purpose in being. Remembering, thinking of, and loving the supreme nature is the purpose for which the soul was created in its image. By remembering, thinking of and loving the supreme good, the soul is renewed in its image:

> It is quite obvious that every rational thing exists in order that it might love something more or less... according as its rational discernment judges... Now it cannot love (the supreme being) unless it strives to remember and understand it. It is therefore clear that the rational creature ought to devote all its power and will to remembering and understanding and loving the supreme good, for which purpose it knows it has its very existence (c. 68).

If the human soul is made in the image of the supreme good, and that image may approach the supreme good by remembering, thinking of, and loving it, then the point of the *Monologion* becomes evident by its end, when Anselm finally calls the supreme being he has been describing 'God' (c. 80). With every detail the mind has attained, the more it has come to mirror that which it is reflecting upon. To acquire the reason of faith, is to internalise the logos, making the Word of God flesh within oneself. The *Proslogion* represents a direct continuation of this project: to renew the image of God within the soul.

In the *Proslogion* Anselm stresses the importance of 'faith seeking understanding', but again he does not refer to scriptural authorities in support of his conclusions. The idea is once again to arrive at an understanding of what is believed on faith by means of reason. Just because he uses reason to find truths that he already believes on faith does not make the *Proslogion* non-rational or merely 'theological'. It simply means that what is expected of reason is quite different for Anselm than for Descartes or, for that matter, Karl Barth. What has changed from the *Monologion* is the form in which the *Proslogion* is written (this time as a prayer rather than as a meditation), the audience for whom it is written (this time for patrons outside as well as for his brethren within the monastery), and above all, the fact that Anselm now seeks to show in one argument what, in the *Monologion*, he had shown in 'a connected chain of many arguments'.[5]

In the prologue to the *Proslogion*, Anselm noted that after he composed the *Monologion*, he began to wonder if he could 'find one single argument, needing no other proof than itself, to prove that God truly exists' (*vere esse*). As several scholars have noted, the expression 'truly exists' is significant for Anselm, because it is an expression that he uses to distinguish God's existence from the plane of ordinary existence.[6] In a sense, the argument of the *Proslogion* is an exercise in understanding how God is distinguished from ordinary existence. In the *Monologion* Anselm noted that in comparison to the supreme nature, created things do not truly exist at all, because all created things depend upon the creator for their existence (*Monologion*, c. 28). Anselm wants to find an argument that shows not merely that God exists, but that somehow shows the way God exists – by focusing on God's mode of existence, rather than that of God's creatures. Having found the thing he had been searching for, said Anselm, he decided that 'this thing' which had given him 'so much joy to discover' would, if it were written down, 'give pleasure to any who might read it' (prologue).

A central role of the monastery in the early Middle Ages was to pray for the salvation of its royal or aristocratic patrons in return for their material support and protection. Monks had been composing prayers or at least selecting psalms for the edification of the royal and aristocratic patrons of their monasteries since the ninth century. During the eleventh century, however, the practice had become more widespread, with aristocratic patrons desiring to take a more active part in securing their own salvation. Anselm is credited with developing a more personal, emotional expression of the genre when he was asked to compose prayers and meditations by aristocratic female patrons of Bec, like Adelaide, daughter of William the Conqueror.[7] The *Proslogion* is representative of Anselm's other prayers and meditations composed for this audience. It was 'private' in the sense that it was written in the form of a prayer, for personal use, and was devotional as well as contemplative. In any case, it was certainly not directed against an external adversary but rather toward the inner transformation of the believer.

The ideal of attaining salvation by personal efforts dominated late eleventh-century lay spirituality.[8] The aristocratic readers of Anselm's prayers and meditations were not subject to the discipline of the *Rule* or to the consequent 'trials and hardships' through which, St Benedict wrote, the monk 'travels to God'.[9] However, the desire for a more active spirituality led, in Anselm's prayers and meditations, to the imitation of a central feature of monastic devotion – the *compunctio cordis* or 'compunction of heart'. In the sacred season of Lent, St Benedict wrote, monks ought to 'expiate the negligence of other times' by applying themselves 'to prayer with tears, to reading, to compunction of heart, and to abstinence'.[10] The argument of the *Proslogion*, as all of Anselm's prayers composed for patrons of the monastery, functioned in the context of this form of devotion, which he may have felt particularly appropriate for women.

The *Proslogion* begins by exhorting the 'inner person' to turn aside from external cares, and to concentrate on seeking God within the heart. The emphasis of such a passage is to prompt concentration upon personal responsibility and interior motivation: an emphasis that sets the scene for the emotional opening chapter:

> Come now little man, turn aside from your little occupations, flee awhile from the tumult of your thoughts. Put away your heavy burdens, and leave aside your petty distractions. Free yourself a while in God, and rest a while in him. 'Enter the little

> room' of your mind, shut out everything except God and what you need for finding him, 'close the door', and seek him.

The inner person to which Anselm appeals in the opening chapter of the *Proslogion* is not the unique individual of modern self-identity. Rather, it is a person which 'finds' him or herself in God and in the narrative of God's self-revelation: the soul searches for God within itself so that it might find itself in God. It is God that Anselm seeks:

> Now say my whole heart, say now to God: 'It is your face I seek, Lord, it is your face I desire.'

Nonetheless, God seems to be absent. The *Proslogion* begins at the heart of the *Monologion*, with the problem of the divine ineffability, this time stated in existential rather than merely linguistic terms:

> Teach me my Lord God, teach my heart where and how to seek you, where and how to find you. Lord, if you are not here, where should I seek you in your absence? But if you are everywhere, why are you not present? But surely you dwell in 'light inaccessible' ... What can your servant do?

The quest for God, Anselm says, is the very purpose for which he was created:

> You are my God, and you are my Lord, and yet I have never seen you. You have made me and re-made me, and all the good things I have I have from you, and still I do not know you. I was made for the purpose of seeing you and I have not yet been able to do that for which I was made (c. 1).

The opening chapter continues with a long meditation on the narrative of the fall that has caused God to seem absent. The *Proslogion* thus locates the identity of its reader firmly within the Christian narrative according to St Benedict; that is, a narrative of human purpose thwarted by the Fall. It is an identity that is bound up with suffering; suffering that is the consequence of separation from God. Anselm admits that there is no way that he could rise to see God in God's self. Nonetheless, he may 'see' God if God restores the divine image within his heart:[11]

> I confess, Lord, with thanksgiving, that you have made me in your image, so that I can remember you, think of you, and love you. But that image is so worn and blotted out by faults, so darkened by the smoke of sin, that it cannot do that for which it was made, unless you renew and refashion it.

Throughout the opening chapter, Anselm's language is charged with bitter regret and sorrowful longing for reparation. What is significant about this emotion, however, is that it is inseparable from reason. The emotional intensity of *compunctio cordis* fuels the rational quest while, as we shall see, the rational quest fuels the intensity of the devotion. The dialectic of love and reason permeating the *Proslogion*, stem from its central theme: that of remembering, knowing and loving God. As it pursues these ends, the image of God is renewed. At the end of the first chapter, Anselm asks God to help him understand what he believes, for without belief, he cannot understand:

> I do not seek to understand so that I may believe, but I believe so that I may understand; and what is more, I believe that unless I do believe I shall not understand (c. 1).

In the light of the first chapter of the *Proslogion* Anselm's quest appears not to be that of proving God's existence but of looking for, finding and recognising God's very face. By coming to understand what he believes about God, Anselm hopes to catch a glimpse of God through the image that is within him:

> Now Lord, since it is you who gives understanding to faith, grant me to understand as well as you think fit, that you exist as we believe, and that you are what we believe you to be (c. 2).

The focus of the request and of the argument in chapters 2, 3 and 4 of the *Proslogion* is to understand that God is that than which no greater can be thought, and God exists in such a way that God exists 'truly'. The movement of the argument is not from doubt to faith, but from faith to understanding. However, this does not stop the prayer from being a rational quest. Anselm seeks to understand what he believes about God by means of reason – just as he had done in the *Monologion*:

> We believe that you are something than which nothing greater can be thought.

Anselm has gone from talking about a 'supreme being' in the *Monologion* to a being 'than which no greater can be conceived'. The key to understanding this expression is provided by the participational and hierarchical scheme expressed in the *Monologion*. As Anton Pegis writes, the phrase compresses the dialectic of participation and hierarchy into a form that is internal to thought.[12] 'That than which no greater can be thought' is not so much a definition of God as a definition of what all other things cannot be and which all other things presuppose by necessity. It is a way of summarising the experience of participation and hierarchy through the maximal object that is their source. All other things are good through something that is good through itself. Moreover since there are degrees of greatness and goodness among things, that through which all other things are great and good and have existence must be 'that than which no greater can be conceived'.

There are three distinct stages in the argument of chapters 2-3 of the *Proslogion*.[13] The first part (c. 2) involves the Fool who says in his heart 'there is no God'. Anselm says that when the Fool hears 'that than which nothing greater can be thought' he understands what he hears, even if he thinks that it does not exist. Yet something which exists in the understanding and in reality is greater than something which exists in the understanding alone. In other words, it is greater, since its existence depends upon God only, and not merely upon the mind of someone thinking of it. Therefore that than which no greater can be thought must exist in both reality and understanding. If it did not it would not be that than which no greater can be thought – which is absurd. Therefore, that than which no greater can be thought must exist in the understanding and in reality.

To exist in both understanding and reality, however, is to exist as other things exist. Anselm has not arrived at God – or at least, he has not yet understood the distinctive way in which God 'truly exists'.

The second stage of the argument (c. 3, 1st half) mirrors the first stage, in that it employs again the dialectic of hierarchy and participation and the comparative clause 'greater than' to distinguish God's existence. The second stage is concerned to show that this thing than which no greater can be conceived cannot even be thought not to exist. Something that cannot even be thought not to exist is greater than something that can be thought not to exist. Something that can be thought of as not existing might not exist at all, even if it does exist. The ability of the mind to imagine it as not being mirrors the dependency of such a thing upon something other than itself. Something than which no greater can be thought must, therefore, be incapable of being thought not to be, for if it could be thought not to exist it would be possible to think of something greater – which is absurd. Therefore, that than which no greater can be thought cannot even be thought not to exist. It exists 'truly' in the sense that, everything can be thought of as not existing – except that than which no greater can be conceived.

It is in the third stage of the argument (c. 3, 2nd half) that Anselm argues that something that cannot be thought not to exist is none other than God. He offers two reasons. God is a reality that the soul cannot surpass in thought and cannot judge by trying to think of something greater. The creature that could do this would think of something greater, than God; which is absurd. Moreover, the human mind can think of any created reality as not existing because every created reality is limited either in time, space or both. If anything can be thought of as not existing in some place or at some time, then it can be imagined as not existing at all. However, when the mind thinks of something that cannot be thought not to exist, it is thinking of something that does not owe its existence to anything and is not bound by time or space. This being must be God.

It is after Anselm has shown that God cannot be thought not to exist that he turns back to the Fool of the thirteenth and fifty-second psalm (of the Latin

Vulgate) who says in his heart, 'there is no god'. If faith believes God to be something that cannot be thought not to be, how can the Scriptures contradict faith? This is the hermeneutical question raised by the Fool, and it is this that Anselm tackles in the fourth chapter of the *Proslogion.* Anselm argues that there are two ways of thinking: one way is to think the words alone; the other is to think the thing signified by the words. It is possible therefore to think that 'God' does not exist if one thinks the words but not what they signify. Anyone who truly understands what God is – whether they think the words 'with none or with some extraneous significance' – cannot think that God does not exist, for God is 'that than which no greater can be conceived' (c. 4).

In the *Monologion*, Anselm had noted that while it is possible for the mind to arrive at a knowledge that the supreme being exists, and to a knowledge that the supreme being is just and good etc., it cannot know what kind of being the supreme being is. The supreme being transcends the power of human language that is necessarily derived from human experience of objects in the world. We know God from God's effects, in other words, but not as God is in God's self. Now, in the *Proslogion*, Anselm appears to be claiming a knowledge of the distinctive character of God's existence. Has he now caught a glimpse of God as God is, in the way that he deemed impossible in the *Monologion*? Gregory Schufreider, for one, has argued that he has.[14] Another look at the text, however, reveals why this interpretation is mistaken. As Anselm later explained in the ninth chapter of his reply to Gaunilo, 'inconceivable' and 'ineffable', are both conceivable, even if that to which they are applied cannot be spoken of or conceived.[15] Back in the fourth chapter of the *Proslogion*, Anselm already invokes that same distinction when he talks of anyone truly understanding what God is 'whether they think the words with none or with some extraneous significance'. That is, the words allow us to understand that God truly exists, even though we either cannot imagine at all or have only some limited image of what they tell us about God in God's self.

By the same token, it is a mistake to think of the argument of the *Proslogion* depending upon a definition of God. The phrase 'that than which no greater can be thought', derives not from a definition of God, but from the scheme of participation and hierarchy that designates God as that which all other beings cannot be but which they all presuppose. In that sense, it is apophatic: it leads us to a knowledge of God by telling us what God is not. Moreover, the very implication of the argument – 'that than which no greater can be thought cannot be thought not to exist' – is itself apophatic. It tells us not what can, but only what cannot be thought about God. It is partly for those reasons that the argument of *Proslogion*, 2-3, cannot be seen as an argument going from the definition to the existence of God.

The mechanism of the 'greater than' formula should not be seen as a mechanism for allowing the argument to go from thought to existence. Nor, however, is it a mechanism that *depends upon* faith. Rather it is a mechanism that operates within existence itself. As Pegis writes, Anselm's argument is an argument from presence to existence – for it depends upon a particular experience of reality wherein the maximal object is already implied in the mind's apprehension of different degrees of being.[16]

Anselm has not attained a vision of what God is in God's self, but what God is in thought; that is, in the image of God. Even if the argument begins in experience, it is within thought that the implication of experience is realised. Indeed, a change has taken place here; a change of some permanence. While giving thanks to God, Anselm declares that now, even if he did not want to believe that God exists, he could not help but understand it (c. 4). Hence, the image within has been reformed, even if Anselm still has not seen God's essence.

To read Anselm as having attained a direct vision of God is to misread the *Proslogion* as a whole, for the distinction between our limited conception of God and what God is in God's self permeates the whole prayer. While 'that than which no greater can be conceived' remains a vehicle for Anselm's search, it cannot carry him all the way to God's face. The knowledge that God is that than which no greater can be thought serves the numinous encounter with God precisely because it leads the mind to a greater awareness of its own inadequacy in the face of God.[17]

The remainder of the *Proslogion* further pursues the consequences of the conclusion of chapters 3-4. First of all, since God is that than which no greater can be conceived, then the rest of the doctrine of God follows, for God must be whatever it is better to be than not to be (c. 5). Hence, the *Proslogion* continues the work of renewing the image within the soul, even if this time it begins from God rather than from creatures. Chapter five begins an analysis of the divine attributes that can be derived from that principle: it is better to be percipient, omnipotent, merciful and impassible than not (c. 6). The appearance of contradiction involved in the combination of these attributes lies in the usage of our language, not in the thing to which the words apply (cc. 6-8). The same is said for the attributes of God's justice and mercy (cc. 9-11). God does not have the attributes through another, but through God's self. The attributes are therefore not other than God, but each attribute is God: God is the wisdom by which God is wise, the justice by which God is just (c. 12). Finally, that being, which is everything that it is better to be than not to be, is everywhere and eternal and eternally everywhere (c. 13).

Having found all those things about God, Anselm returns to the ambiguity with which he began and which permeates the whole prayer: 'How and why God is both seen and not seen by those who seek him?' Again, Anselm is left asking, 'why does my soul not perceive you, O Lord God, if it has found you?' (c. 14). As in the *Monologion*, the *Proslogion* communicates the sense of expressing something and yet not expressing it, seeing something and yet seeing only a likeness. Having attained the limits of its own comprehension, the soul has still not seen that for which it was made. Anselm has caught a glimpse of the vastness of this eternal and omnipresent truth which 'in one glance... sees all created things'. 'Truly', he says, 'it is more than any creature can understand' (c. 14). Yet in this very thought, the soul is carried to its highest insight yet.

> Therefore O Lord, not only are you that than which no greater can be thought, but you are something greater than is possible to be thought. For seeing that something of this kind is able to be thought: if you are not this thing, it would be possible to think something greater than you, which cannot be (c. 15).

With this, Anselm has returned to the place from which he began: 'This is the light inaccessible, which God inhabits' (c. 16). Yet it is a return, and not merely a beginning. Anselm now understands why God is both found and not found; why God both is present everywhere and always and yet dwells in light inaccessible. The same argument that causes the soul to realise that it cannot think of God as not being also causes the soul to realise that it cannot think of that which God is: for God is greater than can be thought. In the remainder of the prayer, Anselm considers the greatness of God's goodness. The more the soul understands of God the more it understands what it cannot see; and the more it knows what it cannot see, the more it desires to see.

Anselm laments that he is unable to sense God's harmony, fragrance, savour, softness and beauty although all these things belong to God in some 'ineffable way' for all things that have them have them from God (c. 17). Now when he laments his inability to see God he does so with understanding. If the soul derives joy from the goods that it does know, how much more must it seek after and love that good that encompasses and is source of all others: 'Consider then what and how great is this good that God is' (c. 24). The whole point of the prayer is that in seeking God one understands something of God's inexhaustible greatness, but to understand that is to desire more of God's greatness. In the case of God, to understand is to desire, for God is the maximal object. To understand anything of God and to remain unaffected by it is impossible. Indeed, there is a sense in which the soul at the end of the argument is more afflicted than it was at the beginning, for now it sees more clearly how far it is from God and yet how all good things come from God.

Whatever Anselm's intentions in writing and circulating the argument of the *Proslogion*, he did not quite succeed in bringing joy to all that read it. As Eadmar, his biographer, explains, after God had 'illumined' his mind to the argument during the recitation of the psalms at matins, Anselm copied it down on wax tablets and gave them to another monk for safe keeping. After finding that this first copy had been stolen, Anselm wrote the argument once more upon tablets of wax. This time they were broken and the wax scattered over the floor of the dormitory. 'With difficulty' Anselm 'pieced together the wax and recovered the writing' before having it copied upon parchment.[18] Perhaps an early, unknown reader had become jealous of Anselm; or perhaps the apparent originality of the argument offended him. However original the argument may have seemed then, as indeed it may seem now, it is important to realise that 'originality' was not what Anselm had been searching for. God had already been described in Patristic tradition as that which 'cannot be thought not to exist', and as that which 'truly exists'.[19] In the argument of the *Proslogion*, Anselm 'found' reasons embedded in the human heart and in the whole structure of reality that explained why this was so even if the Fool of the psalms had said in his heart 'there is no God'. The argument was, therefore, a 'discovery' of God in and through the Creation rather than a 'creation' in itself.

Rather than going beyond, let alone reversing, the conclusions of his earlier meditation, Anselm saw the prayer as expressing the many arguments of the *Monologion* in one single argument. The obsession with finding such an argument not only kept Anselm from eating it seems, it even distracted him from the daily recitation of the psalmody itself.[20] Anselm later recalled that having at one point despaired of ever finding the argument, he tried to put it out of his thoughts altogether. Yet the more he resisted the thought, the more it forced itself upon him until finally the argument presented itself to his mind and he 'embraced it eagerly'.[21] Anselm's motive for finding a single argument was simple: one argument is easier to remember than several. What better way to find and restore the trinity within the soul than by an argument whereby God may be understood, loved, *and* remembered? More urgently, without doing all three, how can the soul do even one?

## Anselm's Earliest Critic

Anselm's biographer and confidant, Eadmar, described the contents of the *Proslogion* but nowhere mentioned a proof for the existence of God. Instead, he talked about how the work discussed the attributes of God and how they were united in God.[22] Given that description, Anselm was either not concerned at all with proving God's existence or such an issue only arose in the course of trying to understand the nature of God's existence. None of Anselm's pupils who cited the *Proslogion* employed it to prove that God exists. Gilbert Crispin, abbot of Westminster (from 1085-1117), used the concept of 'that than which no greater can be conceived' to show in the course of his *Dialogue of a Christian With a Gentile* (c. 1093) that there cannot be more than one God. In his *Dialogue of a Christian and a Jew* (c. 1093), which is thought to reflect actual conversations, he used the same concept to present a possible Jewish objection to the incarnation![23] When one of Anselm's followers did compose an argument for God's existence in the course of a dialogue, he did so by showing the existence of a first cause and not by adapting Anselm's argument from the *Proslogion*.[24]

Even if his friends and pupils did not treat the argument of the *Proslogion* as an argument for God's existence, however, Anselm's earliest philosophical critic certainly did. Gaunilo, a monk of Marmoutier, a rival monastery in northern France, offered a reply on behalf of the Fool which rendered the argument in ways that anticipated the mistakes of later readers. Thus, Gaunilo credited Anselm with arguing from the conception of a 'being greater than everything' to the existence of such a being. In his response, Anselm said that while it is not possible to derive 'that than which no greater can be thought' from the concept of 'a being greater than everything', it is possible to derive the latter from the former.[25]

For the same reason, Anselm said that his argument could not be applied to some other kind of being, such as the lost island, suggested by Gaunilo.[26] An island cannot be that than which no greater can be conceived, since it is necessarily limited. Only something without beginning or end and which exists everywhere and at all times can be a candidate for 'that than which no greater can be conceived'. Anselm was not deriving the existence of something merely from a definition that includes existence. Rather, given hierarchic and participational presuppositions, even someone without faith would have to concede, as Anselm says to Gaunilo, that if 'that than which no greater can be thought' can be thought at all, it necessarily exists.[27]

Why this is so is shown by Anselm's response to Gaunilo's complaint that 'something than which no greater can be thought' cannot even be thought. When he thinks of this thing, Gaunilo says, he cannot conceive of anything. Anselm calls upon Gaunilo's faith as witness to the thinkability of that than which no greater can be thought. However, he also states that the mind can think of that than which nothing greater can be conceived simply by thinking of goods in the world. Something that has a beginning but no end is better than something that has both beginning and end. Better still is something that has neither beginning nor end. Similarly, something which has no beginning or end and exists everywhere at all times is better than something which has neither beginning nor end but cannot be everywhere. Is it possible to think of something greater? Or is this to form an idea of that than which no greater can be thought from things that can be thought?[28] Hence, if 'that than which no greater can be thought' is thinkable it must necessarily exist: the condition of the thought lies in the very presence of God to things as the source of their being and perfection.[29]

Anselm seemed to have intended that faith alone be sufficient to provide the argument of the *Proslogion* with the conception of God as 'that than which no greater can be conceived'. Since the argument was not being used to provide a self-sufficient proof for belief, this did not represent hopeless circularity. In any case, the same notion was implied all along by the logic of participation: it was ultimately derived from the experience of goods in the world, or at the very least, the framework within which goods are understood. The argument is indeed an argument within faith. However, it does not *depend* upon faith, in the Barthian sense. It is only an argument 'within' faith because faith already contains reality. The argument actually depends upon the acceptance of participation, not of faith. In the framework of participation, God is present within creation as that through which all things exist and have their goodness. Hence, as Pegis argues, it is more nearly an argument from presence to existence than from definition to existence: a presence that is implied by the very nature of things.[30]

It was perhaps because Anselm appended Gaunilo's reply on behalf of the Fool and his own response to Gaunilo that future readers of the prayer were to concentrate on chapters two and three in isolation from the rest of the prayer.[31] This perhaps also explains the tendency of some scholars to read the *Proslogion* in the light of Anselm's later works, such as the *Cur Deus Homo* (1097-1098) composed after he had left the monastery and had become archbishop of Canterbury in 1093.[32] Similarly, Anselm's own editorial decision to divide the *Proslogion* into separate chapters with their own headings also had a profound influence on the way in which the argument has been read.[33] Nonetheless, during the twelfth century, Anselm's *Proslogion* continued to be read within devotional contexts, while the twelfth-century schools that preceded the universities took more interest in works like the *Cur Deus Homo*.[34] As far as the transition between the eleventh and thirteenth centuries was concerned, the most decisive fact was that Anselm's thirteenth-century readers belonged to a quite different milieu from that of the aristocratic female patrons who formed the original audience for his prayers and meditations. The new readers of the *Proslogion* belonged to an academic institution that was fundamentally public and adversarial in nature rather than private and devotional.

## The Twelfth Century

The century that separated Anselm and the Friars can be said to have experienced in different ways, but to a comparable degree, the social, economic, technical, political and religious developments which sociologists are inclined to identify as quintessentially 'modern'.[35] One aspect of that period was the massive proliferation of popular religious groups, often following charismatic, wandering preachers. While such groups may be taken to represent dissent from the religious establishment, and a reaction to adverse social conditions, it is important to see that new religious movements were also the expressions of the quest for new forms of community, and new models of the self.[36] As Norman Cohn has pointed out, the attraction of wandering preachers lay principally with newly emerging urban groups of craftsmen, merchants and factory workers, or the peasants who had fled to the cities in search of a living:

> Typically, [persons] of this kind tend to flourish not amongst the poor and oppressed as such, but amongst the poor and oppressed whose traditional way of life has broken down and who have lost faith in their traditional values. Now, during the Middle Ages certain areas of western Europe experienced just such crises of mass disorientation. This was particularly the case from the end of the eleventh century onwards.[37]

In this context, new religious movements expressed a desire to secure a social and religious niche where traditional models for life and security had ceased to be empowering. The apostolic life not only presented a model of practical life in which followers of Christ lived by the labour of their own hands, but it was the model of the earliest and therefore most authentic Christians. It is not surprising, therefore, that the most powerful moral source by which new urban groups might authenticate their own identity was by imitation of the earliest Christian narratives. The model of the self-supporting itinerant apostle appealed to the new migrant population of urban labourers and professionals.[38] By the same token, the popular religious movements of the twelfth century represented a rejection of the enclosed life sponsored by Anselm's aristocratic patrons.

The emergence of new religious movements during the period, such as Waldensians, and more controversially, Cathars, provides one side of the coin for understanding the context of medieval scholasticism. The other side of that coin was the need for governments who defined their authority in traditional religious terms to respond to the threat of religious pluralism that such groups presented.[39] Schools emerged in northern France to provide twelfth-century rulers (secular and ecclesiastical alike) with the literary tools for centralising government by means of classifying persons.[40] Theology became a part of this process because the prerequisite for membership in Christian society was Christian belief. Theology provided a technology of control by providing a means to detect and to classify deviants.[41] By defining the authentic truth of the Church, the schools simultaneously defined deviancy, and the means of detecting it.

The growth of scholastic method in the twelfth century reflects the professionalisation of theology and the creation of mechanisms for monitoring new religious groups.[42] The background of the scholastic method is provided by the proliferation of freelance teachers in and around the Cathedral schools of Paris, Rheims and Laon – whom Helen Waddell called 'wandering scholars'.[43] They were able to sell instruction to students ambitious for careers in ecclesiastical and secular government – a development which reflects not only the economic changes of the time, but also a revolution in government which involved a more intensive use of written records.[44]

Scholastic method involved the technique of the 'quaestio' designed to identify and reconcile contradictions in the authorities of the Christian faith. The educational methods of the twelfth-century schools therefore encouraged a very different attitude to the text from that cultivated in Anselm's monastery. The 'quaestio' encouraged the fragmentation of the texts of tradition by identifying individual statements (isolated from the original works to which they belonged), which appeared to contradict one another in the context of expressing key Christian doctrines, such as the Trinity or the nature of the sacraments.[45] In this respect, the anthologising of texts and arguments was as much a hallmark of the medieval as it is of the modern academy.[46]

The practical expression of the 'quaestio' in the classroom involved students taking part in 'disputations'. In the course of disputing questions it was incumbent upon the student to resolve arguments not only by stating arguments in favour of a preferred position, but also to respond to each and every objection, from reason and from authority, brought against it. At least part of the reason for this was that objections were derived from within the tradition itself. If tradition was to be consolidated, such objections could not merely be rejected, or ignored: they would also need to be conserved in ways that could be harmonised with the position defended. Such methods of enquiry arose in a society where objections to the teaching of the Church could be derived from within the tradition itself.

In time, each question had a number of standard objections and responses, the best of which would be presented in books of 'sentences' or 'opinions' circulating from the cathedral schools in Northern France. Scholastic education involved the memorisation of such standard arguments, and the acquisition of an expertise in discussing the sources of Christian society. In acquiring that expertise, students were acquiring the skills required for preaching within Christian society.

Although the enterprise of the wandering scholars therefore reflects the development of a commercial economy as well as the emergence of a more pluralistic society, the demand for teachers also reflected changes in the nature of power and authority. The authorities themselves did not allow the development of professional education to go unregulated: by the middle of the twelfth century teachers of theology had to be licensed by the local bishop. The foundation of the University of Paris in the first third of the thirteenth century was the outcome of local politics but also, and above all, the outcome of papal policy to ensure that Paris was preserved as a centre for theological studies.[47] Admission to the Faculty of Theology was strictly regulated, with students first being required to graduate in the Faculty of Arts, whose curriculum was based upon the seven liberal arts that St Augustine had taught were necessary for the study of Scripture. Only after incepting as a Master in Arts and teaching there for two years, were students admitted to the long and arduous training of the Faculty of Theology.[48] The supremacy and monopoly of Theology within the curriculum of the University of Paris reflected the aspirations of ecclesiastical power within society more generally: in this context, society had come to depend as much upon theological as upon legal principle. The theology of the schools was itself judicial rather than contemplative, and it was professional rather than aristocratic.

The aims of the theological profession are already illustrated by the most important and famous work of twelfth-century scholasticism, the *Four Books of Sentences* composed at Paris in the late 1140s by Peter Lombard (c. 1100-1160).[49] This contains a systematic account of Christian doctrine from the doctrine of the Trinity to the sacraments of the Church. Its breadth is matched also by its detail, where broad doctrines are broken down into separate *quaestiones* whereby points of ambiguity could be debated in the interests of tradition. In the prologue to the work the author explains the task that presupposed his enquiries: to promote the truth of a Church endangered by heresy and superstition.[50] What such a statement obscures, however, is the extent to which the discourse of orthodoxy did not simply arise from the awareness of religious pluralism, but was itself necessary for the creation of deviancy in the first place and for legitimising its suppression.

Anselm's meditative and devotional texts were not likely to fare well in this atmosphere. The audience of such texts was not made up of female, aristocratic patrons seeking spiritual edification, but of students who paid teachers in return for skills that could serve public careers. The grand harmony between reason and authority that had inspired Anselm was displaced by a concern over discrepancies within tradition itself. Reason was here used not for personal edification, but for deciding between rival teachings and rival interpretations of doctrine. Academic theology was concerned to provide precise formulations of such doctrines as the Trinity, the incarnation and the virgin birth, as well as the nature of the sacraments.

By the beginning of the thirteenth century, however, scholastic texts mark a renewed interest not just in the details of Christian authorities, but also in the broader relationship between authority (what might be called 'supernatural reason') and natural reason. The circumstances that led to this did not mark a resuscitation of Anselm's project, however, even if it did mark a new interest in the *Proslogion.* The circumstances that fuelled the interest in the relationship of reason and faith, revealed and natural routes to truth, was the encounter with a new intellectual challenge, this time one that originated from outside Christendom. That challenge was provided by Aristotelian natural philosophy.

Historians of thirteenth-century philosophy place their subject within an intellectual context that is informed not just by Aristotle, but also by his Jewish and Muslim commentators. In particular, when the Latins confronted Aristotle's works they often did so alongside the commentaries of the Spanish Muslim Averroës of Cordoba (1126-1198) who became known among the Latins simply as 'the Commentator' (just as Aristotle was known as 'the Philosopher'). By the middle of the thirteenth century, Christian scholars were also reading *The Guide for the Perplexed* composed by Averroës' Jewish compatriot and contemporary, Maimonides of Cordoba (1135-1204). These writers were interesting to Christians not least because they had already dealt with the Aristotelian challenge to monotheism from within the contexts of their own communities.

However, as Alasdair MacIntyre notes, Christians faced even greater difficulties than their Jewish and Muslim counterparts, in attempting to integrate Aristotelian thought.[51] As well as the problems of consistency between philosophical truths and prophetic narrative which had already engaged Averroës and Maimonides, they confronted problems arising from the fact that the dogmatic theology of Latin Christianity was already pervasively informed by philosophical theories and conclusions deriving from St Augustine.[52] The relationship of Christian and Aristotelian truths, therefore, was in part a relationship of one philosophical perspective to another. In particular, it was a question of a religious dogma deeply informed by a Platonism to which Aristotle offered important objections.

The question arises, of course, why Christians would have been so concerned to integrate Aristotle within Christian learning if the difficulties of doing so were so great? Why not, after all, simply declare Aristotle's teaching heretical and ban him from the schools? To a degree, this is precisely what the ecclesiastical authorities in Paris did. Throughout the thirteenth century, the Aristotelian 'books of nature', and their Arab commentators, were the subject of papal and episcopal prohibitions, in 1215 and 1231 in particular, culminating in 1277 with the condemnation of 219 theses allegedly taught in Paris.[53] Nonetheless, although earlier prohibitions had never been revoked, the works that 'the Latins had recently received from the Arabs', were being read privately and, by the 1240s, taught openly.[54] That bans upon Aristotle were partial, and that they were often ignored in any case, is a mark of the fact that Aristotle was a subject of intense interest during the period as well as of intense suspicion. The reasons for this interest were partly to do with the very philosophical presuppositions of Augustinian Christianity that had made engagement with Aristotle so difficult in the first place.

Central to the Augustinian tradition was the claim that the vindication of the universal and absolute truth of Christianity was its ability to integrate and correct all other forms of knowledge potential and actual within its depiction of reality. Given that the Scriptures are themselves the revelation of Truth, from the source of all truth, it is clear why it might be claimed that Christian teaching was, in principle, never in conflict with reason (even if reason could not comprehend what God had revealed). That claim was implicit within Anselm's 'faith seeking understanding' in the eleventh century, in the encyclopaedic projects of the twelfth-century school of St Victor in Paris, and once again in the very curriculum of the University of Paris itself in the thirteenth century. To a degree then, the integration of Aristotle was essential to the maintenance of a Christian idea of truth – one that claimed that all available forms of knowledge were properly attained only through faith. Like the authorities of the tradition, therefore, the claims of reason also needed to be conserved within the course of the dialectical *quaestio*. The integrity of the tradition required that conflicts of reason and faith be explained in ways that conserved both. Despite the problems of engaging with Aristotle, therefore, his exclusion from the curriculum would only serve to invalidate the Christian tradition by its own standards. In a sense, therefore, Christian scholars were bound to take the Aristotelian corpus seriously to the extent that they were Christians.

There was another reason, however, why Christian scholars could not simply ignore or ban Aristotle outright. That this reason generally goes unnoticed by scholars, even those as perceptive as MacIntyre himself, is due perhaps to the fact that it only becomes apparent when we understand the broader religious context of the period. Scholars note the importance of Islamic and Jewish thinkers to Christians because they had read Aristotle. Yet Aristotle was important to Christendom precisely because he had been read by Jews and Muslims, and Jews and Muslims had already absorbed the challenges which he presented to their communities. Hence Aristotle's challenge to Christian teachings was worth engaging in not so much because he represented a living threat, but because by engaging with Aristotle Christians were entering upon a discourse which Jews and Muslims were already conducting. The vindication of Christian claims *vis-à-vis* Aristotle was necessary for the defence of its claims against its chief rivals within monotheism. In the context of the Crusades and the expansion of medieval Europe, the Christian response to Aristotle had to be acceptable not just within the Christian community, but also beyond it.

It is in the light of this explanation that the timing of Aristotle's entry into the schools of Western Christendom becomes more understandable. Though the first wave of Aristotelian translations was completed during the twelfth century in Sicily and Spain – lands re-conquered from Muslims and containing a significant Arab population – they succeeded in making only a slight impact upon Christian schools. It was not until the middle of the thirteenth century that the Aristotelian corpus and its commentaries were brought to the centre of academic debate.[55] The persons responsible belonged to the Orders of the Dominican and Franciscan Friars.

The Franciscans and Dominicans were in a sense reflective of the popular religious currents of the period in that they were imitators of the apostles, dedicated to the life of wandering preaching among urban communities. However, in contrast with other such groups, both were endorsed and promoted by papal authority, and had been led to embrace the methods of the schools. Directly subject to the papacy in Rome, the Friars were integral to the revolution in ecclesiastical government in which the papacy sought to supervise the faith of Christendom, and extend its government throughout the known world.[56] Within Christendom they represented one of the specialised agencies for the enforcement of order, which, R. I. Moore has written, always appear when 'rulers begin to assert themselves, and to create a recognisable apparatus of state'.[57] Toward Jews and toward Muslims and other 'unbelievers', this involved the systematic application of scholastic methods in the pursuit of conversion as well as repression.[58]

Once again, the Aristotelian corpus was valuable to the Friars precisely because it had already been absorbed by the Muslim and Jewish communities. Aristotle in particular and philosophical argumentation in general, provided the possibility for a discourse that was capable of crossing cultural and religious boundaries. Moreover, in writers like Averroës and Maimonides the Friars had access to philosophical arguments that were at least already recognised, if not always accepted, within the very communities with which the Friars wanted to engage. If the *Sentence* tradition had been formulated to affirm the integrity and universality of Christian truth within Christendom, the philosophical developments of the thirteenth century were in part a response to the need to fulfil that agenda beyond the Christian frontiers.

The motive for serious engagement with Aristotle was therefore internal to Christian identity, but also a part of the broader religious and political agenda of Christendom *vis-à-vis* its neighbours. The absorption of Aristotle was very much a piecemeal process, not least because the Friars themselves adopted at first the very conservatism toward Aristotle already displayed by the ecclesiastical authorities.[59] It was in the context of that process that interest in Anselm's *Proslogion* was revived: a context very different from that for which it had been originally formulated. Why was Anselm's argument useful in that context?

## From the Monastery to the Schools

The Franciscan Alexander of Hales (c. 1170-1245) is usually credited with fostering a revival of interest in the works of Anselm, and in the *Proslogion* in particular.[60] It is now clear, however, that an interest in Anselm's *Proslogion* was in evidence before the end of the twelfth century. After the work of Gilbert Crispin, the earliest explicit citation of Anselm's argument in a scholastic text is found in the *Speculum Speculationum* of Alexander Nequam (d. 1217). This work summarised the notes of lectures that he had heard in Paris and Oxford by 1201, and illustrates the anthologising approach to texts and arguments of the medieval school.[61] Nequam's sophisticated summary of Anselm's argument – 'Whoever understands God rightly, understands that God exists' – may well reflect an older tradition.[62] In any case, when the Franciscans adapted Anselm's argument to their own purposes they were not the first to make use of it in the scholastic context.

Nequam's discussion of Anselm's argument comes in the context of a discussion about the character of divinity, and in particular after a discussion of divinity as 'the light that illumines everyone coming to the world'.[63] Nonetheless, he argues, it is a light that lies beyond human comprehension: it is *incircumscriptibilis.*[64]

What is interesting about Nequam's use of Anselm's argument, is that he is obviously adapting it for public and adversarial ends. Nequam refers to the foolishness of the Jews, who deny that the incarnated Christ may be God (a reference perhaps to Gilbert Crispin's *Disputation of a Jew*?). He then connects Anselm's argument to the mind's apprehension of truth: if it is true that God does not exist then there must be truth, which is God.[65] Nequam then goes on to draw out other attributes from the nature of God: since God cannot be thought as other than eternal, God cannot be thought not to exist.[66] The materialist theology of Epicurus is cited as an example of an account of God that must be less than that than which no greater can be thought.[67] Anyone who thinks that God does not punish the wicked is thinking of something that is less than God, and is a figment of their imagination. They do this because they want to believe that they can sin with impunity, yet what they think is literally absurd.[68] The soul that denies that God exists denies to itself the existence of that of which it is the image.[69]

Thus, in the work of an Augustinian canon, the *Proslogion* is half way from its origins in the private, devotional context of the monastery of Bec to its place in the public and adversarial environment of the thirteenth-century universities. Most of what is said here will be repeated by various proponents of

Anselm's argument during the thirteenth century, although in many cases, Anselm's argument will take on a more central role than it does here. The argument is now being used to defend a Christian account of God against accounts of God that originate from outwith Christendom. Such rational accounts suggest that God is not interested in punishing wrong-doers, or that God is a body rather than an incorporeal substance. There is also the hint in Alexander Nequam that the light of God in the soul is connected with the soul's knowledge of God found in thought itself.

The most profound challenge to the Christian doctrine of God was of course provided by Aristotle, and it is the Parisian master, William of Auxerre (d. 1231), who represents the first clear citation of Anselm's argument in the context of that concern. William was appointed by Pope Gregory IX in 1231 to head a commission to expunge the Aristotelian texts of error to make them fit for use at Paris; a commission that was cut short by William's death.[70] In the *Summa Aurea* or *Golden Summa* that he composed at Paris in the 1220s, he made faith the key to knowledge in an account that pitted an Augustinian account of reason directly against an Aristotelian one:

> It is well said by a certain master (Simon of Tournai) that in Aristotle, proof is reason producing belief in a matter doubted, but in Christ proof is belief producing reason.[71]

William argued that faith is responsible for purifying the mind and enabling it to turn from those things closest to the senses to those closest to God.[72] Such an account of knowledge, however, presupposes a particular account of the relationship between God and the rational creature. The use of Anselm's argument in the *Summa Aurea* helps provide that account.[73]

In Aristotle's universe, God puts the world into motion but is not the source of its existence. In that sense, Aristotle provides for the twelfth and thirteenth centuries the closest equivalent of the atheism of the modern period. He provides an account of the universe which depicts the world as eternal, rather than as created in time and as moved by one among several first movers which has no knowledge of that which it moves; an account that also rules out the separate immaterial existence of the individual soul. The first mover does not know, and therefore cannot love the world, and nor can the first mover care for the reward or punishment of human beings – who evidently do not survive death as individual souls. The questions of the eternity and mutability of the world, the nature of the human soul, and the significance of Christian faith for natural understanding were to become the pivotal questions of debate raised by Aristotle's thought in the thirteenth century. The whole contrast between Christian and Aristotelian accounts of the universe ultimately devolved upon a cluster of issues relating to the nature of God and to the nature of the human soul made in God's image: concerns which Christians shared with the other monotheistic communities.

It is, in part, against the kind of 'unbelief' represented by Aristotle that Anselm's argument is used in the *Golden Summa*, and in later works of the thirteenth century. William uses Anselm's argument to emphasise how God underlies all existence and is intimately related to all existing things, because God is being itself:

> From the aforesaid, it is clear that the highest good is such a good that it is not able to be thought not to be for three reasons. In the first place, by that which I call the highest I understand that which truly exists (*vere esse*). And so whoever would think that the highest does not exist thinks what is not possible. In the second place, that which is the highest good, from necessity, is the highest; but greater is that which is separable from being neither in reason nor in actuality; therefore being is not separable from the highest good, either in thought, understanding or in actuality; and so the highest good is being itself. For that reason just as the understanding is not able to be separated from itself, so neither in understanding is it able to be separated from that which is being itself. And so the highest good, or God, is not able to be thought not to exist.[74]

There is a sense in which Anselm's argument is being used here in a debate about the rationality of belief in God – but not in the sense that belief required rational foundations. Rather, it is more a question of the kind of God and the kind of rationality that such a monotheism entails. The God of Anselm's argument – at least as it is rendered here – is irreducible to the distant final cause of the Aristotelian system. Anselm's argument designates God as a unique being, as being itself, and as that which cannot be thought not to be. On the other hand, in contrast with Aristotle, William argues that the knowledge of God is found within the soul: the soul cannot separate itself from being anymore than it can be separate from itself.[75] The natural knowledge of God, therefore, already anticipates an account of the soul, and of the relationship of God to the world.

The reception of Aristotle's work forced medieval thinkers to reflect on the nature of philosophy and its relationship with revealed knowledge. In this context, clarifying the nature of the first principles of knowledge and how these are known to the soul became critical to defining the relationship between Christianity and the Aristotelian philosophy.[76] In William's account, God is the first principle of knowledge, through reason *and* faith. The argument was thus used in the context of affirming the mind's inadequacy by itself; its dependence upon faith rather than upon mere sense experience alone for its knowledge of being and truth. It was an account designed to affirm the primacy of theology in matters of learning, and the necessity of faith in the pursuit of understanding. In a sense, Anselm's argument is used here to defend a 'descending' account of knowledge, rather than an account which 'ascends' by way of a knowledge derived from the senses.

Not everyone shared William of Auxerre's approach to reason, to the knowledge of the senses, or to natural explanation, however. During the twelfth century, Abelard emphasised the importance of distinguishing between faith and reason, while scholars of the so-called 'school of Chartres', pursued naturalistic explanations which were independent of faith and which emphasised the importance of evidence derived from the senses. They represented a tradition of enquiry which, in some ways, anticipated the very approach to nature supplied by Aristotle, as a self-contained and self-sufficient organism, to be understood in its own terms.[77] By contrast, scholars of the school of St Victor in Paris, such as Hugh of St Victor (c. 1096-1141), and his pupil Richard of St Victor (d. 1173), followed Anselm's emphasis upon faith as a prerequisite for understanding, and the existence of 'necessary reasons' in the nature of things. There were therefore already competing accounts of the relationship of reason and faith and of the dependency of creation upon God before the thirteenth century. The attitude of the *Golden Summa*, therefore, was by no means the only option available to Christian scholars, and perhaps just as important, it was not the only attitude available to non-Christian Aristotelians.

The key figures in the creation of the Franciscan and Dominican schools – Alexander of Hales and Hugh of St Cher – both sat at the feet of William of Auxerre when he taught in Paris.[78] William appears to have been admired equally by Franciscan and Dominican alike, but not to have influenced them in the same way. It is important to realise that, throughout the period, the Friars were as concerned with institutional as with intellectual challenges. Living at a time when claims to religious authenticity were hotly contested, they were often to be treated with jealousy and suspicion by the secular clergy. Both orders claimed to recover the authentic Christian vision by imitating the apostles' communal living and public preaching. When they were accorded papal privileges immunising them from episcopal intervention, the orders had to defend their vision of the authentic Christian life against increasingly intense and sophisticated criticism.[79] It was partly because of these intellectual and institutional challenges that the disputational methods of the schools were to play a large part in the history of the orders. It was partly because their spiritual outlooks and institutional histories differed significantly, however, that their intellectual responses to the challenges they faced were also different.

## Conclusion: From Private Prayer to Public Discourse

In the late eleventh century, Anselm composed the *Proslogion* for the edification of his aristocratic patrons and brethren in the private, devotional context of the monastery of Bec. In its original formulation the argument formed an integral part of a prayer in which reason and emotion worked together. Comprising twenty-six chapters and composed in the context of the Rule of St Benedict, the argument contributed to the renewal of the image within the soul through the supplicant's compunction of heart. By the first third of the thirteenth century, Anselm's *Proslogion* was subject to a very different kind of reading by a very different kind of audience. With its 2nd and 3rd chapters separated from the work as a whole and anthologised alongside other arguments within the public and adversarial context of the schools, it was employed to show the existence of God in a context of conflicting intellectual possibilities. The rival possibilities, however, did not include atheism. What they did comprise, were different ways of understanding God's relationship to the world. The issue was raised in part by the discovery of Aristotle in the context of Christendom's relations with its monotheistic rivals. Anselm's argument came to be employed as a way of conceiving God and God's relationship to nature and to human understanding. As we shall see in the next chapter, the Franciscans had particular religious reasons for conceiving these issues in ways that made them receptive to Anselm's argument, and for developing the route to God already suggested by William of Auxerre.

## Notes

1. J. Leclercq, *The Love of Learning and the Desire for God* (Fordham, 1961), p. 78.
2. Ibid.
3. Anselm, *Monologion*, 1, in Anselm, *Opera Omnia*, ed. by F. S. Schmitt, 6 vols (Stuttgart, 1968), I, 7-87. Henceforth, citations from the *Monologion* will be noted in the main text as e.g. (c. 1) for *Monologion*, chapter 1.
4. In the prologue to the *Proslogion*, Anselm explains that the title *Monologion* had been suggested to him by the apostolic legate in Gaul, archbishop Hugh of Lyon, in place of a previous title 'Exemplum meditandi de ratione fidei'. Anselm, *Opera Omnia*, I, 94.
5. Anselm describes in the prologue to the prayer the energy and anxiety he expended trying to find one argument, 'which required no other than itself alone for showing that God truly exists'. See the prologue to the *Proslogion*, in Anselm, *Opera Omnia*, I, 93-122. Henceforth, references to the *Proslogion* will be cited in the text. *Proslogion*, prologue, for example, will be cited as (prologue) and chapter 1 as (c. 1).
6. See for example K. Barth, *Anselm: Fides Quaerens Intellectum*, trans. by I. W. Robertson (Cleveland; New York, 1962; 1st pub. in 1931), pp. 132ff.
7. For the audience of Anselm's prayers and meditations, see B. Ward, *The Prayers and Meditations of St Anselm* (London, 1973), introduction.
8. This constituted the major attraction of crusading during this period. See for example, Jonathan Riley-Smith, *The Crusades* (London, 1987), ch. 1.
9. St Benedict, *Rule of St Benedict*, ed. by J. McCann (London, 1951), c. 58.
10. St Benedict, c. 20.
11. Compare Anselm, *Monologion*, c. 67. St Augustine located the rational soul as the image of God within the heart. Compare St Augustine, *De Trinitate*, 15, 23-24 (44),

in *Corpus Christianorum Series Latina*, vol. 50, ed. W. J. Mountain (Turnholt, 1968). See also St Augustine, *De Tractatu Johanini*, tract 18, caput 5, n. 10, in *Patrologia Latina*, ed. by J. P. Migne et al., 217 vols (Paris, 1844-1879), xxxv, col. 1541: 'Redi ad cor; vide ibi quid sentias forte de Deo, quia ibi est imago Dei ... in interiore homine renovaris ad imaginem Dei, in imagine sua cognosce auctorem eius.'

12. A. C. Pegis, 'St Anselm and the Argument of the *Proslogion*', in *Medieval Studies*, vol. 28 (1966), 228-267, 259.
13. McGill suggests this tripartite division of chapters 2-3: A. C. McGill, 'Recent discussions of Anselm's argument', in *The Many-Faced Argument*, ed. by J. Hick and A. C. McGill (London, 1968), pp. 39-40.
14. G. Schufreider, *An Introduction to Anselm's Argument* (Philadelphia, 1978), pp. 90-94.
15. Anselm, *Response to Gaunilo*, c. 9, in Anselm, *Opera Omnia*, I, 130-139 (p. 138).
16. Pegis, 'St Anselm and the Argument…', pp. 259-261.
17. Compare N. Smart, *Reasons and Faiths* (London, 1958), pp. 20ff.
18. Eadmar, *The Life of St Anselm*, ed. and trans. by R. W. Southern (Oxford, 1962), I, c. 19.
19. For the concept of *vere esse* in the works of Augustine, see for example, A. Stolz, 'Anselm's Theology in the *Proslogion*', in J. Hick and A. C. McGill (eds), *The Many-Faced Argument* (London, 1968), pp. 183-206. For the notion of God as that which cannot be thought not to exist, see St Hilary, *On the Trinity*: 'Deo proprium esse id quod est, non ambigens sensus est, quia id quod est, non potest intelligi dicique non esse. Esse enim et non esse contraria sunt.' St Hilary, *De Trinitate*, c. xii, 24, in *Patrologia Latina*, ed. by P. Migne et al., 217 vols (Paris 1844-1879) X, col. 447.
20. Eadmar, *The Life of St Anselm*, I, c. 19.
21. Anselm, *Proslogion*, prologue.
22. Eadmar, *The Life of St Anselm*, I, c. 19.
23. Gilbert Crispin uses the definition of God as 'that than which no greater can be conceived' in his *Disputatio Christiani cum gentili de fide Christi*, ix, to show that there cannot be more than one God: 'Deus est quo nichil maius ac melius est, et quod super omnia est. Plura uero esse non possunt quorum unumquodque sit quo nichil maius ac melius sit, et quod super omnia sit.' In his *Disputatio Iudei et Christiani*, c. 81, he modifies the definition slightly in presenting an objection to the incarnation: 'Si Deus est, quo nichil maius sive sufficientius cogitari potest, qua necessitate coactus humane calamitatis particeps et tantorum factus est consors et patiens malorum?' See A. S. Abulafia and G. R. Evans, *The Works of Gilbert Crispin, Abbot of Westminster* (London, 1986), pp. 64 and 27. On the background of the *Disputatio Iudei*, see ibid., pp. xxviiff. Later in the twelfth century, Achard of St Victor employed Anselm's argument for the purposes of showing not that God exists, but that the Trinitarian God was also the supreme Unity. See M. Th d'Alverny, 'Achard de Saint Victor, Eveque d'Avranches – Disciple de Saint Anselme', in *Analecta Anselmiana*, 2 (1970), 217-222.
24. See Richard W. Southern 'St Anselm and His English Pupils', in *Medieval and Renaissance Studies*, 1 (1941), 14-17; M. J. Charlesworth, *St Anselm's Proslogion*

(Oxford, 1965), pp. 3-4. The manuscript of the dialogue between *Sciens et Nesciens* by the monk Rodolfus is found in the Bodleian, ms. *Laud. misc.* 363. At fol. 34 there is also a *Meditatio Cuiusdam Christiani de Fide.* Neither of these refers to Anselm's *Proslogion.*

25. Anselm, *Response to Gaunilo*, c. 5, p. 135.
26. Ibid., c. 3, p. 133.
27. Ibid., cc. 1 and 8, pp. 131, 137-138. See also A. C. Pegis, 'St Anselm and the Argument...', pp. 253-261.
28. Anselm, *Response*, c. 8, pp. 137-138.
29. Pegis, 'St Anselm and the argument..', pp. 260-261.
30. Ibid., pp. 253-261.
31. J. Clayton, 'The Otherness of Anselm', in *Neue Zeitschrift Für Systematische Theologie und Religionsphilosophie*, 37 (1995), 125-143 (p. 127).
32. See, for example, M. J. Charlesworth, *St Anselm's Proslogion* (Oxford, 1965).
33. See, for example, A. Stolz, 'Anselm's Theology in the *Proslogion*', in *The Many-Faced Argument*, ed. by Hick and McGill (London, 1968), pp. 183-206.
34. For a Cistercian reader of St Anselm's *Proslogion*, see J. Lewicki, 'Saint Anselm et les Doctrines des Cisterciens du XIIe siècle', in *Analecta Anselmiana*, 2 (1970), 209-216. See also M. Th d'Alverny, 'Achard de Saint Victor, Eveque d'Avranches – Disciple de Saint Anselme', in ibid., pp. 217-222. For the fortunes of Anselm's works in the schools of the twelfth century, see G. R. Evans, *Anselm and a New Generation* (Oxford, 1980).
35. For an overview of the effects of change in the high Middle Ages see Richard W. Southern, *Western Society and the Church in the Middle Ages* (London, 1970). Jacques Le Goff, *Intellectuals in the Middle Ages* (Blackball, 1993) gives a clear account of the intellectual repercussions of twelfth-century modernity, while Brenda Bolton, *The Medieval Reformation* (London, 1983), and Rosalind B. Brooke, *The Coming of the Friars* (London, 1975) focus on religious developments; cf. A. Giddens, *The Consequences of Modernity* (Stanford, 1990).
36. See Colin Morris, *The Discovery of the Individual, 1050-1200* (London, 1972); Caroline Walker Bynum, 'Did the Twelfth Century Discover the Individual?', in *Journal of Ecclesiastical History*, 31, 1 (1980), 1-18, and C. Morris, 'Individualism in Twelfth Century Religion: Some Further Reflections', in *Journal of Ecclesiastical History*, 31, 2 (1980), 195-206.
37. Norman Cohn, *The Pursüit of the Millennium* (London, 1957), p. 52.
38. For another account of the crises of identity created by economic and political changes of eleventh- and twelfth-century society, and their role in the emergence of new religious movements, see R. I. Moore, *The Origins of European Dissent* (Toronto, 1994; 1st pub. in 1977). See also Janet Nelson, 'Society, Theodicy and the origins of heresy: towards a reassessment of the medieval evidence', in *Schism, Heresy and Religious Protest*, ed. by D. Baker, Studies in Church History, 9 (Cambridge, 1972), pp. 65-77.
39. See R. I. Moore, *The Formation of a Persecuting Society*, for the awareness of pluralism within Christendom. For Christendom's increasing awareness of the Non-

Christian Other beyond its debated frontiers see, for example, Scott D. Westrem (ed.), *Discovering New Worlds* (New York, 1991); Norman Kedar, *Crusade and Mission: European Approaches to the Muslims* (Princeton, 1984); John Muldoon, *Popes, Lawyers, and Infidels: The Church and The Non-Christian World 1250-1550* (Philadelphia, 1979); Gavin Langmuir, *History, Religion, and Antisemitism* (Berkeley, 1990) and Idem, *Toward a Definition of Antisemitism* (Berkeley, 1990).

40. This interpretation of the rise of the *literati* is that of Moore, *Formation.*
41. See for example a test put to the Waldensians at the Roman Curia recorded in Walter Mapp's *De Nugis Curialium*, dist. 1, c. 31, trans. in Rosalind B. Brooke, *The Coming of the Friars* (London, 1975), pp. 151-152.
42. For an institutional and intellectual account of the invention of theology in the twelfth century, see G. R. Evans, *Old Arts and New Theology: The Beginnings of Theology as an Academic Discipline* (Oxford, 1980).
43. Helen Waddell, *The Wandering Scholars* (London, 1953; 1st pub. 1927). On the schools of Paris, as well as the so-called 'school of Chartres', see R. W. Southern, 'The Schools of Paris and the School of Chartres', in *Renaissance and Renewal in the Twelfth Century*, ed. by R. L. Benson et al. (Harvard, 1982), pp. 113-137.
44. See for example, M. T. Clanchy, *From Memory to Written Record: England, 1066-1307*, 2nd ed. (Oxford, 1993). For other aspects of the revolution in government, see Moore, *Formation of a Persecuting Society.*
45. See Le Goff, *Intellectuals*, p. 45. In the case of Abelard's *Sic et Non* conflicts between texts were listed and left unresolved; not because Abelard believed there were no resolutions but because he was writing for the purpose of instruction. The conflicts were left for the pupil to resolve. Abelard wrote in the prologue to the work: 'It seems right that we should begin to collect diverse sayings of the holy Fathers which we remember, some from the discrepancy which they seem to have which causes a question. This is a great stimulus to young students in their search after the truth and the enquiry itself sharpens their intellect... By doubting, indeed, we come to enquiry, and by enquiry we arrive at the truth.' Abelard, *Sic et Non*, 'prologue', ed. by B. B. Boyer and R. McKeon (Chicago, 1976-1977), p. 103.
46. M. J. P. Robson, 'Saint Anselm's Influence Upon Saint Bonaventure's Theology of Redemption' (Unpublished Ph.D. thesis, University of Cambridge, 1988), makes some useful remarks on the treatment of texts in medieval scholasticism. On this subject, see also R. H. Rouse and M. A. Rouse, '*Statim invenire: Schools, Preachers, and New Attitudes to the Page*', in *Renaissance and Renewal in the Twelfth Century*, ed. by R. L. Benson et al. (Harvard, 1982), pp. 201-228.
47. The University of Paris was an institution that arose out of the attempts of Masters and Scholars to gain independence from the chancellor of Notre Dame. They did so by appeal to Rome. Rome had its own agenda in granting that independence, particularly in the bull *Parens Scientiarum* of 1231. In a bull of 1219, for example, Pope Honourius III forbade the study of civil law 'since we insist on a more thorough study of Holy Scriptures…'. See H. Wieruszowski, *The Medieval University: Masters, Students, Learning* (Princeton, 1966), pp. 37 and 144-145. See also, G. Post, 'Alexander III, the Licentia Docendi and the Rise of the Universities', in *Anniversary*

*Essays in Medieval History by Students of Charles Homer Haskins* (Boston, 1929), pp. 255-277; Idem, 'Parisian Masters as a Corporation, 1200-1246', *Speculum*, 9 (1934), 421-445; and P. R. McKeon, 'The Status of the University of Paris as Parens Scientiarum: an Episode in the Development of its Autonomy', *Speculum*, 39 (1964), 651-675.

48. For the organisation of the faculties at Paris, see G. Leff, *Paris and Oxford Universities in the Thirteenth and Fourteenth Centuries. An Institutional and Intellectual History* (New York, 1968), pp. 138ff. On the historical background of the Christian curriculum, see A. B. Cobban, *The Medieval Universities: Their Development and Organisation* (New York, 1975), pp. 9ff.
49. The fullest study to date is that of Marcia L. Colish, *Peter Lombard*, 2 vols (Leiden, 1994).
50. Peter Lombard, *Sententiae in IV Libris Distinctae* ed. by Collegium S. Bonaventurae, ad Claras Aquas (Rome, 1971), prologue.
51. A. MacIntyre, *Three Rival Versions of Moral Inquiry, Encyclopaedia, Genealogy, and Tradition* (London, 1990), pp. 106-107ff.
52. Ibid.
53. See, for example, F. C. Copleston, *A History of Medieval Philosophy* (London, 1972), pp. 154-155.
54. See for example, G. Leff, *Paris and Oxford*, pp. 137ff. The line concerning the reception of Aristotle comes from a poem celebrating the English scholar John Blund cit. in J. Marenbon, *Later Medieval Philosophy (1150-1350)* (London; New York, 1991), p. 55.
55. B. G. Dod, 'Aristoteles Latinus', in *The Cambridge History of Later Medieval Philosophy*, ed. by Norman Kretzmann (Cambridge, 1982), pp. 45-79 (pp. 50-53).
56. On the global scale of papal ambitions and policy, see Kedar, *Crusade and Mission*; J. Muldoon, *Popes, Lawyers, and Infidels*, and Idem, 'The Nature of the Infidel: The Anthropology of the Canon Lawyers', in *Discovering New Worlds: Essays on Medieval Exploration and Imagination*, ed. by S. D. Westrem (New York; London, 1991), pp. 115-124. See also C. Dawson, *The Mongol Mission: Narratives and Letters of the Franciscan Missionaries in Mongolia and China in the Thirteenth and Fourteenth Centuries* (London, 1955).
57. Moore, *The Formation of a Persecuting Society*, p. 109.
58. See for example, Kedar, *Crusade and Mission* (Princeton, 1984); R. Chazan, 'From Friar Paul to Friar Raymond: Development of Innovative Missionising Arguments', *Harvard Theological Review*, 73: 3 (1985), 289-306; Idem, 'Confrontation In The Synagogue of Narbonne: A Christian Sermon and a Jewish Reply', *Harvard Theological Review*, 67 (1974), 437-457; Idem, 'The Barcelona 'Disputation' of 1263: Christian Missionising and Jewish Response', *Speculum*, 52 (1977), 824-842; Idem, *Daggers of Faith: Thirteenth-Century Christian Missionising and Jewish Response* (Berkeley, 1989); Idem, *Barcelona and Beyond: The Disputation of 1263 and Its Aftermath* (Berkeley, 1992); and J. Cohen, *The Friars and The Jews* (Cornell, 1982). See also Cutler, A. H. and Cutler, H. E., *The Jew as Ally of the Muslim: The Medieval Roots of Anti-Semitism* (Notre Dame, 1986).

59. See, for example, Wieruszowski, pp. 147-148.
60. Alexander of Hales, *Doctoris Irrefragabilis Alexandri de Hales, Summa Theologica*, ed. by V. Doucet (Quaracchi, 1924), V, 91, and J. de Ghellinck, *Le Mouvement Théologique du xiie siécle* (Paris, 1914), pp. 61-63, credit the *Summa Halensis* with an important role in making Anselm known to the thirteenth century and with making him an authority.
61. Alexander Nequam, *Speculum Speculationum*, ed. R. M. Thomson (Oxford, 1988), p. 56.
62. Alexander Nequam, lib. I, xviii, 4: 'Deus enim est id quo nichil potest intelligi esse melius, siue hec dictio 'melius' teneatur nominaliter siue aduerbialiter. Qui ergo recte intelligit Deum, intelligit Deum esse. Maius enim est rem intelligi et esse quam rem intelligi et non esse. Maius item est Deum esse in re et in intellectu et non posset intelligi non esse. Deus ergo est id quod est in re et in intellectu et non potest intelligi non esse.'
63. Ibid., lib. I, xvii.
64. Ibid., lib. I, xviii.
65. Ibid., lib. I, xviii, 5.
66. Ibid., lib. I, xviii 5.
67. Ibid., lib. I, xviii, 7-8.
68. Ibid., lib. I, xviii, 9.
69. Ibid., lib. I, xviii, 6: 'Numquid ergo anima que est imago Dei dictat sibi quod summa natura non est.'
70. Copleston, p. 155, n. 3.
71. William of Auxerre, *Summa Aurea*, ed. by J. Ribaillier, 5 vols (Paris; Rome, 1980-1987), Lib. I, prologus.
72. Ibid., I, prologus: 'Quia vero debilem habet hominem visum spiritualem propter corruptionem que est a primo peccato, ideo etiam in fide gradus sunt ut animus claris incipiat et exercita fides in claris possit purgata magis et magis procedere ad magis clara, ut tandem possit aspectum dirigere in ipsam eternam claritatem. Incipit autem ab articulis fidei magis propinquis sensui, ut quod Filius Dei factus est homo et quod fuit humilis, mansuetus et patiens et huiusmodi. Unde Apostolus, ad Cor. ii: Nichil iudicavi me scire inter vos nisi Ihesum Christum et hunc crucifixum, ut per illa clara purgetur et exercitur et solidetur intellectus ad videndum clariora, ut quod filii Dei sumus, heredes (Dei), cohere autem Christi, Rom. viii. Ad ultimum ipsum Deum.'
73. Ibid., I, tractatus primus: Hic probatur Quod Deus est.
74. Ibid., I: 'Ex predictis patet quod summum bonum tale bonum sit quod non potest intelligi non esse tribus de causis. Prima est quia in hoc quod dico optimum, intelligo vere esse. Et ita qui intelligeret illud optimum non esse quod non potest. Secunda est quia summum bonum ex necessitate summe est; sed illud maius est a quo esse non est separabile ratione etsi non actu; ergo a summo bono non potest separari esse actu vel ratione sive in intellectu; et ita summum bonum est ipsum esse; et ideo sicut intellectus non potest separari a se, ita nec intellectu potest separari ab eo quod est esse. Et ita non potest intelligi summum bonum sive Deum non esse.'
75. Ibid.

76. Jan Aertsen, *Medieval Philosophy and the Transcendentals: The Case of Thomas Aquinas* (Brill, 1996), p. 20.
77. In Thierry of Chartres' *De Sex Dierum Operibus*, God the Father acts as the efficient, the Son as the formal, and the Spirit as the final cause, with matter as the material cause of creation. Once this initial creation was accomplished, according to Thierry, everything else occurred naturally: see Richard C. Dales, 'A Twelfth-Century Concept of Natural Order' in Viator, 9 (1978), 179-192, esp. p. 184. J. Newell, 'Rationalism at the School of Chartres' in Vivarium, 21, 2 (1983), 108-126, says that 'explaining the Trinity in terms of its creative activity rather than its internal nature reveals the focus of Chartrean thought' (pp. 120-121).
78. See K. F. Lynch, 'Some fontes of the commentary of Hugh de Saint Cher: William of Auxerre, Guy d'Orchelles, Alexander of Hales', *Franciscan Studies*, 13: 2-3 (1953), 119-146.
79. For an account of the secular criticism of the Friars, and in particular criticism of the Friars at the University of Paris, see G. Leff, *Paris and Oxford Universities in the Thirteenth and Fourteenth Centuries: An Institutional and Intellectual History* (New York, 1968), and also D. L. Douie, *The Conflict Between The Seculars and the Mendicants at The University of Paris in the Thirteenth Century* (London, 1954).

## Chapter 2

# Encountering God Within: Anselm's Argument Among the Early Franciscans in Paris

Religious life for Anselm consisted of retreat and enclosure. Religious life for both orders of Friars (founded a century after Anselm's death) was a life of encounter and public engagement. For the Dominican order, study and preaching by verbal persuasion were from the beginning central to their understanding of the apostolic life. St Francis (1181/2-1226), on the other hand, considered verbal persuasion to be secondary (even detrimental) to the practical fulfilment of poor and humble living, and the pursuit of studies a hindrance to the call of the apostolic life and its challenge to the unbeliever. If anything, St Francis was reacting as much against the rise of professional theology in his day, as he was against the professions of banking and commerce. The 'unbeliever' for St Francis was not just anyone who did not accept the doctrines of the Church. Rather it was anyone who failed to be charitable to the poor and the sick and who yet claimed to call themselves Christians. For St Francis, preaching was far more a matter of practical demonstration than of words. While teachings or doctrines may be accepted intellectually, 'conversion' was a matter of realising one's sin and living a changed life. For those reasons, only preaching by example could bring about the inner conversion of the unbeliever.

Despite St Francis's own feelings on the matter, the Franciscans – like the Dominicans – went on to develop a highly sophisticated educational structure that included a lecturer in every significant residence of the order. The schooling received by Franciscan Friars was hierarchical, with each province of the order having major schools for theological instruction and the best students from each province being sent to the Faculties of Theology at Oxford and Paris, where the Friars were exempted from the requirement of first graduating in Arts.[1] After receiving the licence of teaching, graduated Friars would in turn supply the houses of the order with lecturers.[2] The integrated character of this educational system explains why Franciscan and Dominican Masters in Theology only remained in their Chairs at Paris and Oxford for a brief period before moving on to found another school and allowing a newly-graduated candidate to take their place. Such was the extent of this educational system (again, mirrored by the Dominicans) that by the 1260s, the two mendicant or 'begging' orders were coming to be known instead as the 'student orders'.[3]

The school of the Franciscans at Paris was already in existence when in 1236 a member of the Faculty of Theology at the University joined the order, bringing his faculty chair with him. Once inside the school, the chair remained among the Franciscans, as at least two other chairs of the Faculty were to remain among the Dominicans – a situation that served to heighten tensions with contemporary secular masters (i.e. teachers who belonged to the ordinary clergy). Henceforth, the Franciscan master shared the Faculty with about eleven other masters, comprising Dominican Friars as well as representatives from other religious houses, and the secular masters themselves. The Faculty was responsible for overseeing academic standards and examinations within its schools, examinations that involved public disputations – sometimes involving masters and students from different schools. This was a context where Franciscans and Dominicans rubbed shoulders and both orders came into close proximity to secular masters and their students.[4] It is no coincidence, therefore, that it was at the universities that the secular clergy's criticism of the Friars was to receive both sophisticated expression in the form of critiques of the apostolic life and somewhat less sophisticated expression, in the form of open violence against student Friars.[5]

In the light of their tenuous institutional position, it is easy to see why the Franciscans were inclined from the beginning to adopt theologically conservative positions. External criticisms also served to exacerbate tensions within the order itself. Academic Franciscans had good reason to believe that studies and training were critical to the survival of the order. Yet they needed to define and defend the nature of education to others within their order in a way that was never required of Dominican Friars. Those promoting studies had to persuade radical imitators of St Francis's teaching that the pursuit of studies was not opposed to the interests of their founder, but rather represented a favourable and necessary development of the way of life he wanted his followers to lead.[6] It was an issue that went straight to the heart of the religious life as St Francis conceived it. It was this internal conflict, together with external criticism of the order, that provided the backdrop for the early Franciscan school at Paris.

## I

It is usually regarded as a matter of unquestionable fact that the clericalisation and introduction of studies into the Franciscan order by an educated elite represented a departure from the ideals of St Francis. This was certainly what opponents of studies and clericalisation believed.[7] It would be wrong to assume, however, that this was what academics within the order took themselves to be doing. That they were attracted to the Franciscans in the first place suggests that they regarded any differences between St Francis and themselves over the question of education and clericalisation as peripheral to other concerns that they identified with St Francis and that they took to be central to their lives.

Besides the *Rule* which St Francis composed for the order, the obvious sources for identifying the concerns of the followers of St Francis are the 'Lives' of the saint drawn up at intervals after the death of St Francis. Far more than the particular teachings of St Francis, the physical example of the saint was of chief significance for his followers. Following in 'the footprints of Christ' was Francis's favourite metaphor for the life of the wandering preacher.[8] Much has been written concerning the way accounts of St Francis's life composed during the thirteenth century reflect the political interests of the writers within the Franciscan order. The *Second Life* of Thomas of Celano and the *Writings of Leo* for example, reflect a radical concern with the literal observance of the *Rule* and the betrayal (as they saw it) of St Francis's ideals of poverty and simplicity.[9] The *Greater Legend* of Bonaventure, on the other hand, scrupulously omits any detail that would suggest discrepancy between the ideals of the order as he saw them and the intentions of its founder.[10]

What each of these accounts share, however, is perhaps more significant than what divided them. Any of them could be easily distinguished from an account of the life of St Dominic by the emphasis which they place upon Francis's yearning to conform to the model of Christ as the means of both inner conversion and the conversion of others. All the biographers of St Francis, whether written by literal observers of the *Rule* or not, recognise Francis by the same central concern: a personal relationship with God that he experienced both through supernatural visions and also through a mystical experience of nature itself. Francis's challenge in word and example to both Christians and non-Christians alike was penitence – by which means the soul might be restored to God. As E. R. Daniel explains, 'the Franciscan missionary had first to experience renewal himself, to develop a spiritual life within and an evangelical conduct without, before he could hope to set an example for others or preach to them'.[11]

What the *Rule* of the order does not convey is the charisma of the example set by St Francis. It is a charisma that is evident throughout his life, especially in two episodes from the beginning and the middle of his career. In 1206, Francis was brought by his father before the bishop of Assisi in an effort to stop him selling cloth from the family business in order to feed the local poor. Unabashed, St Francis stripped himself naked before the whole town, and declared that his only Father from now on was his Father in heaven. In 1219 Francis accompanied the soldiers of the Fifth Crusade to Egypt not to resume his former occupation as a soldier, but to preach directly to the Muslim Sultan himself. The Sultan was not converted, but was impressed enough by Francis to allow him to escape with his life. The point of the exercise was evidently to 'shock' his hearers into repentance, by a 'stark' imitation of Christ. R. I. Burns has described Francis's missionary strategy as 'outrageous, consciously ineffective, yet designed to engage the forces of heaven at some mystical level'.[12] Underpinning that missionary strategy was a spirituality of intimate relationship with God – a relationship which demonstrated itself to others by means of outward conduct.

The most famous and controversial example of Francis's imitative spirituality was his reception of the marks of Christ's wounds in 1224. St Francis received the stigmata during a mystical vision which occurred to him while praying on Mount La Verna. St Francis saw the crucified Christ being held aloft by seraphim. It was an event which both encapsulated the essence of Francis's spirituality, but which also highlighted why it seemed so dangerous. In a society where all authority was legitimised in terms of divine grace, it was a form of spirituality that had deeply subversive possibilities. In that respect, St Francis embodied the most radical aspects of contemporary popular spirituality. The reception of the stigmata was claimed by some of his more radical followers to confirm the authenticity of his teaching as having been dictated directly to him from God. This in fact is what Francis himself claimed about the way of life which he instructed his followers to follow when, in his *Testament*, he tried to bind them to literal observation of the simplicity and poverty of the *Rule.*[13]

The efforts which St Francis himself took to ensure that his followers remained obedient to established authorities were not considered adequate to deal with the problems which he raised. The period between 1150-1216 represented one of the most prolific periods in the growth of popular religious movements: it also marked a transition of papal policy towards those groups from tolerance to repression.[14] The Fourth Lateran Council decreed that no new religious communities were permitted to form unless they adopt an existing religious rule.[15] Any existing communities fell in danger of the harshest ecclesiastical penalties were any part of them found to preach unorthodox teachings. It was precisely because there were already several well-known groups who had fallen prey to ecclesiastical investigation in this way that it was imperative that the Franciscans as much as the Dominicans equip themselves with accurate doctrinal knowledge. Hence, Robert Grosseteste, the first lector to the Franciscans in Oxford, argued that if the Friars Minor did not study, they would quickly degenerate and become like other orders that were now walking in darkness.[16] His contemporary in Paris, John de la Rochelle (d. 1245), the second Franciscan master in the Faculty of Theology at Paris, preached that those who opposed studies within the order were acting under the influence of Satan.[17] As far as the academics within the order were concerned, theological articulation was a condition of the Franciscans' very survival.

The turning point in the academic history of the Franciscan order came when Alexander of Hales (c. 1170-1245) entered the order in the 1230s, taking his chair in the Faculty of Theology with him. Besides his academic work within the order, Alexander joined other academics in the Franciscan schools throughout Europe in opposing the Minister General, Elias of Cortona (c. 1180-1253) who ruled the order from 1232 until 1239. On account of a luxurious living style that was bringing the whole order into disrepute, Elias incurred the opposition of both the academics and the radical Franciscans opposed to studies. Hence, while articulating the theological assumptions of the Franciscan order in the public contexts of the universities, the same masters were also aligning themselves politically with the sympathies of the most radical elements in the order. An indication of their success is the fact that one of several academics that had been active with Alexander in the campaign to have Elias deposed – Haymo of Faversham (d. 1244) – was elected Minister General in 1240 shortly after the campaign succeeded.[18]

In any case, about ten years after the death of St Francis, the Franciscans, like the Dominicans, had a chair in the Faculty of Theology at the University of Paris. The appeal of the Franciscan life was as strong among academics as anywhere else in society. Just as studies were to play an important role in shaping the Friars Preachers, the emergence of Franciscan schools and the advance of education also had an enormous impact upon the Friars Minor. The nature of the enquiries that the Franciscans undertook reflected the spiritual preoccupations of the founder of the order – but this time expressed in terms of the theological authorities of ecclesiastical tradition. In other words, part of what the academics within the order were doing was legitimating Franciscan spirituality. In many ways the rational enquiries of the school in Paris represented the theological counterpart to its defence of the Franciscan life against secular criticisms. However, it also represented a continuing dialogue with those within the order who continued to insist that studies represented a betrayal of St Francis and all that he stood for.[19] In continuing that dialogue, the academics somehow had to overcome the contradiction of articulating a spirituality that rejected theological articulation.

## II

The most significant product of the early Franciscan school in Paris was the *Summa Theologica* ascribed to Alexander of Hales, which was probably begun in the 1230s and not finally completed until the end of the 1250s. This massive work is interesting not because it represents the original thinking of the first Franciscan master in Paris. Rather, it is interesting precisely because it is the product of the Franciscan school as a whole: originality was no more a goal of the early Franciscans than it had been for Anselm. Rather, the goal of the early Franciscan school was to develop a teaching which not only harmonised Franciscan assumptions with the sources of Christian tradition, but also with their own assumptions about the place of studies within the religious life. The key to doing this involved the interpretation of the sources provided by tradition: they had to 'find themselves' within those sources. The evidence of the manuscripts of the early Franciscan school in the 1240s suggests that Anselm's argument had begun to enter that tradition. More than a century and a half after it had been composed, and employed in a very different context, the *Proslogion* was coming to represent not only an argument from reason, but a voice of authority within tradition.

The early Franciscan manuscripts are interesting for us precisely because of the obscurity of their authors: they were not to be remembered as were

Alexander or later, Bonaventure. In some cases, we do not know the names of the authors. It is by comparison with such texts, however, that the relationship of key figures to their wider communities can be more readily appreciated. The significance of that relationship lay in the fact that teaching at Paris was both the pinnacle of teaching within the order, and also a source for the distribution of teaching throughout the order: it was therefore in Paris that the conflict over Franciscan identity had to be fought.

Even before Alexander of Hales became a Franciscan in 1236, he had already been lecturing to the Franciscans in Paris. His teachings were to have a profound influence on the intellectual positions adopted by the Franciscan masters in Paris throughout the thirteenth century. In the last chapter it was noted that Peter Lombard's *Four Books of Sentences* represents the classic expression of the teaching methods of the twelfth century. Alexander adopted this text as a text-book for his students. Henceforth students within the order would be required to comment on the *Sentences* before they could matriculate as Masters in the Faculty of Theology: a practice which was soon adopted throughout the Faculty as a whole.[20]

Marcia Colish's study of Peter Lombard's *Sentences* suggests many reasons why Alexander would have been attracted to this text for the instruction of his students. It covered the full range of Christian teaching in four books, starting with the doctrine of God as Trinity and Unity, then dealing the doctrine of Creation and the Fall, the doctrines of Incarnation and Redemption, and then finally the Sacraments. In the first chapter of the first book, Peter established an organising schema by means of the Augustinian distinctions between signs and things, use and enjoyment. 'God alone is to be enjoyed in and for Himself. He is the supreme being and the supreme good, to which everything else points and in relation to which everything else, and not least, systematic theology itself, is to be used.'[21] More significant, however, was the manner in which the *Sentences* dealt with the topic of divine nature.

Peter Lombard is concerned, like other twelfth century theologians, with what can and cannot be properly said of God. The first book of the *Sentences* is devoted to the Divine Unity and Trinity. The discussion begins in the second chapter of the second book by listing briefly the testimonies of the Trinity in the Old and New Testaments.[22] Almost the entire discussion of book one is concerned, however, not with how God reveals himself to the rational creature, but how the rational creature can understand God from the standpoint of metaphysical reality.[23] Peter provides, in effect, a grammar for talking about God in philosophical, and hence rationally contestable language.[24]

The problem of how human language derived from mundane experience could convey divine reality is the central problem of such a grammar. Peter launches his discussion with rational proofs for God's existence in the third distinction of the first book. The chapter begins from the scriptural reference in Romans, that 'since the creation of the world the invisible qualities of God – his eternal power and divine nature – have been clearly seen from the things that were made' (Rom. 1: 20). It then presents four arguments for God's existence, each of which begins from an examination of created nature. These yield a deity that is first cause, intelligent, immutable, one and simple. By analysing their implications Lombard claims that the attributes of omnipotence, wisdom and goodness, can also be extracted.[25]

Though he takes his cue from St Paul's remarks about the things that are made, Lombard's proofs are metaphysical as well as physical. 'He is concerned less', in Colish's words 'with examining the ways in which created beings act than with considering the structure of created being and what it requires as a necessary metaphysical substratum':

> In treating the deity as that necessary ground of being, he is as interested in delineating the respects in which the divine mode of being is radically different from, and transcendent of, the world of created being as he is in showing the ways in which the world of created being is ontologically dependent upon God and connected to Him.[26]

As we have seen already, in the context of the newly discovered Aristotelian works, the issues of the natural knowledge of God, how God was related to the world, how God was to be named from creatures, and the issue of the status of revelation in relation to natural knowledge all became matters of particular importance. Given St Francis's personal experience of God, and also his suspicions about the dangers of knowledge for the Christian soul, however, the issue was of particular significance for the Franciscan order.

Alexander of Hales' *Glossa on the Sentences* probably reflects his earliest instruction to the Franciscans during the late 1220s and early 1230s before he formally entered the order.[27] The text is somewhat fragmentary, designed to prompt oral teaching rather than to present systematic exposition, but there is already an indication of the direction that the Franciscan school was going to take, and the fact that Anselm's argument was already being highlighted as a key text.

After discussing the issues raised by Lombard's schema of signs and things, use and enjoyment, in the first distinction, Alexander begins the second with the dictum Augustine drew from Isaiah, 'unless you believe you shall not understand'. On the contrary, Alexander replies, it is better to understand what is believed than merely to believe.[28] According to Alexander, the soul may apprehend, but not comprehend God. It is one thing to see, Alexander states, another to comprehend entirely. Indeed, it is not in our power to see God; but it is in God's. Nevertheless, though we have no power to see God, we have the power to make ourselves worthy.[29] Augustine's *On The Greatness of The Soul* states that there are three stages of the soul's cleansing/expiation:

> The first stage is when it is removed from contemplating the senses, the second when it is removed from the contemplation of itself, and the third when it is elevated above itself.[30]

This teaching was to have an important future within the Franciscan order. It ties the natural knowledge of God to the spiritual life. The knowledge of God involves more than intellectual appreciation alone: it also involves purification from bodily desire, purification of the soul within, and then a turning above to contemplation. Notably, when Alexander discusses the knowledge of God, he also discusses the nature of the soul: the knowledge of one is integral to the knowledge of the other.

The treatment of the soul's natural knowledge of God lacks the cohesiveness of the *Summa Aurea* of William of Auxerre. This may in part be due to the idiom of the *Glossa* but, since it ascribes the knowledge of God to many sources, it may have also been quantity and variety that Alexander wanted to communicate to his students rather than a unitary systematic approach to the sources of the natural knowledge of God.[31] In any case, what makes that quantity and variety of ways to God possible is a participational and hierarchical scheme supplemented by divine illumination. Augustine, for example, states that different goods are good according to one good; and the mind is able to discern between better and lesser goods, because the knowledge of the Good is impressed on the soul by nature.[32] The interior impression of God thus underpins the soul's apprehension of God more generally. It is this teaching above all that fundamentally expresses Francis's experience of God, as immanent within nature and intimately related to the soul.

When Alexander cites Anselm's argument he does so in order to show not merely that God exists, but that God cannot be thought not to exist. This may not seem so significant in itself, but it may have been so in his oral delivery of the text: at the very least, later Franciscans made a close link between a natural impression in the soul as a basis for knowledge, and the Anselmian argument that God cannot be thought not to be. Moreover, Alexander uses the Anselmian text as a bridge between talking about the natural knowledge of God and the image of the Trinity within the soul. His close identification between the two is reflected in his explanation for the title of Anselm's work:

> In the book *De personislogion*, that is, 'the divine persons', Anselm says that that than which no greater can be thought is God. But greater is that which is thought to exist in reality and in the intellect, than what is thought in the intellect alone. Greater still is that which can be thought of as being and cannot be thought of as not being, than what can be thought not to be when it is. Therefore, God is a good which exists not only in the mind [but also in reality], and which cannot be thought not to be.

The Fool is able to deny the existence of God, says Alexander, only in so far as he can say the exterior words. He cannot, however, think the interior thoughts.[33] Alexander goes on to discuss whether God is knowable by God alone or also by creatures. While God is known fully only to God, we are able to see God through faith in the mind, and through charity in practice.[34] When we see God through creatures, we do not see God in essence. Rather, we see the highest goodness through the goodness that is in creatures.[35]

Alexander's approach to the natural knowledge of God encapsulates the assumptions that are basic to all of St Francis's religious experiences: that God is encountered in the world but the encounter takes place primarily within the soul itself. The manuscript evidence of four surviving sentence commentaries dating from the 1240s illustrates the ways in which the concerns of the early *Glossa* are developed by students within the Franciscan school.[36] All but one of these manuscripts, ascribed to Odo Rigaud and his disciples, use Anselm's argument to discuss the natural knowledge of God, and the fourth takes up issues pertinent to those raised in the other commentaries.[37] Like the *Glossa* of Alexander of Hales, their treatment of the questions of the first book is cursory. Nonetheless, it is significant that Anselm's argument, apparently neglected in the schools of the twelfth century, is found in a cluster of works connected with the earliest scholars of the Franciscan school: it was becoming integral to a Franciscan way of thinking.

This is shown first of all by the presence of the argument within the sentence commentary of Odo Rigaud (d. 1275). After the death of the second Franciscan chair, John de la Rochelle (d. 1245), Odo Rigaud became regent in the school until 1247.[38] Soon afterwards he was consecrated archbishop of Rouen by Pope Innocent IV in 1148 – a fact that is indicative of the growing influence of the Franciscans in Christian society more generally as well as their allegiance to the cause of papal reform.[39] Odo's sentence commentary dates from 1241-1242 perhaps while he was still under the instruction of Alexander of Hales.[40] It treats of Anselm's argument in the course of the second distinction of Peter Lombard's first book.[41] The second distinction, as Odo states, is concerned with showing evidence for the Trinity from the Old and New Testaments. Yet, because unbelievers do not accept authorities, we should not hesitate to provide reasons, where we seem able, for those things that the catholic faith holds most certain concerning God.[42]

The way to God outlined by Odo is one that implies a particular attitude toward natural knowledge. Anselm's argument provides the conclusion to an exposition of God's presence in nature through participation and hierarchy. God is shown to be the first cause, a simple or pure being, the highest good, wise, and immutable. Echoing the preface to the *Proslogion*, Odo says, all these things are able to be proved by one unique argument that Anselm makes in the *Proslogion*. Odo, therefore, approaches Anselm's argument in terms of Anselm's own claims: since something that exists in reality is better than something that only exists in the understanding, that than which no greater can be thought exists in reality.

Moreover, since that than which no greater can be thought exists, it must be simple, eternal, omnipotent and, finally, incapable of being thought not to be.[43]

Having argued that the nature of God's existence is such that God cannot be thought not to exist, Odo then considers objections to his position. Here he elaborates on what he finds in Anselm's text concerning the Fool, and in the reply on behalf of the Fool, by Gaunilo of Marmoutier. In the first place, it would seem that God is not that than which no greater can be thought, for God's existence, as the Fool shows, can be denied.[44] In the second place, anyone who thinks that evil is pleasing to God thinks that God is not just. To think in this way is to think that God is not God, and yet there are people who think like that, such as the Jews who persecuted the apostles.[45] Finally, Odo discusses the objection found in Gaunilo's counter-argument of the lost island. If one could imagine a lost island 'than which no greater could be thought' it would also, by the same argument, be incapable of being thought not to be.[46]

To sustain his position, Odo needs to respond to the arguments not just in ways that show the Anselmian argument to be more coherent than the objections put to it, but also in ways which do not compromise the authority of the Scriptures which mention the Fool. Odo begins his response by explaining the Fool's denial of God as an error on the part of the Fool rather than some defect on the part of God, which would make God less than something than which no greater can be thought. The cause of error, in fact, is an impediment within human intellects generally, caused by the Fall. More significantly still, the impediment concerns our ability to read the book of nature. As the philosopher says, just as eyes accustomed to the darkness of night are blinded by the light of day, so our intellects are blinded to the most manifest things of nature.[47]

The first thing to note about Odo's response is that it involves an account of error. The second thing to note is that having explained the cause of error, Odo responds to the erroneous objections in ways that depend upon a view of the ontological and epistemological order as one and the same. Only that which has beginning or end or a conjunction of parts can be thought not to be. God, however, has none of these. Thought, he says, finds God always and everywhere.[48] The identity of the ontological and the epistemological order is underlined later in Odo's treatment of the divine simplicity. In the eighth distinction of the sentence commentary, *On the truth and properties of the divine essence*, Odo ties the identification of God's being and essence with the Anselmian argument that God alone cannot be thought of as not existing. It is because creatures do not have being from themselves that they can be understood not to be. Only that which is without a beginning cannot be thought not to exist.[49]

As it is for Alexander of Hales, so it is also for Odo: God is evident to the mind because the very nature of being is participational and hierarchical. God cannot be thought not to exist because God is the head of the hierarchy, the maximal being to which all other things owe their being. It is an account of reality that expresses in rational terms the divine immanence of St Francis's religious experience. Yet, while God is encountered in creation as that which creation presupposes, Odo's account of error makes clear that creation can also lead the mind astray. Precisely because the Fool abstracts from God's effects, he assumes that there is no justice in the world, and if no justice, no God.[50] Returning to the lost island, Odo responds to the last objection. To understand the meaning of that than which no greater can be thought is to understand why there is no comparison between God and something limited and finite.[51] The key to reading nature aright would appear to lie within the soul itself, in its appreciation of the infinite source of all that is.

Significantly, Odo's treatment of Anselm's argument is followed and developed by his own students within the Franciscan school. One of those students, Odo de Rosny, a later regent in the Franciscan school, follows Odo's text word for word on this distinction.[52] Not all were to be so repetitious, however. Another manuscript belonging to a second disciple of Odo Rigaud, whose name is unknown, explores the natural impression of the divine being upon the human understanding.[53] This commentary follows Odo in providing separate arguments to show that God is the first cause, simple, immutable, omnipotent, the highest good etc., and then putting forward Anselm's argument as one single argument proving all of the above.[54] It also follows Odo's commentary concerning the counter argument of the island than which no greater can be thought.[55] Where it develops another position is in its explanation for the error of the Fool. What is interesting about this commentary is the way it employs other texts and arguments alongside that of Anselm to develop a thesis that was to permeate the school as a whole: the knowledge of God begins in the very self-consciousness of the soul.

The commentary of the second disciple does not refer to Odo Rigaud's arguments about divine justice and the apprehension of divine effects. Instead, it makes more forthright statements about knowledge from the senses, and the importance of an inner orientation of the soul. By distinguishing between a superior and an inferior reason within the soul, the second disciple teaches that the soul has a naturally inserted or impressed knowledge of God's existence. It is by inward turning and elevation that it attains certainty regarding its divine source – a certainty that it is unable to ignore. This passage refers to an argument employed by the twelfth-century schoolman Hugh of St Victor (1096-1141). Hugh's work was to be valued by the Franciscan community both for his account of human sciences as subordinate to, and integrated within, the knowledge of the Scriptures and for his development of an approach to creatures as symbols of God.[56] Though the argument is from causation, it is nonetheless an introspective argument: when the soul inspects itself, it recognises that it did not always exist and that it could not bring itself into existence. The soul cannot be ignorant, therefore, of its origins in God.[57] Alternatively, if the soul does not elevate itself and relies only upon sense knowledge it will lose sight of its divine source. Hence, the superior part of reason, which is a similitude of the First Truth, is unable to be ignorant of the knowledge of God's existence because the soul recognises that it must have a Creator. The inferior part, however, which is for the purpose of contemplating creatures, has been so darkened by sin that God is hidden from it. It is for this reason that the Fool is able to say there is no God.[58]

In the course of such reasoning, it is possible to discern a very particular way of reconciling the vocation of the academic Franciscan, both with the sources of Christian tradition, but also with the priorities of Franciscan life. Instead of Franciscan life being opposed to the acquisition of knowledge, it is rather the necessary pre-requisite for the acquisition of knowledge. A true perspective on nature is impossible without an awareness of their participation and dependency upon God. Knowledge must begin in an awareness of God, and must also lead the soul back to a knowledge of God. The teaching of the early Franciscan school – that the encounter with God in the world depends upon an inner orientation within the soul – provides the metaphysical foundations of an account of understanding that is related to faith. The Franciscan account of knowledge is deeply tied to moral and spiritual progress. A soul cannot be persuaded by reason to see God in creation: it either does so, or it does not because reason follows the spiritual orientation of the soul. The proof of God's existence is from God's presence. Those who are unable to raise themselves above the contemplation of what is immediate to the senses are blind to that presence, for it requires seeing things in terms of that which lies above them, and to which the soul only has access through superior reason.

What is important in these commentaries is not just the development of views between them, but also the recurrence of standard arguments and the development of fundamental perspectives which they share in common: an indication that they thought not as isolated individuals, but as a community. This does not mean to say that there was no room for differences within that community, however. The third commentary ascribed to a disciple of Odo Rigaud suggests a slightly different perspective on the issues: a perspective that is more insistent upon the claims of a natural knowledge derived from the senses.[59] Unlike Odo, Alexander or the other representatives of the school whose commentaries survive, the commentary of Odo's third disciple begins the third distinction with the question 'Whether God exists'. Its division of the question into 'solution' and 'response' may represent an abbreviation of the arguments *pro* and *contra* presented in oral discussion. What is interesting about this manuscript is that it represents a contrast with the other commentaries of the early Franciscan school.

The first thing to note is that despite a reference to the Fool of the psalms, the third disciple does not deal directly with Anselm's argument. Instead of identifying God as that than which no greater can be thought, he argues instead to the existence of God as the unique first cause.[60] Nevertheless, under the question 'Whether God is knowable?' the third disciple explores some of the issues raised by his contemporaries. Answering that God is knowable in the highest degree, he employs Augustine's distinction between things and signs, enjoyment and use. God is to be enjoyed: enjoyment presupposes love and love, knowledge. Just as the highest good is loved by the affective soul, so the highest truth is loved by the intellect. Since the image of God within the soul consists in a potency of knowing its cause, it would be vain for God to make the rational creature in the divine image unless it was able to know God. Furthermore, it is only by seeing the highest good that the soul can be beatified. Moreover, since it is this in which eternal life consists, God's goodness requires that God render the divine being visible to the rational creature.[61]

However, having looked at the knowledge of God from a theological point of view, the third commentary looks at the issue again from the perspective of a natural knowledge derived from the senses. The third disciple asks the question 'Whether the knowledge of God is more easily obtained than the knowledge of creatures?' He states that there are two ways of considering the knowledge of God and of creatures: in their own natures or by comparison of their status within our knowledge. God is more knowable according to the nature of God, since God is the light and principle of all our knowledge. By comparison with other knowable things, however, God is less easily known than creatures. This is because, in this life, we come to know God through the knowledge of the creature that is acquired by way of the senses. In heaven, however, the knowledge of God will be easier than the knowledge of creatures. In heaven God is known first and all else is known through God.[62]

As well as asserting the dependency of the soul upon the bodily senses for a natural knowledge of God, the third disciple points to a central difficulty in any perspective which does not do so: unless God is only knowable in this life through effects, God's transcendence is compromised. If God was known more easily in this life than creatures, then God must be known without the medium of creatures. If so, God must be known directly. Yet if this is so, we must all live in beatitude – the condition of those who are blessed with the vision of God in the next life: a contention not only absurd, but also heretical. In effect, the commentary of the third disciple inserts a distinction between our knowledge of God, and the nature of God in God's self: a distinction that was to become a central part of Thomas Aquinas's approach to the natural knowledge of God about ten years later. Like Thomas, Odo's third disciple makes the knowledge of the highest good in this life begin from sense knowledge of the creature. Unlike Thomas, however, the third disciple nowhere mentions Anselm's argument to affirm or deny it. Instead, he discusses the 'certainty' of the knowledge of God and in the course of doing so draws himself closer once again to his Franciscan contemporaries.

The third disciple asks 'Whether the knowledge of God is more certain than the knowledge of creatures or the same', and in his response distinguishes between 'actual' and a 'habitual' knowledge. Habitual knowledge of God is more certain than the knowledge of creatures, he argues, since habitual knowledge is innate within the soul.[63] What he means by the distinction between 'habitual' and 'actual' knowledge and what he means by 'habitual' knowledge only becomes clear by the end of the question. The commentary describes actual knowledge as knowledge of experience and of cause. The knowledge through experience is divided into the experience of the intellect and experience of the senses. Knowledge by means of the senses is more certain where creatures are concerned.

Knowledge by means of the intellect, however, is more certain concerning God since God is the highest intelligible thing.[64]

Hence, the question of certainty regarding the intelligible knowledge of God duplicates the answer to the prior question: since God in nature is the highest intelligible, God is experienced by the intellect as more certain. In terms of sense knowledge, however, the creature is both more easily known and known with greater certainty. Finally, and by reference to the argument with which the third distinction began, actual knowledge acquired by means of causes is more certain regarding God since the knowledge of God is innate within the soul.[65]

For the third commentary, habitual knowledge is a subset of actual knowledge. It is set apart from other forms of actual knowledge in that it is innate within the soul. The significant thing about the fourth commentary is that innate habitual knowledge only becomes actual in and through experience. The image of God within the soul is a potential for knowing its cause – not an actual knowledge. The knowledge of God's existence becomes actual when the soul inspects the process of causation by which it came to be. Those who deny God's existence are fools because they assert an opinion that is obviously false – not, it seems, because they think the unthinkable.

Perhaps the views of the third commentary reflect a sympathy with the claims of argument and persuasion and with the knowledge of the senses as opposed to less tangible, interior sources of knowledge. If it does, then the difference between these early Franciscan masters is more than a matter of disagreement about an abstruse point in natural theology. It is a difference that runs to the heart of the Franciscan life itself: is conversion a matter of rational persuasion or an inner transformation? Is reason led by or is it the leader of will?

The question is not about how one is persuaded to believe in God – no one required such persuasion – rather, the question is more nearly about how the soul encounters God or, even, what kind of God the soul encounters. Anselm's argument, used to show that God cannot be thought, alongside the idea that the soul is an image of the first truth, appears to signify that God is found within the soul itself. More precisely, it signifies that the arguments which had been brought forward for the existence of God in the original *Sentences* of Peter Lombard already presuppose that which they set out to prove. The innate knowledge of the existence of God is the condition of the acquisition of such knowledge.

In addition to this, the Franciscan concern to explain the position of the Fool identifies sin as an obstacle to the awareness of God within the soul. The question is not about the rational foundations of Franciscan life, but about the rational claims of competing accounts of Franciscan life. The tension was created by the historical situation of the Franciscan community, whose leader was committed to simplicity, but whose circumstances demanded education and articulacy. The claim in favour of education and theological training was in part made by the circumstances of a new order living in a climate often hostile to new and especially radical accounts of the religious life. However, in the course of theological training, the Franciscans recognised yet another claim – that of the natural knowledge with which Aristotle was already confronting Christendom. The commentary of Odo Rigaud's third disciple reflects the tension more fully than the others, as it struggles to reconcile the soul's dependency upon the bodily senses for its knowledge, with a need to see the spiritual life as the prerequisite for the knowledge of God.

## III

Officially entitled the *Summa fratris Alexandri Halensis*, it seems more appropriate, not to say more simple, to refer to the major product of the early Franciscan school as the *Summa minorum.* The extent to which the *Summa* was more nearly the compilation of the efforts of a whole group of Franciscan scholars, including Odo Rigaud, John de la Rochelle, and Odo's successor in Paris, William of Melitona (d. 1257), has long since been known among historians. When we turn from looking at the manuscripts of the early school to the *Summa* we therefore find not so much a development away from the positions that we have already seen, but a re-statement in more sophisticated and detailed ways, of those same positions, and the recurrence of arguments we have already found among the manuscripts of the school. The following account of the treatment of the natural knowledge of God in the *Summa* is interesting for our purposes, therefore, not because it represents the thinking of one person, but rather, because it represents the thinking of the early Franciscan community in Paris as a whole.

As late as 1256, William of Melitona was ordered by the Pope to work on the completion of the *Summa*.[66] That the Pope should intervene in such a project is indicative of the importance of the *Summa* for the Franciscan community whose position and justification within Christian society had been under attack for some time. The *Summa* represents the theological and metaphysical counterpart of the defence of the Franciscan life itself; a defence with which Franciscan masters were to be preoccupied throughout the period.[67]

The significance of a *Summa* was not merely that it summarised the best arguments available within the tradition – in this case, the best arguments available within the Franciscan school. The importance of a *Summa* also lay in the overall organisational scheme it gave to those arguments. That scheme was not in itself justified by demonstrative or dialectical arguments, as MacIntyre points out, but 'by its capacity to remedy the defects, transcend the limitations, and extend the reach of the tradition of which it is so far the best outcome'.[68] It is significant then, that in its introductory treatise, the *Summa* deals at length with the questions about the natural knowledge of God that have already been observed in the somewhat less conspicuous sentence commentaries of the school. What is also interesting about the *Summa* is not that it expresses new positions, but rather that it gives prominence to positions already found in those commentaries. Such positions therefore provided an overall perspective for the organisation of the

*Summa* and for the Franciscan school as a whole in the face of challenges that were at once institutional, political and religious as well as intellectual.

The introductory treatise does not cite Anselm's argument. It does cite many of the arguments used beside it in the commentaries of the school, however, and it provides an account of the knowledge of God that anticipates its use of Anselm's argument in the first question of the *Summa* proper. That account needs to be examined to appreciate the role of Anselm's argument and the thesis defended in the opening question of the *Summa.*

Divided in two parts, the first tract of the introduction is concerned with the teaching of the scriptures as a body of knowledge transcending all others, being different in source, procedure and means of transmission, and above all others in certainty since it is inspired directly by God.[69] Its first question emphasises that no human reasoning has any role in establishing the body of knowledge itself. The teaching of theology alone is wisdom as wisdom (*sapientia ut sapientia*).[70] Nonetheless, human understanding of the teaching is possible, but the teachings of faith must be believed first and then understood.[71] Since divine things can be understood by those who are humble in heart, it is not inconsistent therefore, for the doctrine of theology to be both knowledge and belief.[72] The teaching of theology, or sacred scripture, first generates faith and afterward, operating in a humble heart through love, generates understanding. And this is the difference between this doctrine and all others. In science belief follows understanding, in wisdom understanding follows belief.[73]

Having established the overall perspective of the *Summa*, the introduction goes on to deal, in the second treatise, with 'the knowledge of God in this life'.[74] The doctrine that permeates the *Summa's* teaching is that of the soul's commensurability with God as a rational being. Such is God's relationship with the soul and the soul's spiritual and rational nature that the soul knows that God exists more certainly than it knows anything else. The discussion of the knowledge of God in this life is divided into three. The first part concerns what is knowable, the second concerns the nature of the knower, and the third part concerns the medium of knowing.

In the first part, concerned with what is knowable about God, the treatise begins with the fundamental point that God's being is infinitely greater than the soul, and as such is incomprehensible to it.[75] It goes on to say, however, that incomprehensible does not mean unknowable.[76] It is one thing to see, another to totally comprehend. The very immateriality and spiritual simplicity of the mind means that it is able to know something better and more excellent than itself: the divine substance.[77] Though there is an infinite gap in being between the finite and the infinite, there is a certain compatibility between the mind and the object. This is because the mind bears the image of God. The image of God is in the mind both as its ability to grasp the infinite and as its partner (*capax et particeps*). The *Summa* connects knowledge and love: the image of God is in the mind through its infinite potential for knowledge, and as its partner through love.[78]

Yet, the nature of knowledge is limited. Just as Francis had considered 'conversion' primarily a moral rather than an intellectual affair, the *Summa* emphasises that the decisive factor in our knowledge of God – even where our natural knowledge is concerned – is our status as fallen creatures. The rational mind cannot know the Trinity without some gift of grace, namely revelation. This is because the intellect has been darkened through original sin, and is deficient in those very things that most truly are.[79]

In the second stage of this enquiry into the knowledge of God in this life, the *Summa* passes on to the nature of the knower. We are able to know *that* God is through natural reason, but not *what* God is.[80] In the course of supporting this contention, the *Summa* cites a number of authorities and arguments from the Christian tradition. Quoting *On the Sacraments*, by the twelfth-century Augustinian canon, Hugh of St Victor, the *Summa* states that God restrained the mind of the human creature. Though it would never comprehend what God is, it could not be ignorant of God's existence.[81] The *Summa* then cites a passage from the Greek theologian John of Damascus (c. 675-c. 749) that was also to be constantly associated with Anselm's argument in the thirteenth century. John states that, because the universe declares the greatness of the divine nature, the knowledge of God's existence has been naturally inserted in everyone.[82] The difference between the saved and the unsaved in this life is that whilst for both natural knowledge is limited to the existence of God through God's effects, those who are saved, because their minds are purified, can discern the supernatural as well as the natural effects.[83]

Like Odo's second disciple, the *Summa* distinguishes between different powers of knowing. Reason divides itself into superior and inferior powers. The superior part is for the contemplation of God and eternal things, the inferior for the contemplation of creatures and temporal things. The superior part pertains to wisdom, the inferior to science.[84] The superior mode, or the mode of *intelligentia* is in turn divided into two. There is intelligence by the mode of intelligence and intelligence by the mode of reason. The apprehension of God through intelligence by the mode of intelligence is not open to the rational mind in this life. In this life the intelligence apprehends God by the mode of reason as the universal cause of effects.[85]

The third and final part of the enquiry into the knowledge of God in this life concerns the medium of knowledge and follows the discussion of inferior and superior parts of the soul. God cannot be known in this life as God is. The mind requires the medium of creatures for the natural knowledge of God.[86] Creatures supply a similitude of the thing, although there is in one sense no direct comparison between the infinite and the finite.[87] There can, however, be analogical comparison.[88] The knowledge of God is never complete, but always in a process of becoming in this life, and requires instruments and similitudes.[89]

After discussing the knowledge of God through creatures, the *Summa* goes on to discuss the knowledge of God through the grace of faith, before discussing the proof of things believed through reason.[90] Here it draws together the considerations of the first part of the introduction with those of the second. In accordance with dialectical method, the *Summa* lists objections to the possibility of proving by reason things believed by faith. Once again, the objective is not merely to refute the objections, but to show how the arguments brought forward from authority and from reason make more sense in the light of the position defended. The significance of the penultimate question in the introduction is realised when it is appreciated that the *Summa* tackles directly the conflict over studies within the order. There is a sense in which St Francis's own objections to learning are expressed here in terms of standard objections found within Christian tradition itself.

The first of these authorities is found in the teaching of St Gregory (c. 540-604): 'Faith has no merit where human reason supplies its experience.' Therefore, to prove the doctrines of faith is to empty faith of its merit.[91] In the second place, and like William of Auxerre, the *Summa* states that faith is its own proof and not the conclusion of proof.[92] In the third place, since there is nothing more certain to the human creature than faith, it is vain and empty to use reason to try and prove the things of faith.[93] Finally, and in the fourth place, since faith is above all understanding and reason and whatever natural reason supplies is within reason and understanding, things believed cannot be proved by natural reason.[94]

The *Summa* then states another authority, this time in favour of the position that it wants to defend. That authority is provided by Richard of St Victor, successor to Hugh in the twelfth-century Augustinian school at Paris, and advocate of Anselm's belief in 'necessary reasons'. In *De Trinitate* Richard wrote that for necessary things there must also exist necessary, and not merely probable arguments. The more necessary a thing is, the more necessary are the arguments proving it: an authority that identifies the ontological order with the epistemological order.[95]

Responding to the contradiction of authorities, the *Summa* follows William of Auxerre and states three arguments in favour of trying to show by natural reason what is believed in faith.[96] The first reason is on account of believers themselves, who ought always to investigate the understanding of things believed through the self-revelation or 'face' of God. It is a kind of spiritual duty, enjoined on the believer by Scripture: the psalmist says, 'Seek his face always' (Ps. 104, 4).[97] Hence, reason adds to faith, and deepens it by making the enquirer more familiar with the things already believed. In that sense, then, not only does enquiry begin in an awareness of God, but it leads the enquirer closer to God.

Similarly, and in the second place, just as the enjoyment of temporal goods promotes divine love, so reasons can help raise the simple to perfect or greater faith.[98]

Finally, in the third place, reasons ought to be used for recalling the unfaithful to the true faith. This is why John of Damascus says that although the knowledge of the existence of God has been naturally inserted in the rational mind, the pernicious malice of human nature prevails over it so that some say that God does not exist, just like the Fool in the psalms who says in his heart 'there is no

God'. As if to confirm the argument of Richard of St Victor, the passage concludes that for the recalling of such people, necessary reasons do in fact exist.[99]

In response to the arguments against reason, the *Summa* states that it is only faith based on reason that is without merit. Faith that is held on account of itself as the first truth can supply reasons, but these do not remove its merit.[100] To the second objection, and like William of Auxerre, the *Summa* distinguishes between the reason of logic that makes certain a thing doubted, and faith which is a certainty producing reasons. Faith is itself the light of the soul. The more the soul is illumined by its power the greater is the soul's perspicacity for finding reasons that prove the things believed.[101] To the third objection, the *Summa* agrees that nothing is more certain to the human creature than faith to those who have it, the certitude of reason has to be distinguished from certitude of the will and the heart. Nothing is more certain than faith in the second sense, but not in the first. Therefore, there is room for rational proof.[102]

Finally, and in response to the fourth objection, that faith is above reason and therefore cannot be understood, the *Summa* argues that this entails only that certain forms of argumentation are inappropriate for the proof of divine things. Since the things of faith transcend reason and understanding, proof cannot depend upon prior argumentation that has its medium and what it proves within the intellect. The proof of things believed must depend upon posterior reasons, which are external to the human mind and, hence, do not prohibit the mind from proving truths that are above reason. This, therefore, is the reason the Scriptures speak of human reason coming to understand the invisible things of God through the things that are made.[103]

The last question of the introduction asks, like Odo Rigaud's third disciple, 'whether the knowledge of God through natural reason is more certain than the knowledge of creatures?' In addressing this question, the *Summa* resolves the conflict that is implicit in its discussion between the necessity for creatures as a medium for the mind in knowing God, and the knowledge of God that is naturally inserted in the mind. While it may seem that the knowledge of creatures, known directly to the senses, ought to be more certain in this life than the knowledge of God, the *Summa* argues that God is more certain because God is the light by which creatures are comprehended in the mind. Just as light is seen more certainly than the things that are illumined by it, so God is to intelligible things as light is to the visible. 'In this way therefore', Augustine says, 'just as we consider the sun in three ways: that it is, that it shines, that it illumines, so we ought to consider the most hidden God in three ways: that God is, that God understands, that God makes other things intelligible.'[104] Therefore, God is known more certainly than creatures.

The *Summa* thus presents the knowledge of God as arising from the knowledge of creatures – but not as an inference from the knowledge of creatures. Rather, it is in the very act of the intelligence that God is to be known. God is not known as an innate idea, but in the act of the intellect itself when it understands creatures.[105] In its response to objections, the very last part of the introduction employs the notion of habitual knowledge already found in the commentary of Odo's third disciple. By means of this device the *Summa* addresses a key difficulty of the early school: how can the mind depend upon God to know creatures if it requires the medium of creatures to know God? Moreover, if the knowledge of God is more certain than creatures, how can the knowledge of creatures lead the mind astray?

The *Summa* introduces a three-fold distinction into its account of habitual knowledge. There is, it says, knowledge according to an innate disposition, knowledge according to an infused disposition, and knowledge according to a disposition acquired by way of the senses. Knowledge of creatures is more certain than the knowledge of God according to the disposition acquired by way of the senses. God, however, is known more certainly in two ways. The first is through an innate disposition; the second is through an infused disposition. The infused disposition is faith and available only to the faithful. The innate disposition, however, mentioned for the first time in the *Summa* is the same for everyone. The knowledge of God is therefore a natural certainty, and not only a matter for faith. However, when the intellect knows God by means of the disposition acquired through the senses, using creatures as a medium, the knowledge of creatures is more certain than the knowledge of God. When the knowledge is from an infused or innate disposition, the knowledge of God is more certain.[106]

The *Summa* argues a specific case about the nature of all enquiry directed toward God: where it must begin, what is its medium, and what the proper end of that enquiry must be. Without a proper beginning, however, the end of enquiry will never be attained. The beginning, as the *Summa* makes clear, is faith and humility. Without these, reason will not attain the ultimate truths. Similarly, since all rational knowledge depends upon the light of God's illumination, the very proof of God presupposes what it sets out to prove. Nonetheless, it does so only in an implicit way, according to an innate disposition of habitual knowledge.

The *Summa* also wants to claim that the medium of creatures is necessary if the mind is to arrive at a knowledge of God. It is not enough to resolve the apparent contradiction here by saying that the soul is itself a creature, and is therefore able to be its own medium for knowing God. The problem is that the *Summa* makes a stronger claim than that about the soul. It claims that there is a habitual knowledge of God by an innate disposition. To reconcile the need for a medium with the innate disposition it is necessary merely to recognise that a disposition is not itself an object of knowledge – rather it points the soul in a certain direction. Thus the soul is disposed to find God through the medium of creatures.

Finally, the end of inquiry is the understanding of things – or at least some of the things – believed by faith. Just as the innate disposition directs the soul to God, so the end of knowledge is the knowledge of God. This does not serve to rob faith of its merit, however, but rather to draw the believer closer to God, its partner both in love and in its infinite capacity. The life of humility and faith is not only a pre-requisite for attaining knowledge, therefore, but also the effect of its attainment.

## IV

It is in the context of its account of the beginning, medium and end of enquiry that the *Summa* turns to the necessary existence of the divine being and, in a separate section, to the conclusion of Anselm's argument that God cannot be thought not to exist. The arguments which the *Summa* employs to show the necessity of God's existence indicate that God's existence is implicit within the principles of the mind's knowledge: being, causality, truth, goodness and hierarchy. Thus, for the *Summa*, the transcendentals that lie at the source of knowledge, reflect the source of being, causality, truth, goodness and hierarchy itself.[107] The ontological order is also the epistemological order. The mind that sets out to prove the existence of the first principle of things must already possess, in an implicit way, a knowledge of that which it sets out to prove. More importantly, the mind attains the existence of God not as an inference from the existence of creatures, but within the very nature of existence itself, according to the transcendentals of being, causality, truth, goodness and hierarchy. Anselm's argument is employed both to confirm and to complete an account of God that is also an account of the nature of knowledge and, as we shall see, of human nature more generally.

The first part of the first question deals with the necessity of God's existence. The first argument of the *Summa* concerns the transcendental 'being', and is taken from Richard of St Victor's *De trinitate*. When being is considered it must be considered in one of three ways, Richard argues. A being must exist from itself and from eternity, from another and from eternity or from another and from within time. (A fourth possibility is discounted: something cannot be from itself and from within time, for there would have been a time when it did not exist. If it did not exist, it could not produce itself.) Richard of St Victor then introduces the notion of 'superior reason' to describe the way the soul comes to a knowledge of God from ordinary experience. Daily experience shows us that there are innumerable things that are not from eternity. The superior reason understands that whatever is not from eternity is not able to be from itself. But if there was nothing from itself, it would not be possible in any way for those things to exist which did not and were not able to have their being from themselves. There must exist something, therefore, that exists from itself and also from eternity: this we call the divine substance. Thus Richard of St Victor establishes that the very possibility of beings depends upon the necessary being that has being from eternity and from itself and is the source of all being.[108]

Interestingly, the *Summa* adds that something could exist from eternity and yet still owe its being to another being. If the rays of corporeal light are coeval with their source, the sun, why not also the rays of that spiritual and inaccessible light? Nonetheless, they depend upon a being existing from itself.

The *Summa* is already looking forward to its treatment of Aristotle's doctrine of the eternity of the world. That it does not discount the rational possibility of a coeval world here is indicative of its 'accommodationist' strategy *vis-à-vis* Aristotle, despite the fact that the opening topic of the *Summa* indicates that it ties its colours firmly to the mast of Platonic participation. Like the Chartreans of the twelfth century, the *Summa* tends to regard contradictions between philosophers and Christian doctrine as more apparent than real, and thus avoid the problem of contradictions between ancient philosophy and Christian truth.[109] This was one aspect of the *Summa* from which later Franciscans at Paris were to depart.

Having progressed through the transcendental 'being' to God, the next article progresses to God through causation.[110] The *Summa* adds a quotation from the book of *Wisdom* stating that from the wonder of creatures their maker can be known.[111] The *Summa* employs arguments once again from John of Damascus and from Hugh of St Victor. The argument of Hugh of St Victor has already been alluded to in the sentence commentaries of the school. It states that since the soul is not able to doubt concerning itself that it exists (since it is not able to ignore itself) and it knows that it did not always have existence, it cannot deny that it was made by some other. The *Summa* draws on a Scripture to confirm this: 'Know that the Lord is God, Who made us (Vulgate Ps. 99, 3).'[112]

Articles three and four of the first part of the question concern the knowledge of God's substance according to the transcendentals of truth and goodness. Just as being must depend upon eternal being, truth itself must be considered as eternal. If one considers that there was a time when there is no truth, then either this will have been true or will not have been true. Similarly, if there is a time in the future when there will no longer be truth, then either this will be true or it will not. In both cases truth necessarily is. Truth cannot be understood except as eternal. This is what is understood by the divine essence.[113]

The *Summa* then turns to Anselm's argument to pursue God through the transcendental 'good', and it is at this point that the argument first appears in the *Summa*. Just as truth cannot be understood except as eternal, so the highest goodness cannot be understood except as existing.[114] That than which no greater can be thought cannot be understood except as existing in reality. If it was understood to exist in the mind alone, then it would be possible to think of something greater – something which did exist in reality. Therefore that than which no greater can be conceived would not be that than which no greater can be conceived – which is impossible.[115]

The arguments concerning the eternal existence of being, truth and the good than which no greater can be conceived show not just the necessity of God's existence, but also the participation of all things in the highest being. If there were no eternal being, truth or highest goodness, there would be no being, truth or goodness at all. The first part of the first question concludes by an enquiry into the hierarchy of goods in the world. From ordinary experience it is obvious that some beings are better than others. There must exist some being which is greater than all others and over which there is no superior. Otherwise this multitude of natures would have no end, which is absurd. The last argument demonstrates the necessity of a highest nature than which nothing is greater. Again, citing Richard of St Victor, the *Summa* states, 'we call the highest of all things, that than which there is nothing greater or better'.[116]

The necessity of God's existence is thus proclaimed by the participation of things in being, truth and goodness, and by the necessity of a highest being in the hierarchy of things. It is by virtue of the mind's knowledge of the transcendentals that it can know things in the universe: a universe that exists by participation is unknowable without God. The very experience that the mind draws upon to prove God's existence already presupposes, in some implicit way, that God is known to the mind. Anselm's argument is drawn into this discussion to confirm this account of human knowledge, as well as an account of God that is present to the soul and in all creation.[117]

Following neatly on the argument from goodness and eminence in the first part of the first question, the second part of the first question asks whether God can be thought not to be. Having employed the second chapter of the *Proslogion* in the first part, the *Summa* responds to this question with the *Proslogion*'s third chapter:

> If it is possible to think that there is something that cannot be thought not to exist, it will be greater than something which can be thought not to exist. If, therefore, that than which no greater can be conceived can be thought not to exist, this very thing than which no greater can be conceived is not that than which no greater can be conceived; which is clearly impossible. Therefore, there truly exists something than which no greater can be thought, so that it cannot be thought not to exist; and this is you, Lord our God. For if the mind were able to think something better than you, the creature would ascend over the Creator: which is clearly absurd.[118]

The *Summa* then discusses the knowledge of God's existence as a 'natural impression', immutable, universal, and the same in all. John of Damascus taught that the knowledge of God's existence is naturally inserted within us. Therefore, it is a knowledge that is universal and the same in all, and cannot be ignored by the rational creature.[119] In the third place, the *Summa* adapts the third chapter of Anselm's argument again. The most true essence is something that cannot not exist, nor can it be thought of as not existing. Since the divine essence is the most truly existing and most true essence it cannot not exist, nor can it be thought not to exist.[120]

The fourth affirmative argument adopted by the *Summa* is from the continual presence of being to the thinking subject. Here the argument of Hugh of St Victor is employed to unite the idea of the necessity of a first cause with the soul's knowledge of itself and the unthinkability of God's non-being. No one is able to be ignorant of their existence, nor equally of the fact that they did not always exist. Since the soul knows that it exists and that it did not always have existence, it knows by necessity that it has its being from another that is the principle of its being. Therefore it is impossible to be ignorant of God's existence.[121]

The use of Anselm's argument (11th century) alongside the teaching of John of Damascus (8th century) concerning the naturally inserted knowledge of God, and alongside the argument of Hugh of St Victor (12th century) that the soul cannot be ignorant of God's existence, typifies the way the thirteenth-century academy, no less than its counterpart in the twentieth century, de-contextualises and anthologises texts. The process has implications for the way the texts are read. In Anselm's case, the argument has not only been detached from the prayer of which it was originally a part, but it has also been separated from the context of the arguments from participation and hierarchy. Although those elements are present elsewhere in the *Summa*, the Anselmian argument itself lends itself to confusion with a quite different teaching – that the knowledge of God's existence is somehow already present within the soul. However, it would be wrong to think that the *Summa* is itself merely confused about what it is doing, however. Unlike modern anthologies, the *Summa* is adapting its texts toward the deliberate expression of a particular thesis about the nature of knowledge. What that thesis is only becomes apparent in the *Summa*'s response to objections listed against the view that God's non-existence is unthinkable.

In any case, the *Summa* has to consider the possibility that the position it has defended so far is in fact wrong: there are at least five arguments showing that God's non-being is thinkable. First of all, John of Damascus himself has said that though the knowledge of God's existence is impressed upon us naturally, the pernicious evil of men prevails to such a degree that they say that God does not exist. Hence David reports in the psalms that the Fool says within his heart 'there is no God'. The divine essence, therefore, is able to be ignored by the foolish and to be thought not to exist.[122]

In the second place the *Summa* adapts the fourth chapter of Anselm's argument. Since it is the same to say in the heart and to think, it is possible to think, like the Fool, that God does not exist.[123] In the third place, the *Summa* cites the existence of idolaters who say that the God of the faithful does not exist. Yet this God alone exists and is the true God. Therefore, the non-existence of God can be thought.[124] The fourth argument against the favoured position cites the Scripture that God dwells in inaccessible light which no one sees or can see (1 Tim. 6:16). Since the mind can think the non-existence of created things that it can see, how much more is it able to think that the divine being does not exist?[125] Finally, the fifth objection is drawn from Boethius. Our intellect can perceive that things exist, it does not perceive the existence of some highest thing. From this it would appear, therefore, that it is possible to think that the highest good does not exist.[126]

The *Summa Minorum* provides a *solutio* to these conflicting arguments: that is, it attempts to show that the contradictions between them are merely apparent. Once again, like the third disciple of Odo Riguad, it states that there are two kinds of knowledge concerning God. There is active (*cognitio actu*) and habitual or dispositional knowledge (*cognitio habitu*). The habitual or dispositional knowledge of God is naturally impressed upon us as the similitude or image of the first truth in the intellect by which the intellect is able to infer that this very being exists. The rational animal cannot ignore this knowledge. Active knowledge is two-fold. The first kind is the movement of the soul according to the superior part of reason impressed by the image of the first truth. The soul recognises the existence of its creator through the fact that it did not have existence from itself. And so in this way also it is not able to ignore that God exists. The other kind of active knowledge is the movement of the soul according to inferior reason, whose purpose is to contemplate creatures. And in this way it is possible to be ignorant of God's existence, since through sin and error the mind has been darkened so that it is turned away from God. In this way the Apostle says, 'Although they knew God, they did not glorify God as God, but became futile in their thinking, and their foolish hearts were darkened, and they served creatures rather than the Creator (Rom. 1: 21)'.

Hence, by the introduction of superior and inferior reason the Franciscan school can maintain that God is indubitable in one sense, though not in another. Moreover, this is an account of the knowledge of God that establishes a particular approach to the knowledge of nature. When seen in themselves instead of as images of God, creatures are capable of leading the soul astray. Understanding the differences between the superior and inferior parts of reason is to understand the sense in which the knowledge of God is innate within the soul, and yet requires the inspection of creatures to be actualised.

There is a sense in which the talk of natural impression suggests that the knowledge of God is an innate idea. However, the talk of the impression as a reflection of the first truth ought to be seen in the light of the earlier arguments for the necessity of God's existence. It is not that the knowledge of God's existence is innate, but that the image of the first truth guides the mind toward understanding so that God is known in the soul's very act of knowing truth, goodness and being. It is in the reflection of creatures that God is known – but God is reflected in creatures because God is the source of the mind's knowing. Like Anselm himself, the Franciscans encounter God in the divine presence within the world – since the world exists by participation in God. Yet, with the Franciscans, the encounter with God, and Anselm's argument itself, is more deeply internalised. God is encountered in creation because creation participates in God, but also because the soul itself functions by participation in the first truth. It is when the mind is not guided by the image of the first truth that it is in danger of seeing creatures in themselves, without reference to their participation in the first and maximal being. But just how could the soul fail to see the most necessary being, if knowledge depends upon the illumination of that being?

To answer this question, the *Summa* introduces another distinction: a distinction between knowledge that is common to all minds, and the realisation of that knowledge by particular minds. In making this distinction, the *Summa* explains the pre-requisites for the knowledge of God – pre-requisites that are grounded in the spiritual life.

The knowledge and appetite for beatitude, which is 'the perfect aggregate of all goods', is common to all minds. Nevertheless many are ignorant of beatitude according to their own particular reasoning. Hence, they posit beatitude in diverse places: some in honours, others in riches, still others in sensual pleasures. Similarly idolaters are not ignorant of God according to the reason common to all, that God is being, Principle, Omnipotent, *etc.* Nevertheless, under their own particular reasoning they are ignorant and say concerning God, Who is Trinity and Unity and Truth, that this is not God and say instead that an idol is God.[127]

Later, Thomas Aquinas will argue that it is the obscurity of the first truth which prevents the majority from reaching it without Revelation.[128] For the Franciscan school it is rather impediments within the understanding caused by sin which hinders a knowledge of the first truth. The knowledge of God is acquired by encountering God in things – but this requires a prior orientation of the soul: an orientation of desire or appetite for beatitude. Otherwise the soul remains blind to what is most present and most obvious to it. For the summists of the Franciscan school, knowledge is led by desire; and the attainment of knowledge incites desire. In that sense, therefore, the problems represented by Aristotle, which are implicit rather than explicit within the *Summa*, are dealt with by an extension of the principle of 'faith seeking understanding' to knowledge generally, and not just to revelation. Understanding comes to depend upon faith, and in this context reason operates within faith by drawing the soul closer to that in whose image it is made. In ultimate terms, education is justified within the Franciscan order, not because it enables the Franciscans to enter into disputations with the unbeliever, but partly because it contributes to the practical effort of purifying the soul and imitating Christ, by enhancing its personal awareness of God.

## V

The teaching of the early Franciscan school seeks to render a clear account of the Christian tradition, yet like all such accounts, it is necessarily rendered according to a perspective. The *Summa minorum* and the whole host of other texts discussed here end up by giving articulation to the spirituality of St Francis in terms supplied by the sources of the mainstream Christian tradition. In that sense, Anselm's argument (in conjunction with other texts employed alongside it) presents not the rational foundations of Franciscan life, but the rationality internal to the life itself: and this is the crucial distinction for understanding the role of argument within the Franciscan community. The presence of Anselm's argument, together with the recurrence of arguments and authorities from John of Damascus and the Victorine scholars, within the school at large indicates that the Franciscans were thinking as a community, and not merely as a group of scholars who happened to be working in the same institution.

The agenda of the Franciscan school was shaped by the need to reconcile the spirituality of St Francis with the requirements of academic contestability. This was partly because St Francis's vision was capable of legitimation only if it could be articulated in terms of the sources of the mainstream Christian tradition. In this sense, the early Franciscan school was searching for reasons that would count as reasons within its own community, but which were already accepted within the wider Christian community. Ironically it was the apparent novelty or radicality of Francis's teaching that made this project necessary – even if a central part of Francis's teaching involved the rejection of learning and argument. Without the work of the academics, the Franciscans could not have succeeded in overcoming opposition from secular clergy – particularly when they started to receive privileges from the papal see at clerical expense. However, even before the academics could argue on behalf of their community, they had to overcome the contradiction of articulating a spirituality that rejected theological articulation.

They attempted to overcome that contradiction by uncovering the idea of God implicit within St Francis's own teaching, an idea shared by both the academics and the more radical or 'spiritual' wing of the order when they both opposed the corruption of St Francis's successor, Elias of Cortona. The enquiry into the natural knowledge of God, was in a sense therefore, an enquiry into the first principle of the religious life. The aim of the academics with respect to the debate within their own order, was ultimately to show that the pursuit of theological learning was not only compatible with the idea of God implicit within the Franciscan life, but necessary for its realisation in practice. Although St Francis promoted simplicity within his order, it was a simplicity that in itself involved a profound awareness. In a sense, St Francis was himself battling against ignorance of God and of God's requirements for human beings. This was ignorance of the most manifest and most necessary thing, and like St Francis, the academics ascribed the cause of that ignorance to sin or, to put it another way, the love of sensual things. Knowledge by itself will not lead the soul to a true understanding of the nature of things. Knowledge requires a re-orientation of the soul, or penitence.

Odo Rigaud's third disciple explained that God is known because God is loved. When love is turned towards objects of sensual desire, or beatitude is sought in worldly goods, the soul ceases to see God through creatures and sees only the creatures themselves. True knowledge springs from a love of God – because that love sees everything in the light of God. It is for this reason that even the natural knowledge of God depends upon faith. In this context, faith is an attitude of the soul as well as a body of doctrine. Above all else, the knowledge of God may begin in sensible experience, but it is realised through an interior journey of purification and ascent.

It is not a case of providing a proof for the existence of God from nature therefore, but of explaining what nature is in terms of God, and how knowledge is dependent upon inner purification. Anselm's argument was validated within the Franciscan convent in Paris, not just because of its place within a broader doctrinal scheme which the community accepted, but because that doctrinal scheme expressed the encounter with God in nature and in the soul that was peculiar to Franciscan spirituality. God cannot be thought not to exist both because the very structure of nature requires the presence of God, but also because God is present to the rational soul. Moreover, the problem of the Fool indicates that the awareness of God is nonetheless extinguished by sin. In such an account of God it is the example of penitence rather than verbal persuasion that is required to draw the soul to an awareness of itself in the presence of God. Anselm's argument was significant therefore because the God that cannot be thought not to exist helps explain both the precondition of the Franciscan mission, and also the reason why its distinctive form of mission is necessary. As we shall see however, the Dominicans and even elements within the Franciscan order in Oxford had other ways of conceptualising the relationship between God and the world. This was in part because Dominicans encountered God in ways unlike their Franciscan contemporaries.

## Notes

1. For an account of the organisation of the Faculty of Theology, its relationship to the Faculty of Arts, and the exceptions made for the admission of the Friars at the University of Paris, see G. Leff, *Paris and Oxford Universities in the Thirteenth and Fourteenth Centuries: An institutional and Intellectual History* (New York, 1968), On the exemption of Friars from the requirement of studying in the lower Faculty, see Leff, pp. 162 and 164-167.
2. See, for example, H. Felder, *Histoire des Études dans L'Ordre de S. Francois*, trans. into French by E. de Bar-Le-Duc (Paris, 1908; 1st pub. in 1904), pp. 335-345.
3. Little, A. G., 'The Franciscan School at Oxford', in A. G. Little, *Franciscan Papers, Lists and Documents* (Manchester, 1943), pp. 55-71 (55). See also Felder, *Histoire*, pp. 322, 335-345.
4. See Leff, *Paris and Oxford Universities*, esp. pp. 160-173.
5. On the origins of the struggle between seculars and mendicants see Leff, pp. 34ff, and D. L. Douie, *The Conflict Between The Seculars and the Mendicants at the University of Paris in the Thirteenth Century* (London, 1954).
6. See on this, Felder, *Histoire des Études dans L'Ordre de S. Francois*.
7. See ibid., esp. pp. 480ff.
8. See the *Early Rule*, c. xxii, 2, trans. in R. J. Armstrong and I. C. Brady, *Francis and Clare: The Complete Works* (Paulist Press, 1982).

9. See Duncan Nimmo, *Reform and Division in the Franciscan Order* (Rome, 1987), p. 83. For an overview of the sources of the life of St Francis see J. R. H. Moorman, *Sources for the Life of St Francis* (Manchester, 1940).
10. Nimmo, pp. 70-76.
11. See E. R. Daniel, *The Franciscan Concept of Mission in the High Middle Ages* (Kentucky 1975), p. 40.
12. R. I. Burns, 'Christian-Islamic confrontation in the West: The thirteenth-century dream of conversion', in the *American History Review*, vol. 86, 4-5 (1976), 1395-1396.
13. See, for example, J. R. H. Moorman, *A History of the Franciscan Order, From its Origins to the Year 1517* (Oxford, 1968), pp. 77ff.
14. See Brenda Bolton, 'Tradition and Temerity: Papal Attitudes to Deviants, 1159-1216', in *Schism, Heresy and Religious Protest*, ed. by D. Baker, Studies in Church History, ix (Cambridge, 1972), pp. 79-91.
15. Ibid., p. 90.
16. M. W. Sheehan, 'The Religious Orders, 1220-1370', in J. I. Catto, *The History of the University of Oxford* (Oxford, 1984), I, 197.
17. Cit. in É. Gilson, *History of Christian Philosophy in the Middle Ages* (London, 1978), p. 329.
18. Moorman, *History*, pp. 100, 131ff.
19. Cit. in J. G. Bougerol, *Introduction to the works of Bonaventure*, trans. by J. de Vinck (New Jersey, 1963), p. 13.
20. See I. Brady, 'The Distinctions of Lombard's Book of Sentences and Alexander of Hales', *Franciscan Studies*, 25 (1965), 90-116.
21. M. Colish, *Peter Lombard*, 2 vols (Brill, 1994), II, 719.
22. Ibid., I, 79.
23. Ibid., I, 79-80.
24. Ibid., I, 80: 'Peter is deeply interested in the terminology appropriate to the description of the attributes of the individual members of the unmanifested Trinity as well as in the terms apposite to the general divine attributes which They share. He is sensitive to the need for terminological distinctions in this connection, and is far more successful than his contemporaries and immediate predecessors in making the lexical specifications which he needs here and in applying his chosen vocabulary consistently.'
25. Ibid., I, 241.
26. Ibid.
27. See Alexander of Hales, *Glossa in Quatuor Libros Sententiarum Petri Lombardi* (Quaracchi, 1951), I, which contains brief notices relating to the life of Alexander.
28. Alexander of Hales *Glossa*, I, 27-28.
29. Ibid., I, 28.
30. Ibid., I, 28.
31. Ibid., I, 37-74.
32. Ibid., I, 39-42, Lib. I, distinction iii, articles 4, 5, 10, 11.
33. Ibid., I, 42, Lib. 1, dist. iii, art. 12, i, 'Ad primam quaestionem absolvendam dicit Anselmus libro De personislogion id est divinis personis: Quo maius excogitari non

potest, est Deus. Sed maius est quod cogitatur esse in re et intellectu, quam quod cogitatur intellectu solum. Maius est iterum illud quod cogitari potest esse et non potest cogitari non esse, quam quod cogitari potest non esse cum sit. Erit ergo Deus bonum quod non est tantum in intellectu et non est cogitari non esse. Quod quidem dicitur in Psalmo: Dixit insipiens in corde suo non est Deus, nota: est dupliciter dicere: verbo exteriori, et sic verum est: vel interiori, quod est verbum rei, et sic est impossibile.'

34. Ibid., I, 42-43, Lib. I, dist. iii, art. 12, ii.
35. Ibid., I, 43-44, Lib. I, dist. iii, art. 12, iii.
36. On the dates and influence of two of these early Franciscan commentaries see P. F. M. Henquinet, 'Eudes de Rosny, O.F.M., Eudes Rigaud et La Somme d'Alexandre de Hales', in *Archivum Franciscanum Historicum*, 33 (1940), 3-54.
37. See P. Glorieux, *Répertoire des Maîtres en Théologie de Paris au XIIIe Siécle*, 2 vols (Paris, 1933), II, n. 303a, and Frederick Stegmueller, *Repertorium Commentariorum in Sententias Petri Lombardi* (Wurzburg, 1947), pp. 607-611.
38. On the dates see P. Basilius Pergamo, 'De Quaestionibus Ineditis Fr. Odonis Rigaud, fr. Gulielmi de Melitona et Codicis Vat Lat. 782 Circa Naturam Theologiae deque earum relatione ad Summam Theologicam Fr. Alexandri Halensis', in *Archivum Franciscanum Historicum*, 29 (1936), 3-54, 308-364 (p. 16), Glorieux, *Répertoire*, II, nos 302-303, and Henquinet 'Eudes de Rosny…', p. 3. Historians are unsure as to whether John de La Rochelle and Alexander of Hales both held chairs in the faculty during this period. See Alexander of Hales, *Glossa*, I, 15*.
39. See also R. W. Southern, *Western Society and the Church in the Middle Ages* (London, 1970), pp. 190-193, for Odo's administration of the archiepiscopal see at Rouen.
40. Pergamo, 16, Glorieux, II, 303, and Henquinet, 3.
41. Odo's commentary was consulted at Paris, Bibliothèque Nationale, MS. Lat. 14910. The second distinction is found on fols 6v-10r.
42. Ibid., fol. 6v. 'Quod de deo tenet catholica fides... contra heretici et mundatiorum confictori qui auctores non recipiunt rationibus probare posse videamus.'
43. Ibid., fol. 7r. 'Item, omnia predicta possunt probari unico argumento quid facit anselmus in proslogion sicut: deus est quo melius excogitari non potest. Tale est quemlibet fingit esse deum tale aut est aut non est. Si est habeo propositum. Si non est, cum quemlibet ens sit melius non ente, quemlibet ens est melius eo quo melius excogitari non potest. Hoc autem est impossibilis. Ergo necesse est ponire esse deus. Ergo est tale quo melius excogitari non potest. Ergo est simplicitas aeterna, omnipotens etc... Ergo patet quod possunt praedicta probari quae de deo tendit fides catholica.'
44. Ibid., fol. 7r. 'Melior est quod non potest excogitari non esse quam quod potest cogitari non esse. Sed deus potest cogitari non esse: Secundum Psalm, dixit inspiens in corde suo non est deus. Et aliquid potest cogitari tale quod non possit cogitari non esse. Ergo aliquid potest cogitari melius ipso deo. Ergo ipse non est deus.'
45. Ibid. 'Aliquis quis putat malam placere deo putat deum non esse deum. Sed multa sunt tales sicut illi qui persequendo apostoles putabant se obsequi [et] placere deo (Job

xvi). Ergo Deus potest putari non esse. Sed melior esset si non possit putari non esse. Ergo ipse non est id quo melius excogitari non potest. Ergo non est deus.'

46. Ibid., fol. 7r. 'Item utrum queritur ratio anselmi non valeat. Possum et ego intelligere aliquam insulam qua melior excogitari non possit et dicitur insulam perditam est et a nemine cognita. Probo per similem rationam quod hanc insulam est sic. Insula qua melior excogitari non potest aut est aut non est. Si est habeo propositionem. Si non est, tunc aliqua insula est. Omne autem est melius non ente. Ergo aliqua insula est melior illa insula qua melior cogitari non potest. Hoc autem est impossibile. Ergo necesse est hanc insulam esse. Sed hoc est manifeste falsum. Ergo constat quod argumentum non valde. Nec quod facit anselmus de deo.'
47. Ibid., fol. 7v. 'Sit ex defecto nostro, quia sicut dicit philosophus sicut se habet occulus noctae ad lucem, sic intellectus noster ad manifestissima naturae.'
48. Ibid. 'Dicit ansemlus in libro contra inspiente omnia illae et sola possunt cogitari non esse quod habet initium et finem et partium coniunctionem. Hoc autem solum non potest cogitari melius in quo nec initionem est nec finem nec partium coniunctionem. Et quod non est nisi semper et ubique totum invenit cogitatio. Sed hoc ergo dominus quia nemo potest simpliciter cogitare deum non esse.'
49. Ibid., fol. 23v. 'Dicendum ... quod in deo non differunt sua existens et sua essentia. Sed in creaturis differunt... quia non habent suus esse ex se ipsiis sed a causa efficiente... Ergo possunt intelligi omnes creaturae non esse. Ipse autem deus non... quia solum id potest intelligi non esse quod habuit principium.'
50. Ibid., fol. 7v. 'Sed prout videmus et cognoscemus eum in creaturis in effectibus suis sic possumus abstrahere et sic potest putari non esse iustus ratione alicuius occulti effectis... Et sic dixit insipiens in corde suo non deum esse.'
51. Ibid. 'Nec est simile de deo et de insula. Deus enim de ratione sua importat quo melius excogitari non potest.'
52. Troyes MS. Lat. 1245 (Clairvaux), fols 1-67. The exposition of the argument is found in fols 4v-5r. The manuscript is listed in Stegmueller, *Reportorium*, nn. 607-608. On Odo de Rosny and the dating of his work to 1244-5, see Henquinet 'Eudes de Rosny..', pp. 4ff.
53. Paris, Bibliothèque Nationale, MS lat. 3424.
54. Ibid., fol. 12r.
55. Ibid., fol. 12r.
56. See, for example, G., A. Zinn, 'Book and Word: The Victorine Background of Bonaventure's Use of Symbols', in *S. Bonaventura 1274-1974*, ed. by J. G. Bougerol, 5 vols (Grottaferrata, 1973-4), II, 143-169.
57. Compare Hugh of St Victor, *Eruditionis Didascalicae*, lib. vii, cap. xvii, in *Patrologia Latina*, ed. by J. P. Migne et al., 217 vols (Paris, 1844-79), CLXXVI, cols 824-826.
58. Paris, BN, MS. Lat. 3424, fols. 12r-12v. 'Ad Illud quod ultimus queritur utrum anima possit ignorare deum. Dicendum [est] quod cognitio de deo habitus naturaliter est impressus nobis quia naturaliter impressa in intellectu est similitudo primae veritatis quae potest cognoscere deum esse et non potest ignorari ab anima rationali. Cognitio uero in actu duplex est. Unum est cum movetur anima superiore parti rationis et habitus similitudini primae veritatis superiore parti rationis impressus. Eo modo ergo

[anima] recolit suum principium et per hoc videt se non esse a se et hoc est modo non potest ignorare deum esse... Alium est cum movetur anima inferiore parti rationis qui est ad contemplandas creaturis et in hoc modo potest non cognoscere deum esse omnino si per peccatum in errorem auersa a deo obtenebatur. Et in hoc modo dixit insipiens in corde suo non est deus.'

59. Paris, Bibliothèque Nationale, MS lat. 10640.

60. Ibid., fol. 4r: 'Queritur utrum deus est. Solutio: deus est et stultus fuit qui dixit in corde suo non est deus. Respondeo: .. nos dicamus esse deum quia si non esset unam primam causam quam dicamus esse deum...etc.' 'Queritur utrum unam primam causam vel plures. Solutio: dicendum est unam primam causam est.'

61. Ibid., fol. 4v: 'Queritur utrum deus sit cognoscibilis. Solutio: dicitur quia deus est summa cognoscibilis. Respondeo: hoc est quia est frui. Fruitio presupponit delectationem; delectatio amorem; amor cognitionem et ideo quod fruibilis cognoscibilis est. Alia ratio: quia summa bonitas est diligibilis ab affecta propria, ideo summa veritas dilgibilis ab intellecta. Alio ratio: quia anima sit ymago dei et ymago consistat in potentia congnoscendi. Frugis cassus esset deus facere hominem ad ymaginem eius nisi homo deum cognoscere posset. Item, alia ratio: quod deus cogniscibilis est cum sit summum bonum et ipsam animam creavit ad beatitudinem et ipsa non possit beatificari nisi videndo eum. Videtur in hoc esse vitam eternam etc. Exigit eius bonitas quae ipsem reddat suae creaturae rationabili visibilem.'

62. Ibid., fol. 5v: 'Queritur utrum cognoscendum deum sit facilior quam de creatura vel non. Solutio: de cognitione dei et creaturae contingit loqui dupliciter: aut in se aut in comparatione ad cognita. Dico ergo quia cognitio dei quae est de se facilior est quam cognitio de creatura. Ratio: hoc est quia ipse est summum lux et principium omnis cognitionis. ... Loquendo vero de cognitione dei in comparatione ad cognita necesse est distinguere quam vel est cognitionem viae aut patriae. Loquendo primo modo: cognitio de creatura facilior est quam de deo... Ratio est dum summus in via cognitio creaturae incipit a sensibus et ideo facilior. Secondo modo: facilior est cognitio de deo quam de creatura, eo quod in Patria cognoscitur deus in se primo et principaliter et in ipso cognoscetur alia.'

63. Ibid., fol. 4v: 'Queritur utrum cognitio de deo sit certior quam de creatura. Solutio: Iste duo cognitiones possit considerari ut disperate vel ut invicem ordinate. Si ut disperate sic una non ordinatur ad alteram et sic distingeundum quae aut est cognitio actualis aut habitualis. Si habitualis sic de deo certior est quam de creatura, eo quod innata sit animae rationali – notio dei non creaturae.'

64. Ibid., fol. 4v: 'Si uero sit cognitio actualis distinguo aut per experientiam aut per causam. Si per experientiam: aut sensus aut intellectus. Si per experientiam sensus sic cognitio de creatura certior eo quod creatura est obiectum sensus. Si vero sit cognitio per experientia intellectus sic cognitio de deo certior eo quod ipse est summe intelligibilis.'

65. Ibid., fol. 4v: 'Si uero sit cognitio actualis quae est per causam distinguo aut [ ] aut respectu eius demonstrationis: una certior altera eo quod non different per experientia sed solum in ratione et ita cognoscuntur principia prima... cognitio dei est certior (eo

quod innata sit animae rationali) quam de creatura. Unde mobilior est lapis rotundus maioris ponderis quam quodratu minoris.'

66. See the Doucet's discussion concerning the authorship of the Summa in Alexander of Hales, *Summa Theologica*, ed. by V. Doucet, 5 vols (Quaracchi, 1924), V; and K. P. Keane, 'The Logic of Self-Diffusive Goodness in the Trinitarian Theory of the Summa Fratris Alexandri' (unpublished doctoral thesis, Fordham University, 1978), pp. 18ff.
67. See, for example, D. L. Douie, *The Conflict Between The Seculars and the Mendicants at The University of Paris in the Thirteenth Century* (London, 1954).
68. MacIntyre, A., *Three Rival Versions of Moral Inquiry, Encyclopaedia, Genealogy, and Tradition* (London, 1990), p. 125. MacIntyre is referring in this passage specifically to the *Summa Theologiae* of Thomas Aquinas. It would be my contention, however, that what MacIntyre credits Thomas with is really embodied by the scholastic tradition as a whole and by the *Summae* produced in that tradition.
69. See the summary in B. P. Gaybba, Aspects of the Medieval History of Theology (Pretoria, 1988), pp. 73-75.
70. Alexander of Hales, *Summa Theologica*, I, Tractatus Introductorius, q. I, 'De Doctrinae Theologiae', cap. i, solutio.
71. Ibid., q. I, cap. i, ad obiecta 3. Following William of Auxerre and Alexander's *Glossa*, the *Summa* cites the scriptural injunction, 'unless you believe, you cannot understand (Isaiah, 7, 19)'.
72. Ibid., q. I, cap. i, ad obiecta 3.
73. Ibid., q. I, cap. i, ad obiecta 4.
74. Ibid., I, Tractatus Introductorius, Quaest. II, 'De cognitione Dei in via', pp. 14-36.
75. Ibid., q. II, m. i, c. i, ad quod sic, 3-4.
76. Ibid., q. II, m. i, c. i, ad obiecta, 3-4.
77. Ibid., q. II, m. i, c. i, ad obiecta, 5.
78. Ibid. 'Et in hoc imago eius est, secundum Augustinum, in libro De Trinitate: 'Imago Dei est in hoc quod capax eius et particeps esse potest: capax per cognitionem, particeps per amorem.'
79. Ibid., q. II, m. i, c. iii, respondeo.
80. Ibid., q. II, m. ii, c. i, respondeo.
81. Ibid., q. II, m. ii, c. i, respondeo: 'Deus notitiam suam ab homine sic ab initio temperavit, ut sicut nunquam "quid esset" poterat comprehendi, nunquam "quia esset" poterat ignorari.' (Cf. Hugh of St Victor, *De Sacramentis*, lib. I, c.1 in Migne, *Patrologia Latina*, ed. by J. P. Mighne, 217 vols (Paris 1844-1879), CLXXXVI, cols 217-218.)
82. Alexander of Hales, *Summa Theologica*, I, Tractatus Intro., q. II, m. ii, c. i.
83. Ibid., q. II, m. ii, c. ii, ad obiecta 2.
84. Ibid., q. II, m. ii, c. iv, respondeo 1.
85. Ibid.
86. Ibid., q. II, m. iii, c. i, contra 1.
87. Ibid., q. II, m. iii, c. ii, et videtur quod non 1-2.
88. Ibid., q. II, m. iii, c. ii, respondeo 1.

89. Ibid., q. II, m. iii, c. ii, respondeo 3: 'Dicendum ergo quod est cognitio in fieri et in facto esse: cognitio de Deo semper est in fieri in vita ista, sed in futuro erit facta.' 'Indigemus in praesenti dispensationis similitudinis.' (Cf. Augustine, De Trinitate, XV, c. 9 (16), in *Corpus Christianorum Series Latina*, vol. 50, ed. W. J. Mountain (Turnholt, 1968).)
90. Ibid., m. iii, c. iii-iv.
91. Ibid., m. iii, c. iv, 1.
92. Ibid., m. iii, c. iv, 2. See William of Auxerre, *Summa Aurea*, ed. by J. Ribaillier, 5 vols (Paris; Rome, 1980-1987), I, prologue.
93. Alexander of Hales, *Summa Theologica*, I, Tractatus Intro., q. II, m. iii, c. iv, 3.
94. Ibid., q. II, m. iii, c. iv, 4.
95. Ibid., q. II, m. iii, c. iv, contra.
96. William of Auxerre, *Summa*, I, prologue.
97. Alexander, *Summa*, I, Tract. Intro. q. ii. m. iii, cap. iv, respondeo.
98. William, *Summa*, I, prologue.
99. Alexander, *Summa*, I, Tract. Intro. q. ii. m. iii, c. iv, respondeo: 'Tertia ratio est revocatio infidelium ad fidem: sicut enim dicit Ioannes Damascenus, I libro, "quamvis cognitio existendi Deum naturaliter nobis inserta sit, tamen in tantum praevaluit perniciosa malitia hominum naturae, aut dicant non esse Deum, secundum quod dicit David: Dixit insipiens in corde suo: non est Deus". Propterea, ad tales revocandos necessariae sunt rationes.'
100. Ibid., q. II, m. iii, c. iv, ad obiecta 1.
101. Ibid., q. II, m. iii, c. iv, ad obiecta 2.
102. Ibid., q. II, m. iii, c. iv, ad obiecta 3.
103. Ibid., q. II, m. iii, c. iv, ad obiecta 4.
104. Ibid., q. II, m. iii, c. v, contra: 'Certius videtur lux quam ea quae lumine videmus; sed ipse Deus se habet ad intelligibilia sicut lux ad visibilia, ut dicit Augustinus, in I Soliloquiorum: "Quomodo in hoc sole tria animadvertimus: quod est, quod fulget, quod illuminat, sic in secretissimo Deo tria animadvertere debemus: quod est, quod intelligit, quod cetera intelligere facit".'
105. See Ibid., q. II, m. iii c. iii-iv.
106. Ibid. Ibid., q. ii, m. iii, c. v, ad obiecta 3.
107. As Jan Aertsen has pointed out, the third treatise of the first book of the *Summa* is a highly sophisticated account of the transcendentals – the principles of knowledge – ordered according to a theological scheme. See J. Aertsen, *Medieval Philosophy and the Transcendentals, The case of Thomas Aquinas* (Brill, 1996), pp. 40ff.
108. Alexander, *Summa*, I, Lib. i, pars i, inquisitio i, tract. i; q. i, c. i, art. i.
109. See Richard C. Dales, *Medieval Discussions of the Eternity of the World* (Brill, 1990), pp. 68ff. Dales terms the strategy 'accomodationist'.
110. Alexander, *Summa*, I, Lib. i, tract. i, q. i, c. i, art. ii.
111. Ibid. Lib. I, q. i, c. i, art. ii. The quotation is from the book of Wisdom, 13, 4-5.
112. Ibid.: '"Cum anima de se dubitare non possit quoniam est (quia se ignorare non potest), cogitur ex se et hoc credere (quia aliquando coepisse se meminit) quoniam non semper est. Cum ergo non per se coepisse et initium habuisse se videat, non

potest ignorare" quia non fuit sibi initium. "Ut ergo inciperet quod non erat, ab alio factum est, qui erat": et illum dicimus Deum.' (Cf. Hugh of St Victor, I *De sacramentis*, i, cc. 8 et 9 in *Patrologia Latina*, ed. by J. P. Migne et al. 217 vols (Paris 1844-1879), CLXXVI, col. 219.)

113. Alexander, *Summa*, I, Lib. I, q. i, c. i, art. iii.
114. Ibid., Lib. I, q. i, art. iv. Compare William of Auxerre, *Summa*, I, tr. I, c. i.
115. Alexander, *Summa*, Lib. I, q. i, art. iv.
116. Ibid., Lib. I, q. i, c. i, art. v.
117. Ibid., Lib. I, q. i, c. ii, art. i.
118. Ibid., Lib. I, q. i, c. ii, art. i, a: 'Ad quod arguit Anselmus, in Proslogion: "Si potest cogitari esse aliquid quod non possit cogitari non esse, maius erit quam illud quod non esse potest cogitari. Si ergo id quo maius cogitari nequit potest cogitari non esse, id ipsum quo maius cogitari nequit non est id quo maius cogitari nequit; quod convenire non potest. Sic ergo vere est aliquid quo maius excogitari non potest, ut nec cogitari possit non esse; et hoc es, tu, Domine Deus noster. Si enim mens aliqua possit cogitare aliquid melius te, ascenderet creatura super Creatorem: quod valde absurdum est."'
119. Ibid., Lib. I, q. i, c. ii, art. i, c.
120. Ibid., Lib. I, q. i, c. ii, art. i, d.
121. Ibid., Lib. I, q. i, c. ii, art. i, d.
122. Ibid., Lib. I, q. i, c. ii, art. i, contra 1.
123. Ibid., Lib. I, q. i, c. ii, art. i, contra 2.
124. Ibid., Lib. I, q. i, c. ii, art. i, contra 3.
125. Ibid., Lib. I, q. i, c. ii, art. i, contra 4.
126. Ibid., Lib., I, q. i, c. ii, art. i, contra 5: 'Boethius, in libro De hebdomadibus: Intellecto paulisper, gratia disputandi, quod non sit summum bonum, adhuc intelligetur aliquid esse album, aliquid esse magnum, sed tamen non intelligetur aliquid esse bonum. Potest ergo intellectus noster accipere de rebus esse, non intellecto summo bono esse. Ex quo videtur relinqui: posse cogitari summum bonum non esse.'
127. Ibid., Lib. I, q. i, c. ii, art. i, contra 3: 'Ad tertium dicendum quod cognitio alicuius potest esse duobus modis: in ratione communi et in ratione propria. Potest ergo aliquid cognosci in ratione communi et tamen ignorari sub ratione propria: sicut cum aliquis cognoscit mel sub ratione communi, videlicet quia est corpus molle, rubeum, ignorat autem ipsum sub ratione propria; et ideo, cum videt fel esse corpus molle, rubeum, deceptus credit ipsum esse mel. Similiter cognitio beatitudinis et appetitus ipsius nobis innatus est in ratione communi, quae "est status omnium bonorum aggregatione perfectus"; tamen in ratione propria ab aliquibus ignoratur. Unde diversi in diversis ponunt et aestimant beatitudinem: quidam in voluptatibus, quidam in divitiis, quidam in honoribus. Hinc patet quod ipsi ignorant beatitudinem in propria ratione. Similiter dicendum quod idolatrae in ratione communi Deum non ignorant, quod est ens, principium, omnipotens; Deum tamen sub ratione propria ignorant, et ideo dicunt de Deo, qui est trinus et unus et verus, quia non est Deus et de idolo quia est Deus.'
128. For Aquinas's teaching, see chapter five.

## Chapter 3

# Other Ways to God: Anselm, the Early Dominicans and the Friars in Oxford

> Whilst God's vassal, Dominic, was in Rome and was pouring out his prayers in the presence of God in the basilica of St Peter for the preservation and extension of the order which God's right hand was propagating by his care, the hand of God came upon him. He saw Peter and Paul, those princes full of glory, appear. The first, Peter, gave him the staff; Paul, the book; and both added, 'Go and preach; for God has chosen you for this ministry'. Then in a flash it seemed to him that he saw his sons scattered throughout the world, going off two by two to preach to the people the word of God.[1]

This story was almost certainly added to the biography of St Dominic in an effort to paint him in the image of St Francis, his more charismatic contemporary. Nonetheless, it is indicative of the differences between Dominic and Francis, that Dominic should experience visions of the apostles rather than of Christ himself. Moreover, Dominic's vision had a highly specific symbolism and message: Peter and Paul symbolised the Roman Church, while the staff and the book they carried were symbolic of the messenger of God and of the doctrine the messenger taught.[2] Dominic's conception of the true Preacher was someone who went out among people 'speaking only with God or of God, in himself or with his neighbour' – a conception which contrasts with St Francis's emphasis upon preaching by deeds.[3]

### I

St Francis and St Dominic both founded their religious orders in the course of the first two decades of the thirteenth century, approximately a century after the death of St Anselm. In comparison to St Francis (d. 1226), however, St Dominic (d. 1221) cut a dry figure. Whereas there existed historical accounts of Francis's activities during his own lifetime, contemporary references to Dominic were strictly limited to official documents and charters.[4] Similarly, modern biographers of St Dominic have been unable to provide accounts of a rich inner life or of the 'divine familiarity' readily associated with St Francis.[5] Instead they have tended to concentrate almost entirely upon outward events, encounters and projects motivated less by mystical experience than by direct encounter with heresy. If Francis was struck by the greed and violence of his surroundings and influenced by popular spiritual ideals, Dominic was struck by the nature of unbelief and the failure of the establishment in dealing with it.

Unlike St Francis (the son of a cloth-merchant and a former soldier), St Dominic was always destined for a career in the clergy. Brought up and educated on a Christian-Muslim frontier in Castile, Dominic was inbred with a consciousness of the presence of unbelief. Yet, it was only later, as a canon of the Cathedral of Osma in Northern Spain, that he was to experience events that were to shape his view of the apostolic life. While in the entourage of his bishop, Diego, who had been sent to Denmark on an embassy from the king in 1203, Dominic stayed a night in the Languedoc only to discover that his landlord was a member of the Cathar sect. After a night spent in debate, Dominic returned his landlord to the faith.[6] Later, at Parmiers in 1207, Dominic helped his bishop, Diego, conduct a debate with leading Waldensians in which he succeeded in returning the 'heretics' to the Church, after their opponents had been impressed by the poverty of Diego and Dominic as well as by their words.[7] It was not until after Diego had died, however, and Dominic had decided to dedicate himself to preaching that the Order of Preachers was to receive official sanction from Pope Honorius III in 1216. Nonetheless, it is hardly surprising that Dominic immediately sent his followers to the newly-founded University of Paris for training in biblical studies and the art of disputation.[8] Indeed, it might even be said that within Dominic's early experiences of debate lay the origins of Thomas Aquinas's *Summa contra gentiles*, begun some fifty years later!

By contrast with the unruly and spontaneous Francis, Dominic's approach to his order was organised and pragmatic. He founded his community within the context of established institutions, and instead of insisting upon a rule of his own (as Francis had), he rigorously adapted the existing *Rule of the Augustinian Canons of Premontré*.[9] The contrast was already obvious in their attitudes toward poverty. Whereas Francis had adopted the life of poverty from the time of his conversion, and had employed it in part to 'shock' his audience into repentance by a literal imitation of Christ, Dominic adopted it only after the creation of his community and for precisely the opposite reason. As far as the Cathars in the Languedoc were concerned, poverty was the mark of authenticity of any preacher. Dominic imitated the poverty of the heretics as a means of getting his audience to listen to the gospel. It had been the very opulence of previous Christian missionaries, argued Dominic, which explained their lack of success in fighting the Cathars.[10] It was later that Dominic found sanction for his interpretation of the apostolic life, in the gospels themselves.[11] Although Franciscans and Dominicans adopted the same outward appearance, therefore, they did so for remarkably different reasons.[12]

The most obvious contrast with Francis, however, lay in Dominic's attitude toward learning. Where Francis saw it as imperative for the apostolic life that learning be resisted, Dominic felt that study was second only to preaching in the hierarchy of spiritual duties.[13] Deliberately recruiting among, and sending his Friars to, the universities, Dominic decreed in 1220 that no new Dominican foundation could be made without a continual lecturer, and the constitutions of the order made studies an integral part of the regular life.[14]

It was St Dominic's coolness toward the cultivation of a more personal, and interior spiritual relationship with God, however, that represented the key contrast with St Francis. As Simon Tugwell has written, 'the early Dominicans were not particularly concerned, either for themselves or for others, with what has come to be called the "interior life"'.[15] The lack of concern with an interior spirituality has often been understood to mean that the early Dominicans did not really possess a spirituality at all. Tugwell points out, however, that the absence of 'interiority' was deliberate policy, and not a mark of spiritual impoverishment. Indeed it is in the rejection of 'interiority' that that the key to Dominican spirituality is found.[16] At the beginning of the Dominican constitutions the attitude of working for 'the sake of preaching and salvation of souls' was enshrined within the community:

> And all our concern should be primarily and passionately directed to this all-important goal, that we should be able to be useful to the souls of our neighbours...[17]

As Tugwell again writes, personal spiritual growth was never a legitimate goal in its own right for the early Dominicans, but was rather a kind of 'spin-off' from their service of others.[18] The Dominicans inherited a spirituality from the early Church Fathers that is less obvious to our eyes, partly because it does not conform to a modern idea of spirituality that derives from the Romantic notions of introspection and the uniqueness of the inner person.[19] Above all, early Dominican spirituality remains hidden precisely because it is self-effacing by its very nature.

Their different attitudes toward the interior life underpinned the differences between St Francis and St Dominic over preaching, poverty, and toward the advancement of studies. It was a contrast that ultimately reflected their very different social origins. Whereas St Francis was representative of a popular spirituality which emphasised personal experience of God, St Dominic was representative of the suspicion and fear which that spirituality engendered within the establishment.[20] What St Dominic meant by 'helping the souls of others' was precisely to return the attention and obedience of those all too influenced by popular preaching back to the external teaching authority of Mother Church.

## II

The interests of the early Dominican community help explain the direction of its school in Paris. Hugh of St Cher (d. 1263), who held one of two chairs in the Faculty of Theology acquired by the Dominican convent of St Jacques between 1230-1235, led and organised a whole movement to provide concordances to Scripture, and other tools of Biblical study. Beryl Smalley sees the project as having been part of an overall strategy within the order to create the materials necessary for their work – which they could not, as mendicants, buy for themselves.[21] It was perhaps also the case that the early Dominican community's attempts to guarantee the textual integrity of the sacred texts at their schools complimented their emphasis upon the authority of those texts within society.

The preoccupations of the Dominican school in Paris may be a factor explaining the paucity of commentaries on Peter Lombard's *Sentences* emanating from there before the arrival of Albertus Magnus in the 1240s.[22] Perhaps the whole sentence commentary format was suited to the interests of the Franciscan order more than to the Dominicans. The sentence commentary of Hugh of St Cher himself is the only complete commentary on Lombard's sentences that can be ascribed definitively to a Dominican Regent Master before Albertus Magnus.[23] A Burgundian by origin, Hugh was a Master of Laws at Paris before entering the Friars Preachers in 1226.[24] He studied theology from this time before becoming himself a Master of the Dominican school between 1230 and 1235 as a replacement for Roland of Cremona.[25]

Hugh's treatment of the natural knowledge of God is considerably more cursory than anything found at the Franciscan school of the 1240s. Hugh preferred brief summaries of Lombard's own arguments from effects to a first cause, from mutability to the necessity of an immutable first being, and from the hierarchy of goods and beauty to a highest good and a highest beauty. He makes no reference to innate knowledge or an argument showing that God cannot be thought not to exist.[26] Hugh's arguments, however, do have the slightly distinctive feature of being presented as arguments showing that God is one – a feature that perhaps reflects the continuing concern with the dualist heresy of the Cathars against which the Dominicans began their preaching. The glosses of Hugh's commentary composed by his pupils, however, barely glance at the question at all.[27]

The work of another Dominican who composed a *Compendium of Theology* at Paris between 1235 and 1244, but who was never himself a Master of the school, shows that Anselm's argument was certainly known to the Dominicans.[28] John of Treviso cited Anselm's argument at the beginning of his *Compendium* based largely on the sentence commentary of Hugh of St Cher and the *Golden Summa* of William of Auxerre.[29] Perhaps once again the interest was in demonstrating the uniqueness of God – something to which Anselm's argument would have been appropriate. In a brief opening passage dealing with the existence of God, John names rather than states his arguments. We can show that God exists from the existence of mutable beings: they presuppose the existence of a necessary and immutable first being. Moreover, we can show the existence of a highest good from the existence of a hierarchy of goods. We can also show the existence in reality of that than which no greater can be thought from its existence in the understanding. Finally, reason shows that God cannot be thought not to exist, since neither in actuality nor in the understanding is the highest good separable from that which is Being itself.[30]

The very presence of Anselm's argument in this text, however, makes its absence elsewhere among the Dominicans conspicuous. They knew the argument, but did not employ it. Like Alexander, Hugh of St Cher had been a pupil of William of Auxerre but while John of Treviso followed William in his statement of the Anselmian argument, Hugh did not. Neither, for that matter did the Master that Hugh of St Cher replaced in the chair of Paris.

Roland of Cremona (d. 1259) was a Master of Arts at Bologna when he took the Dominican habit in 1219 and began studying theology.[31] Coming to Paris in 1228, he was made a Master of Theology in May 1229 before being sent to the new University of Toulouse where he lectured between 1230 and 1233.[32] Roland's *Summa* is the product of that teaching. He did not discuss arguments for God's existence there, nor did he cite Anselm's *Proslogion.*[33] What Roland's *Summa* did contain, however, was a more cosmopolitan approach to theology than anything demonstrated at Paris during this period. As one scholar has argued, 'Roland was the first of his time to make an abundant and enthusiastic use of the non-theological works just becoming available', and he was 'certainly given permission to study further the philosophy with which he had become familiar before he had entered the Order'.[34]

It was perhaps in accordance with his learning that Roland was sent to Toulouse in the first place. In 1229 the ecclesiastical authorities in Toulouse had declared to Christendom that 'those who wished to scrutinise the bosom of nature to the inmost can hear the books of Aristotle which were forbidden at Paris'.[35] It is significant that enquiry into Aristotle was permitted in a university that was both on the borders of Muslim Spain and at the heart of the Languedoc where the Dominicans had been involved from their origins in preaching against the Cathars. Was it already thought that philosophical learning might provide tools for defending the faith? In any case it is fitting that the first *Summa* of the Dominican order reflected the dualist Cathar challenge.[36] Roland of Cremona does not deal with the question of God's existence, but rather with a more pressing question: whether there is one principle of the world or two.[37]

Roland uses both Scriptures and argument to show the impossibility of interpreting the Scriptures dualistically, and the logical impossibility of two principles.[38] That Roland approached the question by means of authorities, arguments from causation and the nature of created being was indicative of a specific end: the conviction of heretics who appealed to the evidence of nature in defence of their dualistic claims and interpretation of the Scriptures. To show the unity of a first cause, Roland used an argument from causation that he openly ascribes to Aristotle:

> A thing has a cause and that thing has another cause; and lest this account proceeds into an infinity (since it is not possible to pass beyond an infinity) it should be anchored in one principle.[39]

In contrast with the teaching of the Franciscans, the natural knowledge of God is not generated by God's presence within nature. Rather, the first principle of things is an inference from causation to an extrinsic first cause of things.

Another contrast with the Franciscans is Roland's treatment of the relationship of natural knowledge and faith. Reason is significant for Roland not because it can function within faith, but precisely because it is separate from it. Roland accepts that the same truths may be believed by faith and known by reason, but he is careful to divide the two. In contrast to the Franciscans, Roland does not teach that faith leads the soul to knowledge, nor that knowledge may deepen faith: rather, they are quite different things.[40] The nature of the unbeliever in this particular case raised the significance of natural knowledge and natural philosophy. Roland recognised the potential of natural reason as a means of settling arguments over the interpretation of Scripture or as an authority in itself precisely because of its independence from the Scriptures not recognised by unbelievers.

The role of natural philosophy in the defence of the faith is perhaps muted in Roland because the order, concerned as it was to promote the authority of the Bible, initially took a very conservative stance toward philosophy. The Dominican General Chapter of 1228 issued a constitution forbidding students and masters within the order from studying 'the books of the Gentiles and the philosophers', and forbidding them to learn 'secular sciences nor even the arts which are called liberal', unless granted dispensation by the Master of the Order.[41] What Roland began, however, was taken a stage further in the sentence commentary of Albertus Magnus composed in the 1240s.

Albertus Magnus (c. 1206-1280) joined the Dominican order as a young man in 1223. He was sent to Paris in 1242 under the aegis of the German, John of Wildeshausen (elected Master General of the order at Paris in 1241), and of Hugh of St Cher (in charge of the French province of the order between 1236 and 1244). Having been educated through the Dominican schooling system and having himself lectured within the minor Dominican schools of Hildesheim, Freiberg, Regensberg and Strasbourg, Albert was now selected by order for promotion to its most important school.[42] Albert arrived in Paris in 1242 to become, by 1245, the first German Master of the Dominican school.[43] As with all Masters in the order, Albert attained his position by passing through the ranks with the approval of present and former Masters – an indication that his perspectives on theology would not have been unrepresentative of the wider order.[44]

The product of his teaching at Paris was explicit both about the role of natural reason as a primary means of defending the faith and about the role of natural philosophy in discoursing the contents of faith with the unbeliever. Albert's commentary on Lombard's *Sentences* is almost entirely concerned with the role of argument as an instrument for defending the faith against its adversaries. Although he does not employ Anselm's argument either to endorse or dispute it, his sentence commentary is valuable for us both as an indication of the teaching in the Dominican school, and as a contrast with the approach adopted by the Franciscans in Paris at this very time. It is in the light of this contrast that the very absence of Anselm's argument becomes significant.

Like the Franciscans, Albert begins his commentary by considering the nature of theology as a body of knowledge. Interestingly, he accords reason a different role from his Franciscan contemporaries. Every science has its own ruling habitual knowledge, and its own instrument. The ruling habitual knowledge of theology is the single light of faith. Nonetheless, theology has two instruments according to its two ends: exhortation of the faithful in true doctrine, and recalling to faith those who reject it.[45]

The instrument of exhortation is Scripture.[46] To recall the detractors of faith, theology employs the instrument of argumentation. Arguments may be drawn from authority or from natural reason, or from a combination of the two. Whereas the instrument of exhortation is to be found in Scripture, the instrument of argument is to be observed in the sentence commentary.[47]

For Albert, reason is justified in matters of faith not because it deepens faith or is a reward for faith, but because it allows for discourse with unbelievers. In the first article of the third distinction, following Peter Lombard, Albert asks whether the ancient philosophers knew that there is one God. Instead of focusing upon Christian arguments, therefore, Albert focuses on those that are drawn from non-Christian literature. He is concerned to ask what the philosophers knew and what they did not know; and how their knowledge is to be distinguished from faith. Like the Franciscans, he sees the question as having biblical roots in Paul's letter to the Romans: 'From the creation of the world, God's invisible qualities – his eternal power and divine nature – have been clearly seen, being understood from what has been made' (Rom. 1. 20). Yet his reading of this text has a different emphasis from his Franciscan contemporaries.[48]

Citing a number of ancient texts (including both Plato's *Timaeus* and an unnamed text of Aristotle) Albert concludes that the philosophers were able to have a knowledge of God through natural reason.[49] They were able to know God from creatures, *a posteriori*, but while they were able to say that God was the glorious creator of all things and eminently above them, they were unable to determine the nature of that eminence and the nature of the divine properties.[50]

In the second article, Albert considers what the philosophers were able to say concerning God besides that God exists. Albert considers arguments that aim to show that the philosophers could not know anything of God besides the divine existence.[51] Albert argues in objection that the books of the Gentiles not only show a knowledge of the existence of God but also of properties or attributes of God.[52] In solution, Albert says that besides a knowledge that God exists, the philosophers were also able to attain a knowledge of what God is not. They knew some of God's attributes but not with certainty. For example, knowing God to have knowledge, some enquired after the nature of God's knowledge and said that God did not know particulars. From this, it might seem that created intellects are unable to know the attributes of God.[53] In view of this allusion to Aristotle's First Mover, it is perhaps worthy of note that Albert does not, by contrast with William of Auxerre, employ Anselm's argument to show that God is being itself.

In response to the objections, Albert actually stresses that God can be understood from creatures, but that creatures are not understood from God. In other words he stresses that the basis of knowledge in natural theology is inferential rather than participational. It is not that Albert is denying participation; but if creatures do exist by participation, then this is known as an inference from, and not as the cause of, the knowledge of God.[54] What the evidence of creatures show is not merely that the world is the product of design, but that the world represents a sustained order. Whereas the work of the designer is distanced and separate from the design, the work of God is not separated from the Creation: the universe requires an eternal governor to whom all time is present completely and at once.[55] Albert also stresses that there is only one governor of this order: evil and corruption are not due to another principle, nor to error on the part of the governor, but to the fact that creatures were created from nothing.[56] Albert later presents an argument that can sustain an inference to *this* kind of world-governor.

In the third article, Albert considers whether natural knowledge differs from the knowledge of faith.[57] Hence, the issue of the natural knowledge of God impinges on the relationship between natural to revealed knowledge. Albert argues that these forms of knowledge differ in at least five respects.[58] The principal difference is that whereas the process of nature falls under reason, faith transcends it.[59] In the second place, whereas the principles of natural cognition are self-evident, in faith an infused light informs the conscience and convinces reason more through the love of the will than by rational proof to which things of faith are not apparent.[60] Thus, Albert affirms the Aristotelian view that a first principle of knowledge is self-evident and it is upon first principles that enquiry depends.

Albert carries the separation of faith and reason a step further in recounting the third difference. Whereas in natural cognition it is the creature that causes the object for the rational creature, in faith it is the first truth that is the efficient and final cause of faith.[61] Hence, Albert presupposes in this discussion, that all truth comes from the first truth. Yet, in natural knowledge, the mind arrives at a knowledge of the first truth by looking at its derivatives. The order of knowledge is the reverse of the causal order by which created truths are generated. Moreover, just as the beginning of reason and faith are different, so too are their ends: natural knowledge does not approach, as faith does (through revelation), a knowledge of what God is.[62]

Finally, there is a difference on the part of the subject. Faith is in the affective intellect while the knowledge of natural reason is in the speculative intellect. Though faith informs the speculative intellect it is more voluntary than rational and it is moved by love and fear while neither fear nor love affects those things which are in the speculative intellect.[63] Whereas the Franciscans were interested in the relationship of faith, reason and desire within the believer, Albert is more concerned with stressing the independence of reason. Whereas the Franciscan arguments demand a prior ordering of the soul to the object of its quest, Albert's arguments presuppose that no such prior ordering is necessary for the perception of rational truth.

In some places in his writings, Albert assents to the view that the knowledge of God and of the soul are present to the soul through itself; whilst elsewhere he asserts that 'all our knowledge is founded in the senses'.[64] For Albert's most famous pupil in the 1250s, Thomas Aquinas, the apparent conflict in Albert's writings would be resolved very much in favour of a knowledge of God that is derived from the senses. Other students, such as Ulrich of Strasbourg in the 1260s, were to stress the self-evidence of God's existence to the human mind. In any case, the proofs that Albert presents in his own sentence commentary begin in the senses. The basic argument that he employs is the one found in the *Summa* of Roland of Cremona. That there is causation is clear to the senses. Therefore there must be a first uncaused, uncreated cause and this we call God.[65]

Having shown the existence of a First Mover, Albert moves on to discuss the attributes and nature of God, and here the differences between Albert and his contemporary Franciscans in Paris become more apparent. For the Franciscans God's attributes could be deducted as soon as the existence of 'that than which no greater can be thought' had been found, implied in the nature of things. For Albert God's uniqueness is not implied within creation, it must be argued dialectically, by means of arguments from experience and from self-evident first principles. The first attribute of the First Mover is its infinity. Since no creature is able to create, creation requires an infinite potency. The distance between something and nothing is infinite and therefore it requires an infinite potency to draw something from nothing. Since the supposition of all natural things is from nothing, nothing is able to come into existence according to finite nature alone.[66] Dispositions within creatures show that God is incorporeal. The reason for this is found in Aristotle's *Physics* and is founded upon two propositions which are not proven, but are received as self-evident principles (*per se notae*). No body moves unless it is moved. Every mover is moved according to a mover. Since a moving body is moved according to a mover and since God is the first cause not moved, God is not able to be a body.[67]

Moreover, God is not a mutable spirit. Every mutable spirit is moved through itself or through an accident: the first mover is not moved through itself and is not moved by an accident. Therefore the first mover is not a mutable spirit. The reason for this is that the first mover is a mover not moved in any way. If the first mover were receptable to movement it would not be the first mover. The first mover is in every way the same and always in possession of itself.[68]

God is the highest good – and *per consequens* one, since the highest good cannot be otherwise. The argument showing this depends upon two divisions, each of which is self evident (*per se patet*). In the division of being into substance and accident, it remains that the substance is better than accidents since the accident depends upon the substance, yet nothing exists simply like God. Similarly the soul is the perfection and the act of some body. The soul is therefore better than the body. The cause of the soul, however, will be infinitely better than the soul.[69]

Albert says that the ancient Greek theologian, Pseudo-Dionysius, teaches another way to come from the order of all existing things to a knowledge of that which is above all ways and orders: we ascend to God by negation, eminence and by causation. We come to a knowledge of what God is by denying what God is not. Hence, God is not a body: God is incorporeal. Similarly, as the cause of creatures God is not what they are: a rock, a lion etc. Yet, in some sense, as God is maker they must reflect in their natures something more eminent within the Creator.[70] Albert is impressed by a Christian author who has enquired into the ways in which God is named from creatures. Yet there is no hint that God is known immediately in the encounter with creation: rather, God is the conclusion of an argument from the existence of creatures and then named analogically. As we shall see later, 'the three ways' of the Pseudo-Dionysius were to be cited as consistently in the writings of the Parisian Dominicans as Anselm's argument was among the Parisian Franciscans.

Albert comments on Lombard's fourth argument, that God is the species of all created species. He divides the text into two questions, 'whether prime matter is nothing', and 'whether from perpetuity eternity is shown and from magnitude an infinite potency'. If prime matter has no form, but is entirely in potency, it is nothing. But if it is nothing how can God be its principle? Albert argues, following Augustine, that prime matter is unformed but ordered to form, since its very privation makes it desire form so that it has, in some way, a mode of species in its appetite for species and order. Hence for that reason, prime matter is nothing in one sense (in that it is yet to receive a form), but in another it is not nothing.[71] Prime matter, therefore, requires a cause.

Turning to the second question, it is objected that the finitude of creatures entails that they have an end – not that they require a beginning. Similarly, the magnitude of creatures is not infinite: therefore, the infinite potency of God is not able to be inferred. Albert responds that nothing creates itself. For something which makes acts, and something that acts is in act. Something that becomes something else is in potency to become what it becomes. For something to make itself it must be both in act and in potency at the same time, which is impossible. Therefore, there must be a first cause of things that exists without having a beginning. In response to the second part of the second question, Albert says that the Creator did not display all of the divine power in Creation. Nonetheless, that the Creator brought forth such magnitude without requiring pre-existing matter or instruments shows that the Maker is omnipotent.

Finally, the order of each individual thing to its appropriate perfection is demonstrable of the divine goodness, and the government of the whole in generation and corruption demonstrates the divine wisdom.[72] It is important to note that Albert is not moving here by analogy from design to the need for a designer. Such an argument is an argument from the concept of a design to the existence of a designer – hence, if the world is an artefact, it requires a cosmic artificer. The operator in Albert's argument is not the presence of design, but the evidence of *direction* and of government. Albert's argument goes from the observed necessities within things to the source of their necessity within a first principle that is necessary by its nature. Albert's proof does not presuppose some prior acquaintance with that which it sets out to prove: the knowledge of the absolute is not a precondition of knowing the relative. Rather, the absolute is an inference from a nature that is understood in terms of its own necessity. Even before Albert began his project of 'making Aristotle intelligible to the Latins', therefore, he provided an account of the Christian God – or at least the God of monotheism – from within an Aristotelian understanding of nature.

Albert began work on the *Physics* of Aristotle at the behest of his fellow Dominicans.[73] What was the source of the attraction? For one thing, Albert's God is not nearly so immanent as the God of the Franciscan school. There is no emphasis upon the presence of god to the soul, but instead a need for discussion from shared philosophical sources, and from shared experience. The attraction to Aristotle reflected a particular Dominican encounter with God, or more accurately, the Dominican encounter with the unbeliever who had already acquired Aristotelian science. Rational enquiry had a practical result for Albert as much as for the Franciscans, but this time the praxis lay in discourse with the other and not in the rectification of the soul. In particular, the practical end of rational enquiry lay in providing a means of contesting and defending the content of belief with the unbeliever in the absence of shared religious authorities.

In contrast with modern approaches to the philosophy of religion, reason was not used here to test tradition, to replace it with the universal deity of reason, nor was it used to provide necessary foundations for beliefs already held. Instead it was used to sustain a discourse that was capable of expressing religious differences in terms that were capable of being understood beyond the frontiers of those religious differences. Hence, Albert's proofs establish the God of faith, but his faith does not depend upon those proofs. The thing that depends upon the proofs is the very discourse itself.

Albert's commentary is more sophisticated than any of those we have examined in the contemporary Franciscan school partly because it was an *ordinatio*, that is, a text edited and distributed around the order and not merely a set of individual lecture notes. Probably begun upon his arrival in Paris in 1242, it was not completed until shortly after 1248.[74] It was in that year that Albert was sent to organise a new Dominican *studium* in Cologne, to which place he took the young student-friar Thomas Aquinas.[75] Albert's account of the natural knowledge of God and its relationship with revealed knowledge has an emphasis different from that of his Franciscan contemporaries in Paris. His choice to focus upon a knowledge of God inferred from nature, and his concern with the separation of natural knowledge and faith would certainly appear to have been conditioned by the concerns of his contemporaries within the Dominican order.

## III

When we turn to Albert's most prominent rival in the acquisition of the Aristotelian corpus among the Franciscans in Oxford, however, we find a different approach to the book of nature, and a different form of encounter with God – both in terms of how that enquiry can begin, and what marks the proper end of that enquiry. Robert Grosseteste (d. 1253) never formally entered the Franciscan order but was nonetheless secured as the first lector of the Oxford school, within six years of the Franciscans' arrival there in 1224.[76] Although Grosseteste was to leave Oxford in 1235 to become the bishop of Lincoln, his influence among the Franciscans there continued to be strong. As we shall soon see, Grosseteste was to have an influence among the Dominicans as well as among the Franciscans in Oxford before the 1250s. The place of Grosseteste within the Franciscan school, however, was particularly important, partly because of his differences with the Franciscan school in Paris; but partly also because of the continuities that existed in spite of those differences.

Whereas Alexander of Hales championed the use of Peter Lombard's *Sentences* as a text of instruction within Paris and among the Friars Minor there, Grosseteste openly disliked the commentary on the *Sentences* as a method of teaching, preferring instead to promote the incorporation of all enquiry within biblical commentary. In addition, at least one historian has considered the Parisian *Summa* and Grosseteste's *Hexaëmeron* to be representative of two different approaches to Aristotle in general and to the question of the eternity of the world in particular.[77] Whilst in the integrative strategy of the *Summa* an attempt is made to show differences between Aristotle and Christian teaching to be more apparent than real, Grosseteste virulently rejects such an approach.[78] As far as Grosseteste is concerned, those attempting 'to make Aristotle a catholic' should beware lest 'they make themselves heretics'.[79]

In common with Albertus Magnus, Grosseteste emphasised the dependence upon the senses for knowledge. Yet in Grosseteste's account, explained in his commentary upon Aristotle's *Posterior Analytics*, human dependency upon sense knowledge was not due to the sufficiency of the senses for understanding. Rather, it was consequent upon the fall and the derailment of the higher faculties; only through doctrine and experience could those higher faculties be restored:

> Nevertheless, I say that it is possible to have some knowledge without the help of the senses, for in the divine mind all knowledge, not only of universals but also of all particulars, exists eternally ... and intelligences which have received illumination from that source of light see all knowable things both universal and particular and this would be the case with all human beings, if they were not weighed down under the load of a corrupt body.[80]

Hence, while Grosseteste places greater emphasis upon sensual knowledge than his Parisian counterparts, he does so because he shares one of their fundamental assumptions: that human intellectual faculties have been corrupted by the fall. For Grosseteste the senses provide the occasion rather than the source of our knowledge which is, as the Franciscans in Paris also taught, properly sourced within the divine light.[81] The foundation upon which this conclusion rests, as McEvoy explains, is Grosseteste's favourite doctrine, and one to which he returns at every opportunity and in all his works. The mind can only claim complete knowledge concerning any individual thing when it can see, not only the object itself, but the exemplar in the divine word that is its standard.[82] Our knowledge is in fact restored rather than acquired and marks a reversal of the effects of the fall.[83] As the soul achieves understanding through faith, so it attains perfection.

The soul's gaze is clouded and burdened with a corrupt body because its affection (*affectus*) and sight (*aspectus*) are not separated off from each other. The soul's gaze only reaches out to, lays hold of, those things to which its love and affection devote themselves. As Lawrence Lynch explains:

> Since the soul's love and affection are turned to the body and the snares of the body, they drag along with them the soul's gaze and turn it from its own light, a light which is related to the soul as the sun is related to the external eyes. In this way the mind's gaze is necessarily turned towards darkness and laziness until, going out in a certain fashion, through the external senses into the sensible light, it receives after a fashion a vestige of the light that is native to it. And being once aroused it tries to rise to that light.[84]

Robert Grosseteste's emphasis upon sense knowledge does not serve to separate spiritual contemplation from natural science, but to draw them together. Above all, we find in his account of creation in the *Hexaëmeron* a different Pseudo-Dionysius. This is less the Pseudo-Dionysius that provides us with conceptual tools for naming God from creatures, than the one who provides Grosseteste with a conception of the divine nature flowing through Creation and drawing all things back to their source. In Grosseteste's account, every detail of nature is a symbol of the Trinity.[85] Grosseteste's scientific studies are not directed toward the discovery of universal laws or a universal order in nature – as in the work of Albertus Magnus. Rather, Grosseteste's whole concern is with the properties of individual things, how they symbolise the Creator and how they symbolise the unity of Creator and Creation:

> Wherever we look… we find vestiges of God, not only as a necessary first cause, but as a Trinity of power, wisdom and love. If we had nothing else to contemplate but a speck of dust, it would display in its essence the nature of God. Similarly, if

> we had any part of the universe, or the whole of the universe, or just the human mind, the same characteristics of the divine nature could be found. God, nature, and the human mind all lead to the same conclusion.[86]

In Robert Grosseteste's thought the order of knowledge is the same as the order of being, for the divine exemplar that is the cause of the being of things is also the source of human knowledge of them. Moreover, the divine ideas or exemplars perform another task – they are '*regulae* exercising a normative function in the order of being and knowledge and making for truth in both realms'.[87] The divine word is the truth of things that is both the truth that is perceptible to the mind, and also the form that preserves things from slipping into non-being. The exemplar is 'not only the pattern on which the world was fashioned but also the power that conserves it in being'.[88] If Albertus Magnus emphasises the laws of nature that lead us to a knowledge of the governor of things, Robert Grosseteste – like the Parisian Franciscans – emphasises the transience and mutability both of creation and of the created intellect. It is in the existential instability of created things that we know the necessity of the absolute being preserving things in existence, and facilitating the judgement of the mind. While Robert does not cite Anselm's argument in the context of explaining his exemplarism, that doctrine provides the conceptual context within which the argument was to operate among the Franciscans for most of the thirteenth century. Anselm's argument that God 'cannot be thought not to exist' contributes toward an account of the natural knowledge of God as something presupposed in all of the intellect's activities.

Surprisingly, perhaps, when we turn to the first commentary on Peter Lombard's *Sentences* of the Oxford school, composed by a Dominican, we find the account of the natural knowledge of God presupposed by Grosseteste's exemplarist approach to natural knowledge. Its author, Richard Fishacre (d. 1248), uses Anselm's argument to provide an account of the natural knowledge of God which expresses Grosseteste's central convictions: the corruption of the human intellect by the fall; the role of divine illumination in human knowing; and the participation of created beings in the being of God.[89] According to Richard Fishacre (about whom hardly anything is known), the knowledge of God's existence is indubitable since it is through God that we know all else. All created things have their being, goodness and truth by participation in the *Summum Bonum*. Hence, a proper knowledge of the principles of knowledge is also a knowledge of the principles of being. Fishacre's treatment of the question of God's existence articulates the God of Grosseteste's science: in Fishacre's doctrine, God is the reality of which Creation is the reflection. Moreover, God is the key to knowledge.

Fishacre begins by defining God as the Good containing all other goods beyond which there is nothing greater.[90] This is the good in which all things participate and by which the human soul recognises and judges all other goods.

Whoever judges greater or lesser goods sees something within all goods which is the highest or something which is greater than all goods.[91] Every name given to multiple things signifies that concerning which it is first and most properly said. If that being did not exist it could only signify non-being.[92] Privation or lack of something is known by a prior knowledge of something that is not lacking. Hence, a privation of the good is known only through a knowledge of something that is better, and so on *ad infinitum*. Therefore, some good is known that is the highest good, by which all other goods are known.[93]

Fishacre then employs a variety of arguments from the necessity of a first cause, from the nature of the divine being itself and from the nature of truth. Since there is something caused, there must be something that is both cause and caused: therefore, there must be something that is the very cause itself.[94] Fishacre then moves to the nature of the divine being. Since it is most simple it must be identical with its being. Therefore the most simple divine being must exist.[95] Fishacre adds the second chapter of Anselm's argument to this. If God exists there exists that than which no greater can be thought. Since it is greater to exist both in reality as well as in the understanding, God must exist both in understanding and in reality.[96] Just as we cannot recognise Snub-nose without a nose, he says jokingly, so God cannot be understood without existence![97]

Before returning to the proof from causation, Fishacre states the Augustinian argument from the identification of God and Truth: if it is true that God does not exist then there must exist truth. Either this is true from eternity and eternal truth is God or it is not true and its opposite is true: that God exists from eternity.[98]

Having used arguments which emphasise the participation of created being and intellect in God, Fishacre ends his list of arguments with one from causation emphasising God's transcendence over creation: the universe of causes requires a cause beyond itself which is uncaused and this is called God.[99]

Fishacre concludes from the foregoing that God cannot be thought not to exist. Why then does the Fool say in his heart there is no God? The Fool speaks concerning something that is less than God – something that is less than what is comprehended in the term 'God'. Similarly those who speak of 'gods' do not understand by this 'God' but something inferior to God – something not unique, but appropriate to more than one thing.[100] With Grosseteste, however, Fishacre also affirms the role of sin within human knowledge. If God cannot be thought not to exist, and if also the knowledge of God is naturally inserted within us – as John of Damascus teaches – then we surely waste our time in trying to prove God's existence: it is corruption and malice that lead anyone to doubt that God exists.[101] Reform of the will rather than argument, Fishacre implies, precedes right understanding.

The first sentence commentary composed by a Dominican in Oxford would seem to accord well with the teaching both of Robert Grosseteste as well as with the *Summa* of the Franciscan school in Paris. When we turn to the first Franciscan sentence commentary in Oxford composed only a few years later, however, we find teaching that is not only very different from Grosseteste but also from all other Franciscan commentaries of the period. Though Richard Rufus of Cornwall had the works of Robert Grosseteste and the commentary of Richard Fishacre before him when he composed his commentary, he represented, according to Peter Raedts, 'a totally different outlook'.[102]

## IV

After the demise of Elias of Cortona, the hated Minister General of the Franciscan order during the 1230s, the Franciscan leadership continued with efforts to draw the Franciscan community together on concerns that were shared by both the 'spirituals' (or radical Franciscans) and the academics. John of Parma tried to foster the acceptance of studies as a part of Franciscan life, as well as promote stricter observance of the rule of poverty.[103] At the General Chapter of Genoa in 1251, the Minister General called upon one of Francis's companions to bear witness to the truth of the stigmata.[104] It also appears that, having himself been trained in theology at Bologna, and perhaps also at Paris, John of Parma intervened in the school at Oxford during this period.[105] During a visit to England in 1248, Thomas of Eccleston reports, he held a chapter in Oxford 'to recall some of the Friars to unity who had began to go beyond the rest in wrong opinions'.[106] The same source recalls that 'John used to say that the Order was built on two walls, right conduct and right learning, but some Friars make the wall of learning reach higher than the heavens in as much as they ask "Whether God exists", and at the same time they allow the wall of conduct to be so low that it is considered great praise when it is said of a brother "He is a sound man".'[107] Does Eccleston's comment reflect an actual criticism?

Not all scholars within the Franciscan order agreed with the Parisian doctrines of the *Summa Minorum*. At least one master in Oxford who had been influential in the demise of Elias, Richard Rufus (d. circa 1260?), offered a very different approach to God. John of Parma's complaint may have signalled the beginning of difficulties for Richard Rufus, the first Oxford Franciscan responsible for posing the question 'whether God exists'. The Minister General apparently issued Rufus with letters obliging him to study in Paris, but from which he was released on the grounds of 'weak health'.[108] Did he think that Rufus would find in Paris a more appropriate form of teaching?

Rufus's approach to argument appears to differ from that of both Grosseteste and the Parisian school. According to Rufus, faith and reason must remain separate. Reason has its limits that it cannot transgress without danger: that is, it cannot reach those things that pertain to grace.[109] Gone from Rufus is the view that argument is meant to edify the soul. For Grosseteste the whole of nature is the theatre of God's creative power and love, with the properties of every individual thing symbolising the Creator. For Rufus the problem of theology is 'how, in a universe governed by the laws of nature, he can find a new way to define God's place in it.'[110] For Rufus, the visible world was a largely autonomous system governed by strict laws.[111]

Whatever might be said with respect to Rufus' spirituality his account of the natural knowledge of God manifests an approach more adversarial than contemplative.[112] Rufus begins by stating that Peter Lombard does not ask 'Whether God exists' and rightly so, because it is the teaching of John of Damascus that 'the knowledge of God's existence is naturally inserted in everyone'. Yet, he responds, that knowledge has been corrupted. Whereas in Fishacre's approach human corruption makes argument superfluous, however, in Rufus's commentary it is human corruption that makes argument and disputation necessary. For this reason, the question of 'Whether God exists' can properly be asked.[113] Rufus then proceeds to problematise the three sources of indubitable knowledge in Fishacre's commentary: divine illumination, participation, and the unthinkability of God's non-existence.

By reference to suppositional logic, Rufus offers doubts about that which is supposed to be beyond doubt. With reference to divine illumination, Augustine says that all unchanging principles of truth are common to all created minds, and therefore all minds see them in one light which is both unchanging and one and the same for all.[114] How can one and each of the principles known by the created mind be the same as God, asks Rufus, if they are different even from one another? They are identified with God by means of a 'formal predication'.[115] Rufus is not necessarily denying the reality of divine illumination or the divine origins of principles, merely that we know God directly in knowing those principles. Rather we attribute those principles to God by means of argument.

Rufus makes the same kind of criticism with reference to the participational arguments found in Fishacre. Referring to Anselm's argument that greater and lesser created goods are good by virtue of their participation in that which is Good itself, Rufus asks, how can this name 'good' which is said concerning many singular goods be the highest good? He replies that it cannot, for no universal can be the highest good.[116] Once again Rufus does not deny the reality of participation. He merely denies that our knowledge of created goods is a knowledge of the supreme Good. The universal term 'good' by which we refer to multifarious goods is not the same as the Good which stands for the supreme goodness itself or divine essence through which all other goods exist by participation: the universal term is derived from the goods in the world, not the Supreme Good.

Rufus also attacks the argument from participation with another example. Of two straight lines equal to one another, are they equal through some third line or are they both just one line? In the first instance the two lines are placed next to a third, and if a third there must also be a fourth, and so on *ad infinitum*... If the second is true, then there is really only one line. Which is correct? 'I don't know', says Rufus, 'respond if you can.'[117]

Finally, Rufus interrogates at great length Anselm's argument from the 'description of God', 'that than which no greater can be thought'.[118] Even if we concede the hypothesis, says Rufus in anticipation of Aquinas, we can still deny that there is any such being to which the description applies. Therefore, Rufus argues, Anselm has not been able to show the necessity of God's existence.[119] To move from the definition of a thing to the nature of things in reality is to incur the fallacy of the accident.[120] The realm of conception is different from the realm of existence.

Rufus does not say explicitly that he rejects Anselm's argument – either out of reverence for Anselm, or at least for others within the Franciscan order. Nonetheless, his view that 'anyone who truly sees God will see infinite conditions explicitly and most expressly' concedes no more than that Anselm's argument will be valid in the next life when God enters our direct experience.[121] In terms of this life, Rufus at least raises doubts about Anselm's argument, and also about the exemplarist account of knowledge so favoured by Robert Grosseteste, in which the mind knows truths through the first light that is God.

The arguments for God's existence that Rufus does put forward nonetheless reflect a Franciscan sensibility to the divine immanence. By presupposing that the relative always depends upon the absolute, Rufus presents a series of inferences which depend upon a scheme of participation. Rufus begins by stating that 'if there is something deficient, there is something sufficient. Again, if there is something flowing, there is something stable or permanent. If there is something in motion, there is something fixed. If there is something respective, there is something absolute.'[122] Yet the basis of these inferences is not exemplarist divine illumination. While he does not return explicitly to Anselm's argument, he employs a modal argument that concerns not the possibilities of thought, but the possibility of God's existence itself. Since for God to be and to be able to be are the same, God must either necessarily exist or necessarily not exist.[123] Hence, if it is possible that God exists, then God must exist. It is in this sense that Rufus is able to draw the absolute from the relative – the existence of the relative shows that the absolute is possible, and if it is possible, it necessarily exists.

When Richard Rufus finally left for Paris in 1253 his decision to quit Oxford came suddenly and during a period of emotional crisis.[124] Although there is no clear statement as to what caused the crisis, Raedts has argued that Rufus was edged out of the Oxford mastership by a younger candidate, Thomas of York, who had been promoted by his Franciscan superiors.[125] It is notable that the treatment of the natural knowledge of God in Thomas of York's work resembled more closely the doctrine of the *Summa* at Paris, as well as that of Richard Fishacre in Oxford.[126]

Thomas of York (d. 1260?) never composed a commentary on Peter Lombard's *Sentences*. His treatment of the question of God's existence occurs instead within the course of his metaphysical *Summa*, the *Sapientiale*. In the course of this, Thomas teaches that God is known to exist through a natural impression on the mind, by the appetites of the soul, and by the arguments of the philosophers.[127] From the general impression on the mind, Thomas writes,

Epicurus describes God as that than which nothing more blessed, nothing greater nor anything more flowing with all goods is able to be thought. From that conception Anselm formulates an argument that is called the *Proslogion.*[128]

Thomas defends Anselm's argument against detractors who would say (as Rufus said they could) that there is no such thing as something than which no greater can be thought. In response, Thomas shifts the emphasis back to the possibility of what can and cannot be thought, and the light that underpins human thought more generally. Like Anselm, Thomas of York declares that there are two ways of thinking something – thinking the words or thinking the thing signified by the words. In the first way something than which no greater can be thought can be thought not to exist, but not in the second. Thomas goes on to argue that the signification of the words is such that if the thing is thinkable at all it follows by necessity that it exists both in understanding and in reality.[129] For 'that than which no greater can be thought' is the precondition of existence and of thought itself.

Thomas shows that the conception of 'that than which no greater can be thought' can only be given to something that is without beginning.[130] Moreover, it can only be given to a being that is without any constraint in time and place.[131] After employing Augustinian arguments from the necessity of truth, Thomas argues that although there are philosophers who have doubted the existence of God or who have said, like the Fool, 'there is no God', the name of God has been impressed upon everyone.[132] Those denying or doubting God's existence have made errors regarding the nature of God and thereby deny that God is God. In doing so they confess that if God *is* God then God must exist.[133]

The identification of the impressed knowledge of God and the argument from Anselm is interesting not least because of Thomas of York's position on divine illumination. As well as the knowledge of universals derived through the senses, Thomas pointed out that the mind acquired universals by another route. The influence of Grosseteste is unmistakable:

> There are two ways of knowing. One of these is derived from below. This is the way of the senses. One who asserted that this was the only way of knowledge, as we have seen, is Aristotle, since he said that all knowledge is from the senses. We, on the other hand, according to the wisdom of Christians and of philosophers, know that there is clearly another way, from above and not from the senses. This is by way of the influence and reception from the First (Principle), and this knowledge is more certain than all others, and this is the way which comes from the (divine) idea into the (created) idea, which is not through exterior teaching, but through interior illumination.[134]

Thomas tells us that this light is none other than the formal essence of the soul made in the image of God. Within this, all knowable species exist like the colours in material light.[135] In the context of his wider doctrine, then, Anselm's argument does not make an illicit move from the realm of ideas to the realm of existence. Rather it forms part of an account of how God is already present to the mind when it apprehends the realm of existence. Here Anselm's argument presupposes a particular contention about the role of divine illumination in natural knowledge and a particular account of the soul as the image of God. Moreover, what Thomas of York supplies, and what Rufus singularly did not, was an account of Aristotle's error. Aristotle's ignorance concerning illumination, according to Thomas, is fatal for his account of the soul more generally.[136]

Thomas of York tends more than his colleagues in Paris toward an account of the natural knowledge of God as an innate idea. Nonetheless, their lines of enquiry are more than sufficiently alike to suggest that it was the spiritual interests of the Franciscan order itself which made Franciscans from two different locations receptive to Anselm's argument at about the same time. In the context of the encounter with Aristotle, of course, Anselm's argument had come a long way from its original role in the devotional context of the monastery of Bec and its patrons. In the writings of Thomas of York and in those of the Parisian Franciscans, Anselm's argument became instrumental in the attempt to integrate the knowledge of nature more fully within a particular theological scheme. More basically, the particular approach to God in the majority of Franciscan texts reflects something basic to Franciscan religious experience itself: divine immanence in nature and in the soul of the individual.

Richard Rufus's disposition to use the idiom of the sentence commentary has suggested to some commentators that it was he, far more than Robert Grosseteste, who represented the real father of the Franciscan theological tradition at Oxford.[137] A brief examination of the wider Franciscan community – and of the masters who actually taught at Oxford after Richard Rufus – suggests that quite the opposite is true. It is well known that while never formally entering the order himself, Robert Grosseteste held a very powerful and direct influence upon the earliest Franciscan master at Oxford in Adam Marsh and that he was later also followed by Roger Bacon – arch-critic of Richard Rufus. When we look to other Franciscan masters at Oxford during the period, we find little or no interest in Lombard's *Sentences.* John of Wales, 1259-1262, Thomas Docking, c. 1262-1265, Henry of Brisingham c. 1265-1267 and William of Hedley c. 1267-1267 are all known for biblical commentaries and for a degree of scientific interest – but not for commentaries on the *Sentences*.[138]

The first extant commentary of an Oxford Franciscan after Richard Rufus is that of John Peckham – the product of his education and teaching at Paris in the 1260s and early 1270s.[139] Peckham was one of the first Franciscan masters to speak of a Franciscan tradition of thought and he named Alexander of Hales and Bonaventure after St Francis himself as its founding fathers.[140] By contrast, as Raedts himself has said, 'Rufus would probably have been forgotten completely but for the fact that Roger Bacon saved him from oblivion by violently attacking him in his *Compendium of Theological Studies*'.[141] If an Oxford tradition of thought was manifest in the next generation of Franciscans at Oxford and at Paris, it was more nearly represented by Robert Grosseteste than by Richard Rufus.[142] Only in the much later work of Duns Scotus, after a great deal of change within the intellectual contexts of Paris and Oxford, was the approach of Richard Rufus to the natural knowledge of God to be revived. Ironically, perhaps, Richard Rufus was less successful than his contemporary Thomas of York, precisely because he was more original. In a context where tradition is the final arbiter of truth, anything that is worth saying has been said before. Whether Richard Rufus really did fall from grace and whether he did so on account of 'exceeding others in wrong opinions' – as Roger Bacon later put it – it is clear that upon his arrival in Paris in 1253 he spent time studying the opinions of another of his more successful contemporaries, Bonaventure.[143]

## V

By the time of the sentence commentary of Albertus Magnus there were two distinct ways of attaining the knowledge of God in Paris. Both began in sources that lay outside the soul – in the senses. Nevertheless, the approach epitomised in the use of Anselm's argument by the Parisian Franciscans and by Richard Fishacre in Oxford represented a journey toward the first principle of knowledge that lay within the soul. The approach adopted by Albertus proceeded from the knowledge of the senses as *from* the first principles of knowledge toward a conclusion dependent upon those principles. Whereas the God of the Franciscan community is encountered within the nature of things, and within the soul itself, the God of Albert's commentary is found only as an inference from nature. Those differences represented not only a different account of the first principles of knowledge, but a different account of how those first principles are found and how they operate within knowledge. Yet, to express an account of reason in this way, is to suggest not only an account of God, but also of human nature itself, as made in God's image.

What is important to note about the proofs for God's existence employed by the likes of Albertus Magnus, Richard Fishacre, Thomas of York and Richard Rufus, was that they presented alternatives within both communities. Already in the case of the Franciscan community there was an evident preference for the approach of Thomas of York over that of Richard Rufus. That preference was to receive its vindication above all in the writings of Bonaventure and his followers. In the work of Thomas Aquinas, Richard Fishacre's thesis that the knowledge of God was somehow so obvious to the mind that it lay beyond argument was to receive decisive refutation in favour of a dialectical approach involving the Aristotelian arguments employed by Roland of Cremona and Albertus Magnus. What these intellectual decisions reflect are the presence of rational standards internal to the communities, standards embedded within the interests of the orders themselves.

Theistic arguments were not validated in terms of rational principles that owed nothing to the time or place in which they were put forward, therefore. The Franciscan and Albertian arguments, along with the account of knowledge that those arguments represented, were validated in terms of the account of God, or of reason itself, that was already embedded in the religious ideals to which the Franciscans and Dominicans aspired. The proofs mirrored and articulated the encounter with God that the communities embodied: one in which God was encountered within the self, and another in which God was encountered outwardly, and particularly in the encounter with 'the other'. The natural knowledge of God is the metaphysical counterpart of an account of what the authentic religious life ought to be. In that sense, the proofs were concerned far more with a debate about the ends of religious life, than about its foundations. As we shall see, the ideals of Franciscan and Dominican life were to receive clearer articulation in the next generation of Franciscan and Dominican enquiry. In that context, Anselm's argument was to become critical in opening up the space within shared Christian teaching where differences of interpretation were already being lived out.

## Notes

1. Cit. in M.-H. Vicaire, *Saint Dominic and His Times*, trans. by K. Pond (New York; London, 1964), p. 230.
2. Ibid.
3. Ibid.
4. See, for example, J. R. H. Moorman, *Sources for the Life of St Francis* (Manchester, 1940), pp. 55-56 and Vicaire, p. 382.
5. See the remarks of Vicaire, p. 229.
6. Simon Tugwell, *Early Dominicans* (New York, 1982), p. 11.
7. Tugwell, p. 17.
8. Ibid., pp. 14-15.
9. Ibid., pp. 19ff.
10. Vicaire, p. 88.
11. Tugwell, pp. 18-19.
12. Tugwell writes of Diego and Dominic's adoption of poverty: 'They were responding to an external need, not just following the impulses of their own spirituality.' Ibid.
13. Vicaire, p. 312, and Tugwell, p. 24.
14. Vicaire, p. 312, and Tugwell, p. 25.
15. Tugwell, p. 3.
16. Ibid., p. 5.
17. Cit. in Tugwell, p. 457. Tugwell's introduction to the translated documents collected here offers a fascinating account of Dominican spirituality which he has also elaborated in *Ways of Imperfection: An Exploration of Christian Spirituality* (London, 1984), and in 'The Dominicans' in *The Study of Spirituality*, ed. by C. Jones et al. (London, 1984), pp. 296-300.

18. Tugwell, *Early Dominicans*, p. 4.
19. For an account of the ways in which spirituality has, in modern times, come to be associated with the individual's interior life and self-expression, see Charles Taylor, *Sources of the Self: The Making of the Modern Identity* (Cambridge, 1989), esp. pp. 368ff.
20. For the role of individualism and interiority in contemporary spirituality see Colin Morris, *The Discovery of the Individual, 1050-1200* (London, 1972); C. W. Bynum, 'Did the Twelfth Century Discover the Individual?', *Journal of Ecclesiastical History*, 31: 1 (1980), 1-18, and C. Morris, 'Individualism in Twelfth Century Religion: Some Further Reflections', *Journal of Ecclesiastical History*, 31: 2 (1980), 195-206. For the fears of the establishment surrounding popular religious groups see B. Bolton, 'Tradition and Temerity: Papal Attitudes to Deviants, 1159-1216', in *Schism, Heresy and Religious Protest*, ed. by D. Baker, Studies in Church History, ix (Cambridge, 1972), pp. 79-91.
21. Beryl Smalley, *The Study of the Bible in the Middle Ages* (Oxford, 1952), pp. 270-273.
22. Smalley, p. 274.
23. Fragments of the commentary of Guerric de St Quentino (Albert's immediate predecessor and teacher) are listed in T. Kaeppelli, *Scriptores Ordinis Praedicatorum Medii Aevi*, 4 vols (Rome, 1970-93), II, 61-70. Those fragments cover the fourth book of the *Sentences*, as do the fragmentary remains of the commentaries of the Dominicans, John Pointlasne and Stephan of Venizy, found in Paris, Bibliothèque Nationale MS. Lat. 15652, fols 81-88.
24. P. Glorieux, *Répertoire des Maîtres en Théologie de Paris au XIIIe Siècle*, 2 vols (Paris, 1933), I, n. 2.
25. Ibid.
26. Paris, BN, MS. Lat. 3073, fol. 8r. Hugh of St Cher's arguments are extremely cursory, and basically reiterate the Lombard's arguments from causation, from mutability, from the hierarchy of goods and of beauty. The following is a partial reconstruction of the text before it goes on to discuss evidences for God as Trinity: 'Nunc probit per rationes. Primo ergo hic probat quia unus deus est et per nostra argumenta. Primus sunt creaturas et ergo creator est... si sumat id quid est creatura est ab creatore vel relatore... Si enim creatura est ab alio id aliud aut est ab alio aut a non alio et ita proceditur in infinitum vel dabitur quid aliquid est a nullo et est Creator sui, deus. Scilicet argumentum est aliquid est mutabile ergo aliquid est immutabile... et item de illo queritur utrum est mutabilis aut non et sic proceditur in infinitum vel pervenitur ad aliquid quid est immutabilis et id est deus. Nunc vero est bonus et aliquid est melius eo et sit ab aliquo ergo et illud est optime. Item est aliquid pulcritudinem et aliquid est pulchritudius eo et id est pulchritudissimus.'
27. The glosses of Hugh's disciples on the commentary, namely Paris, Bibliothèque nationale MS. Lat. 3423, and Assisi MS. Lat. 131, barely mention the natural knowledge of God's existence let alone Anselm's *Proslogion.*
28. F. Stegmueller, *Repertorium Commentariorum in Sententias Petri Lombardi*, 2 vols (Wurzburg, 1947), I, n. 503.

29. Ibid.
30. John of Treviso, *Compendium Theologiae*, Vatican ms. lat. 1187, fols 1r-1v: 'Ita nec intellectu nec in actu potest summum bonum separabile ab eo quid est esse.'
31. Glorieux, I, n. 1.
32. Ibid.
33. Roland of Cremona's *Summa* is found in two manuscripts, Vatican MS. Barb. Lat. 729, and Paris, Mazarine MS. Lat. 331.
34. C. R. Hess, 'Roland of Cremona's Place in the Current of Thought', in *Angelicum*, 45 (1968), 429-477. The quotations are from pp. 433 and 434.
35. Gordon Leff, *Paris and Oxford Universities in the Thirteenth and Fourteenth Centuries: An Institutional and Intellectual History* (New York, 1968), p. 203.
36. F. Ehrle, 'S. Dominico, Le Origini del Primo Studio Generale del suo Ordine a Parigi e la Somma Teologia del primo Maestro, Rolando da Cremona', in *Miscellanea Dominicana*, 1 (1924), 85-134.
37. G. Gremacoli, 'La Summa di Rolando da Cremona, Il Testo del Prologo', in *Studi Medievali*, 16 (1975), 825-76: 'An sit principium rerum unum an plura...' (pp. 860ff.).
38. Gremacoli, pp. 860-863.
39. Ibid., p. 861: 'Quod sit unum principium omnium divina Scriptura demonstrat, tamen propter Grecos qui querunt sapientiam oportet istud probari. Hoc modo probaverunt philosophi: hoc habet causam et illud aliud causam, et sic non procedatur in infinitum quia infinita non est pertransire: ergo stabitur in uno principio.'
40. Roland of Cremona, *Summa Theologiae Liber Tercius*, ed. A. Cortesi in *Monumenta Bergomensia* [vol. 7] (Bergamo, 1962), p. 307, C. Utrum idem sit Creditum et Scitum, 11: 'Ad ea que obiecta sunt dicimus quod idem potest esse scitum et creditum, sed non secundum idem. Hoc est dictu: circa idem potest attendi scientia et fides, sed respectu diversorum, ita quod non est scitum secundum quod est creditum, ut posuimus exemplum in eo quod est *Deum esse*, quoniam illud potest esse creditum in quantum assentitur ei sine aliquo amminiculo forinseco, sed fides que est in corde, scilicet habitus asserit illud et probat, sicut et alios articulos probat; et est scitum secundum quod non exit ab illo habitu, sed ex cognitione causatorum.'
41. Cit. in Leff, *Paris and Oxford*, p. 201.
42. J. A. Weisheipl, 'The Life and Works of St Albert the Great', in *Albertus Magnus and the Sciences*, ed. by J. A. Weisheipl (Toronto, 1980), pp. 20-21.
43. Ibid.
44. For the organisation of the Friars schools, see the introductions to vols 1 and 2 of *Glorieux*, *Repertoire*, and H. Rashdall, *The Universities of Europe in the Middle Ages*, rev. ed. by F. M. Powicke and A. B. Emden, 3 vols (Oxford, 1987; 1st pub. in 1936).
45. Albertus Magnus, *Opera Omnia*, ed. by A. Borgnet, 38 vols (Paris, 1890-1895), xxv. *Commentarii in Sententiarum*, Lib. I, dist. i, art. v.
46. Ibid.
47. Ibid.
48. Ibid., I, dist. iii, art. i.
49. Ibid., dist. iii, art. i, 1-8, solutio.

50. Ibid., solutio, ad aliud: 'Dicendum, quod in Philosophia causa physica proportionata est causato, et motor mobili: Sed quia proportionatum in virtute causandi non potest esse primum quod habet influentiam ad omnia, ideo extendit se ratio ad probandum illud esse, licet non probet nisi quia est tantum, et non possit determinare proprietates eius. Unde etiam circa talia attributa inveniuntur Philosophi multos errores dixisse: circa esse vero Deum, sive quia est, et quod unus est, pauci Philosophi qui vere erant Philosophi, erraverunt.' Ibid., Ad ultimum: 'Et licet positio Deo non ponatur necessario creatura: tamen posita creatura tanquam effectu Dei, necesse est Deum creatorem poni: et sic a posteriori ex creatura potest Deus cognosci.'
51. Ibid., dist. iii, art. ii, 1-5.
52. Ibid., Sed contra: 'In libris Gentilium legimus, quod non tantum probant Deum esse, sed ipsum esse primum, ipsum esse ens necesse quod non cadit in praedicamento, ens simplex cuius substantia sit intellectus et voluntas et actio eius: ergo videtur, quod non tantum cognoverunt quia est, sed etiam proprietates, vel attributa eius, et quid est ipse.'
53. Ibid., Solutio: 'Dicendum, quod non cognoverunt quaedam attributa ipsius: non tamen habuerunt de ipsis cognitionem certam: sicut invenimus quosdam cognovisse sapientiam ipsius, et cum hoc dicere quod non haberet scientiam particularium: et ita etiam est de aliis. Et ita de Deo attributa taliter cognoscere, non facit cognitionem quid est, praecipue cum definiti termini illorum attributorum non sint cogniti a quoquam intellectu creato. Et per hoc patet solutio ad ultimum.'
54. For example, see ibid., lib. I, dist. iii, art. ii, Ad aliud: 'Dicendum, quod licet non sequatur creaturam esse si Deus sit: tamen e converso sequitur Creatorem esse si sit creatura.'
55. Ibid.: 'Nec est simile de fabro lignorum et domo, et Deo: quia faber lignorum separatur a domo, et opus eius similiter, et transit. Unde etiam sequitur: si domus est, faber lignarius est, vel fuit. Sed in Deo opus universaliter non separatur a creatura: quia postquam creata est, adhuc in nihilum caderet nisi contineretur ab ipso: et ordo eius in universo corrumperetur, nisi ab ipso gubernaretur. Non tamen dico, quod sequatur, quod Deus fuit: sed sequatur, quod ipse est propter rationem aeternitatis quae est tota simul et perfecta.'
56. Ibid.: 'Ad aliud dicendum, quod in creatura mutabilitas et corruptio incidunt et non causantur proprie ab aliquo, sed incidunt ex hoc quod creatura est ex nihilo ut supra notatum est in quaestione de duobus principiis: et ideo quantum est de se, non inducit errorem.'
57. Ibid., lib. I, dist. iii, art. iii.
58. Ibid.
59. Ibid.
60. Ibid.
61. Ibid.
62. Ibid.
63. Ibid.
64. See J. Owens, 'Faith, ideas, illumination, and experience', in *The Cambridge History of Later Medieval Philosophy*, ed. by N. Kretzmann, et al. (Cambridge, 1982), pp.

440-459, 448. In his commentary on the *De anima*, Albert teaches 'omnis nostra scientia oritur ex sensibilibus'. Cited in Owens, ibid., p. 48, n. 31.

65. Albertus Magnus, *Commentarii*, lib. I, dist. iii, art. vi.
66. Ibid., art. vii.
67. Ibid., art. viii, prima.
68. Ibid., art. viii, secunda.
69. Ibid., art. ix.
70. Ibid., art. x.
71. Ibid., art. xi.
72. Ibid., art. xii.
73. See E. A. Synan, 'Albertus Magnus and the Sciences', in *Albertus Magnus and the Sciences*, ed. by J. A. Weisheipl (Toronto, 1980), pp. 9-10.
74. Synan, p. 22.
75. Ibid., pp. 28-29.
76. D. E. Sharp, *Franciscan Philosophy at Oxford in the Thirteenth Century* (New York, 1964), p. 1.
77. See R. C. Dales, *Medieval Discussions of the Eternity of the World* (New York, 1990), pp. 68-71.
78. Ibid.
79. Robert Grosseteste, *Hexaëmeron*, ed. by R. C. Dales and S. Gieben (Oxford, 1982), I, viii, 4: 'Ex hiis et multis que afferri possent nisi prohiberet prolixitas, evidenter patet quod plurimi philosophorum simul cum Aristotile asseruerunt mundum carere temporis principio; quos unius verbi ictu percutit et elidit Moyses dicens: *In principio.* Hec adduximus contra quosdam modernos, qui nituntur contra ipsum Aristotilem et suos expositores et sacros simul expositores de Aristotile heretico facere catholicum, mira cecitate et presumpcione putantes selimpidius intelligere et verius interpretari Aristotilem ex litera latina corrupta quam philosophos, tam gentiles quam catholicos, qui eius literam incorruptam originalem greceam plenissime noverunt. Non igitur se decipiant et frustra desudent ut Aristotilem faciant catholicum, ne inutiliter tempus suum et vires ingenii consumant, et Aristotilem catholicum constitudendo, se ipsos hereticos faciant. Sed de hiis actenus.'
80. Cit. in R. W. Southern, *Robert Grosseteste: The Growth of An English Mind in Medieval Europe*, 2nd ed. (Oxford, 1992), p. 165.
81. See J. McEvoy, *The Philosophy of Robert Grosseteste* (Oxford, 1982), p. 321.
82. Ibid.
83. Southern, *Robert Grosseteste*, p. 165.
84. L. E. Lynch, 'The Doctrine of Divine Ideas and Illumination in Robert Grosseteste, Bishop of Lincoln', in *Medieval Studies*, 3 (1941), 161-73 (p. 169).
85. See, for example, S. Gieben, 'Traces of God in Nature according to Robert Grosseteste: with the text of the Dictum "Omnis creatura speculum est"', *Franciscan Studies*, 24 (1964), 144-158.
86. Cit. in Southern, *Robert Grosseteste*, p. 217.
87. Lynch, 'The Doctrine of Divine Ideas', p. 170.
88. Ibid., p. 172.

89. The text of Richard's treatment of the question is published in P. A. Daniels, *Quellenbeiträge und Untersuchungen zur Geschichte der Gottesbeweise im Dreizehnten Jahrhundert* (Münster, 1909), pp. 21-24. References to Fishacre's commentary will be to Daniels, and to Richard Fishacre, *Com. in I sent. libro*, dist. iii.
90. Ibid., 21-24: Richard Fishacre, *Commentarius in I Sententiarum libro*, dist. iii, 1: 'Item, quodlibet erit summum bonum. *Probatio:* quia, si hoc est bonum bonitate infinita, continet omnem bonitatem in se, quia si aliquo caruerit, non erit dicere non tantum quin amplius, nec erit dicere extra quod nihil.'
91. Ibid., dist. iii, 2: 'Item quicumque iudicat hoc illo melius, videt aut unum eorum esse optimum aut aliquid melius utroque, ut patet in visu dicentis hoc illo rectius. Ut enim dicit Augustinus *De doctrina Christiana* illud quo iudicas est praestantius eis de quibus iudicas. Ergo qui dicit vel iudicat hoc esse de minimis bonis, videt aliquid in omnibus bonis quod est optimum aut aliquid omnibus melius bonis. Hoc voco Deum. Per habitus enim congnoscuntur privationes; sed minus bonum, unde minus privatio est.'
92. Ibid., dist. iii, 3: 'Item, omne nomen multipliciter dictum, significat illud de quo primo dicitur: ergo aut est primum bonum, aut bonum significat non-ens: ergo de nullo ente praedicaretur.'
93. Ibid., dist. iii, 4: 'Item, privatio non cognoscitur nisi per habitum. In hoc ergo minus bono est aliquid de privatione et non cognoscitur nisi per habitum suum. Sed si habitus ille importatur per illud quod est proximo melius illo, illud etiam habet aliquid de privatione boni, et ideo non nisi per melius cognoscitur, et sic in infinitum. Ergo cognitio cuiuslibet boni dependet ex infinitis: ergo nullum eorum cognoscitur. Aut igitur non congnoscis aliquid bonum, aut est aliquid summum bonum, quo omnia alia cognoscis.'
94. Ibid., dist. iii, 5: 'Item, est aliquid tantum causatum, et aliquid quod est causa et causatum: ergo est aliquid quod est causa tantum.'
95. Ibid., dist. iii, 6: 'Item, si aliquid esset simplicissimum, non differret ab esse suo sed esset suum esse; quia si non, iam haberet esse et aliquid amplius, et tunc non esset simplicissimum. Igitur si aliquid esset simplicissimum, illud esset; sed simplicissimum est simplicissimum: ergo est.'
96. Ibid., dist. iii, 7: 'Item, si Deus esset, esset quo maius cogitari non potest; sed aliquis hoc audiens cogitat quid quo magis cogitari non potesst: si dico verba, intelligit. Hoc quod ipse cogitat, aut in cogitatione eius tantum aut in re: si in re est, hoc volui; si in cogitatione eius tantum aut in re: si in re est, hoc volui; si in cogitatione tantum, iam illo cognito aliquid erit maius, quia illud quod est in cogitatione et in re est maius quam illud quod est in cogitatione tantum.'
97. Ibid., dist. iii, 8: 'Ergo sicut simus non potest intelligi sine naso, sic nec optimum sine esse.'
98. Ibid., dist. iii, 9: 'Item, si Deus non est, *Deum non esse* est verum: ergo veritas aliqua est. Haec aut fuit ab aeterno et tunc ipsa Deus, quod volo; aut non, et tunc eius oppositum fuit verum, siciliet *Deus est*, ab aeterno.'
99. Ibid., dist. iii, 10: 'Item, universitas causatorum vocetur *A*. Constat ergo *A* est causatum, cum sit universitas causatorum; sed omne causatum habet causam extra se:

ergo *A* habet causam extra se: ergo causa eius quod est *A* est causa non causata; sed hoc dico Deum: ergo Deus est.'

100. Ibid.: 'Cum hoc dicit, non de Deo dicit, sed de aliquo quod est minus Deo, quod comprehenditur per hoc quod dico *Deus*; sicut dicens *dii* non intelligit Deum sed aliquid Deo inferius, quod potest cogitari convenire pluribus.'
101. Ibid.: 'Item, si non potest cogitari non esse et etiam innata est nobis cognitio existendi Deum, ut dicit Damascenus cap. 1, non dereliquit nos Deus omnimoda ignorantia. Omnibus enim cognitio existendi Deum ab ipso naturaliter inserta est: ergo probando ipsum esse stulto labore consumimur. Ergo in malitia quosdam corrumpit ut quod naturaliter est certissimum fiat eis dubium. Damascenus cap. 3: "In tantum praevaluit malitia hominum naturae, ut quosdam in irrationabilissimum et omnium malorum pessimum perditionis deduceret barathrum, ut dicant non esse Deum, de quorum insipientia ait sacrorum enuntiator David: *Dixit insipiens in corde* etc." Et bene subiungitur: *corupti sunt et abdominabilies.*'
102. P. Raedts, *Richard Rufus of Cornwall and the Tradition of Oxford Theology* (Oxford, 1987), pp. 208 and 247.
103. See Thomas of Eccleston, *De Adventu Fratrum Minorum in Angliam*, ed. A. G. Little (Manchester, 1951), col. xiii 'De successione Ministrorum Generalium', pp. 73-74. See also Moorman, *Sources for the Life of St Francis* (Manchester, 1940), pp. 136-140.
104. R. B. Brooke, *Early Franciscan Government* (Cambridge, 1959), p. 257.
105. See Thomas of Eccleston, col. xiii 'De successione Ministrorum Generalium', pp. 73-74.
106. Ibid.: 'Et provinciale capitulum celebravit Oxoniae, et fratres ad unitatem revocavit, qui praecedere ceteros in sententiis singularibus inceperant.'
107. Ibid.: 'Dixit autem idem pater, quod cum ex duobus parietibus construatur eadificium ordinis, scilicet moribus bonis et scientia, parietem scientiae fecerunt fratres ultra coelos et coelestia sublimem, in tantum ut quaererent an Deus sit; parietem vero morum permiserunt ita bassum esse, ut pro laude magna dicatur de fratre: "Securus homo est"...' Compare also J. R. H. Moorman, *A History of the Franciscan Order, From its Origins to the Year 1517* (Oxford, 1968), p. 247.
108. A. G. Little, *The Grey Friars in Oxford* (Oxford, 1892), p. 142.
109. Cit. in G. Gál, 'Viae ad exsistentiam Dei Probandam in Doctrina Richardi Rufi, O. F. M.', in *Franziskanische Studien*, 38 (1956), 177-202: 'Inventio enim naturalis ingenii quod naturae est non transcendit; ergo ad id quod mere gratiae est, pertingere nequit, ad fidem sciliciet et Verbi incarnationem' (p. 181).
110. Raedts, *Richard Rufus*, p. 169.
111. Ibid., p. 161.
112. Richard Rufus's proofs for God's existence have been edited in Gál.
113. Gál., p. 187: Richard Rufus, *Commentarius in I libro Sententiarum*, dist. ii: 'Dicet aliquis quid non probabile vel quaestio an sit Deus, quia *omnibus naturaliter inserta est ab ipso cognitio existendi Deum*, ut ait Damascenus, capitulo 1. Sed istud ipse idem solvit capitulo 3, dicens: "In tantum praevaluit naturae perniciosa malitia hominum, ut dicant quidam non esse Deum; quorum insipientiam manifestans

sacrorum enuntiator ait: *Dixit insipiens in corde suo*" etc. Est ergo quaestio an sit Deus, sed omnino non esset nisi perversa anima praeexsistente a casu liberi arbitrii. – A superioribus ergo inchoetur et quaeratur an sit Deus.'

114. Ibid., p. 188, dist. ii, 2-3: 'Item, haec omnia, tam numeri quam sapientiae vera incommutabilia, omnibus ratiocinantibus et intelligentibus ad videndum sunt communia; ergo ad nullius unius creaturae naturam sunt pertinentia, ergo ab omnibus creaturis sunt segregata: ergo sunt immutabilia, nam omne mutabile creaturae. Item, omne quod videtur, in lumine videtur. Haec et talia omnia ab omnibus et communiter videntur; ergo in aliquo lumine uno et eodem omnia haec illuminante videntur; et illud unum lumen, quando haec incommutabilia sunt, mutabile esse non potest.'

115. Ibid., p. 189, dist. ii, dubitatio: 'Sed de illis multis incommutabilibus quae narrat Augustinus, *De libero arbitrio*, quid dicam? Numquid unumquodque illorum est Deus, cum tamen nullum illorum sit alterum? Nescio, an singulum istorum, secundum esse quod habent verbo aeterno, sit Deus et ratio aliqua idealis, ex parte qua est idea, distinguibile est. Alia est enim et differens idea ab idea. Unde Augustinus, *De 83 quaestionibus*, 46 quaestione: "Restat ut omnia ratione sint condita. Nec eadem ratione homo qua equus. Singula igitur propriis sunt creata rationibus. Has autem, inquit rationes ubi esse arbitrandum est, nisi in ipsa mente Creatoris?" – Unde etsi nullum illorum aliud sit quam Deus, nullum tamen illorum est alterum secundum formalem, dico, preadicationem.'

116. Ibid., p. 189, dist. ii, 2, dubitatio: 'Sed numquid ex regula ista sequitur quod illud commune univocum quod per hoc nomen "homo" praedicatur de singulis hominibus sit maxime homo, sicut probat Philosophus. Si enim illud esset homo, esset aliquis singularis homo; et tunc esset commune significatum nominis appellativi aliquod appellatum eiusdem nominis appellativi; quod non est intelligibile. Similiter dico: numquid commune quod per hoc nomen 'bonum' dicitur de singulis bonis erit maxime bonum? Nequaquam. Nullum enim universale est summe bonum...'

117. Ibid., p. 191, dubitatio 2: 'Sed in hac ultima ratione dubitatur: duae lineae rectae sibi aequales numquid per unum aliquid tertium ab illis erunt aequales, aut per unum et idem quod sit hoc quod ipsae sunt? Si primo modo, ergo si ponantur duae aequales ponteur et tertia, et si tres quarta et ita in infinitum. Si secundo modo, iam non duae lineae, sed una essentia, una linea. Nescio; responde si potes. Duae lineae in materia, duae in imaginiatione, scilicet aequales, mensurantur et sibi invicem sunt aequales et pares per unicam intelligibilem illis aequalem in mensura, immo quae est ipsa mensura talium, sibi aequalium, etsi infinitarum.'

118. Ibid., p. 191.

119. Ibid., p. 193: 'Dicamus in proposito: differt dicere "aliquid, quo maius cogitari non potest, potest cogitari non esse" et "potest cogitari nullum entium esse, quo maius cogitari non potest". Prima positio est impossibilis, nam subiectum repugnat praedicato. Ipsa enim significat per "aliquid": quod non potest cogitari non esse, potest cogitari non esse. Et propter hoc illa hypothesi dicta, bene arguit Anselmus, et concludit opposita contradictorie, cui, ut aestimo, nullus potest resistere. Sed ego illam secundam darem hypothesim, scilicet: aliquis cogitat nihil entium esse quo maius cogitari non potest. Quaerat ergo: cum hoc cogitat, aut cogitat aliquid, quo

maius cogitari non potest aut non. Dico non. Ergo dicet: non cogitat aliquid, quo maius cogitari non potest, non esse. Verum est. Non enim fuit illa hypothesis, nec ex hoc sequitur: ergo cogitat omne illud, quo maius cogitari non potest, esse. De nullo enim quo maius cogitari non potest, cogitat esse nec non esse, sed de omni ente cogitat ipsum non esse quo maius cogitari non potest. Ergo secundum istam viam non videtur probari de necessitate Deum esse.'

120. Ibid.: 'Sed nec secundum priorem ut videtur. Nam non sequitur, etsi haec ratio, quae in substantiae termino, sciliciet, "aliquid, quo maius excogitari non potest" opponitur huic praedicato, potens cogitari non esse, et haec est ratio Dei, ergo Deus opponitur eidem praedicato. Sed est accidens, quia nomen "Deus" ipsam naturam dicit absolutam, illa autem ratio dicit intentionem, cui est alia intentio opposita.'

121. Ibid., p. 193: 'Aut forte, sicut prius dixi, qui vere videret deum, infintas conditiones explicite et expressissimas videret, quarum unquaeque repugnaret eidem praedicato.' Ibid., p. 202: 'Et qui negat Deum esse vel veritatem esse, nec ens ponit omnino, nec rem, nec sermone, nec intellectum, nec opinionem. Vir Dei, istud dico salva reverentia beati Anselmi et aliorum Sanctorum qui praedicto modo arguunt.' Rufus liked to hedge his bets, although he toyed with positions that would later be considered 'radical' among Franciscans: see, for example, D. Callus, 'Two Early Oxford Masters on the Problem of Plurality of Forms, Adam of Buckfield, Richard Rufus of Cornwall', in *Revue néo-scolastique de philosophie*, 42 (1940), 411-445.

122. Gál, p. 194.

123. Ibid.: 'Sed forte dicet adversarius, quod per hoc ipsum "ab alio" non innuitur quod sit alius modus, sed quod possit esse. Hoc mihi sufficit. Nam sic potest esse ens quod habet esse non ab alio; potest igitur esse Deus. Sed si potest, et est, quia ipsum esse vel est necessarium vel impossibile. In talibus enim non differt esse et posse esse.'

124. See Raedts, pp. 5-7, who cites a letter of Adam Marsh referring to Richard's decision: 'A few days ago the aforementioned Brother R., because he found himself in a state of utter confusion, came to the irreversible decision that he wished to transfer to the province of France, availing himself of the permission given to him by the Minister-General some time ago. God willing, he desires to stay in Paris for some time.'

125. See ibid., pp. 7-8.

126. On the manuscripts of the *Sapientiale* consulted for this chapter, see P. Éphrem Longpre, 'Fr. Thomas d' York, O.F.M., La Première Somme Métaphysique du xiii siècle', in *Archivum Franciscanum Historicum,* 19 (1926), 875-930. For other aspects of Thomas of York's thought and its relationship to that of Robert Grosseteste, see D. E. Sharp, *Franciscan Philosophy at Oxford in the Thirteenth Century* (Oxford, 1930).

127. See Longpré, p. 907 (5b).

128. Thomas of York, *Sapientiale*, Vatican Lat. MS. lat. 4301 fols 8r-8v, and Vatican Lat. MS. 6771 f. 23v: 'Ex diffinitione vel descripcione aut dei pronuntiatione altera nomina quae ponit Epicurus et recitat Cicero in *de natura deorum*, lib. I cap. 8, arguitur deum esse. Ergo deus secundum Epicurum est quo nihil beatius, nihil maius, nihil omnibus bonis affluensius, excogitari potest. Argumenta igitur ex hac diffinitione est quod arguit theologus Anselmus in libro quod nominavit *Proslogion:*

quo maius excogitari potest non tam est in intellectu sed etiam in effectu quia arguitur maius eo excogitari potest. Maius est quod est in effectu et in intellectu quam quod in intellectu tantum. Cum ergo deus est quo maius excogitari non potest, ipse non tantum est in intellectu sed in effectu.'

129. Ibid.: 'Sed forte hoc argumento respondet alius et dicet quia non est tale aliquid quo maius excogitari non potest in effectu sed tantum in intellectu nam quamuis non habet suppositum in re significata [at]tam[en] potest esse in intellectu vel cogitacione prout dicit anselmus in eodem quia aliter res cum vox ea significata cogitur et [aliter] cum id ipsum quod res intelligitur. Primo modo intelligens quod deus est quo maius excogitari non potest potest cogitare quia non est sicut dixit insipiens in corde suo non est deus. Secundo modo non.

Contra igitur hanc responsionem insipientis interest anselmo declarare rationem supradictam neccessariam in tractatu de redargumentatione insipientis demonstranti manifestive quia tanta vis est significatio huius quo maius excogitari non potest ut si cogitat sequitur necessitate quod sit in effectu.'

130. Ibid.: 'Quicquid excogitari potest esse et non est potest excogitari esse per initium. Quo maius excogitari nequit non potest cogitari esse per initium. Ergo quo maius excogitari nequit non potest cogitari esse et non est. Sed si potest excogiatri esse necessitate est. ... Minoris probatio tale est: si quo maius excogitari nequit potest excogitari esse per initium possit id quo maius excogitari nequit et non esset id quo maius excogitari nequit. Hoc autem est impossibile. Ergo et per consequencia est manifestum quod maius est id quod non potest cogitari esse per initium quam id quo potest excogitari esse per initium. Et ideo, si quo maius excogitari non potest possit excogitari esse per initium possit esse id quo maius excogitari potest et ideo, non esset id quo maius excogitari nequit, quae est impossibile per se.'

131. Ibid.: 'Quartus sillogismus tale est quicquid alicubi et alio non est et si est alicubi et alio non potest cogitari nusquam esse et numquam esse. Si non est alicubi aut alio illud potest cogitari non esse. Sed quo maius cogitari nequit vero est non potest cogitari non esse. Alioquin "a" (quo maius cogitari non possit) non esset "a" quia non est quo maius excogitari non possit. Ergo "a" aut alicubi aut alio non est. Ergo semper et ubique est.'

132. Ibid.: 'Hiis ergo sunt modis quibus sapientes devenerunt in cognitionem dei...maxime cum divinitatis nominatio omnibus impressa sit...'

133. Ibid.: 'Nam qui dicit deum in corde suo non esse dixit deum non esse deum et tunc actione modo fatetur esse deum.'

134. This passage is cited from Sharp, *Franciscan Philosophy in the Thirteenth Century*, p. 100, and is derived from the manuscript Florence, Biblioteca Nazionale, Conv. Sopp. A. 6. 437, f. 36r: 'Duplex est via cognoscendi, quarum una est ab inferiori, hoc est per viam sensus, cuius solus assertor, sicut videtur, fuit Aristoteles, cum dicit quod omnis cognitio est a sensu: nos autem, secundum sapientiam christianorum et philosophorum, scimus esse aliam, videlicet a superiori et non a sensu, hoc est per viam influentiae et receptionis a Primo, et haec cognitio est certior alia, et haec est via quae currit ab idea in ideam, quae non est per doctrinam exteriorem, sed tantum illuminationem interiorem, sicut ostenditur tibi infra.'

135. Florence, BN, Conv. Sopp. A. 6. 437, fol. 206v. cit. in Sharp, p. 100.
136. Florence, BN, Conv. Sopp. A. 6. 437, fol. 213r, cit. in ibid.: 'Scientia de anima non est perfecte tradita in libro quem edidit Aristoteles *De Anima*, in quo non tractat de anima nisi secundum quod anima.' Cit. in ibid.
137. See, for example, Southern, *Robert Grosseteste*, p. 296, who says of Grosseteste, 'His name was revered, but his influence on the main stream of even Franciscan Theology was small.' C. H. Lawrence, 'The Letters of Adam Marsh and the Franciscan School at Oxford', in *Journal of Ecclesiastical History*, 42 (1991), 237, says that 'Rufus differed sharply from Grosseteste; and in the later Franciscan theological tradition at Oxford it was Rufus, not Grosseteste, who was followed'. Compare the judgement of A. G. Little, 'The Franciscan School at Oxford in the Thirteenth Century', in *Archivum Franciscanum Historicum*, 19 (1926), 845: 'After Thomas of York and Richard of Cornwall, there seems to have been a reaction against philosophy in the Franciscan School.'
138. All these masters are listed and discussed in Little, 'The Franciscan School', pp. 845-850. Although Thomas Docking may have composed a sentence commentary now lost, he was known to his contemporaries as a commentator on the Scriptures. See also A. G. Little, 'Thomas Docking', in *Franciscan Papers, Lists and Documents* (Manchester, 1943), pp. 98-121.
139. Little, 'Franciscan School in Oxford', pp. 852-885.
140. John Peckham, *Registra Epistolarum*, 3 vols, in *Rerum Britannicarum Scriptores*, n. 77 (London, 1885), iii, 902: 'Sit ergo solidior et sanior doctrina. filiorum Beati Francisci sanctae scilicet memoriae fratris Alexandri ac fratris Bonaventurae et consimilium, qui in suis tractatibus ab omni calumnia alienis sanctis et philosophis innituntur....'
141. Bacon's attack concerned the content of his logic. 'The one I knew best was the worst and most stupid of them all. He was the inventor of these errors. His name is Richard of Cornwall, very famous among the stupid masses, but the wise thought he was absurd. And he was rejected in Paris for the errors he had invented and promulgated, while lecturing there on the *Sentences* solemnly from the year 1250 onwards, after he had lectured on the *Sentences* at Oxford. From that time, 1250, on, therefore, most people persistently followed this master in his errors, and it has mainly weakened Oxford, where all this nonesense started.' Cit. in Raedts, pp. 1-2.
142. For the place of Thomas of York within the Franciscan tradition at Oxford, see Sharp, *Franciscan Philosophy*.
143. Opinion over Rufus among the English Franciscans was certainly divided: Roger Bacon reserved some of his severest criticisms for Rufus, while Thomas of Eccleston praised him and states that in Paris he was regarded as a great and admirable philosopher. For Rufus's period of study at Paris and his introduction of Bonaventure's work into Oxford, see Raedts, pp. 5, 9, and infra, chapter 4.

Chapter 4

# Bonaventure and the Franciscan Community

Alasdair MacIntyre defines 'a living tradition' as 'an historically extended, socially embodied argument, and an argument precisely in part about the goods which constitute that tradition'.[1] The idea of the good within monotheistic communities is none other than the idea of God. Far from being disconnected from the lives of the communities involved, theistic debate in the Franciscan school was debate about the good or the experience of God that defined the aims of the community. By the 1250s Anselm's argument became a key text for expressing the idea of the good embodied by Franciscan tradition, an idea that emerged from the conflicts between radical and academic imitators of St Francis. The 1250s saw an intensification of those conflicts. On the one hand, the Franciscans and the Dominicans were both to become targets of criticism from outwith their communities. On the other hand, criticisms made from outside the Franciscan order served to exacerbate tensions within it, by seeming to vindicate the view held by radical Franciscans, that the academic leadership represented a betrayal of St Francis.

It was in this context that Bonaventure (1221-1274) was not only elevated to the Master's chair at Paris, but also to the leadership of the whole order. He attained a position of long-term significance not merely because he followed the positions of his predecessors, however. Bonaventure's importance lay in the fact that he was able to use the resources provided by the Franciscan traditions at Paris and Oxford to vindicate Christian claims more generally against Arabian and Aristotelian challenges. That Bonaventure was inescapably involved in the conflicts central to the historical development of the Franciscan community is not, therefore, a fact merely accidental or peripheral to his philosophical thought. The historical context of tradition, time, place and conflict, is critical for understanding the significance of what he taught and its impact within the context in which he taught.

Like Richard Rufus, Bonaventure entered the Franciscan order under Haymo of Faversham while a Master of Arts. Studying under Alexander of Hales and John of La Rochelle (d. 1245), Bonaventure made a point of expressing his indebtedness and loyalty to his former teachers, referring to Alexander as 'his father and master'.[2] Between 1248 and 1250 Bonaventure delivered his course of lectures on the Bible and between 1250 and 1252 delivered his course of lectures on the Sentences, probably under the instruction of William of Melitona (d. 1257) whose own works are now lost.[3] Although he had therefore completed his course on the *Sentences* by the time Rufus arrived in Paris in 1253, it is likely that the final version of his commentary belongs to his years as regent in the Franciscan school. Although he received his licence to teach at the beginning of 1254, he was not admitted to the Master's chair in the Faculty of Theology at the University of Paris until 1257. This period of delay between the reception of the teaching licence and admission to the Faculty as a Master (1253-1257) was also experienced by Bonaventure's direct contemporary in the Dominican school, Thomas Aquinas (c. 1225-1274). The delay was the product of the intense opposition of secular Masters within the Faculty of Theology toward both Orders of Friars, who resented their growing influence within the Faculty as well as within society as a whole. In the same year as his inception as a Master, Bonaventure was elected Minister General of the Order of Franciscans, and in the context of this position, continued to publish his writings while, as leader of the order, consolidating its academic organisation.[4]

## I

At the beginning of his commentary on the *Sentences*, Bonaventure solemnly affirmed that he intended not to depart from the traditional teachings he himself had received from his masters.[5] At the beginning of the second book he also affirmed that just as he had adhered in the first book to the common opinions of the masters and especially to 'our master and father' Alexander, so in the remainder he would not turn back from their footsteps.[6] Despite deeming himself a mere 'compiler', Bonaventure's treatment of the natural knowledge of God already reveals that his approach to natural knowledge in general was to be somewhat more expansive than that of his predecessors – even if it was to employ the same sources and point to the same conclusions.

For Bonaventure, the realms of faith and reason are separate from each other.[7] Theology brings them together: by the addition of reason it turns what is believed through faith into something known in the understanding.[8] In the prologue to his commentary, Bonaventure ascribes to ratiocination the traditional functions of supporting faith and defending the Church, but he also added something further: understanding what one believes is itself a kind of spiritual exercise:

> The investigatory method is of value first of all for the refutation of adversaries... Secondly, for assisting the weak... Thirdly, for the delight of those perfected (in faith). For it is wonderful how the soul can take delight in understanding what it with perfect faith believes. For as St Bernard teaches, 'nothing is understood more freely, than what faith believes'.[9]

Like Robert Grosseteste, Bonaventure links the pursuit of understanding in theology to faith and love. For Bonaventure, understanding effects a renewal within the soul. It does not empty faith of its merit. When something believed becomes understood it does not cease to be a matter of belief. Faith that depends upon reason, or assents on account of reason alone, has no merit. Faith that assents on account of love, however, desires to have reasons: these do not empty faith of merit, but rather provide comfort.[10] Faith is able to lead reason beyond its human limits. For though revelation is above reason, faith elevates human reason through its gift of knowledge and understanding so that it might understand those things that are already believed.[11]

The third distinction of the commentary is, in a way, a concise re-statement of the introduction to the *Summa minorum.* The Augustinian conception of theology, adopted by Lombard, as a single science embracing all things and signs of things in as much as they are related to God permeates Bonaventure's thought and is presented as the key to natural knowledge.[12] The thread that permeates his thinking here is that unless creatures are considered as signs of God and not merely in themselves they lead the mind astray.[13]

For Bonaventure, the first question is whether the created intellect can know God. As usual, Bonaventure states the objections to his preferred position, and then offers arguments from authority and reason in favour of the proposition. He concludes why the objections with which he began ultimately support rather than undermine his favoured position. Bonaventure begins his consideration with the proclamation of the Pseudo-Dionysius that the mind cannot know God:

> For the understanding understands only that which is proportional to it, and that which is united to it in some way, and that of which it judges, and that by which the vision of its understanding is informed.[14]

Since there is no proportion between the finite and the infinite, no union (since the infinite cannot be in the finite), no judgement (since the finite has no power over the infinite) there can be no knowledge of God. Moreover, the soul cannot be informed by a likeness of God because any knowledge by way of likeness is a knowledge by means of abstraction. An abstracted likeness is always more spiritual than the substantial form from which it has been abstracted. Since nothing is, nor can be, more spiritual than God, however, there can be no abstracted likeness either.[15]

Following the *Summa minorum*, Bonaventure states the contrasting teaching of Augustine, that the rational soul is formed to the image of God: 'The soul is the image of God in that by which it is capable of possessing God, and in that by which it can partake in God.' The soul is capable of possessing and partaking in God by knowledge and love. All spiritual knowledge is made by reason of light and by uncreated light, and light is knowable in the highest degree.

God therefore is knowable to the soul in the highest degree since God is the greatest light.[16]

Furthermore, Augustine teaches that things known by presence are known more truly than those that are known only by likeness. God, however, is united to the soul itself, and so must be more truly knowable than anything known by likeness. Moreover if the supreme truth is related to knowledge as the supreme good is related to love then the supreme truth must be supremely knowable to the understanding, just as the supreme good is supremely loveable by the affection. Finally, since the understanding is supremely ordered to the knowledge of the supreme light, the supreme light is knowable to the highest degree.[17]

Resolving the tensions between the arguments and authorities, he explains that while God is intrinsically knowable in the highest degree, God would be intrinsically knowable to us were it not for something impeding the soul or deficient within it.[18] To understand the soul's ability to gain an incomplete knowledge of God it is necessary to distinguish apprehension from comprehension. There can be a knowledge by means of apprehension for this requires not an equality but a proportion of agreement. The soul and God are proportionate in the sense that both are spiritual; both are intelligibles. Quoting Aristotle, Bonaventure states that since 'the soul is in a certain manner all things', it can know all things by assimilation. It can be assimilated to God because it is an image of God.[19] There can be apprehension, therefore, but not comprehension, since the latter would require that the soul and God were proportionate as equals. It is in this sense that the Pseudo-Dionysius taught that God was beyond words and understanding.[20]

In terms of assimilation the mind can apprehend God since God is a simple, and not a complex, being. So although the infinite cannot be comprehended, it can be apprehended in its infinity – since God is everywhere completely, and completely the same everywhere.[21] The soul cannot judge God, but as truth, God assists the mind in all its judgements, since the mind judges by means of truth.[22] Similarly, the soul does not need to be informed by an abstracted likeness of God since the soul is already a likeness of God. The likeness is not abstracted, but impressed, inferior to God because it is in an inferior nature, but superior to the soul because it makes the soul better.[23] In order to enquire into God, Bonaventure, like his Franciscan predecessors, must enquire into the soul.

The same method of comparing pro and contra arguments is used in addressing Bonaventure's next question. He goes on to ask, 'whether God is knowable through creatures'. Bonaventure's treatment of the question expresses the Franciscan ambivalence toward natural knowledge – that although the senses can lead the soul to God, the senses can also lead the soul astray. Once again, the dilemma is presented as one embedded in Christian authority. Bonaventure lists the authorities and arguments that suggest that sense knowledge is not only inferior, but harmful, to spiritual knowledge. In doing so he includes objections found previously within the Franciscan convent at Paris. The book of *Wisdom* states that 'the creatures of God are for deception and hatred and as a trap to the feet of fools'. Bonaventure also employs Augustine who speaks to God of those preoccupied with creatures: 'they turn their back to you, they are fastened firmly in corporeal work, as in their own shadows.'[24] Creatures are darkness compared with the light of God.[25] Moreover, creatures are an inadequate medium for knowing God because the medium must have something in common with the object of knowledge and must approach that object in some way. Yet creatures have nothing in common with God and are separated from God to an infinite degree.[26]

By contrast, says Bonaventure, the Book of *Wisdom* also states, that 'from the greatness of the species and the creation it will be possible that the Creator of them will be seen in knowledge'. Moreover, the seventh-century Spanish authority Isidore of Seville says that 'from the beauty of the circumscribed creature God makes his beauty, which cannot be circumscribed, to be understood'. The cause may be known through the effect, and the sensible is the way of knowing the intelligible. Finally, every creature is a trace or image of God.[27]

Bonaventure affirms that the Creator is known through the creature both because of agreement and because of need, and proceeds to resolve the tensions raised by the objections. Human intelligence requires the medium of creatures because God cannot be known in God's spirituality by a mind that is almost material. Creatures may be dealt with in two ways, either with respect to their special properties or with respect to their general conditions. In terms of special properties, creatures may only lead to God by denial – that is, by denying their limited attributes of God. Otherwise they will lead the mind astray. In terms of general conditions – that is, qualities as perfections – the creature may lead the mind to or away from God depending on whether the creature is considered as a picture or as an image. If considered as a picture, creatures will lead the mind astray. However, if considered as an image, they can assist the mind in knowing God in so far as the noble qualities of creatures must be attributed to God in the highest degree.

Thus, viewed in the right way, creatures lead to God. Moreover, this is the only way the mind can come to know God. In so far as the eye cannot bear the light of the sun in itself, so the mind can only see the light of God by means of the shadow of creatures. There is nothing in common between creatures and God in univocal terms, but there is an analogical community between them. Though there are infinite steps between God and creatures in terms of equality, there are but three in terms of the sight of God's presence. The first step is the consideration of sensible things, while the second is the consideration of invisible or spiritual things. The third step is from soul (the highest creature), to God, 'because', says Bonaventure quoting Augustine, 'the image within the soul is formed by truth itself and is joined immediately to God'. Hence, the image of God within the soul is created by God's very presence. Exploring the differences between creatures as shadow, trace and image of God, Bonaventure concludes that whilst all creatures are shadows or traces, only the human soul is an image of God – for the human soul alone 'is capable of possessing God by knowledge and love'.[28]

Although the knowledge of God in creatures is proper fully only to those who are blessed (for 'they praise God in creatures') the knowledge of God through creatures is proper to those in this life. Whereas the soul knew God through the creature clearly in the state of innocence, in the state of sin it knows God through the creature as through a dark or stained mirror, because of the darkening of the understanding and the deterioration of things.[29] Creatures act as media for the soul in its path to God but, Bonaventure concludes enigmatically, the media must be left behind if the soul is to reach God, like a ladder that is kicked away once a wall has been scaled.[30] Thus, the soul begins its apprehension of God not within the soul, but in creatures, and ends by transcending them.

Bonaventure appears to have enriched the Parisian account of the natural knowledge of God with what he found in the Oxford Friars – perhaps through Thomas of York who came to Paris during this period to defend the Franciscans alongside Bonaventure against secular critics. In any case, had he looked to Robert Grosseteste he would have found an account of creatures in which each contains an image of the Creator. The exemplar causality which Bonaventure expresses, like that of Robert Grosseteste, involves an account of the source of being that is also the source of the knowledge of being.

At no stage in the third distinction does Bonaventure attempt to use natural knowledge to prove either God's existence or anything else about God.[31] Bonaventure is concerned rather with discerning the ways in which creatures symbolise God as Being and as Trinity.[32] In contemplation, creatures are necessary for the soul to know God in this life.[33] The understanding, which is almost material, cannot know God as Spirit.[34] The soul must rise to the apprehension of God's presence through the creature, as through a ladder.[35] Yet the soul itself is a creature – but one that is an image joined immediately to God. For Bonaventure, as for Robert Grosseteste, to see God in nature the soul must be properly orientated in its desires.

It is important to note that when Bonaventure employs Anselm's argument in the commentary it is not to discuss the natural knowledge of God, but rather, in the eighth distinction, to discuss the properties of God, including, truth, simplicity, immutability etc. This is significant because Anselm's argument is not employed as a proof of God's existence, but rather as a way of elucidating the attributes of God's being. What is particular about this account of God has already been explained in the third distinction – it is a God that is present to the soul, and also within creation such that the Creator is symbolised by creatures as shadow, vestige and as image. Anselm's argument is employed in the service of answering the question, 'what kind of God is this?'

Once again, while enquiring into God, Bonaventure enquires into the soul. Having affirmed in the first question of the eighth distinction that truth belongs to the essence of God, and that created truth is truth by participation in Truth Itself (God), he goes on to consider whether God is such that God cannot be thought not to exist.[36] This time, he presents the arguments in favour of the proposition he wants to defend, before the objections.

In Bonaventure's reading, and like Thomas of York, 'that than which no greater can be conceived' has become a 'common conception of the mind'.[37] Hence, it is no longer merely a description one might find in a prayer – it is a conception present within every soul. Something whose non-being is unthinkable is better than something whose non-being is thinkable. (The latter is certainly a dependent being.) Since the divine being is such that no greater can be thought, it must be incapable of being thought not to exist.[38] Like the *Summa minorum*, Bonaventure adds other arguments to this, from John of Damascus and Augustine in particular. John of Damascus teaches that the knowledge of God is naturally impressed upon us. Since a natural impression cannot be relinquished or denied, it is inseparable from the soul itself.[39] Bonaventure compares the truth in the divine being with the truth of a *dignitas* or necessary proposition, such as a whole is greater than its part. Since this cannot be denied in the heart, with all the more reason therefore neither can the first truth be denied in the heart.[40] Again, our intellect understands nothing except through the first truth. When it thinks that something does not exist, or not to be true, it thinks this through the first light; how can it possibly think that the first light does not exist or is not true?[41]

Bonaventure also employs the participational arguments found in the commentary of Richard Rufus: all affirmations imply the existence of God. Whenever we say 'this' being we speak of a limited, finite being; and so there is always implied something which is not finite or limited.[42] In Bonaventure's work, this is grafted into an exemplarist and participational account of knowledge in which every negation implies the existence of God. Why is this so? There is no greater negation than the denial of truth itself. If it is true that there is no truth, however, there is something that is true: therefore truth is affirmed.[43]

Does this mean that Bonaventure thinks that God is a self-evident proposition? Pegis argues that the existence of God is not self-evident for Bonaventure, but it is, nonetheless, indubitable.[44] On the one hand, there are ways in which God's existence seems capable of being denied. Listing these objections, Bonaventure notes first the teaching of John of Damascus that the pernicious evil of the human heart has so darkened the understanding of some that they say, like the Fool, 'there is no God'.[45] There are idolaters for example, who call an idol God and therefore deny that God is God.[46] Since things hidden from our intellect are able to be denied, God must also be capable of being denied since he 'dwells in light inaccessible'.[47] The non-being of God can be thought as a falsehood, in which case it is no different from other truths.[48] Finally, what can be said can be thought – neither the denial of God nor the denial of truth imply their contraries. The positing of nothing infers nothing.[49]

It is in his resolution of the tensions between his favoured position (that God's existence is indubitable) and the objections to it that we gain greater insight into the place of the knowledge of God within human knowledge more generally. Bonaventure affirms that the divine being is such that it is not possible 'with assent' to be thought not to exist.[50] In other words, it is possible to think the words but not actually to think their meaning. Deficiency on the part of the understanding – ignorance of *what* God is – leads to confusion as to the existence of God.[51] Citing Hugh of St Victor, Bonaventure states that God has so tempered the human creature that while it can never comprehend *what* God is, it can never be ignorant *that* God is.[52] Just as the idolater is mistaken as to what God is, so the idolater can think that God is not just. Since he or she thinks God is not just, so he or she thinks that God does not exist.[53] This is a defect on the part of the intelligence, not on the part of the object.

A defect on the part of the object would take the form of a defect in presence or in evidence. Once again, like the commentary of Odo Rigaud, Bonaventure argues that only those things which have a beginning and an end and which are not everywhere are able to be thought not to exist. They have, Bonaventure argues, a defect of presence. Citing the same passage as Odo Rigaud, from Anselm's *Response to Gaunilo*, Bonaventure argues God alone is eternal and omnipresent: and for that reason, God cannot be thought not to be.[54] Bonaventure concludes, therefore, that God has no defect of presence.

Like his contemporary, Thomas Aquinas, Bonaventure thinks that the existence of the divine truth is evident in itself: the predicate is included in the subject. In the second place, he thinks that the existence of the divine truth is also affirmed by the evidence of created things: beings that exist through another eventually insist upon the existence of a being that exists through itself. Moreover, Bonaventure asserts that every understanding has been impressed by the knowledge of the first truth, and it is through the first truth that every intelligence understands. Hence, having shown that God is Truth, the unthinkability of God's non-being reflects the mind's dependence upon God for its knowledge of truth. Finally, he concludes that God is so evident and so present, in fact, that God cannot even be thought not to be.[55] Nonetheless, although God's existence is self-evident in and of itself, Bonaventure's position implies that it is not self-evident to us. The denial of God's existence, shows that this is so, but from what Bonaventure has said, it is clear that this is due to a particular ignorance of what 'God' actually signifies.[56]

Next, Bonaventure responds to each of the objections to his favoured position. Once again, his aim is to show how the arguments brought against the indubitability of God's existence either support the resolution he has just outlined or are unsound. Bonaventure points out that John of Damascus talks of those denying God as having been overcome by malice.[57] An idolater still affirms that God exists, even if he or she is wrong as to what God is.[58] It may be possible to think that God does not exist, but not while assenting to the meaning of the proposition.[59] The knowledge of what God is remains hidden from us, but the knowledge *that* God exists, is present to the understanding of every rational creature.[60] While it is possible to think many things untruthfully, it is not even possible to think that God does not exist. The certainty of a creature may be limited to those to whom it is present, but the first light is present equally to all.[61] Finally, turning to the objection that what can be expressed can be thought, Bonaventure argues that while it may be possible to express outwardly the proposition that God does not exist, it cannot be thought with the interior reason – that is, with assent to the meaning of the words.[62]

The sentence commentary thus outlines a doctrine of God as the exemplar cause of being and knowing. Creatures represent signs and images of God both because God is the cause of their being, but also because God is the cause of the mind's knowledge of their truth. Anselm's argument represents a key move in the Franciscan approach to natural knowledge partly because it explains the epistemic status of the knowledge of God: since God is the very light of the intellect, God cannot be thought not to be. In this sense Bonaventure's early work represents a synthesis of the best arguments available within the Franciscan schools. What is equally important to note, however, is that Anselm's argument places God in the centre of all knowing, for without God there is no true knowledge. The first article of the disputed questions *On the Mystery of the Trinity* expands upon the argument of the eighth distinction of the commentary.[63] Once again, we encounter familiar themes: Franciscan spirituality is not anathema to learning; it is, rather, its prerequisite.

## II

The disputed questions *On the Mystery of the Trinity* belong to the period just after Bonaventure received the licence to teach in 1254 and began acting as Regent Master within the Franciscan school. They probably represent a carefully edited version of questions actually disputed between Bonaventure and one or more of his own students. Bonaventure states that his reflections upon the Trinity will begin with a preamble of two articles – the first dealing with 'the foundation of all certain knowledge', the second with 'the foundation of all faith'. The first deals with the indubitability of God's existence, the second with the credibility of the truth that God is a Trinity. The arguments in the first article are not themselves set up – in the Cartesian manner – as foundations for knowledge in themselves. Rather, they reveal what the foundation of knowledge is – ultimately the presence of God to the soul. Why should this concern Bonaventure in a discussion of the Trinity? In the first place it must be stressed that Bonaventure does not think that the arguments in the first article themselves provide any form of rational justification for belief in the Trinity. Instead he has two other reasons for proceeding in this way. It is in part at least because the foundation of all knowledge is itself the image of the Trinity impressed upon the mind. Hence, the foundation of all knowledge is the trinity in the soul that mirrors the foundation of all faith, which is belief in the Trinity. It is also in part because faith presupposes a rational nature which itself is properly fulfilled in faith. The first article of the disputed questions *On the Trinity* thus provides, in effect, an anthropology in which the need for faith is internal to human rationality itself and its encounter with nature.

The first article of the preamble concerns the indubitability of God's existence, as the foundation of all knowledge. Bonaventure divides his arguments into three separate paths. The three ways again correspond to the purgative ascent of the soul found in Alexander's *Glossa* as the soul moves beyond itself, within itself and above itself. Bonaventure does not intend to identify each of the three ways with a particular person of the Trinity. Nonetheless, the three stages in the soul's purgative ascent, like so many things in Bonaventure's world, represent an image of the Trinity. More precisely, the three ways reflect the trinitarian character of the soul, made in God's image.

In the account that Bonaventure provides here, the order of the soul's purgative ascent is changed slightly from its original statement in the teaching of Alexander of Hales. Bonaventure places the soul's ascent within itself, *before* the ascent beyond itself. This often goes unnoted by commentators. Bonaventure does not appear to regard the order as arbitrary – for he would never have placed the soul's ascent 'above itself' before its ascent within or beyond itself. It is the noetic structure of the mind that concerns Bonaventure in the first article of the disputed questions *On the Mystery of the Trinity* not the actual stages by which the mind would arrive at the knowledge of God. When he does compose a systematic account of the mind's approach to the knowledge of God, in his *Journey of the Soul* he begins, as Alexander did, with the soul's journey from outside itself.

The three ways of the disputed questions *On the Mystery of the Trinity* begin with the knowledge of God that is implied within human desires and instinct. The three ways end in consideration of those who, like the Fool, say 'there is no God'. In a sense, the whole point of the three ways is to explain why this is possible, why it is the work of a fool and what foolishness is. Bonaventure is as much concerned with the ignorance of God's existence as with the knowledge of God. He concludes that the error of the Fool is wilful. Just as the knowledge of truth is implied by desire, so the rejection of God involves a struggle against the very instincts of the soul. This account of the indubitable knowledge of God is the metaphysical assumption of Franciscan life: the soul is convicted by outward imitation of Christ because Christ as Truth is already present to it. When Thomas Aquinas attacks the indubitability thesis, therefore, he attacks an assumption that underpins Franciscan life itself (see below, chapter 5).

The first way, in a sense, 'unpacks' the teaching of John of Damascus that the knowledge of God is naturally inserted within the soul, and of Hugh of St Victor that the human soul cannot be ignorant of God, even if it cannot know what God is. The soul is implicitly aware of God by its innate desires for goodness, truth, wisdom, happiness, beatitude, its hatred of error and love of truth. All of these imply a knowledge of God since desire presupposes knowledge of the object desired, and all those objects are identifiable as God. Moreover, God is most present to the soul and most knowable whilst the soul is impressed by the image of God. If it knows itself, therefore, the soul knows God.[64] Bonaventure's account of the foundations of natural knowledge already implies an account of human nature: the source of human life and destiny is to be found in something deeper than the intellect, in the spiritual desires of the soul. The knowledge of God implanted within the soul – the divine image, in fact – is not a dormant intellectual principle; it is the functional operation of the mind itself in knowledge, memory and will.

In the second way, Bonaventure turns to creatures. When the soul inspects creatures it makes an ineliminable reference to their condition in terms of temporality, mutability, participation, relativity, qualification, potentiality, composition, etc. Yet, to know what these are, one must already possess, in some sense, a knowledge of a being that is first, simple, absolute, immutable, active, being in essence and without qualification.[65] In Bonaventure's thought, the true knowledge of creatures involves an ineliminable reference to their exemplars or archetypes in the mind of God. The second way thus points us back to the first: the presence of God to the soul.

In the third way – the ascent of the soul above itself – Bonaventure employs Anselm's argument together with arguments from Augustine, Aristotle and Boethius, to show that God cannot be thought not to be, for any truth that cannot be thought not to be is indubitable. Bonaventure's fundamental position is this: since God is that than which no greater can be thought, God cannot be thought not to exist. That which cannot be thought not to be is more true than something which can be thought not to be. Moreover, all truths are known through some first truth, and that truth is the most indubitable truth. Since God is that than which no greater can be conceived, God is a truth than which none is more indubitable. Bonaventure identifies the truth of God's existence with the first axioms or transcendentals of the mind, so that the principle of being is also the principle of knowledge:

> The more prior and universal a truth is, the more evident it is. But that truth by which the existence of the first being is affirmed is the first of all truths, not only in reality but also in our knowledge of reality. Therefore, it is necessarily the most certain and most evident truth. But the truth of the axioms or the first concepts of the mind are so evident because of their priority that they cannot be thought not to be. Therefore, no intellect can think that there is no first truth, nor can it be in doubt about this.[66]

Like Thomas of York, Bonaventure argues that it is impossible to say that God does not exist without saying simultaneously that God does exist, since to deny God is to deny truth, which is self-contradictory. Finally, if God is truth and being itself, then there can be no proposition more true than the proposition in which the existence or truth of God is affirmed.

Does this all mean that Bonaventure thinks the existence of God is self-evident to the mind? This is the position that his direct contemporary Thomas Aquinas argues against, and would appear to ascribe to Bonaventure. In this respect, Bonaventure's objections to the indubitable knowledge of God are illuminating. He cites the Fool, St Paul on mistaking idols for God, John of Damascus's teaching about the corruption of human knowledge through sin, Gaunilo's lost island, and Pseudo-Dionysius on God's supreme hiddenness, to show that God's existence is capable of being doubted. More interestingly, perhaps, he also cites favourite arguments of Thomas Aquinas: the proposition 'the whole is greater than its part' is self-evident but not to anyone who does not know the nature of its terms. Yet no one knows the nature of God. Moreover, if God's existence is indubitable, then proofs would be futile. Finally, if God's existence were indubitable, faith would lack merit.[67]

By contrast, Bonaventure distinguishes between two different senses of doubtful. A thing is said to be doubtful either because of the process of reasoning, or because of a defect in reason itself. The first way of doubt refers both to the knower and to the thing known; the second refers only to the knower. In terms of the process of reason there is no room for doubt. There is innate to the mind, Bonaventure says, 'a natural desire for, together with a knowledge and memory of, that reality in whose image it is made, and to which it naturally tends for its beatitude'. In this sense, Bonaventure's account of the natural knowledge of God frames a Franciscan conception of human nature. Moreover, his account also expresses a Franciscan sense of God's immanent presence. All creatures, Bonaventure says, 'in voices loud and strong, cry out the existence of God whom they need because of their deficiency and from whom they receive their perfection'. Finally, 'to say that a being which possesses the highest degree of existence is non-existent involves a most evident fallacy'.[68] In terms of the process of reasoning, God's being is a truth that cannot be doubted:

> If we understand the indubitable in the sense of removing doubt in the procedure of reason, then the existence of God is an indubitable truth; for whether the intellect enters within itself, or goes outside itself, or looks above itself, provided it proceed rationally, it knows that God exists with certitude and without doubt.[69]

If we look at doubt in the second way, as a doubt arising from a defect of reason, however, then God's existence can be doubted. Bonaventure lists three kinds of error occurring when the indubitable truth of God's existence is not recognised because of human weakness. There are errors of apprehension, comparing and resolving the argument.[70] The mind errs in apprehension when it does not rightly receive the significance of the name 'God', and this is true of the Fool who says in his heart 'there is no God', and of idolaters who call mundane things 'God'.[71] Like Odo Rigaud, Bonaventure also explains that the mind errs in comparing when it concludes from the absence of immediate retribution upon the impious that there is no rule within the universe, and therefore that there is no first and highest governor of the universe.[72] Finally, the error of resolving occurs when the carnal intellect, so tied to the realm of the senses, is unable to raise itself to the incorporeal substance and fails to resolve the argument to a truly first cause.[73] Bonaventure sums up these errors on the part of the knower as a failure to sufficiently understand the meaning of the term 'God'.[74]

Bonaventure argues that, in terms of its proper functioning, the intellect has sufficient light within itself to dispel doubt and rescue itself from such foolishness. He then explains the denial of the Fool, the corruption of the soul taught by John of Damascus, and the reference to the worship of idols in Paul's *Letter to the Corinthians*, in terms of error that has its origin in the will:

> Therefore, in this defective consideration of the foolish man, the mistake of the intellect arises more from the will than from necessity; it comes from a defect in the knower rather than a deficiency in the object known.[75]

The idolater makes the same mistake, thinking that God is something less than which nothing greater can be thought: 'He throws himself into error with stubbornness so that his situation becomes wholly inexcusable.' Yet, the idolater errs even against his or her own instincts. The ignorance is, once again, wilful:

> And yet he is not entirely lacking in the knowledge of God, because even though in his perversity he desires to worship an idol, yet he has a natural instinct to worship the God against whom he fights by throwing himself into voluntary error.[76]

Bonaventure goes on to deal with the arguments brought against Anselm and Augustine. Mere thought without assent is identifiable with external speech. Yet, thought with assent is thought accompanied by understanding and is not synonymous with external speech. It is in this sense that what is said by the Fool is not able to be thought. The denial of truth does imply its opposite, since it claims truth for itself. An island is a limited being, while the implication of that than which no greater can be conceived is proper to the most perfect being, and so it is not surprising that one cannot infer the existence outside the mind of an island than which no greater can be thought.[77]

At the heart of Bonaventure's doctrine is exemplar causality. The same truth that causes knowledge in the mind, is also the cause of being. It is that truth that is proclaimed in and through all things. To apprehend that truth, however, the soul of the knower must be correctly attuned:

> If he desires to think correctly, there is nothing that could separate him from this truth. It is, therefore, a truth that is supremely evident and present, which is absent to no place, time, thing, or thought. Such is not the case with other created truths.[78]

Despite God being above the soul, God is not more doubtful than things below or on a par with the soul. This is because God is with the soul 'in the form of knowledge' and outside the soul 'in the form of representations ... which all creatures contain within themselves, since this truth is contained and understood in every truth'.[79]

In response to the other objections, Bonaventure argues that faith does not preclude knowledge, since the certainty of faith is a certainty of adherence not of understanding. Though God is hidden from us as Trinity, the first thing knowable about God is that God exists, and this is most evident. God's justice and existence are one in God, but not the same in terms of the notions by which they are grasped nor in terms of the effects in which they are reflected. Trying to prove something that is self-evident, says Bonaventure, is pointless. Yet God's existence may still require proof:

> It should be said that this truth, as is clear by now, does not need proof because of any lack of intrinsic evidence, but rather because of the faulty reflection on our part. Hence, arguments of this sort are exercises of the intellect rather than proofs that provide evidence and make the truth manifest as proven.[80]

Hence, while God's existence may be self-evident in itself, it is not so to us. Similarly, in response to the objection that the principles of a demonstration are unknown unless their terms are known, Bonaventure argues that God is known in different ways by different beings – by God, by the blessed, and by those in this life who know God 'imperfectly as through a mirror'. Though God is not known to anyone fully in this life, God is partly known, and anyone who knows that they have not always existed knows also that they must have come from another. In this sense, the knowledge is available to all, and if that is indubitable, so is the existence of God.[81] It is not that the soul knows God as a self-evident proposition, it is rather that the evidence is so manifest and compelling that there is no room for doubt in anyone who desires to think properly.

Finally, Bonaventure considers the objection that faith that is based upon reason is without merit. He argues that belief in God has no merit of itself in any case, unless it is the basis for an article of faith, such as the Trinity. The natural knowledge of God's existence – which is so manifest to the soul – is a foundation for other articles of faith. Faith is built upon this natural foundation, lest unbelievers be excused on account of ignorance.[82] Bonaventure is not saying that faith itself requires a rational proof for its foundation, but that the foundation itself is already prepared within the rational nature of the human soul, the image of God itself.

As Gilson argued, it is the presence of the being of God to the soul that is the metaphysical foundation of Bonaventure's adaption of Anselm's argument. Bonaventure does not move illicitly from an idea to a being. Rather, the idea is the mode by which the soul becomes aware of the divine presence.[83] Like Anselm,

Bonaventure's knowledge of God presupposes the hierarchical and participational scheme in which creatures depend upon God because of their deficiency in being and goodness. Yet in Bonaventure the knowledge of God is also presupposed in the knowledge of creatures itself, because the mind is also deficient: it requires God's light to know truth. Anton Pegis agrees that God's presence to the soul is the source of its indubitable knowledge. Yet Pegis also emphasises that the presence is as a guiding light rather than as an object of direct knowledge. In other words, the knowledge of God implanted within the soul does not render empirical knowledge superfluous but rather is what makes that knowledge possible. Hence, while we may infer the existence of God by looking at creatures, the ability of the mind to attain such knowledge depends upon the presence of God to the mind itself.[84] Yet, the knowledge of creatures is a necessary beginning for the knowledge of God, for the guiding light is not itself an object of knowledge. It is for that reason that God's light is the most manifest thing, and yet capable of being ignored. Knowledge enters through the senses, as Aristotle teaches. From that knowledge it may be possible to arrive at a being that is absolute, immutable and eternal. Nevertheless, if the mind reflects more deeply on how it can know this, it must enter within itself. The implanted knowledge of God – the image of God within the soul – is the *functional principle* of human knowledge.[85]

Thus, in Bonaventure, Anselm's argument is more deeply internalised and concerns an account of knowledge erected in the face of the new intellectual challenge of Aristotelian empiricism. Bonaventure integrates the Aristotelian account of knowledge by abstraction by means of a foundation that is not itself derived from the senses, but from the presence of God to the soul. Anselm's argument reveals that foundation, which is also the foundation of all existence. If the disputed questions contain an account of the noetic basis of human knowledge, the *Journey of the Soul into God* proceeds according to the order of the ascent when the soul tries to rise to a knowledge of God. For this reason, it returns to the original order of the Soul's purgative ascent from beyond itself, from within itself, to above itself (*extra se, intra se, supra se*). It is interesting for us not least of all because it reveals more fully the place of Anselm's argument in Bonaventure's thought when the soul turns to contemplate God above itself, and why the account of reason which it presents is particularly valuable within the Franciscan context.

## III

Understanding the significance of the *Journey* involves reminding ourselves of the conflicts that occasioned it, however. During the 1250s the Franciscans, along with the Dominicans, were forced to defend their commitments to apostolic poverty against the criticism of secular masters led by William of St Amour. What made those criticisms so damaging for the Franciscans in particular, however, was that they tended to reinforce complaints of radical Franciscans about the rise of studies within the order. Matters were brought to a head when a young friar,

Gerard of Borgo San Donnino, wrote an introduction to the prophetic books of Joachim of Fiore, which claimed that St Francis had been divinely appointed to bring in a new order that would replace the authority of the Church. Joachim's prophecies were read widely within the Franciscan order where they were readily taken as confirmations of the order's divine vocation. Secular masters were not slow to point out the heretical implications of Gerard's writings, and the order as a whole was tainted. Pope Alexander IV asked for the resignation of the Minister General, John of Parma, and it was as his replacement that Bonaventure took over the leadership of the order. Bonaventure had to deal not only with the external criticisms caused by the Joachimite affair, but also with the threat of internal schism, as radical Franciscans interpreted John of Parma's demise as yet another defeat for authentic Franciscanism.[86]

The Joachimite controversy was so dangerous to the order not merely because many important Franciscans were tainted with heresy, but because the affair involved claims about the Franciscan order based upon its distinctive, and radical approach to the religious life. *The Soul's Journey into God* was composed in the context of this problem and as such represents a 'tradition conserving' project. The work relocates the most radical experience of St Francis's life, the seraphic vision of Christ, within the central authorities of mainstream Christian mysticism.[87] In doing this, Bonaventure was merely continuing the project of the Franciscan schools as a whole: to validate Franciscan experience in terms of established tradition. In the course of the *Journey*, Franciscan teaching about the natural knowledge of God receives its most elaborate expression. Here exemplarism is not used merely to express the metaphysical structure of the universe. Rather, it becomes the ladder by which the soul actually reaches God.

Bonaventure wrote in the prologue to the work that it was while meditating on Mount La Verna, the site of St Francis's seraphic vision, that he remembered the miracle. 'All at once', Bonaventure wrote, he saw how the six wings of the seraph pointed the way to how the state of contemplation which Francis experienced might be attained through 'the ecstatic transports of Christian wisdom'. The six stages of ascent suggested by the wings of the seraph are actually the three stages of the soul's ascent, *extra*, *intra*, *et supra* first articulated in the Franciscan school by Alexander of Hales.

The key to contemplation, Bonaventure writes, is desire. No one is disposed for contemplation unless, like Daniel, they are 'a man of desires'.[88] The desires that presuppose the knowledge of that which lies behind every desire mark the beginning of the journey, which also presupposes 'grace, justice, knowledge... penetrating meditation, holy living and devout prayer...' (c. 1, 8). Hence, just as mendicant wandering is transformed into a contemplative journey, so the contemplative journey is transformed into an ascetic path. Wolterstorff's account of medieval natural theology fitting into a teleological scheme defined by the quest for happiness fits, in outline, the natural theology of Bonaventure:[89]

> Since happiness, is nothing other than the enjoyment of the highest good and since the highest good is above, no one can be made happy unless they rise above themselves, not by an ascent of the body, but of the heart. But we cannot rise above ourselves unless a higher power lifts us up. No matter how much our interior progress is ordered nothing will come of it unless accompanied by divine aid. Divine aid is available to those who seek it from their hearts, humbly and devoutly; and this means to sigh for it in this valley of tears, through fervent prayer. Prayer, then, is the mother source of the ascent (c. 1, 1).

Having explained what has to be done to attain the happiness that is the enjoyment of the highest good, Bonaventure explains the method of the *Journey* and the stages that it follows:

> By praying in this way, we receive light to discern the steps of the ascent into God. In relation to our position in creation, the universe itself is a ladder by which we can ascend into God. Some created things are vestiges, others images; some are material, others spiritual; some are temporal, others everlasting; some are outside us, others within us. In order to contemplate the First Principle, who is most spiritual, eternal and above us, we must pass through his vestiges, which are material, temporal and outside us... We must enter into our soul, which is God's image, everlasting, spiritual and within us... We must go beyond to what is eternal, most spiritual and above us, by gazing upon the First Principle...

The three stages of the journey, outside, within and above are each divided into two, according to which God may be contemplated through as well as in each stage, or as the alpha and the omega. The first stage begins from outwith the soul. From visible things, Bonaventure says, the 'soul rises to the consideration of the power, wisdom and goodness of God'. The consideration may be extended also to the sevenfold general properties of creatures 'which bear a sevenfold witness to the power, wisdom, and goodness of God'. Their origin, magnitude, multitude, beauty, fullness, activity and order proclaim the power, wisdom and goodness of their creator (1. 14):

> Whoever, therefore, is not enlightened by such splendour of created things is blind; whoever is not awakened by such outcries is deaf; whoever does not praise God because of all these effects is dumb; whoever does not discover the First Principle from such clear signs is a fool (1. 15).

All creation is as a mirror through which we can see God, Bonaventure writes, 'not only through them as through divine vestiges, but also in them as God is in them by essence, power and presence' (2. 1). This consideration, Bonaventure writes, is higher than the previous one, and holds the second level of contemplation 'by which we are led to contemplate God in all creatures which enter our minds through our bodily senses'. Indeed, Bonaventure acknowledges that it is through the five senses that the macrocosm enters the microcosm (2. 2). Once inside the smaller world, or human soul, however, the deliverances of the senses enter upon the process of apprehension, pleasure and judgement. All of these are also 'vestiges in which we can see God' (2. 7). Bonaventure likens the process of apprehension, through the generation of a likeness, to the generation of the Son as an Image of the Father (2. 7). The pleasure in the apprehension leads the soul to the delight that is contained to the highest degree in the Image of God (2. 8). Finally, judgement leads to the eternal truths 'in a more immediate way':

> Judgement takes place through our reason abstracting from place, time and mutability, and thus from dimension, succession and change, through reason which is unchangeable, unlimited and endless. But nothing is absolutely unchangeable, unlimited and endless unless it is eternal. Everything that is eternal is either God or in God. If, therefore, everything which we judge with certainty we judge by such a reason, then it is clear that God is the reason of all things and the infallible rule and light of truth... Therefore we cannot judge with certainty except in view of the Eternal Art which is the form that not only produces all things but also conserves and distinguishes all things, as the being which sustains the form in all things and the rule which directs all things. Through it our mind judges all things that enter it through the senses (2. 9).

These creatures are 'exemplars or rather exemplifications... so that through sensible things' which are seen, the soul 'will be carried over to the intelligible things' which it does not see, 'as through signs to what is signified' (2. 11). The soul is therefore led to contemplate the image of the first truth within the soul itself. We are therefore now placed to understand something of the knowledge of God 'naturally inserted in the soul', for as Bonaventure has already taught, that naturally inserted knowledge is the image of God. That image, of course, is the image of the Trinity. We find ourselves back in the Trinitarian teaching of Augustine of which Anselm makes so much in both the *Monologion* and the *Proslogion*:

> Enter yourself, then and see that your soul loves itself most fervently; that it could not love itself unless it knew itself, nor know itself unless it remembered itself, because our intellects grasp only what is present to our memory (3. 1).

Bonaventure explains the image within the soul in terms of function. The memory function retains both temporal things, and simple principles pertaining to quantities, such as point, instant and unit. In the third place, it also retains immutable principles, such as 'every whole is greater than its part'. In its ability to retain all temporal things, past, present and future, the memory is an image of eternity. In its ability to retain simple forms that cannot have entered the soul from outside through the senses, the memory shows that it is also informed from above as well as from outside. In its retention of immutable principles, the memory is shown to have present to itself an unchangeable light. From the activities of memory, Bonaventure concludes, the soul is seen to be an image of God (3. 2).

The function of the intellect consists in understanding the meaning of terms, propositions and inferences. The intellect grasps those meanings when it comprehends in a definition what a thing is. Definitions, says Bonaventure, are constructed by using more universal terms; and these are defined by more universal terms 'until we come to the highest and most universal'. Without these, we cannot know fully the definition of any particular substance. Here Bonaventure touches on the transcendentals that we encountered in the *Summa minorum*, and also the way in which the knowledge of God underpins the knowledge of things more generally:

> Unless we know what being *per se* is, we cannot fully know the definition of any particular substance. We cannot know being *per se* unless we also know its properties, which are: one, true good... Since privations and defects can in no way be known except through something positive, our intellect does not come to the point of understanding any created being by fully resolving, unless it is aided by a knowledge of the Being which is most pure, most actual, most complete and absolute, which is unqualified and Eternal Being, in which are the principles of all things in their purity (3. 3).

Moreover, the intellect only truly comprehends the meaning of a proposition when it knows with certitude that it is true and when it cannot be deceived. Yet this unchangeable truth must be seen by an unchangeable light which shines in the intellect, for the intellect itself, like other creatures, is changeable. 'From this it is obvious that our intellect is joined to Eternal Truth itself since it can grasp no truth with certitude if it is not taught by this Truth' (3. 3).

The function of will or choice, Bonaventure goes on, is manifest in deliberation, judgement and desire. Deliberation consists in enquiring what is better, but a knowledge of what is better depends upon a prior acquaintance with what is best. The highest good must be imprinted on the mind. Certitude of judgement also depends upon some knowledge of the law through which it judges. The law must be higher than the mind since the mind does not judge the law, but judges by it. Yet nothing is higher than the mind except God. In judging, therefore, 'our deliberative power touches the divine laws if it reaches a solution by a full resolution'. Desire, meanwhile, moves toward what it loves most – happiness. Yet happiness is only found in the best and ultimate end. So great, says Bonaventure, is the power of the ultimate or highest good that nothing can be loved except out of a desire for that highest good. 'Creatures, when they take the image and copy for the Truth', says Bonaventure, 'are deceived and in error' (3. 4):

> See, therefore, how close the soul is to God, and how, in their operations, the memory leads to eternity, the understanding to truth, and the power of choice to the highest good (3. 4).

Thus, the image of God within the soul is not a doctrine of innate ideas, but an account of the way in which the soul is constituted and how it is guided by the presence of God. 'God is the light without which the human soul cannot see or think or love; it cannot define or reason or take counsel or desire without finding the ultimate and justifying ground of its activity in God.'[90]

He begins the fourth stage of contemplation by looking at the reasons for ignorance regarding the most manifest thing, as he considered them in the sentence commentary and disputed questions. 'It seems amazing', Bonaventure reflects, 'when it has been shown that God is so close to our souls that so few should be aware of the First Principle within themselves.' The soul is clouded by sensual distractions, allured away by desires of the flesh. 'Thus lying totally in these things of sense', Bonaventure says, 'it cannot re-enter into itself as into the image of God' (4. 1). In such a situation, the soul must rely on external help:

> And just as, when someone has fallen, they must lie there unless they are raised up by another, so our soul could not be perfectly lifted up out of those things of sense to see itself and the eternal Truth in itself had not Truth, taking the human form in Christ, become a ladder restoring the first ladder that had been broken in Adam. Thus it is that, no matter how enlightened a person may be by the light coming from nature and from acquired knowledge, he cannot enter into himself to delight in the Lord except through the mediation of Christ (4. 2).

This text draws out the full implications of the account of the soul that Bonaventure has already provided. If the soul is not aware of the truth within itself then no amount of argument will persuade it. For it is precisely the failure of the soul to recognise the First Principle in its reasoning that is the problem. It requires an outward image of the Truth, of God, to remind it or draw it back to the Truth within.

Through the mediation of Christ, the soul is clothed over with the three theological virtues, so that it might be purified, enlightened and perfected – as in the three stages of the ascent. Bonaventure enumerates how in receiving Christ, the soul recovers its spiritual senses of hearing, sight, smell, taste and touch, and is made hierarchic in order to mount upward. Just as philosophy had been helpful in the preceding stage, so the Holy Scriptures become helpful when this stage of contemplation is reached. The soul becomes 'filled with intellectual lights' and like the house of God 'is inhabited by Divine Wisdom' (4. 8).

Reformed and illuminated, the soul can turn above itself to contemplate God through the light 'which shines upon our minds, which is the light of Eternal Truth' (5. 1). This is the 'Holy of Holies, where the Cherubim of glory stand over the ark overshadowing the Mercy Seat'. The Cherubim signify the two stages of contemplating the invisible and eternal things of God: the essential attributes of God as Unity, and the essential attributes of God as Trinity. The soul turns to the two names which, according to Moses and to Christ, are God's primary names: Being and Good. The fifth stage, contemplating God as Being and unity draws upon the dictum that 'God cannot be thought not to be', and then 'unpacks' what this means. The contemplation of God as Being reveals that this is synonymous with the intellectual light by which the soul first contemplated creatures:

> He... who wishes to contemplate the invisible things of God in relation to the unity of His essence should fix the attention of his soul on Being Itself and see that Being Itself is so absolutely certain that it cannot be thought not to be... Being, however, does not come to us by means of something else, because everything that is grasped by the intellect is grasped either as non-being, or as being in potency, or as being in act. If therefore, non-being cannot be grasped except though being, and if being in potency cannot be understood except though being in actuality, and if being designates the pure actuality of being, then being is that which first comes into the intellect, and this being is that which is pure act. But this being is not particular being, which is a limited being, since it is mixed with potentiality; nor is it analogous being, for that has the least of act because it least exists. It remains, therefore, that the being that we are considering is the Divine Being (5. 3).

It is important to note that Bonaventure is not confusing the divine light from above with the concept of being which the soul derives from creatures. Once again, the First Principle, or Being Itself, guides the mind, it is not an object of the mind's vision, it is that which guides the mind in its resolving activity:

> Strange, then, is the blindness of the intellect, which does not consider that which it sees first and without which it can know nothing. The eye, concentrating on various differences of colour, does not see the very light by which it sees other things; and if it does see this light, it does not advert to it. In the same

> way, the mind's eye, concentrating on particular and universal being, does not advert to being itself, which is beyond every genus, even though it comes to our minds first and through it we know other things... Thus our mind, accustomed to the darkness of beings and the images of the things of sense, when it glimpses the light of the supreme Being, seems to itself to see nothing. It does not realise that this very darkness is the supreme illumination of our mind, just when the eye sees pure light, it seems to itself to see nothing (5. 4).

The sixth stage considers God as the Trinity in its name that is the good. This time Bonaventure begins his discussion with the other dictum of Anselm's argument: that God is that than which no greater can be thought:

> Behold, therefore, and observe that the highest good is unqualifiedly that in comparison with which a greater cannot be thought. And this good is such that it cannot rightly be thought of as non-existing, since to be is absolutely better than not to be. And this good exists in such a way that it cannot rightly be thought of except as triune. For good is said to be self-diffusive; therefore the highest good must be most self-diffusive (6. 2).

Anselm's argument is tied to the Pseudo-Dionysian theology of self-diffusive goodness; a goodness that is only satisfied in three-fold diffusion. It is in contemplating the emanation of the Son that the soul attains perfect illumination, for here it contemplates the perfect image of God that is the model for humanity. Moreover, it is in contemplation that the soul imitates Christ, since Christ is the Word, or Logos of the Father. It is at this stage, however, that the intellectual capacities of the soul – helped first by philosophy and then by revelation – must themselves be passed over (7. 4). Again, Christ is the way, but Francis also reappears, this time 'as an example of perfect contemplation, just as previously he had been of action' (7. 3). The simplicity of St Francis is reclaimed and is identified with the sleep of Christ upon the cross (7. 6). The simplicity that St Francis had deliberately cultivated has, in Bonaventure, become a learned ignorance:

> And thus, through him, more by example than by word, God would invite all truly spiritual men to this passing over in this transport of the soul... In this passing over, if it is to be perfect, all intellectual activities ought to be relinquished and the most profound affection transported to God, and transformed into Him...

Bonaventure has re-cast the Franciscan journey in a form in which intellectual contemplation plays a central role, but in doing so he has preserved the central assumptions of Franciscan spirituality, using Anselm's argument and the arguments showing the indubitable knowledge of God to help him. Conversion is the key to understanding, not understanding the key to conversion, for understanding requires faith. Because the soul without faith lacks awareness of spiritual truth, it is tied to the realm of the senses and requires a physical image of truth before it will return to the truth that is hidden within. Conversion is possible, however, because the knowledge of truth – however obscured by sin – is implanted within the soul.

Moreover, the truth that lies hidden within the soul is seen and yet not seen. As well as expressing the presence of God in the very uniqueness of God's being, as the absolute ground of being, Anselm's argument also expresses the being that is not seen in itself. In this sense, the apophatic conclusion of Anselm's argument, that God cannot be thought not to be, is doubly appropriate. Wolterstorff is right to see medieval arguments within a teleological context of attaining happiness, yet it is not just any account of happiness that they express.[91] Not all arguments attain their goal by the same means, nor do they express the goal in the same terms. Bonaventure's arguments articulate a particular account of human happiness and the means of getting there.

The God that cannot be thought not to be is the particular goal of Franciscan mendicancy. In Bonaventure's thought, Anselm's argument has been interiorised in order express that goal. The knowledge of God that underpins all knowing, that lies within every soul, requires a particular orientation of the soul if it is to be found. If the soul is to see the world aright it must be orientated toward the first light and not distracted by the flesh. The soul that is weighed down by sensual distractions is incapable of seeing the light. For such a soul argument alone is not enough if it is to be saved. What such a soul requires is an outward image of the truth that can be apprehended by the senses. The image of truth physically embodied reminds unbelievers of the truth they have hidden within themselves. Once again, it is the account of truth, of reason and of human nature that both vindicates Franciscan life, and shows why its particular kind of mission is necessary. In the process, Bonaventure is also showing how the very studies denigrated by radical Franciscans can lead the follower of St Francis to the contemplation of God which St Francis experienced on Mount Alverna.

## IV

Historians of Bonaventure's thought, such as Gilson and Pegis, have both been alert to the extent to which Bonaventure's thought is co-extensive with, and expressive of, his personal spirituality. What tends to be obscured by the concentration on the major figure within the Franciscan order during the mid-thirteenth century, however, is the presence of Anselm's argument within the writings of his lesser-known contemporaries. The importance of the personal experience of God is expressed through Anselm's argument in the work of lesser-known Franciscans Gerard de Prato and Servasanctus Tuscus as well as in the sophisticated expression of Bonaventure and his immediate successors at Paris.[92] This is because the personal experience of God is central to Franciscan spirituality itself, and Anselm's argument had become an indispensable means of expressing this central aspect of Franciscan experience.

Though educated at Paris and Bologna respectively, neither Gerard de Prato nor Servasanctus Tuscus de Faenza themselves taught at the universities. Gerard is remembered in Franciscan tradition for a mission on behalf of the Pope to the Mongols in 1270,[93] while Servasanctus is remembered chiefly as a writer of sermons in thirteenth-century Florence.[94] Once again, however, it is their very obscurity in academic terms that makes them important for us. The citations of Anselm's argument in their writings again illustrates how the argument expresses the way in which God's uniqueness is manifest in nature and within the very soul itself, and how the soul must be properly orientated to experience that presence.

A very brief collection of dogmatic sentences which follow loosely the order of Lombard's *Sentences* survive from Gerard. He rarely employs counter-arguments. His main purpose seems to have been to provide a 'breviloquium' or handbook of doctrine perhaps designed as a preaching aid, perhaps as an aid to memory – in so far as its brief statements refer to texts that will have been known to his Franciscan colleagues. In this sense, it is the emphasis that is important – what Gerard leaves out as well as what he mentions.

The first thing to notice is that the *Breviloquium* misses out a lot – summarising as it does the first book of Lombard's *Sentences* in ten brief chapters. The second thing that is obvious is that the text only follows the structure of the *Sentences*, not the details. It is significant therefore, that though Gerard refers to the argument briefly he does so at two significant points. Not discussing the issue of whether theology is a science, Gerard first cites Anselm at the very beginning of the text – perhaps indicative in itself of the extent to which Anselm's argument provides a key for the Franciscan understanding of God:

> God is that than which no greater can be conceived, as Anselm says. As Cicero puts it, God is a spirit, free and removed from all materiality and mortality, understanding everything and moving all by his eternal command. Again, Augustine says that everyone agrees that God exists, and that God comes first before all other things.[95]

The other citation of Anselm occurs under the fifth heading, dealing with the conditions and properties of the divine essence, and once again in the first line. This chapter comes closest to Bonaventure's eighth distinction in the first book of his commentary. Like Bonaventure, Gerard identifies the unthinkability of God's non-being with truth, before going on immediately to talk about the simplicity of God:

> The divine essence is the highest truth, so that God alone is in no way able not to exist, nor to be thought of as not-existing. God is unchanging; and so is moved neither by place, time nor by affection. God is the highest simplicity, since whatever God has God is neither composed from other things, nor is God mixed with other things.[96]

As with Odo Rigaud and Bonaventure (as well as with Alexander Nequam), Anselm's argument is linked in Gerard's thinking with an account of God's uncircumscribable presence, to all things, and within all things. Following a brief comparison between God's simplicity and the complexion of bodies, Gerard proceeds with the condition of infinity:

> The divine essence is infinite, incomprehensible, and uncircumscribable. Since God is uncircumscribable, God is, for that reason, contained in no place, just as a body is assigned to a place with a beginning, a middle and an end... and a created spirit, which, while it is in one place, cannot simultaneously be in another. But God fills every place and is in all things... in presence, power and essence: in presence… since God is absent from nothing; in power… since God fills all things; and in essence according to the most intimate being, since God is intimate with all things.[97]

Gerard's description of the conditions and properties of the divine essence proceeds from truth, the unthinkability of God's not being, simplicity, omnipresence, to God as the self-diffusive goodness, from which everything flows and toward which everything returns.[98] Gerard's discussion of the properties and conditions of the divine essence ends with a reference to God's timelessness, which he likens to the ray of light flowing from the sun – which knows no succession.[99]

It is in the course of the second book that Gerard discusses briefly the knowledge of God through creatures. The eighteenth chapter of Gerard's commentary on the second book of sentences is reminiscent of the third distinction of Bonaventure's commentary on the first. In Gerard's case, the discussion follows chapters on the days of creation, beginning with the production of things through light, and an account of the powers and conditions of the human soul listed as they are in the first chapter of Bonaventure's *Journey of the Soul into God.* The account of 'syndresis', the highest power in the soul, by which the soul is always naturally inclined toward honesty and virtue, immediately precedes the account of the soul's knowledge of God through the creature. Thus Gerard's discussion links the intellectual with the moral and spiritual aspects of the soul. Though syndresis cannot be extinguished, says Gerard, it can be impeded:

> in Heretics, who believe evil to be good, and what is false to be true, syndresis does not rise against the evil, since they take themselves to be living in piety, when they are in fact rejoicing in themselves. Similarly, syndresis is impeded on account of the licentiousness of pleasure; as when in the sins of the flesh the human is absorbed by the licentiousness of the flesh, so that he/she does not experience remorse.[100]

The Franciscan master is interested in the metaphysics that underpins a particular view of nature, a view of nature in which God is seen everywhere and in all things and therefore cannot be thought not to be. Gerard's metaphysics allows nature to be the medium of knowledge for the soul that, through the image that is within it, has the capacity to be, in some sense, the possessor of God.[101] As the discussion of syndresis indicates, for the soul to see God in nature, it must be properly orientated within itself. Gerard concludes this discussion by saying that the knowledge of God is available through the creature as shadow, trace and image, but also through natural reason, through the grace of faith, the grace of prophecy, through the gift of wisdom and understanding, and also through the grace of rapture.[102]

Returning to the other contemporary of Bonaventure whose career, as we mentioned, lay outside the universities, Servasanctus Tuscus de Faenza, we find Anselm's argument employed in a work listed by Stegmueller as *On the articles of the faith, the sacraments and virtues.* The text begins with the question of whether the existence of God is necessary and the attributes of God as unity.[103] The arguments reflect a different academic background from those of the Parisian and Oxford Franciscans: nonetheless, Anselm's argument is again employed to express the indubitability of God's existence.

Servasanctus's understanding of the necessity of God's existence reveals an unexpected and uncanny sophistication. At the beginning of the text, Servasanctus explains that the necessity of God's existence can only be understood by God's transcendence of that which we understand by 'being'. As a tract concerned with morality, Servasanctus relates goodness to being. Without God as the first cause there could be no goods.[104] All substances and accidents depend on something prior which is neither a body nor some kind of animal nor able to be accidental in any way.[105] This is what we mean by the oft-spoken word 'God'.[106] Every creature declares that God exists; all multitude is reducible to unity, all multiformity to uniformity, every mover to an unmoved mover.[107] Yet, explains Servasanctus, God is not some first substance. God is not to be identified with form that cannot exist without matter or matter that is pure passivity.[108] God is not merely the first being of beings; God is not the first in a series. God can only be that which is beyond being.[109] Having begun with an account of God as the first cause, Servasanctus identifies a problem intrinsic to any argument from natural causation: there is a danger of reducing God to the level of the finite causal system itself.

Identifying the transcendence of God with the notion of a highest good, Servasanctus argues that the existence of the highest good is revealed by the nature of human desire. Having an infinite capacity, the spirit is unable to find satisfaction in any one limited thing and never ceases to seek for more. Yet the more it gathers the less satisfaction it finds in what it has. Given the Aristotelian principle that nature makes nothing in vain, it is necessary to suppose that there is some highest good in which the desire of the spirit is satisfied and the spirit is perfected. That, however, is nothing other than the highest good beyond which the spirit cannot desire.[110]

If the necessity of the highest good is implied by the nature of human desire, it is also implied in human knowledge of comparative goods. The existence of many and varied imperfect goods means that it is necessary that some highest good is presupposed. That good, Servasanctus says, is so far removed from created being that it cannot be thought not to be, for it is that than which no greater can be thought.[111] Hence, the very transcendence of God is at the same time the source of the mind's implicit and indubitable knowledge of God and the implicit end of human desire.

The second chapter of the text explains that the highest good is infinite so that nothing more noble nor better nor more perfect can be thought. In contrast to imperfect beings, the highest good requires nothing and nothing, either in thought or reality, can be added to it since it exceeds all that is able to be said regarding it. If anything could be added, it would not be that than which no greater can be thought.[112]

From this analysis of the nature of God's existence Servasanctus goes on to discuss the divine attributes of goodness and justice which relate directly to his ethical themes. In defining God he simultaneously defines the principle of human morality and a teleological principle at work within nature. God's wisdom, immensity, rectitude, goodness and justice are seen from the operation of God's works. In creating things from diverse elements God gives to them their right order. Just as all good things come from God, so does their rectitude. Thus just as fire has a tendency toward heat so the human creature, made together from diverse elements, is ordered towards the highest good.[113]

By articulating an account of God's being, Servasanctus articulates an account of the human soul and the nature of creation as a whole. He is less concerned with the agenda of the sentence commentary, than with articulating an account of human morality that underpins preaching. Once again, the knowledge of that than which no greater can be thought is implied in the nature of human desire and human capacity to live righteously. Finally, as with the Franciscans at Paris, Anselm's argument sums up all of God's attributes, so that each of these may be extracted eventually from this first principle. If God were lacking in any of these attributes, argues Servasanctus, God would be less than that than which no greater can be thought.[114]

Besides non-academic Franciscans like Gerard and Servasanctus, however, the most striking approximation to Bonaventure's position in this period came from none other than Richard Rufus of Cornwall. When Thomas of York left Oxford to replace William of Melitona at Cambridge, Richard Rufus was finally appointed to the chair at Oxford. His return did not follow a complete capitulation toward the teachings of the Parisian school. His continued independence of mind expressed in his abbreviation of Bonaventure's sentence commentary, however, serves to make conspicuous his modified approach to the natural knowledge of God.[115] That Richard Rufus follows Bonaventure in his teaching in the third and eighth distinctions may be an indication that Rufus was less interested in this topic than he was in others. It seems more likely, however, that it is an indication of the extent to which the Franciscans conducted their enquiries within a community of interests, a community within which there was less room for debate on central points.

Previously, Rufus had shown himself sceptical of the exemplar illuminationist thesis of Robert Grosseteste and Richard Fishacre. In the third distinction of the *abbreviatio*, however, he follows Bonaventure's account of the natural knowledge of God through signs, shadows and images almost word for word.[116] In the eighth distinction, he deviates significantly from Bonaventure, but not by adding the criticisms of Anselm's argument that he had expressed in his earlier sentence commentary. There, he had criticised Anselm's argument on the grounds that it involved an illegitimate step from the order of propositions to the order of reality. Without compromising his earlier view, Rufus nonetheless prefers to stress what he shares in common with Bonaventure and not what might divide them. Although he does not deal directly with Anselm's argument, he does deal with the indubitability of truth. In doing so, he seems to identify the indubitability of truth with the indubitability of God's existence although not, it must be said, without ambiguity: just as God's existence cannot be denied by God, he says, so neither can truth be denied by anyone.[117]

## V

To understand Bonaventure's contribution to the community of thought is to see how he used the traditions he inherited to articulate them in ways that were meaningful to his contemporaries. Bonaventure played a key role in articulating the consciousness of the community by expressing its interests in its own language, using the reasons that counted as reasons for the Franciscan community. In doing so he used the exemplarism of the Oxford school to draw out the full implications of what his predecessors had taught in Paris.

Anselm's argument was important to Franciscans partly because, together with other authorities in the Christian tradition, it helped to articulate the intimate relationship between God and the soul that was a key assumption in Franciscan spirituality. The centrality of this theme was also assured in theology, however, because it provided an effective means of dealing with the reception of Aristotle and new forms of natural knowledge.

Throughout his career, Bonaventure affirmed the theme of the knowledge of God that is common to Christians, Muslims, Jews, and Heretics alike: human beings know the existence, but not the nature of God. It is precisely because God is both the beginning and the end of knowledge, however, that true philosophical understanding depends upon a proper understanding of God. It is in these terms that Bonaventure develops his arguments against the Arab Aristotelians and Averroists in his final work, the *Collationes on the Six Days* delivered to the Franciscan convent in Paris a year before his death in 1274.[118]

His target in these sermons were certainly Masters of Arts at Paris who had been unduly influenced by Aristotle's twelfth-century Muslim commentator, Averroës of Cordoba. Over the course of the thirteenth century, the curriculum within the Faculty of Arts had grown to incorporate the Aristotelian works and the Arab commentaries upon them formally banned in Paris.[119] It is a mark of the fact that medieval Christianity was itself so deeply committed to particular philosophical perspectives that philosophical enquiry could not but touch on issues relating to the faith. The response of the authorities in 1270 and 1277 was to ban 219 propositions reputedly taught within the Faculty of Arts. It was within this atmosphere that St Bonaventure composed his final and most comprehensive statement on the place of natural philosophy within theology in the *Collationes on the Work of Six Days*.[120] Nonetheless, in venting his spleen against Masters in the Faculty of Arts, Bonaventure was merely deploying the position of the Franciscan community more generally in its encounter with Aristotle – particularly as it was found in the work of Robert Grosseteste and Thomas of York as well as in the first book of his own commentary on the *Sentences*. The mistakes of Aristotle's Arabian followers, he argues, are tied to Aristotle's principle error – the denial of exemplarism. That denial entails that reason stops short at images as if they were complete in themselves, instead of leading beyond themselves to God.

Without exemplarism, God does not know singulars (since God does not possess the ideas by which God could know them), and knows only the divine being by itself. In such a universe, all things operate under internally predetermined, and self-sufficient principles, seeking God only as their final cause. In such an eternal, self-sufficient universe, God exercises no providence nor judgement over things and in such a universe there is no reward or punishment for human deeds, and therefore, no morality.[121] A natural knowledge of God that looks beyond creatures to the source of their being and the source of the soul's illumination, will lead the soul beyond philosophy to faith. It is the role which Anselm's argument came to play in articulating the mind's relationship to the source of the divine exemplar that accounts for its importance within Bonaventure's thought. By using Anselm in this way, however, Bonaventure was only drawing out the full implications of what his school had been teaching all along:

> It is said that the light of the intellect is truth, which radiates over the intelligences of men and of angels; which radiates inexhaustibly, since it is not able to be thought not to be. Moreover it radiates in three ways: as the truth of things, as the truth of the word, and as the truth of morals; so that the truth of things is the indivision of essence and existence, as the truth of the voice it is the adequation of voice and understanding, and as the truth of morals it is the rectitude of life.[122]

Hence, it is only by discovering God through the inward path, and the spirituality that goes with it, that the true nature of things and of human destiny can begin to be understood rationally.[123] Anselm's argument thus represents the principle route to the natural knowledge of a God who is the principle of knowing and of being through exemplarism.

Yet Bonaventure remains in dialogue with Aristotle: he did not, as Gilson once claimed, evaluate Aristotelian philosophy 'as one… who saw through it, and passed beyond it'.[124] He accepted central doctrines of Aristotle, including the doctrine of intellectual abstraction from sense experience, but he incorporated them into an account of exemplarist illumination. Nonetheless, in Bonaventure's account, Aristotle's philosophy is in need of correction, precisely because it denied what he, Robert Grosseteste and Thomas of York all thought was central to intellectual knowledge, and what in fact expressed the central assumption in the Franciscan experience of God – divine exemplarism.

Thus, despite the fact that Aristotle's ultimate handicap is his lack of faith, his philosophical failing is a genuine philosophical failing because reason by its very nature shows that God represents both the beginning and the end of understanding. The authenticity of Franciscan life was vindicated in Bonaventure's writings, not just by the fact that he was able to provide a publicly defensible account of the idea of the idea of God embedded in its spirituality. It was vindicated because that same account provided a solution to the contemporary intellectual challenge presented by Aristotle and his Arab followers.

## VI

As we shall see, there were other ways of dealing with the Aristotelian challenge available to western Christians. That Bonaventura's approach to the problem was representative of the broader Franciscan community, however, is illustrated by the works of his contemporaries, and also by the revival of the *Summa minorum* during this period. William of Melitona vacated his chair in Cambridge in 1255 in order to bring the project to completion.[125] The timing of the final stage of the project suggests that it formed part of an attempt to consolidate the order in the face of secular criticism and internal dissension in the 1250s. Under William of Melitona's supervision, for example, Bonaventure's *Questions concerning Evangelical Perfection*, defending the Franciscan life, were incorporated into the fourth book of the *Summa*. The natural theology expressed in the first book thus represented the metaphysical counterpart of the form of life defended in the fourth.

When we turn to Thomas Aquinas we find an account of the natural knowledge of God not only different from that offered by Bonaventure but incompatible with it. Their differences are brought out by their rival interpretations of Anselm's argument and its place in their respective approaches to Aristotle. At stake was not merely a philosophical issue, however, but a religious one: their different approaches to Anselm reflected and expressed competing assumptions about God, about the soul and about the nature of the religious life. Moreover, in each case, Bonaventura and Thomas were articulating wider communities of interpretation, and not merely individual projects.

## Notes

1. A. MacIntyre, *After Virtue* (London, 1981), p. 222.
2. Cit. in J. G. Bougerol, *Introduction to the Works of St Bonaventure*, trans. by J. de Vinck (New Jersey, 1963), p. 4.
3. P. Glorieux, *Répertoire des Maîtres en Théologie de Paris au XIIIe Siécle*, 2 vols (Paris, 1933), II, nn. 304-305.
4. See, for example, J. R. H. Moorman, *A History of the Franciscan Order: From its Origins to the Year 1517* (Oxford, 1968), pp. 140ff, and H. Felder, *Histoire des Études dans L'Ordre de S. Francois*, trans. into French by E. de Bar-Le-Duc (Paris, 1908; 1st pub. in 1904), pp. 335ff. and 361.
5. Bougerol, p. 19.
6. Bonaventure, St., *Comentarium in II librum sententiarum*, in *Opera Omnia*, 10 vols (Quaracchi, 1882-1902), II, Proemii, i: 'Ad quemadmodum in primo libro sententiis adhaesi et communibus opinionibus magistrorum, et potissime magistri et patris nostri bonae memoriae fratris Alexandri, sic in consequentibus libris ad eorum vestigiis non recedam.' Ibid., proemii, ii: 'Et licet fortassis aliquis eum in aliquibus harum opinionum sustineat, verumtamen pater et magister noster bonae memoriae frater Alexander in nulla harum ipsum sustinuit, sed potius contrarium sensit, cuius vestigiis praecipue inhaerere propono.'
7. Bonaventure, *Commentarium in I librum sententiarum*, in *Opera Omnia*, I. Proemii, q. ii, ad ob. 4.
8. Ibid., *proemii*, q. i, respondeo.
9. Ibid., *proemii*, q. ii, respondeo.
10. Ibid., *proemii*, q. ii, ad ob. 6.
11. Ibid., *proemii*, q. ii, ad ob. 5.
12. See É. Gilson, *The Philosophy of St Bonaventure* (London, 1940), p. 116.

13. Bonaventure, *Commentarium in I lib. sent.*, dist. iii, part i, art. i, q. ii, concl. 1.
14. Ibid., dist. iii, part. i, art. i, quaest. i, 2.
15. Ibid., art. i, quaest i, 5.
16. Ibid., q. i, sed contra, 1-2.
17. Ibid., q. i, sed contra, 3-5.
18. Ibid., q. i, concl.
19. Ibid., q. i, concl., 2.
20. Ibid., q. i, concl., 1.
21. Ibid., q. i, concl., 3.
22. Ibid., q. i, concl., 4.
23. Ibid., q. i, concl., 5.
24. Ibid., q. ii, 1.
25. Ibid., q. ii, 2.
26. Ibid., q. ii, 1-4.
27. Ibid., q. ii, sed contra, 1-4.
28. Ibid., q. ii, resp. 1-4.
29. Ibid.
30. Ibid., q. iii, concl. 2.
31. The only place where Bonaventure actually considers proofs for God's existence in the course of the third distinction is in an appendage taken from a separate manuscript and added to the commentary in the critical edition under the title *Dubia circa litteram magistri.* Under this heading the editors added the notes from Bonaventure's *cursorie* reading of the *Sentences* completed around 1245-1247 before he became bachelor. See Bougerol, pp. 59, 87 and 101-105.
32. Bonaventure, *Commentarium in I lib. sent.*, d. iii, part I, q. ii, concl.; q. iv, concl.
33. Ibid., concl.: 'Since God as the supremely spiritual light could not be known in God's spirituality by the understanding, which is almost material, the soul needs to know God through the creature.'
34. Ibid.
35. Ibid., dist. iii, part i, q. iii., concl., and concl. 2.
36. Ibid., d. viii, art. i, q. i.
37. Ibid., q. ii, 1: '...videtur per Anselmum, qui dicit quod Deus secundum communem animi conceptionem est quo nihil maius cogitari non potest.'
38. Ibid., d. viii, art. i, q. ii, 1.
39. Ibid., art. i, q. ii, 2.
40. Ibid., art. i, q. ii, 3.
41. Ibid., art. i, q. ii, 4.
42. Ibid., art. i, q. ii, 6.
43. Ibid., art. i, q. ii, 7.
44. A. C. Pegis, 'The Bonaventurean Way to God', in *Mediaeval Studies*, 29 (1967), 206-242 (pp. 225ff).
45. Bonaventure, *Com. in I lib. Sent.*, d. viii, art. i, q. ii, sed contra, 1.
46. Ibid., art. i, q. ii, sed contra, 2.
47. Ibid., art. i, q. ii, sed contra, 4.

48. Ibid., art. i, q. ii, sed contra, 5.
49. Ibid., art. i, q. ii, sed contra. 6.
50. Ibid., art. i, q. ii, concl.
51. Ibid., cf. Odo Rigaud, Paris Bibliothèque nationale, MS Lat. 14910, fol. 7v: 'Sed prout videmus et cognoscemus eum in creaturis in effectibus suis sic possumus abstrahere et sic potest putari non esse iustus ratione alicuius occulti effectis... Et sic dixit insipiens in corde suo non deum esse.'
52. Bonaventure, *Com. in I lib. sent.*, d. viii, art. i, q. ii, concl.
53. Ibid.
54. Ibid. 'Alio modo potest cogitari, aliquid non esse propter defectum *a parte intelligibilis*, et huiusmodi defectus potest esse dupliciter: aut defectus *praesentiae*, aut defectus evidentiae; defectus *praesentiae*, utpote quia non semper, non ubique, non ubique totaliter. Quod non semper est, aliquando est, aliquando non: et ideo aliquando vere potest cogitari non esse. Similiter de eo quod non est ubique, quia eadem ratione, qua potest cogitari non esse hic, potest cogitari non esse alibi. Similiter de eo quod secundum partem adest, secundum partem abest. Deum autem est semper et ubique et totus semper et ubique: ideo non potest cogitari non esse. Hanc rationem assignat Anselmus in libro contra insipientem.' Cf Odo Rigaud, BN, MS Lat. 14910, 7r.
55. Bonaventure, *Com. in I lib.sent.*, d. viii, art. i, q. ii, concl.
56. Ibid.
57. Ibid., art i, q. ii, ad obj., 1.
58. Ibid., art. i, q. ii, ad obj., 2.
59. Ibid., art. i, q. ii, ad obj., 3.
60. Ibid., art. i, q. ii, ad obj., 4.
61. Ibid., art. i, q. ii, ad obj., 5.
62. Ibid., art. i, q. ii, ad obj., 6.
63. Glorieux, *Répertoire* II, 305c.
64. Bonaventure, *Quaestiones Disputatae de Mysterio Trinitatis*, in *Opera Omnia*, v, pp. 45-115. Quest. i. art. i, *Utrum Deum esse sit verum indubitabile*, i-x.
65. Ibid.
66. Ibid., q. i, art. i, 27.
67. Ibid., q. i, art. i, objections 1-14.
68. Ibid., concl.
69. Ibid.
70. Ibid.
71. Ibid., concl., 1, 2, 3.
72. Ibid., concl., 11.
73. Ibid., concl.
74. Ibid., concl.
75. Ibid., resp. 1, 2, 3.
76. Ibid.
77. Ibid., resp. 4-6.
78. Ibid., resp. 7.

79. Ibid., resp. 10.
80. Ibid., resp. 12.
81. Ibid., resp. 13.
82. Ibid., resp. 14. (Cf. Hugh of St Victor, I *De Sacramentis*, in J. P. Migne, *Patrologia Latina* t. 176 (Paris, 1844-1879), bk III, c.2).
83. Gilson, *Philosophy of St Bonaventure*, p. 129.
84. Pegis, 'The Bonaventurean Way...', pp. 228-229.
85. Ibid.
86. For the Joachimite affair, and the troubles faced by the Franciscans and Dominicans at the University of Paris, see J. R. H. Moorman, *A History of the Franciscan Order* (Oxford, 1968), pp. 114ff and 145ff.
87. See E. H. Cousins, 'Francis of Assisi: Christian Mysticism at the Crossroads', in S. T. Katz, *Mysticism and Religious Traditions* (Oxford, 1983), pp. 163-190.
88. Bonaventure, *Itinerarium mentis in Deum*, in *Opera Omnia*, V, pp. 295-316: prologue. Henceforth, references to the *Itinerarium* will be included in the main text in parenthesis. Hence, (c. 1, 1) refers to the first verse of chapter one.
89. Cf. N. Wolterstorff, 'The Migration of the Theistic Arguments: From Natural Theology to Evidentialist Apologetics', in *Rationality, Religious Belief, and Moral Commitment*, ed. by R. Audi and W. J. Wainright (Cornell, 1986), pp. 38-81 (pp. 56ff).
90. Pegis, 'The Bonaventurean way to God...', p. 233.
91. Wolterstorff, pp. 56ff.
92. The major work of Bonaventure's immediate successor at Paris, Gilbert of Tournai, has been examined sufficiently for us to be sure of its allegiance to the teachings of Bonaventure. See for example, Bérubé, C. and Gieben, S., 'Gilbert de Tournai and Robert Grosseteste Sources Inconnues de Saint Bonaventure, Suivi de L'Édition Critique de Trois Chapitres du *Rudimentum Doctrinae* de Guibert de Tournai', in *S. Bonaventura 1274-1974*, ed. by J. G. Bougerol, 5 vols (Rome, 1973-4), III, 627-654. Gilbert's successor Eustachius of Arras (Master, 1263-1265; d. 1291) employs Anselm's argument in his account of the indubitable truth of God's existence. His sentence commentary is found in Padua, Anton. 158. See Glorieux, II, nos 311 and 313.
93. See C. H. Lawrence, *The Friars* (New York, 1994), 214.
94. See G. Melani, 'Servasanto da Faenza', in *Enciclopedia Cattolica* (Vaticano, 1953), 11, col. 403-404, and D. L. D'Avray, 'Philosophy in Preaching: The Case of a Franciscan Based in Thirteenth-Century Florence', in *Literature and Religion in the Later Middle Ages. Philological Studies in Honor of Siegfried Wenzel*, ed. by R. G. Newhauser and J. A. Alford, Medieval and Renaisance Texts and Studies (New York, 1994), pp. 263-273.
95. Gerard de Prato, in *Breviloquium super librum sententiarum.* Consulted at Paris Mazarine, MS 862, and in Il Breviloquium super Libros Sententiarum di Frate Gherardo da Prato Dell' ordine de' Minori, Pubblicato per la prima volta e corredato di Alcuni Studi dal Padre Marcellino da Civezza O.F.M. (Prato, 1882). The transcriptions and translations use both. 'Caput I, Quid sit Deus, et quid sit persona et

quot sint Personae Divinae: Deus est id quo melius exogitari non potest: sic dicit Anselmus. Item Cicero: Deust est mens quaedam soluta et libera, secreta ab omni concretione mortali, omnia sentiens et movens (ipsaque) praedita nutu sempiterno. Item Augustinus: Deum omnes esse consentiunt, quod coeteris rebus omnibus anteponitur. Deus est unus in essentia et trinus in personis.'

96. Ibid., Cap v, *De conditionis, sive proprietatibus divinae essentiae*: 'Est divina essentia verissime, ita quod nullo modo potest non solum non esse, sed nec cogitari non esse. Est incommutabilis; itaque nec loco, nec tempore, nec affectione movetur. Et simplicissima, quia est quidquid habet, nec est composita ex aliis, nec ipsa componibilis est.'

97. Ibid.: 'Est infinita, incomprehensibilis, incircumscripta; et quia incircumscripta, ideo nullo loco continetur, sicut continetur corpus, cui secundum locum assignatur principium, medium et finis; ante et retro; dextrum et sinistrum; et sursum et deorsum. Et nullo loco circumscribitur, sicut spiritus creatus, qui dum est in uno loco non potest (esse simul) in alio; sed omnem locum implet et omnem locum excedit, et in omni loco adest, et rebus omnibus praesens est, et in omnibus rebus est. Et dicitur Deus esse in rebus diversimode secundum diverso effectu, sive secundum diversas conditiones. Est enim in omnibus praesentialiter, potentialiter et essentialiter: praesentialiter, secundum praesentialitatis indistantiam, quia nulli abest; potentialiter, secundum virtutis indistantiam, quia nulli abest; potentialiter, secundum virtutis influentiam, quia rebus omnibus influit; essentialiter, secundum intimitatis existentiam, quia est intimu omni rei.'

98. Ibid.: 'Est igitur Deus in omnibus rebus per naturam, tribus praedictus modis, secundum quod res exeunt ab deo; in quibusdam vero, secundum quod redeunt ad ipsum.'

99. Ibid.: 'Sicut.. in.. radio exeunte a sole.. est tantum emissi luminis continuatio. Nulla harum subcessionum est in aeternitate.'

100. Ibid., lib. II, cap. xvii: 'Syndresis est quoddam inclinitavum (spirituale) pondus ipsius affectus animae, naturaliter inclinans eam ad bonum honestum, quod est virtus et opus virutis. ... cuius actus quamuis impediri possit, extingui non potest. Impeditur tamen actus eius vel propter obcoecationis, sicut in haereticis, qui malum credunt bonum, et falsum verum in quibus non remurmurat cum credunt se pro pietate mori, sed potius gaudire sibi videtur. Propter lasciviam delectationis similiter impeditur; aliquando enim in peccatis carnalibus ita absorbetur homo carnis lascivia, ut remorsum non sentiat...'

101. Ibid.: 'Sciendum est autem quod anima non tenet rationem imaginis nisi per conversionem sui ad Deum, vel ad se: unde quia anima Deum capit, vel capere potest per memoriam, intelligentiam et voluntatem, eius imago dicitur.'

102. Ibid.: 'Cognoscitur igitur Deus per creaturam, prout consideratur ut umbra, ut vestigium et ut imago; cognoscitur etiam per naturalem rationem, per gratiam fidei, per gratiam prophetiae, per donum sapientiae et intellectus et per gratiam raptus.'

103. The manuscripts, authorship and codicology of Servasanctus's writings are discussed in Martin Grabmann, 'Der *Liber de Exemplis Naturalibus* des Franziskanertheologen Servasanctus' in *Franzkanische Studien*, 7 (1920), 85-117 and in P. L. Oliger,

'Servasanto da Faenza O.F.M. e il suo *Liber de Virtutibus et Vitiis*', in F. Ehrle, *Miscellanea*, ed. by F. Ehrle (Rome, 1924) I, pp. 148-189.

104. Servasanctus Tuscus de Faenza, *On the articles of the faith, the sacraments and the virtues*, was consulted at Paris, in Bibliothèque Nationale, MS Lat. 3436: fol. 1r. 'Occurrit namque primo discutere utrum sit necessarie ponere deum esse. Nihilum debet hoc verti in dubium cum sit stigma fidei sacramenti. Unde philosophus quidam ait si deus non est unde bonum est? Si deus non est quomodo aliquid est? ... At deus secundum suam sentenciam omnis est principia causa et ratio omnis posteriorum. Sicut infra probabit multiplex argumentum ergo si deus non fuerit nichil ex rebus omnibus esse potuit. Sed posterius multiplex est ex illo causatum. Ergo deus est.'

105. Ibid.: 'Nam nonne decem praedicamentarum principium et omnis causa est ipsa substantia qua omnia dependent accidentia et posteriora.'

106. Ibid.: 'Restat ponere principium omnis rerum quod visitato vocabulo dicamus "deum".'

107. Ibid., fol. 1v. 'Omnis creatura predicat deum esse. Item omnis multitudino ad unitatem reducitur et omne multiforme ad uniformem et omne mobile ad unum aliquod immobile sicut constat probatum esse in viii libro *Physicarum* et xv *Metaphysicarum*.'

108. Ibid., fol. 1v. 'Unde Philosophus omnia creata ad decem reduxit praedicata et tandem omnia ista reduxit ad substanciam tamquam ad radicalem omnis causam. At substancia ipsa quae est genus generalissimum, cum sit aliis principiis constituta quod ex materia et forma composita, cum non sit simplicissimum: nec potest esse causa prima. Ergo est aliquod principium reducendum quod est simplicissimum et simpliciter primus. Sed illud principium non potest esse materia vel forma quia forma quantum ad esse dependet materia. Neque etiam in natura absque materia valet esse forma cum sint inter se, teste philosophi, relativa... Prima simplicitas sit absolutissima nulli extraneo omnino relativa. Restat extra genus aliud ponere omnis formam materiae coniungere quod nos dicamus deum esse... Non ergo deus prima vel secunda substancia est.'

109. Ibid., fol. 2r. 'Deus non est substancia composita cum sit substantia simplex. Prima non generata cum non ex aliis extracta cum sit omnis causa. Nec est substancia materia cum materia sit omnino passiva nec habens esse nisi per formam. Nec eciam est substancia forma cum forma non possit esse absque materia in natura et materia potencia est quaedam res imperfecta... Deus ergo cum sit omnis causa prima a nulla habens dependencia non potest probari sub substancia generata quae non causa sed causata. Deus ergo de genere entium non est. Sed super ens et super ipsum esse ens ut philosophus docet.'

110. Ibid., fol. 3r. 'Item ut experiencia docet [animus] naturaliter appetit perfici summo bono propter suam potentiam amantem et eius infinitem capacitatem ut ipsa experiencia probat ut [animus] nullo bono omnino iterato possit impleri quin ultra ergo appetat et semper ad alia se extendat... Semper bona affectat et nova semper investigare non cessat.' Later: 'Animus nullo bono creato complendus (est). Ergo si in natura nichil plantatum est frustra – ut omnis [docet] philosophorum doctrina – necesse est ponere summum bonum ergo quo perficiatur affectus et quo habito sit

perfectus. Illud autem est summum secundum quod bonum. Quo adepto nichil ulterius desiderare queat.'

111. Ibid., fol. 3v. I read Servasancus's expression 'ita habet nullum esse' as, 'so has nothing of created being'. Thus, God is so without dependency that God cannot be thought not to be: 'Ergo omnino est necessariem ponere summum bonum quod ita habet nullum esse ut non possit excogitari non esse. Enim summum bonum sit quo melius sive maius excogitari non possit sicut in sequenti capitulo appearetur et constat quod maius sit illud bonum quod non potest cogitari non esse. Omnino est necesse ut deus est sic habeat nullum esse ut nullo modo posset excogitari non esse. Unde Algazel in *Metaphysica* sua notat deum necesse esse eo quod sic habeat nullum esse et incommunicable esse ut nequeat excogitari non esse.'

112. Ibid., fol. 4r. 'Si infinito aliquid addi possit, simul et semel finitum et infinitum esset – quod est impossibile. Cum ergo summum bonum actu infinitu existat et omnem intellectum excedit plus quam dici valet, necesse est ut nullam prorsus addicionem admitat quia si aliter esset et ei aliquid addi posset non esset quo maius excogitari non posset.'

113. Ibid., folios 4r-v. 'Diligenter hoc attenedum est quod summum bonum est causa omnis et principium. Est esse immensissimum. Est sapientia splendidissima. Est equitate rectissimum. Est eternalitate sempiternalissimum. Nam immensitatem divinum esse nobis ostendit divinorum operum amplitudo. Ineffabile nomen eternae sapientiae nobis probat divinorum operum multitudo. Simul et pulcritudo. Infinitatem divinae potenciae nobis probat divinorum operum magnituodino. Inflexibilitatem suae essenciae patenter ostendit operum divinorum [ ] duratio et incorruptio. Igitur incipientes a primis dicamus quod primum principium sive summum quod dicamus dei nomine est esse omnino immensissimum numquam temporalibus coartatum. Sed omnino non solum potentia sed ipsa sua essencia est presentissimum... Quod summa sapientia sit ille qui variare universa sic potuit et formas distinguentes materiae tam diversas impressit. Nonne sapientia est illae admirabilis quae humanus corpus instituit ex tam diversis compositis. Non solum ex carne et ossibus et hummoribus et elementis sed venis arcanibus et nervis tanta inter se colligacione coniunctis quanta in natura diversis.

Est hoc principium nostrum in summo rectissimo in nullo penitus tortuosum, nec obligatum vel modicum inclinatum. Si enim elementa haec a deo facta habet motus rectissimis propter quod ignis tendit sursum et terra deorsum quomodo obliquus ille poterit esse, quia rebus creatis tantum rectitudinem dedit quantum est rectitudino carnorum ... [Summum bonum] est ergo principium nostrum rectissimum in iusticia consummatum quia si non esset summum bonum esse non potuisset. Nam omne bonum est iustum. Ergo omnino est necessarium ut summum bonum est summum iustum. Non enim est aliud in deo bonitas aliud iusticia sed omnino idem sunt bonitas et iusticia simul cum divina essencia.'

114. Ibid., fols 5r-v. 'Ex hiis quae inventa sunt et probata, euidens trahitur argumentum quod summum bonum sicut est potentia altissima, sapientia calrissima et equitate rectissimum. Sic est eternitate sempiternalissima. Nam si deficiret vel deficire posset summum bonum non esset quia sic esset quo maius aliquid cogitari posset.'

115. G. Gál, 'Opiniones Richard Rufi Cornubiensis a Censore Reprobatae', in *Franciscan Studies*, 35:13 (1975), 136-193, discusses the opprobrium of a censor upon Rufus's teachings in the *abbreviatio*.
116. Richard Rufus's *abbreviatio* of Bonaventure's sentence commentary was consulted in Vatican MS. Lat. 12293 fol. 11r. Dist. iii, 'Queritur utrum deus cognoscibilis per creatura est' only abbreviates Bonaventure's discussion, while elsewhere Rufus is apparently less tied to his text.
117. Ibid., 26v: 'Si non est veritas verum est veritatem non esse. Ergo aliquam veritatem [esse] verum est. Et illa est veritas...' 'Sed aliter ostenditur quod non potest interire veritas quia non potest negari nec est dubitari. Aut hic dubitas veritatem esse aut non dubitas. Si non concedis. Ergo si dubitas verum est te dubitare et hoc verum scis et concedis hanc igitur veritatem concedis... Item ipse deus se ipsum negare non potest ergo veritas omnino a nullo negari potest...'
118. For dates, see Bougerol, p. 15. On the *Collationes*, see H. Van Der Lann, 'The Idea of Christian Philosophy in Bonaventure's *Collationes in Hexaemeron*', in *Bonaventure, 1274-1974*, ed. by J. G. Bougerol, 5 vols (Grottaferrata, 1973-1974), iii, 39-56. The following also emphasise the role of exemplarism within Bonaventure's thought, and its role in explaining the errors of Aristotle: A. C. Pegis, 'St Bonaventure, St Francis and Philosophy', in *Medieval Studies*, 15 (1959), 1-13; and E. Cousins, 'St Bonaventure, St Thomas, and the Movement of Thought in the 13th Century', in *Bonaventure and Aquinas*, ed. by R. W. Shahan and F. J. Kovach (Washington, 1974), pp. 5-23; Gilson, *Philosophy of St Bonaventure*, p. 98.
119. On the growth of the Arts curriculum at the University of Paris during this period, see Leff, *Paris and Oxford*, pp. 138-46.
120. Bonaventure, *Collationes in Hexaemeron*, in *Opera Omnia* (Quaracchi, 1891), v, pp. 327-454.
121. Bonaventure, *Collationes*, c. vi, 2-4.
122. Bonaventure, *Collationes*, c. iv, 1.
123. Gilson, *Philosophy of St Bonaventure*, p. 98.
124. Ibid., pp. 1-10, 24-34.
125. Glorieux, II, n. 304.

Chapter 5

# Thomas Aquinas and the Dominican Community

Châttillon, Pegis and others have remarked that, in approaching Anselm's argument, Thomas was reacting to his contemporaries rather than to Anselm himself.[1] Was Thomas also contributing to a wider picture of God that reflected Dominican experience? Although there are counter-examples, there is evidence to suggest that once again the significance of the key thinker lay in his representing the interests of the wider order. Thomas's arguments were formed within, and on behalf of, a community of interpretation. Though historians have been willing enough to see Bonaventure as expressing a Franciscan spirituality through philosophy, they have generally been less inclined to view Thomas and the Dominican order in quite this way. Pegis, for example, says of Bonaventure:

> There is no way in which we can read St Bonaventure in a purely philosophical way. Unlike St Thomas Aquinas, whose highly technical prose is the work of intelligence pure and simple and can be read in a purely impersonal way, the prose of St Bonaventure is the mirror of a visibly devout theologian.[2]

It would be a mistake to think, however, that Bonaventure was the religious thinker, Thomas the philosopher. As with the spirituality of St Dominic, it is the very impersonal character of Thomas's prose that communicates a particular approach to God. In Thomas's case, as much as in Bonaventure's, the question 'how does the mind arrive at a knowledge of God?' is a theoretical expression of the question to which all forms of religious life provide a practical answer: how does one know God? In Thomas's case, as much as in the case of Bonaventure, the style is both constituted by, and constitutive of, the message. The contrast between the two thinkers is not between a theologian and a philosopher, but between different forms of religious life and two different ways of communicating the Christian message.

## I

Born and brought up in the kingdom of Sicily around 1224, Thomas joined the Dominican order while a student at the cosmopolitan university of Naples.[3]

Thomas first met Albertus Magnus at the convent in Paris and followed him when he was sent to found a new *Studium* at Cologne in 1248.[4] After hearing Albert lecture on the Pseudo-Dionysius and Aristotle's *Physics*, Thomas was allowed – with the help of Hugh of St Cher – to overcome age restrictions and read the sentences in the Dominican school at Paris.[5] David Burrell has argued that it was the dimensions of Thomas's own personal history that led him to be more open to thinkers from the Islamicate than his co-workers from Cologne or Paris might have been.[6] If this is true, then his personal history prepared him to articulate interests that were shared by other Dominicans. What really distinguishes Thomas from his contemporaries in the Franciscan school at Paris was not so much the sources he read, however, but the use which he made of them.

Thomas's treatment of Anselm's argument in the early sentence commentary composed in Paris between 1254 and 1256 represents a key move in his approach to natural knowledge. Unlike Bonaventure, Thomas did not begin his commentary by asking whether reason ought to be used in matters of faith. Instead he began with the question, 'whether beyond physics another teaching is necessary for human beings?'[7] Thomas was less concerned with justifying the use of reason to Christians, than with justifying theological doctrine to natural philosophers. The philosophers he had in mind were actually the Christian, Muslim and Jewish scholars who now shared common traditions of thought. Like Albert, Thomas was interested less in how argument might contribute toward personal religious experience than in how reason might function across religious boundaries.

Thomas argues that another teaching beyond physics is necessary because the purpose of human life is to contemplate God and a knowledge of creatures leads only to an imperfect knowledge of God.[8] We therefore require another science acquired not by natural but by supernatural light. This is higher than anything that can be acquired by the natural light and from this we are able to draw two conclusions. One is that this science – theology – rules all the others as first. Another is that all other sciences are used in obedience to it, like vassals to a lord. Just as a sub-science of medicine is used by the physician for the end of medicine (which is health), so theology draws upon philosophy in attaining its own end (which is the knowledge of faith and salvation).[9]

How does theological knowledge use other sciences? For Thomas, there is no suggestion that faith provides some kind of key for understanding, either in terms of the rational understanding of the principles of faith, or for the understanding of other sciences. Theology does not prove its own principles, any more than any science proves its own principles, but receives them from above. Since theology is higher than all other sciences, however, it is above rational proof.[10] Nonetheless, while the principles of theology may not be proven, they can be defended against detractors. For Thomas, as for Albert, the object of rational inquiry *within* theology is not the edification of the soul through the understanding of what is believed, but the defence of faith against detractors. Thomas does not include any reference to understanding as the delight of the faithful, or even to rational proof as a means of edifying the weak. Finally, Thomas at no point entertains the notion that faith may lead reason beyond its natural limits. Even if Anselm, Bonaventure and Thomas all considered themselves to be engaged in the project of 'faith seeking understanding', they understood that project in very different terms.

Theology rules other sciences not because it is itself the object of natural knowledge, but because it is above knowledge. As for the Franciscans, Thomas regards revealed and natural truth as deriving from the same principle. Unlike the Franciscans, however, he regards the first object of faith to be the last object of natural knowledge. A key move in his account of the relationship between theological and natural knowledge is therefore provided by his treatment of the natural knowledge of God. Whereas in the Franciscan account the knowledge of God underpins all natural knowledge, for Thomas natural knowledge underpins the natural knowledge of God. Thomas makes the natural knowledge of God subsequent, not prior, to the knowledge of nature.

Thomas begins his discourse on the natural knowledge of God in the sentence commentary by examining the arguments of the Lombard himself. Lombard's proofs, Thomas says, can be reduced to the three ways of Pseudo-Dionysius: the ways of causality, denial and eminence.[11] Since creatures have their being from some other there must be some first cause of their being. Creatures receive what they have from their Creator only imperfectly, and hence we come to a knowledge of the Creator by denying of the Creator the imperfections that belong to creatures. God is therefore incorporeal, immutable and in every way perfect. On the other hand, whatever creatures have that is good and noble the Creator will have more perfectly and more eminently. It is from the way of eminence that Lombard draws his last two proofs: there must be some first incomparable being which accounts for the different levels of goodness and stability in created things.[12]

Asking 'whether God is able to be known by the created intellect', Thomas lists many of the same objections as Bonaventure.[13] Dionysius said 'we are neither able to speak of nor to understand God'. Furthermore, cognition concerns existent things, but God is above all existent things, therefore God is above all cognition.[14] In the second place there is a greater distance between God and the created intellect than there is between the senses and the intellect but the sensible is unable to know the intellect. Therefore, the intellect is unable to know God.[15] The Philosopher says that the infinite is unknown.[16] Our intellect is unable to form an image of God: it cannot, therefore, know God.[17]

Like Bonaventure, Thomas argues that a distinction must be made between imperfect and perfect knowledge of God. The question is not whether God in essence is able to be seen directly: this is a different matter altogether. The question is whether God is able to be known in some way. And for that reason we are able to say that God is knowable; but God's essence cannot be comprehended. Every knower has a knowledge concerning the thing known, not according to the mode of the thing known, but according to the mode of the knower. No creature's mode of knowledge attains to the height of the divine majesty. It is fitting, therefore, that God is known by no one perfectly; only God can know God perfectly.[18]

Thomas goes on to ask whether God's existence is self-evident *(per se notum)*. It becomes clear that under this heading Thomas is assessing the very approach to God adopted by Bonaventure and the tradition that he articulated. To begin with, it seems that God's existence is self-evident, for this is said of knowledge that is naturally inserted within us, like the truth of the proposition 'every whole is greater than its part'. According to John of Damascus the knowledge of God's existence is naturally inserted within us. Therefore, God's existence is self-evident.[19] Again, it is also argued that God is to the intelligible soul as the light of the sun is to the eye. Yet the light of the sun is visible in itself; in fact, nothing else can be seen without it. Therefore God is also immediately seen in God's self.[20] Again, all knowledge comes about through a union of the thing known to the knower. Yet God is more present to the soul, through God's very self, than the soul is to itself. Therefore God is able to be known self-evidently.[21] Thomas accepts that a distinguishing feature of a self-evident proposition is that it cannot be denied. If God is not able to be thought not to be, therefore, God's existence is a self-evident truth. Thomas ascribes this argument to Anselm, though Anselm nowhere discussed the existence of God as a self-evident proposition.

Thomas states two arguments against the proposition. The Philosopher says that those things that are self-evident are able to be denied on the exterior by the mouth, but cannot be denied inwardly in the heart. Yet according to the psalmist, this is precisely what the Fool does.[22] Furthermore, whatever is the conclusion of a demonstration can hardly be self-evident. That God exists, however, is demonstrated by philosophers. Therefore, that God exists is not a self-evident truth.[23]

In conclusion, Thomas says there are two ways of talking about the knowledge of a thing: either as the thing is according to the thing itself, or as it is according to us. By speaking, therefore, concerning God according to God's own being, the existence of God is self-evident, and this God understands through God's own self, not through this concept which we make when we attempt to render God intelligible.

Thomas thinks that God's existence is in some sense self-evident in relation to our knowledge. He distinguishes between two ways of talking about God. When talking about God according to the image of God, God's existence is self-evident; for nothing is known except through truth, which is copied from God: that God exists, therefore, is self-evident. Thomas does not deny that our ability to know truth comes from God in so far as we are a likeness of God; but he argues that the knowledge of truth is not a knowledge of God in God's self.

Thomas distinguishes, therefore, between the knowledge of God according to the image of God and the knowledge of God's own nature. God's nature is incorporeal; and in this way God is not known self-evidently. More precisely, there are many who can be found who deny that God exists – all the philosophers who do not posit an agent cause, such as Democritus and certain others. Thomas grounds all knowledge in the senses – including knowledge of divine things. Existent things that are self-evident must be self-evident to the senses. Hence, we see that every whole is greater than its part without any further enquiry. Yet with all those things which appear to the senses we do not come into a knowledge of God except by proceeding along causes to that agent cause by which everything is caused and which is not able to be a body. Thus, we do not come to God, Thomas states, without arguing: and no such thing can be self-evident.[24] Thus Thomas emphasises that it is from God as truth that truth and our knowledge of truth flows; similarly with being, all being flows from God. Thomas teaches however that it is from the derivative that we begin if we are to arrive at a knowledge of God.

Thomas then responds to the arguments by explaining how the authorities brought in favour of the self-evidence of God's existence ought to be interpreted. When John of Damascus said that the knowledge of God was impressed upon the soul, he meant the image of God rather than a knowledge of God's own nature. He was referring to the image of God when he said that all things desire God. Nothing is desired unless some similitude of it is already possessed. Yet nothing is thus known of God in God's own nature.[25] Thomas's emphasis upon the senses as the source of our knowledge explains why, though our sight is proportionate to that which is illuminated by corporeal light, our intellects are only proportionate to natural knowledge which comes from the senses. For that reason the understanding is not able to come to 'pure intelligibles', or beings which are beyond the reach of the senses, except by means of argument.[26] Thomas does not deny that God is present to the soul in essence, presence and power. Nevertheless, God is not in the soul as an object of knowledge: according to Thomas even the soul is not easily known to itself, except by inference.[27]

Finally, Thomas turns back to Anselm's argument. After we understand God, it is not possible to understand what God is and to think that God does not exist. Nevertheless, it does not follow from this that God's existence is not able to be denied in this life. Echoing Richard Rufus, Thomas says that it is always possible to think that there is nothing of any such kind that cannot be thought not to exist (*potest enim cogitare nihil huiusmodi esse quo maius cogitari non possit*).[28] As Aquinas explains elsewhere, existence is originally grasped not through concepts but through a judgement involving sense experience.[29] Judgement and conceptualisation are two different acts of the mind, stemming from radically different sources. Judgement concerns existence, and concepts essences. Even a concept that includes existence does not tell us anything about the actual existence of a thing: the concept 'the existent horse', for example, does not mean that a horse actually exists. Since the existence of something is not given in its conceptualisation, there is no self-contradiction in denying that a thing to which the concept corresponds is in actual existence. That than which no greater can be thought is not grasped by the senses, and its existence, for that very reason, is capable of being doubted. Anselm does not show therefore, that God's existence is self-evident.[30]

For Thomas, a self-evident principle is something that cannot be thought not to be. In asking whether God's existence is self-evident, he is stating his rejection of Anselm's argument, as Pegis put it, for Aristotelian reasons, and in Aristotelian terms. In particular, while he was not rejecting participation or exemplarism in his account of being, he was rejecting the participation and exemplarism as an account of knowledge. To appreciate what this means it is helpful to look beyond the early sentence commentary to another work which he composed around the same time.

In his commentary on Boethius's *De Trinitate* – contemporary with Bonaventure's disputed questions *On the Mystery of the Trinity,* as it happens – Thomas again deals with Anselm's argument. He cites the dictum 'God cannot be thought not to be' and the teaching of John of Damascus concerning the naturally inserted knowledge of God, in favour of the proposition that God is the first object of the human intellect.[31] Here, Thomas addresses the view that the mind knows all that it knows through God or through the illumination of God's light. By contrast, he says, Aristotle teaches that all knowledge is from the senses: since God is most removed from the senses, God is the last thing known by us.[32] Moreover, Aristotle also teaches that those things which are first in nature are last known to us, and those things which are last in nature are known first. God is therefore last known to us.[33] If God were known as the first object of the mind, then everyone would live in beatitude.[34] Moreover, whether the intellectual light is the divine light or not, we do not even perceive that we have an understanding until we perceive that we understand – something that is not attained without great labour.[35]

Just as physical light is not known except by means of its reflection in colour, so the intelligent light is not known except in so far as particular things are known.[36] To arrive at any knowledge whatever, therefore, the intellect operates by means of abstraction from matter – and that which is without matter cannot be the object of abstraction. If God is known at all, therefore, it is only by inference from things that are known by abstraction.[37] In response to Anselm's argument, and to John of Damascus, Thomas again argues that God's existence is self-evident in itself but not to us, since we do not see God's essence. God cannot therefore be the first object of the mind. Furthermore, he argues, the knowledge of God is inserted within us only in as much as the principles through which we are able to perceive that God exists are innate within us.[38]

Thomas affirms that 'truth' and 'being' have a primary referent in God. He also affirms that all truths and beings depend upon that being which is first in the hierarchy of beings. Thomas also affirms that God's knowledge causes things to exist. Nonetheless, in rejecting Anselm's argument, Thomas is rejecting an example of a proof which relies on some kind of contact between divine and created minds.[39] As important as the rejection of exemplarist theories of knowledge, however, is the space provided for a different approach to natural knowledge; one in which the mind is sufficient within its own principles for arriving at knowledge, and one in which the sources of knowledge lie entirely with the senses. In this framework, God is reached only by inference and is the conclusion rather than the first principle of knowledge. In coming to understand the ordering of each being and each truth towards the first in being and truth, natural reason follows the reverse of the order by which they were caused.

Back in the sentence commentary, having cleared the decks, so to speak, Thomas turns to the ways in which the mind can come to a knowledge of God. He argues that since creatures proceed from God as from their cause they must indeed bear some analogous similarity to God, in so far as they imitate God according to the potential of their natures. Thomas concludes his discourse on the created mind's knowledge of God as unity by returning to the three paths with which he began. Like Bonaventure and Alexander of Hales, Thomas adopts the three-fold path of the Pseudo-Dionysius: through causality, negation and eminence.[40] In each of the three ways, the operative principle is not the mind's contact with the divine exemplar, but its direct experience of existence: 'since the existence of a creature is from another, in this manner we are led to the cause from which it comes.'[41] Once again, to understand Thomas's teaching, it is helpful to turn to another early treatise.

The principle which underpins the kind of proof that Aquinas does accept, and which underpins his endorsement of the three ways of the Pseudo-Dionysius, is expressed in his early treatise *On Being and Essence.* Thomas argues there that in created substances, the essence of a thing is separate from its act of existence. Whatever belongs to a being, Aquinas argues, either belongs to the principles of its nature or comes to it from some extrinsic principle. Since existence does not add anything to the nature of a thing, its existence comes from beyond the thing itself. 'Everything which is such that its act of existing is other than its nature must have its act of existing from something else.'[42] It is through existence, therefore, that the mind encounters a path to something that lies beyond finite natures themselves: to the cause of existence, which is God.[43]

The distinction between being and essence is the archimedian point of Thomas's thought. It not only distinguishes him from the general Augustinian tradition that sees being and truth in terms of their relationship to the exemplar form, it also distinguishes Thomas from Aristotle himself.[44] The distinction allows for un-Aristotelian emphases upon God as the source of being and upon God's immanence within creation as the cause of being of each individual thing. Hence, Thomas's distinction between being and essence allows him to adapt an Aristotelian account of nature to a Christian theology. In this account, it is precisely by understanding nature in Aristotelian terms, rather than by rejecting such an account, that one is led to a knowledge of God. Thus the 'five ways' of the *Summa Theologiae* he composed much later, illustrate that the very forms of causality that operate in nature are the very forms of causality that lead the mind to a natural knowledge of God.

At the same time, however, the distinction between being and essence serves to mark the radical distinction between God and creatures: God alone has existence by nature while all other things exist by participation. Hence, the very thing that makes God knowable at all to natural reason, also defines God's radical unknowability.[45] As well as being removed from the senses, God exists in a way that nothing else can. It is for these reasons that it is the three ways of Pseudo-Dionysius that mark out his fundamental scheme for the natural knowledge of God in his major works. What is received from the first cause (the way of causation) is received imperfectly. God is thereby only known by denying the imperfections of God (the way of negation) and by understanding the perfections of created things in an unrestricted way (the way of eminence), a way that requires Thomas's doctrine of analogy.[46] Hence, the teaching on being and essence allows Thomas to combine a Christian doctrine of God with an Aristotelian physics, without compromising God's 'otherness'.

How far does Thomas's approach to God encapsulate the experience of God of the Dominican community? What is perhaps most striking about Thomas's teaching on being and essence is not just that it allows him to combine Aristotelian physics with a Christian doctrine of God, but the fact that its origins lie within the Arabic Aristotelian tradition. Hence, Thomas's central teaching derives from an engagement with the unbelievers who had been trying to make sense of monotheistic assumptions within an Aristotelian framework for themselves. What serves to divide Thomas from his fellow Christians in Paris, makes him philosophically, if not theologically, more akin to his Arab opponents.[47]

Moreover, for Thomas, progress along the paths of causality is unaffected by faith or morality. All are equally dependent upon shared sources of knowledge in the senses: good, evil, faithful and unfaithful alike.[48] In this respect, as in his teaching on the relationship between natural reason and faith, Thomas is as reminiscent of Moses Maimonides, as he is of Roland of Cremona or Albertus Magnus.[49] Yet it is not just a question of influences upon Thomas's thinking that needs to be noted here, but the ends to which his arguments are directed. Thomas's account of the natural knowledge of God involves and underpins an approach to knowledge that is particularly suited to an order whose religious practice involves preaching by rational persuasion, where equal access to sources of knowledge among believers and unbelievers is critical to the whole enterprise. Thomas thus rejects the whole Franciscan account of the natural knowledge of God, not least because its emphasis upon the priority of penitence and faith undermined the very activity of persuasion to which his order was committed.

In any case, Thomas's account stands in sharp contrast with his Franciscan contemporaries. According to Thomas the image of God within the soul is not the point at which the soul is joined to God in its intellectual operations, nor a point of access to truth that is renewed by faith. The image of the first truth is rather the soul's innate principles by means of which it may follow the evidence of the senses. Moreover, just as the soul is sufficient within its own nature to perform its natural operations, so nature as a whole is sufficient for its own operations. Robert Grosseteste had emphasised the role of the exemplar cause in impressing itself upon the creature in order to preserve it from ebbing into nothingness. The same view of creation is implicit within Bonaventure's proofs that reach God's absolute necessity from the mutability of things. In Thomas's scheme, it is not the mutability of nature that leads the mind to an awareness of God's presence. Rather it is the very self-sufficiency of nature, following immutable laws, that leads the mind to an appreciation of God as the immanent governor of things.

The full significance of these points becomes clearer in the *Summa contra gentiles*, but it is worth suggesting that not only Thomas's personal history, but also his Dominican vocation, had something to do with his 'openness' to thinkers from the Islamicate and the methods which he adopted from them. In rejecting Anselm's argument, Thomas was rejecting both the exemplarist account of knowledge, and creating a space to erect a very different knowledge of God. Henceforth, God is not encountered as the necessary principle implied in all thought and being, but as the extrinsic principle that causes the existence of each and every thing. The evidence of Thomas's earliest contemporaries in Paris and Bologna on the issue of Anselm's argument suggests that his teaching was not, as some have suggested, merely a 'personal' project.[50] In the light of these, the text of the *Summa contra gentiles* may be taken as evidence of the broader interests of the community as a whole.

## II

One of Thomas's most important Dominican contemporaries at Paris was Peter of Tarentaise (b. c. 1225-1276) who later became Pope Innocent V (1276).[51] Peter was a bachelor of the *Sentences* between 1257 and 1259 probably under the direct contemporaries of Thomas, Hugh of Metz and Barthelemy of Tours (neither of whose commentaries have been found). They occupied the Dominican chair at the Faculty of Theology in Paris, which was strictly reserved for French masters and their students, and were succeeded in that chair by Peter for a brief period in 1259 and then again between 1267 and 1269. The large number of manuscripts, scattered around European libraries, of the commentary that Peter composed as a bachelor student is indicative that his opinions were valued among his Dominican contemporaries.[52] Interestingly, he illustrates an attempt to retain Anselm's argument while nonetheless, like Thomas, rejecting the participational and exemplarist account of knowledge that it usually presupposed in this period.

Peter's similarities with Thomas are evident in his discussion of the nature of theology. Like Thomas, he considers that theology proceeds from the articles of faith as from first principles that are self-evident to those having faith. This is because in matters of belief all other things are proven through the first principles, though they themselves are incapable of demonstration. Nonetheless, some of the articles are made manifest and defended by reasons.[53] Following discussions of the unity of theology as a science, of God as its subject, and of its status as a speculative and a practical science, Peter asks whether, for the attainment of their proper end, the rational being requires another doctrine beyond other sciences, namely, theology.[54] Once again, it is not merely a case of justifying the use of reason within theology, but of defending against rational agents the need for doctrines that lay above reason.

Peter considers the same objections as Thomas had: philosophy deals with all existent things, speculative and practical philosophy suffice for the perfection of intellect and morality, and since other animals acquire their perfection through their own nature, no science must be necessary for the attainment of human perfection that is not able to be acquired through nature alone.[55] Against these, Peter considers the contrary position in the same way as Thomas. According to Augustine, theology considers those things which pertain to salvation and therefore is most necessary.[56] Since no effect improportionate to its cause leads sufficiently to a knowledge of its cause, it is fitting that there should be some other source of knowledge regarding the first cause than effects alone.[57]

In his response, Peter is almost identical to Thomas. The end of the rational creature is assimilation with its Creator through contemplation. There are two kinds of contemplation. Through creatures the Creator is known obscurely – this is the end of the sciences of philosophy. The Creator may also be known through the Creator's proper essence and this is attained through the way of grace and merit and is only attained in the future through an immediate vision – which is the ultimate end of the rational creature. Since this ultimate end is not able to be attained through natural reason, it is fitting that there is some science concerned with God and which is infused into the finite intellect by the infinite light. Since this science deals with the most noble of causes, it is the most noble science to which all others are inferior and ancillary.[58]

In reply to the objections, Peter states that whereas philosophy deals with knowledge of different kinds of being it is theology that deals with these in the most noble way: according to their return to God as the final cause.[59] Although philosophy is sufficient for the perfection of the intellect according to the mode of nature, nature itself remains imperfect without the gift of grace.[60] Finally, precisely because the human creature is incomparably more noble than animals, its perfection exceeds its nature: therefore its nature does not suffice for its perfection as it does for other creatures.[61]

Before closing his discussion of the nature of theology, Peter considers whether the mode of inquisition through reason and argument is appropriate to this science. Peter argues that authorities cannot be used to defend the Faith against those who reject the authorities: therefore it is fitting that rational arguments are employed.[62] The proper use of reason is not for the demonstrative proof of faith, but for the declaration of its truth against the infidels.[63] Peter had earlier cited John of Damascus's warning that since the Faith is passed down to us by prophets and evangelists we ought to venerate them, not enquire beyond them.[64] Peter responds that it is necessary to answer objections to Scripture where the answer is not explicitly or implicitly contained therein.[65] Reason excludes merit when it stands in place of faith, but not when it is used for the defence of faith and the declaration of its truth.[66] This account of the role of reason in matters of faith expresses the interests of an order committed to defending the faith. Moreover, it is underpinned, it would seem, by a particular account of God.

Peter endorses Thomas's position with regard to the natural knowledge of God. Whilst there is a sense in which an image of God within the soul is known self-evidently, God's own nature cannot be known in this way. Like Thomas, Peter begins by summarising Lombard's proofs for God's existence. Whereas Thomas, however, had represented Lombard's four proofs as corresponding to the Pseudo-Dionysian ways of causality, negation and eminence, Peter already identifies them with the four causes of Aristotle: efficient, material, final and formal.[67]

Peter begins the third distinction proper by asking whether God is knowable by creatures. Peter considers the usual objections: the distance between the creature and the Creator; the lack of proportion between finite and infinite; the inability of the mind to judge that which is superior to it; the ultimate simplicity of God making abstraction of more simple form by the intellect impossible; the inability of the mind to abstract form from something immaterial; the transcendence of God over those things contained within science; and finally, the ultimate transcendence of God over the mind.[68]

In favour of the mind's ability to know God, Peter cites the text from Paul's *Epistle to the Romans* which teaches that God is knowable from God's creatures.[69] Like Thomas, Peter makes much of the Aristotelian principle of nature – that nothing exists in vain. If the most noble creature were unable to attain its end of contemplating God then it would exist in vain.[70] The rest of Peter's arguments in favour of the knowledge of God would appear to bring him close to the position of Bonaventure. The excellence of God is not an impediment to the mind's knowledge, but rather its aid.[71] The mind is an image of God, not just in so far as it is a receptacle of God's presence, but also in so far as it has knowledge of God.[72] Since the spiritual light is that through which all other things are known, the spiritual light must be maximally intelligible.[73]

Responding to the objections Peter draws on the distinction between apprehension and comprehension. The finite can apprehend but not comprehend the infinite. Only God alone can comprehend God. Like Thomas, Peter quotes Boethius: 'every knower has a knowledge of the thing known according to the mode of the knower, not according to the mode of the thing known.[74]

Though there is an infinite distance between the created intellect and the Creator they are both intelligibles.[75] Though there be no proportion between them, they are both immaterial, and therefore the intellect is ordained toward the knowledge of God.[76] With respect to judgement, though the mind cannot judge truth, it judges according to it.[77] Though no species can be abstracted from God, God is known by impression upon the soul and by an irradiation of light within the intelligence.[78] Peter says, concerning phantasms, that though no phantasm of God is available to the created intellect in this life, the phantasms of God's effects can lead to a knowledge of God as cause.[79] Finally, when Dionysius claims that God is above human knowledge he is referring to comprehension, not apprehension.[80]

Peter then asks how it is able to be known and proven that God exists.[81] Peter draws on proofs from Richard of St Victor concerning the necessity of a being existing from itself and from eternity,[82] from Augustine concerning the necessity of truth,[83] from Aristotle concerning the necessity of a first unmoved mover and some first mover which moves another from potency into actuality,[84] and from Anselm concerning the necessary existence in reality of that than which no greater can be thought.[85] Peter then considers four different rejections of proofs for God's existence which also reveal the incompatibility between these different proofs. If the knowledge of God's existence is naturally inserted it is self-evident and therefore incapable of proof.[86] If God illuminates the mind to objects of the understanding then those objects cannot illuminate the mind to God.[87] The existence of evil within the world makes the existence of an infinite and omnipotent Good impossible.[88] Finally, echoing Richard Rufus and Thomas, it is always possible to think that there is simply no such thing that cannot be thought not to exist.[89]

In reply, Peter endorses four modes of knowledge simultaneously. God is the cause of the knowledge of all principles and conclusions as the light of the intellect. The knowledge of God's existence is naturally inserted within the mind and is self-evident. As the conclusion of a demonstration God's goodness, truth, omnipotence etc. can be known from the divine effects. Finally, God can be assented to simply by faith.[90]

Having adopted a form of knowledge that appears closer to Bonaventure than to Thomas, Peter distances himself from the Franciscan view in his replies to the objections. Peter attempts to remove the incompatibility between the implicit knowledge of God as the light of the understanding, and the knowledge of God as a conclusion of demonstration by introducing a distinction between knowing God in a general way and knowing God specifically. The knowledge that is inserted is said to be confused and general inasmuch as there is an inserted knowledge of truth and a love of the good that causes all creatures to desire the good. All creatures, rational and irrational alike, are therefore said to seek God – but they do not know God specifically (*in propria ratione*).[91] Though God illumines the mind for its knowledge of principles it knows God only in a general way – as truth. Again, God is not known specifically (*in propria ratione*).[92] Nor does the problem of evil mitigate God's goodness and omnipotence: these are revealed by God's bringing a greater good from evil.[93]

Peter's distinction between the specific and general knowledge of God corresponds to the teaching of Thomas's sentence commentary in which Thomas discusses the sense in which the existence of God is known self-evidently – in terms of an impressed created image and not in terms of God's own nature. In other words, God is still unknown to the mind without evidence. As we shall see, it is only by arguing from other sources that the mind is able to arrive at a proper knowledge of God. With Peter, as with Thomas, the order of knowing is the reverse of the order of causation.

Finally, Peter draws upon his distinction between the general and specific knowledge of God to present an interpretation of Anselm which, unlike the interpretation of Thomas, is not found among his predecessors or contemporaries. Anselm had said that there were two ways of thinking in the heart – thinking the words or thinking the thing signified by the words. Peter argues that these ways are the ways of specific reason and general reason. God may be considered according to the specific reason (*in ratione speciali*), when God is called 'God', or according to the general reason, when God is called truth, goodness etc. In the first of these ways God is able to be thought not to exist, but not in the second way: for truth is not able to be thought not to exist.[94] The object of knowledge is therefore not God specifically, but the confused reflection of God in the knowledge of truth and goodness naturally inserted within the understanding.

Peter of Tarentaise offers an interpretation of Anselm that succeeds in conserving Anselm's argument (or at least a particular interpretation of it) with Thomas's doctrine that God's existence is neither self-evident nor signified directly by the knowledge of truth. His ability to provide interpretations that more explicitly confirmed the authority of Christian teachers such as Anselm while at the same time endorsing teachings that were closely related to Thomas, may in part explain the popularity of Peter's sentence commentary among his brethren.[95]

Having rejected the idea that God's own nature is self-evident to us, Peter discusses the way God is known to us through the evidence of creatures. Here Peter's position with respect to the illumination of the soul and the limits of the soul's direct knowledge is clarified. Once again, God can be known from creatures according to the triple way of the Pseudo-Dionysius: through cause, negation and eminence.[96] Though there is no univocal proportion or agreement of terms between God and creatures there is nonetheless a proportion of analogy since the creature received its being from God and imitates its cause.[97] If God is more present to the soul than creatures, how can creatures form a medium for the soul's knowledge of the creator?[98] Peter responds that God is present to the soul, but not as an object of knowledge. Similarly, the soul is more present to itself than all other things, but not as an object of knowledge. Only with much work can the soul come to a knowledge of itself.[99] Finally, though the mind knows all else through God, it knows other things through God as through an efficient light – but creatures make God known to the mind in a specific way.[100] Thus, Peter endorses a doctrine of illumination in which the mind receives an initial light sufficient for all of its natural operations. Yet this is not the light of exemplar causality, for in Peter's account truth is not the adequation of human and divine mind's, but rather that of mind and object.[101]

Another indication that Thomas is not nearly so unlike his contemporaries as historians usually suggest, is found in another Parisian sentence commentary surviving from the period – albeit that of Thomas's bachelor student, Annibald d'Annibald, composed between 1258 and 1260.[102] Annibald (d. 1272) became regent in the school, occupying the chair for foreigners between 1260 and 1262, before he was created a cardinal by Pope Urban IV. Annibald's discussion of the nature of Theology reflects a Dominican concern with the unbeliever, and as such internalises and explores the implications of his master's positions. Like Thomas and Peter of Tarentaise, Annibald equates articles of faith with first principles in other sciences. Following Thomas's commentary on the *De Trinitate* of Boethius, Annibald states that the articles of faith are received from God through the mode of belief as from a superior science that God knows but we do not.[103] They are not known by natural reason but through the light of faith.[104] It is a reflection of God's self-knowledge by which we might become God-like, partially in this life and completely in the next.[105] Unlike other first principles, however, the articles of faith are not indubitable for our minds until we are glorified in heaven, when we see God face to face.[106]

Once again, this is the most noble science to which all others must be ordained and subject.[107] God is the interior teacher in so far as God has placed the first principles of all knowledge in the natural light of the soul and has revealed to the soul the articles of faith by the light of grace. Though it was given to the human creature to administer knowledge to others by drawing conclusions from commonly held principles, it is only those assigned by the Church who are permitted to expose scripture, destroy error and correct the faithful.[108]

Annibald goes on to ask whether a teaching that is above the natural light of reason is necessary. Aristotle himself states that the rational creature ought to seek divine things as much as possible. Since divine and immortal things exceed the faculty of reason, the human creature ought to pursue those things that exceed the rational faculty.[109] Yet it would be pointless to pursue those things which lie outside of the rational faculty's comprehension and apprehension. With divine aid, however, the divine things that defy comprehension can be apprehended. According to Aristotle, those small things that might be known concerning the divine are worth more than all that can be known concerning other things.[110]

Annibald then asks whether reason can be used to fortify faith. There are four possible ways in which arguments can be used with respect to faith: demonstration, manifestation, reproof and approbation. Demonstration, however, is not possible as things of faith cannot be comprehended.[111] Faith should not be assented to on account of reason, but reason may be used to defend faith against error and to refute detractors.[112] Though all desire truth, truth is able to offend when it makes manifest iniquity in others.[113]

Annibald next asks whether it is blameworthy when reason follows the will. His Franciscan contemporaries implied that reason did, in that rational perception depended upon prior spiritual orientation. Though in matters of faith, Annibald says, reason must follow the assent of the will, the will ought always to be subject to the good. The good, however, moves the will in accordance with the apprehension of reason. This occurs in two ways. It follows reason explicitly when reason by itself decides that something should be chosen or avoided. It follows reason implicitly when reason judges that something should be chosen or avoided according to the dictates of God – even though God is not known to reason directly. The will therefore implicitly follows the mind in matters of faith, and it is reprehensible when reason follows the will.[114] Diversity of opinion in matters of reason results from complacency. Desiring one opinion the enquirer collects arguments which support that opinion but neglects arguments which support its contrary.[115] As Annibald has already made clear, however, that subjection of reason is wrong. It is indicative of the ways in which Franciscan and Dominican identities were constructed dialogically that the Franciscan priority of the will over intellect was only made explicit from the time of John Peckham, a Franciscan master of the late 1260s and early 1270s. Thenceforth it was to become a key aspect of Franciscan teaching.[116]

In dealing with the natural knowledge of the highest good, the question of proportion between the finite and the infinite again frames the discussion.[117] Annibald endorses the doctrine that the rational soul apprehends but does not comprehend the Creator, and quotes Boethius after Thomas: 'every knower has knowledge concerning a thing known according to the mode of the knower, not according to the mode of the thing known.'[118]

Is the existence of God, therefore, self-evident? It would seem so, since according to John of Damascus the knowledge of God's existence is naturally inserted within the soul, and God is united to the soul through God's self.[119] Moreover, Anselm has said that God cannot be thought not to exist.[120] Annibald responds in the same way as Thomas. When considered by the mode according to God's self, God's existence is self-evident since God's essence is to be. The mode of knowledge according to us, however, is two-fold. God can be known either according to a similitude and participation or according to God's own nature. Though the existence of truth is self-evident to the mind, the mind knows only a similitude of the first truth and not the first truth itself. The knowledge that the mind can have of God's nature is a conclusion from demonstration, and is therefore not a self-evident truth.[121]

The natural insertion within the mind is a created copy of the first truth, and not what is in the nature of God.[122] God is present to the soul, but not as an object of the understanding.[123] Finally, Anselm's argument is not cogent because it presupposes what it is supposed to prove – namely, that God exists.[124] The knowledge of God is gained through God's effects – namely creatures. It is closed only to beasts without reason and to those in heaven who see God in essence. The knowledge of God through the medium of creatures is otherwise open to good and evil alike.[125]

Thomas's bachelor student, Annibald d'Annibald and the bachelor student of his direct contemporaries, Peter of Tarentaise, both suggest that Thomas's teachings were not nearly so radical within the Dominican context as they might have seemed among his Franciscan contemporaries. There is one contemporary of Thomas, however, who was a master at Bologna during the late 1250s and early 1260s who makes this argument somewhat more convincing. Surprisingly, he has been neglected by Thomist scholars and by historians of medieval thought alike. Perhaps possessing the inauspicious name of Bombolognous of Bologna ensured that he would always be doomed to obscurity.[126] In any case, it is once again the obscurity of Bombolognous that makes him interesting. Bombolognous asks similar questions to Thomas and adopts very similar positions. It is of course possible that Bombolognous may yet have been entirely indebted to Thomas for the positions that he adopted. However, in the light of the fact that Thomas never taught at Bologna, it might also be suggested that Thomas himself was addressing questions that already had a wider currency within his order. Besides Albertus Magnus, it is possible to find at least one other former Regent Master of Paris, who anticipated Thomas's concern with the Aristotelian account of nature, and the relationship of faith and reason. Perhaps it is no coincidence to find that Roland of Cremona (d. 1259) had been teaching and preaching in Bologna since his departure from Toulouse in 1233.[127] At the very least, it can be said that Bombolognous's commentary provides support for the view that teachers like Roland of Cremona (and Thomas's contemporaries Barthelemy of Tours and Hugh of Metz also?) had prepared the ground for a wider receptivity to Thomas than is usually appreciated.[128]

Like Thomas, Peter and Annibald, Bombolognous begins his sentence commentary by arguing for the necessity of a science beyond physics, necessary for the perfection of the human creature, which is revealed by God and unattainable by reason alone.[129] Like the others, Bombolognous also argues that theology should use arguments where its adversaries do not accept sacred authorities.[130]

In his discussion of the knowledge of God's existence, Bombolognous considers objections to the created intellect coming to a knowledge of the Creator. Given that intellectual knowledge is derived from the senses and God is not available to the senses, the intellect is unable to know God. Furthermore, given (as Augustine says) that we can only judge concerning inferiors we cannot judge concerning God.[131] The finite cannot reach the infinite but the divine is infinite and the knowledge of the creature is finite.[132] Finally, the distance between the Creator and the created intelligence is greater than the distance between the created intelligence and the senses, yet the senses cannot comprehend the intelligence. How then, can the created intelligence comprehend God?[133] Against this, the Scriptures declare that God is known by reason from the things that are made.[134]

After responding to the objections, like his Parisian contemporaries distinguishing between apprehension and comprehension, Bombolognous turns to the question of whether God's existence is a self-evident truth.[135] It would seem to be so since, as Boethius says, everyone desires the highest good. Yet what is not known cannot be desired.[136] Those things that are self-evident to us are naturally inserted. The knowledge of God, according to John of Damascus is naturally inserted in us.[137] Thirdly, in a derivation of Anselm's argument, Bombolognous states that God is God's own being. Yet it is not possible to think that something both is and is not what it is.[138]

Against this position, Bombolognous argues that the conclusion of a demonstration cannot be self-evident.[139] While Anselm declares that God cannot be thought not to exist, this can be said outwardly.[140] Avicenna, Boethius and Anselm say, God's being is included in God's quiddity; it is not an addition. However, since the quiddity of God is not self-evident to us because of the distance between God and our sensory apprehension, God's existence is not self-evident to us but requires demonstration. Only in heaven, will God be known as self-evidently as the difference between affirmation and negation.[141] In response to the arguments in favour of the proposition, Bombolognous teaches that although all desire the highest good, it is not God that is desired distinctly, but only what is reasonable.[142] To the argument that the knowledge of God's existence is naturally inserted within the soul, Bombolognous argues that what is inserted is the natural reason which is able to come to a knowledge of God's existence through demonstration from effects.[143] To the argument that God's existence is predicated of God's quiddity, Bombolognous reiterates that God's quiddity is unknown to us.[144]

Finally, Bombolognous considers whether the knowledge of God's existence can be known through the medium of creatures. Quoting Romans 1, Bombolognous affirms the existence of creatures as a medium for knowing the existence of God.[145] His consideration of this question and the objections reveal a shared concern with the Dionysian corpus.[146] In response to the objection that the soul itself as the highest creature could not use lesser creatures as a medium to God, Bombolognous insists on the dependence upon inference from sense knowledge not only for knowledge of God, but for the soul's knowledge of its very self.[147]

Peter, Annibald and Bombolognous illustrate that, at the very least, there was a receptivity to Thomas's teaching among his earliest contemporaries. The evidence of the treatment of Anselm's argument, even in Peter's more conciliatory approach, illustrates that the central aspects of Thomas's thought were already being accepted within the Dominican order. The evidence strongly supports one of the central claims of this book, namely that Thomas expressed the interests of the wider Dominican order. He did so by articulating an account of the natural knowledge of God that was the metaphysical counterpart of Dominican religious life. That religious life was one which rejected excessive concern with subjective and personal approaches to God, in favour of one which emphasised the objectivity of the natural knowledge of God and the possibility of edifying the souls of others by leading them to God through argument. That this account provided the metaphysical account of the Dominican imitation of Christ is brought out especially by the *Summa contra gentiles* – a work that was composed within a context in which Thomas's teachings already received broad acceptance.

## III

Just as Bonaventure had given the Franciscan project its most detailed articulation to date in the *Journey of the Soul into God*, Thomas gave the Dominican strategy its most detailed expression in the *Summa contra gentiles* at roughly the same time. Thomas began this work by defining the office of the wise and prefacing his discussion with a proverb ideally suited to a Dominican conception of wisdom: 'My mouth shall meditate truth, and my lips shall hate impiety.'[148] While artisans who know arts that rule other arts appropriate for themselves the title of the wise: 'the name of the absolutely wise is reserved for those whose consideration is directed to the end of the universe, which is also the origin of the universe.'[149]

Since the end of each thing, Thomas says, is that which is intended by its first author or mover and the first author or mover of the universe is an intellect, the ultimate end of the universe must be the good of an intellect. Such a good is truth. 'Truth must consequently be the ultimate end of the whole universe, and the consideration of the wise aims principally at truth.'[150] It is to make the truth known that God came into the world in flesh: 'For this I was born, and for this I came into the world, so that I should give testimony to the truth' (John 18:37). Hence, for Thomas, the most authentic expression of Christianity – Christ himself – is one in which truth is taught:

> Appropriately, therefore, is the twofold office of the wise shown from the mouth of Wisdom in our opening words: to meditate and speak forth of the divine truth, which is truth in person (Wisdom touches on this in the words *my mouth shall meditate truth*), and to refute the opposing error (which Wisdom touches on in the words *my lips shall hate impiety*). By impiety here is meant falsehood against the divine truth.[151]

Having defined the office of the Wise – what is in fact the Dominican 'imitation of Christ' – Thomas states that his intention is to embark upon this office. This is because, despite the weaknesses that would prevent him, the pursuit of wisdom is more perfect, more noble, more useful and more full of joy than all other human pursuits.[152] It is more perfect because in pursuing wisdom the person already has some share in beatitude; more noble because through this pursuit a person more especially approaches the likeness of God. 'And since likeness is the cause of love, the pursuit of wisdom especially joins a person to God in friendship.' It is more useful, for through it a person arrives at immortality, and it is more full of joy because 'her conversation has no bitterness, nor her company any tediousness, but joy and gladness' (Wisdom, 7:16).[153]

Hence, in Thomas's account, like that of Bonaventure, the appropriation of Wisdom entails the acquisition of likeness to God. However, in Thomas's account, the pursuit of Wisdom is not conceived as a turning of the soul towards itself and then into God, but rather as a means of joining the subject to God in friendship and as a 'conversation' that leads to gladness, beatitude and immortality. Echoing St Dominic and Humbert of Romans, Thomas justifies his intentions to pursue Wisdom despite his weaknesses because, 'to use the words of Hilary: I am aware that I owe this to God as the chief duty of my life, that my every word and sense may speak of God'.[154] Thomas specifies the particular parties he would want to address. He mentions Jews and Heretics, but more specifically, the Muslims, for whom, he says, rational argument is particularly necessary.[155] While Jews could be confronted with the Old Testament, and Heretics with the New, Muslims and pagans accepted neither.[156] 'We must, therefore, have recourse to natural reason, to which all men are forced to give their assent.'[157]

This statement in the prologue to the *Summa* has tended to be pushed aside by historians in the wake of René-Antoine Gauthier's demolition of the traditional view that this work was composed at the request of Raymond of Pennyafort for the conversion of Muslims in Spain.[158] Besides the refutation of the textual argument for the missionary legend, Gauthier also stresses, that there is very little within the *Summa* itself to suggest that Aquinas was concerned with refuting the beliefs of either Heretics, Jews, Pagans or Muslims.[159] When Aquinas refers to 'pagans' he is referring exclusively to the pagans of the ancient world, though he is concerned in the *Summa* not with refuting pagan religious beliefs, but the philosophical views of pre-Aristotelian, and especially pre-Socratic, philosophers.[160] After the reference to the refutation of Jews in the second chapter of the first book of *Summa*, Thomas omits to mention the word 'Jews' in the rest of the work. He refers to Jewish philosophers Maimonides and Isaac Israeli only briefly for individual philosophical errors.[161] Even more strikingly, the *Summa* nowhere contains the detailed knowledge and refutation of the errors of the Koran which we would expect if it had been consecrated to the task of converting Muslims. The refutation of Islamic philosophers takes a critical place within the *Summa contra gentiles.* Yet, Gauthier writes, if Aquinas thought that he was contributing to the conversion of Muslims by refuting the philosophical errors of Averroës or Avicenna, he could not have been more wrong. The majority of Muslim people were no more acquainted with philosophical ideas than ordinary Christians. If Thomas was concerned with targeting philosophers they were those who resided in and around Paris itself.[162] The unbelievers with whom Aquinas is most concerned in the *Summa contra gentiles* are heretics – whom, he has said already, could be refuted by reference to Scripture.[163]

Following on from Gauthier, Norman Kretzmann puts forward the additional argument that books I-III of the *Summa* are concerned with theism rather than with specific teachings of Christianity, and as such contain little or nothing that Muslims would object to. If Thomas had intended the work for a Muslim audience, therefore, he was wasting his time until he got to book four which contains probable arguments relating to the doctrines of the Trinity and Incarnation.[164]

In refuting the missionary hypothesis, however, both Gauthier and Kretzmann erect particular accounts of the missionary goal, and assume that the job of apologetics is always to attack and refute the beliefs of unbelievers. Moreover, Kretzmann reads Thomas's natural theology as if it were, and could only be, intended for providing rational foundations for theistic belief.[165] Both sets of assumptions prescribe the roles of natural theology and of apologetics without considering how these actually functioned in the context of the Dominican order during this period. For one thing, Dominican missionaries were in fact mostly concerned with targeting subject peoples in territories already conquered by Christians, usually during and after crusades, and with adding rational arguments to the more physical and material forms of persuasion already applied to the subject population. In such a context, as well as arguing against specific Jewish and Muslim beliefs, the objective was to make Christianity appear more palatable to Jewish and Muslim peoples subject to Christian authority.[166] In such a context, the last thing Thomas would have been concerned to do was insult his audience, or at least, the audience of the preachers he was involved in training – even if, in practice, that is what normally happened.

Top of Thomas's agenda, was overturning the specific objections which Jews and Muslims had against Christianity. Kretzmann is right to point out that neither Thomas nor any of his contemporaries would have felt any need to convince Muslims that God exists. As John Clayton has written, however, it would seem more likely that by rehearsing proof for God's existence, Thomas was defending an account of God's unity so cherished by his Muslim contemporaries, but which was nonetheless compatible with the Christian doctrine of the Trinity. Such arguments would thereby provide a common platform for building more specifically Christian arguments.[167] Indeed, it is noteworthy that when Thomas presented arguments for God's existence in the first book, he did so not in their original Aristotelian form, but in the form they took after they had passed through the hands of near-contemporary Arab commentators.[168] Had such arguments been directed toward Muslims in newly-conquered Christian territories they would have been reassured that becoming Christian did not involve giving up beliefs that they already held, or committing the sin of polytheism.[169]

The very act of setting out the truth of Christian faith in this way serves to set aside errors contrary to Christian belief – particularly errors *about* Christian belief. In this case, the biggest obstacle to Muslims in newly conquered territories accepting Christian belief was the Muslim conviction that Christianity involved compromising the unity of God. It was therefore precisely because of the missionary strategy of the Dominican order, and not in spite of it, that Thomas reserved discussion of the most disputed doctrines between Christians and Muslims until the fourth and last book of the *Summa.* That was after he had expressed the doctrine of God in a way acceptable to both traditions.

This is not an argument for singling out the *Summa contra gentiles* as a missionary work, however, but rather for seeing the *Summa* as an articulation of the approach to the unbeliever embedded in the Dominican vocation generally, and particularly as it was formulated in the natural theology of Thomas and his Dominican contemporaries. At least one merit of this view is that it makes sense of Thomas's explicit references to the conviction of Muslims by means of reason. If his project in the *Summa contra gentiles* was not intended to carry any implications for missionary activity, it is difficult to see why he would have mentioned unbelievers at all, not merely in passing, but in his account of the whole purpose of the office of the wise, and the very purpose of the incarnation itself. Natural theology in Thomas's writing, and in the writings of his near contemporaries at Paris and Bologna, is intrinsically concerned with edifying the souls of others, by directing them to a particular conception of God, or the proper end for human life. In directing others toward that end, he was also directing them away from philosophical conceptions that did no justice to the God of tradition – particularly those of Averroës.

In the third chapter of the *Summa contra gentiles*, Thomas defines the relationship between truths known to natural reason and truths known through revelation in accordance with his conception of the office of the wise and the aims of his discourse. There is a two-fold truth that we profess concerning God – those things known both through revelation and reason, and those things known only through revelation.[170] As with the Dominican sentence commentaries, the *Summa* is concerned to show that it is reasonable to have faith in revelation though it contain things that surpass reason.[171] Since both modes of truth have the same origin, the one cannot contradict the other.[172] Although there are truths of faith which, belonging only to revelation, cannot be proven by means of argument, these can at least be defended against detractors. This is because arguments that contradict revealed truth must be improperly derived from first principles: reason itself cannot contradict the truth revealed by God.[173]

Unlike Bonaventure, for whom articles of faith can also become objects of understanding without ceasing to be objects of faith, Thomas sharply distinguishes between articles of faith and demonstrations of reason. Things demonstrable by reason are included within revelation and can be accepted by faith, but they are no longer accepted on faith once they have been reached by reason. His treatment of the natural knowledge of God again explicitly rejects the view that God's existence may be self-evident and therefore incapable of demonstration. Thus Thomas removes the metaphysical basis of the approach to theology outlined by his Franciscan colleagues. When God is not a direct object of human knowledge, faith cannot be an object of understanding either. God is not the first object of the human mind, but is an inference from nature that is known equally to believers and unbelievers. While faith may temporally precede knowledge it does not contribute to that knowledge epistemically or logically. It is for that reason that natural theology becomes a discourse capable of transcending religious boundaries.

After eliminating the view that God's existence is self-evident, using the arguments we have already examined and with which Thomas's contemporaries were now familiar, Thomas elaborates at length arguments for God's existence of which he does approve. Once again, these reflect a set of religious priorities different from those of Thomas's Franciscan contemporaries. Whereas the Franciscans stressed the priority of the soul's direct relationship with God over its knowledge of all else, Thomas, following Albert, emphasised a different way of 'seeing' God. The natural knowledge of God is attained, for Thomas, not by means of an introspection that transcends the body, but by inference from nature for which the soul is dependent upon the bodily senses. The empirical source of the proof does not emphasise the mutability of things, but rather their inner necessity. God is not related to this world as that which prevents it from slipping into non-being. God has given being to the world and can take that being away, but the being it has been given has necessary and immutable principles in and of itself. The process of generation and corruption is the outworking of necessary, and not merely contingent, principles, although the necessity here is a created necessity.[174]

Moreover, the God inferred from the knowledge of the senses is a God of causation and of government:

> Contrary and discordant things cannot, always or for the most part, be parts of one order except under someone's government, which enables all and each to tend to a definite end. But in the world we find that things of diverse natures come together under one order, and this not rarely or by chance, but always or for the most part. There must therefore be some being by whose providence the world is governed. This we call God.[175]

In the third book of the *Summa contra gentiles*, Thomas states that our supreme glory is to be helpers of God by means of the causality that we exercise. Following the Pseudo-Dionysius, Thomas argues, 'the most divine thing of all is to become a co-operator with God'.[176] It is no coincidence that within Dominican tradition 'God's co-worker' was already becoming an epithet for the preacher.[177] Hence, Thomas's rejection of Anselm's argument was integral to an account of God encapsulating a very different form of spiritual life and an approach to natural knowledge which that form of life entailed. To adopt the office of the wise, as Thomas does in the *Summa contra gentiles*, is in fact to conform to the image of the intellectual agent that governs the world, and to co-operate with God in the act of ruling and ordering things toward their proper end in God. In leading rational creatures to God, the Dominican adopts the office of the wise, and imitates Christ, the incarnated Word.

## IV

Thomas's rejection of Anslem's argument carried conviction within the Dominican order because of its place within a wider account of the natural knowledge of God and the place of that, in turn, within the wider context of the Dominican religious life. Thomas's account of the natural knowledge of God was one that reflected the interests of those sensitive to the central traditions of the Dominican order. Any account of the natural knowledge of God defines the status of natural knowledge and its relationship with revealed knowledge. Thomas's account underpins a particular account of the relationship between natural reason and revealed truth that was essential for the religious life of the Dominican order.

As the last thing known to reason, the existence of God is not a truth that is implied in all the intellect's natural knowledge. Moreover, the presence of God to the world is not proclaimed by the mutability of creatures. The knowledge of God is not a key to the knowledge of nature, therefore, though the very workings of nature point to the existence of God. It is for that reason that understanding nature does not depend upon faith. Furthermore, it is precisely because of its separation from faith that natural reason can be used to defend faith without risk of undermining either faith or reason. Thomas's account of the natural knowledge of God therefore involves an account of reason, and is driven by a strategy with respect to the non-believer that suits an order committed to preaching by word of mouth.

By criticising Anselm's argument as it had been used by his contemporaries, Thomas was questioning the consistency of a particular view of God – both with Christian teaching and with human knowledge more generally. On both counts, Thomas found the Franciscan arguments to be deficient. God is not self-evident to the soul, since – as the Scriptures teach – we have no vision of God in this life. Moreover, God's existence is not a self-evident truth since it is capable of being denied and of being the conclusion of a demonstration. If Thomas was right to reject Anselm's argument, however, not only the Franciscan account of the natural knowledge of God, but a key assumption of Franciscan spirituality would be undermined. And for this reason, before long, Franciscans and others whose spiritual priorities were akin to those of St Francis, sprang to the defence of the argument.

## Notes

1. J. Châtillon, 'De Guillaume d'Auxerre à Saint Thomas d'Aquin: L'Argument de Saint Anselme chez les Premiers Scolastiques du xiii[e] Siècle', in *Spicilegium Beccense*, vol. 1 (1959), 209-231. A. C. Pegis, 'St Anselm and the Argument of the *Proslogion*', in *Medieval Studies*, 28 (1966), 228-267.
2. A. C. Pegis, 'Four Medieval Ways to God', in *The Monist*, 54 (1970), 317-358 (329).
3. For Thomas's early life, see J. A. Weisheipl, *Friar Thomas d'Aquino* (Washington D. C., 1983), pp. 4-36.
4. Ibid., pp. 36-37.
5. Ibid., pp. 49-50. The Dominican order considered the years of biblical study in the convent already completed before a student was sent to Paris, sufficient to allow their

students to forgo the cursory reading of the bible as *baccalaurius biblicus* mandatory upon other students in the Faculty of Theology.

6. D. Burrell, 'Aquinas and Islamic and Jewish Thinkers', in *The Cambridge Companion to Aquinas*, ed. by N. Kretzmann and E. Stump (Cambridge, 1994), pp. 60-84 (62).
7. Thomas Aquinas, St, *Scriptum in primum librum sententiarum*, in *Opera Omnia*, ed. by T. P. Fiaccodori (Parma, 1852-1873; reprinted in Musurgia 1948-1950), VI, Prologus, quaestio i, articulus i.
8. Ibid., prologus q. i, art. i, sed contra, 2, 3.
9. Ibid., q. i, art. i, conclusio; et ad obiecta, 1-3.
10. See, for example, B. P. Gaybba, *Aspects of the Medieval History of Theology* (Pretoria, 1988), p. 135. In other words, Theology is a science subalternated to God's own knowledge.
11. As W. J. Hankey, *God in Himself* (Oxford, 1987), pp. 71-72 and others have pointed out, Aquinas reverses the order in which Pseudo-Dionysius places the ways of eminence, denial and causality to suit a scheme which begins with God's existence as the first part of the process of naming God.
12. Thomas Aquinas, *Scriptum in I sententiarum*, d. iii, div. 1ae partis textus.
13. Ibid., d. iii, q. i, art. i.
14. Ibid., q. i, art. i, 2.
15. Ibid., q. i, art. i, 3.
16. Ibid., q. i, art. i, 4.
17. Ibid., q. i, art. i, 5.
18. Ibid., q. i, art. i, concl.
19. Ibid., q. i, art. ii, 1.
20. Ibid., q. i, art. ii, 2.
21. Ibid., q. i, art. ii, 3.
22. Ibid., q. i, art. ii, sed contra 1.
23. Ibid., q. i, art. ii, sed contra 2.
24. Ibid.
25. Ibid., q. i, art. ii, respondeo 1.
26. Ibid., q. i, art. ii, respondeo 2.
27. Ibid., q. i, art. ii, respondeo 3.
28. Ibid., q. i, art. ii, respondeo 4.
29. On St Thomas's distinction between the judgement and conceptualisation of existence see J. Owens, 'Aquinas on Knowing Existence', in J. Owens, *St Thomas Aquinas on the Existence of God: collected Papers of Joseph Owens, C.Ss.R.*, ed. by J. R. Catan (Albany, 1980), pp. 20-33, esp. 27-28.
30. See also J. Owens, 'Aquinas and the Five Ways', in Owens, *St Thomas*, pp. 132-141, esp. 138ff.
31. Thomas Aquinas, *Expositio in librum Boethii de Trinitate*, ed. by B. Decker (Leiden, 1955), pars i, q. i, art. iii, 1: 'Videtur quod primum, quod a mente cognoscitur, sit deus. illud enim, in quo omnia alia cognoscuntur et per quod de omnibus quae cognoscimus iudicamus, est primo cognitum a nobis sicut, lux est primo nota oculo quam ea, quae per lucem videntur, et principia intellectui prius quam conclusiones.

Sed omnia in prima veritate cognoscuntur et per ipsam de omnibus iudicamus, ut augustinus dicit in libro de trinitate et de vera religione. "ergo prima veritas, scilicet deus, est id quod primo a nobis cognoscitur." Ibid., pars i, q. i, art. iii, 6: "Praeterea naturaliter cognita et quae non possunt intelligi non esse sunt illa quae primo nostrae cognitioni occurrunt. 'Sed cognitio exsistendi deum naturaliter est omnibus inserta', ut dicit damascenus, 'nec potest deus cogitari non esse', ut dicit anselmus. Ergo deus est primum quod a nobis cognoscitur."'

32. Ibid., pars i, q. i, art. iii: sed contra 1.
33. Ibid., sed contra 2.
34. Ibid., conclusio, 1.
35. Ibid., conclusio, 2.
36. Ibid., respondeo 1 and 5.
37. Ibid., conclusio 3.
38. Ibid., respondeo 6.
39. For Thomas's doctrine of participation and the place of exemplarism within his thought, see Wippel, J. F., 'Thomas Aquinas and Participation', in *Studies in Medieval Philosophy*, ed. by J. F. Wippel (Washington, D. C., 1987), pp. 117-158.
40. Thomas Aquinas, *Scriptum in I librum sententiarum*, d. iii, q. i, art. iii, concl., and sed contra 8.
41. Ibid., d. iii, div. 1ae partis textus.
42. Thomas Aquinas, *On Being and Essence*, ed. and trans. by A. Maurer (Toronto, 1949), p. 47.
43. Cf. J. Owens, 'Aquinas and the Five Ways', in Owens, *St Thomas*, p. 138.
44. Cf. J. Owens, 'Aristotle and Aquinas', in *The Cambridge Companion to Aquinas*, ed. by N. Kretzmann and E. Stump (Cambridge, 1993), pp. 38-59.
45. For a broader account of this distinction, as well as its origins, see D. B. Burrell *Knowing the Unknowable God: Ibin Sina, Maimonides, Aquinas* (Notre Dame, 1986).
46. Thomas Aquinas, *Scriptum in I sent.*, d. iii, div. 1ae partis textus.
47. See Burrell, *Knowing the Unknowable* and also, by the same author, 'Aquinas and Islamic and Jewish thinkers', in *The Cambridge Companion to Aquinas*, op. cit., pp. 60-84.
48. Thomas Aquinas, *Scriptum in I sent.*, d. iii, q. i, art. iii, concl., and sed contra 8.
49. On the parallels between Thomas and Moses Maimonides on faith and knowledge, see Burrell's 'Aquinas and Islamic and Jewish thinkers', and *Knowing the Unknowable God.*
50. See, for example, Frederick Van Steenberghen, *The Philosophical Movement in the Thirteenth Century* (Edinburgh, 1955), pp. 94-103.
51. P. Glorieux *Répertoire des Maitres en Théologie de Paris au XIIIe Siècle*, 2 vols (Paris, 1933), I, n. 17.
52. See ibid., I, nos. 15-17.
53. Peter of Tarentaise (Innocentii Quinti), *In IV libros sententiarum commentaria*, ed. by T. Turci and J. B. de Marinis (Toulouse, 1652), lib. I, prol., art. i, ad obi. 3.
54. Ibid., prol. art. v.
55. Ibid., art. v, 1-3.

56. Ibid., art. v, sed contra 1.
57. Ibid., art. v, sed contra 2.
58. Ibid., art. v, respondeo.
59. Ibid., art. v, ad obi. 1.
60. Ibid., art. v, ad obi. 2.
61. Ibid., art. v, ad obi. 3.
62. Ibid., art. vi, sed contra 2.
63. Ibid., art. vi, respondeo.
64. Ibid., art. vi, ad obi. 2.
65. Ibid., art. vi, ad obi. 2.
66. Ibid., art. vi, ad obi. 3-4.
67. See Hankey, p. 139, which discusses Thomas's re-ordering of the four causes to suit his own purposes.
68. Peter of Tarentaise, *In IV libros sent. commentaria*, lib. I, dist. iii, quaest. i, art. i, 1-7.
69. Ibid., dist. iii, q. i, art. i, sed contra 1.
70. Ibid., art. i, sed contra 2.
71. Ibid., art. i, sed contra 3.
72. Ibid., art. i, sed contra 4.
73. Ibid., art. i, sed contra 5.
74. Ibid., art. i, respondeo.
75. Ibid., art. i, ad obi. 1.
76. Ibid., art. i, ad obi. 2.
77. Ibid., art. i, ad obi. 3.
78. Ibid., art. i, ad obi. 4.
79. Ibid., art. i, ad obi. 5.
80. Ibid., art. i, ad obi. 6-7.
81. Ibid., art. ii.
82. Ibid., art. ii, 1.
83. Ibid., art. ii, 2.
84. Ibid., art. ii, 3-4.
85. Ibid., art. ii, 7.
86. Ibid., art. ii, sed contra 1.
87. Ibid., art. ii, sed contra 2.
88. Ibid., art. ii, sed contra 3.
89. Ibid., art. ii, sed contra 4.
90. Ibid., art. ii, respondeo.
91. Ibid., art. ii, ad obi. 1.
92. Ibid., art. ii, ad obi. 2.
93. Ibid., art. ii, ad obi. 3.
94. Ibid., art. ii, ad obi. 4. 'Nihil est, quod non possit cogitari non esse etc. Resp. Cogitari Deum non esse potest intelligi dupliciter secundum Anselmum. Aut quod cogitatur oratio hoc significans, aut quia cogitatur res significata: et hoc dupliciter, aut in ratione speciali, qua dicitur Deus; aut in ratione generali, qua dicitur veritas, bonitas et huiusmodi: duobus primis modis Deus potest cogitari non esse: ultimo modo non

potest, ita quod intelligatur id, quod cogitatur: non enim potest cogitari veritas non esse: cum hoc cogitari non possit, nisi veritate existente.'

95. Though this is difficult to verify, I take it to be evidenced by the massive number of manuscripts containing the work surviving from the period and scattered among libraries throughout Europe. See Glorieux, *Répertoire*, I, n. 17.
96. Peter of Tarentaise *In IV libros*, lib. I, dist. iii, quaest. ii, art. i, respondeo.
97. Ibid., dist. iii, q. ii, art. i, ad obiecta 1.
98. Ibid., art. i, ad obi. 3.
99. Ibid., art. i, ad obi. 3.
100. Ibid., art. i, ad obi. 4.
101. Ibid., dist. viii, quaest. ii, art. ii, respondeo.
102. Glorieux, *Répertoire*, I, n. 19. Annibald d'Annibald's *Scriptum super libris magistri sententiarum* has been published among Thomas Aquinas's *opuscula dubia* in Thomas Aquinas, *Opera Omnia*, ed. by T. P. Fiaccodori (Parma, 1852-1873; reprinted in Musurgia, 1948-1950), XXII.
103. Annibald d'Annibald, *Scriptum super libris magistri sententiarum*, lib. I, prologus, quaest. i, art. i, respondeo.
104. Ibid., prol., q. i, art. i, ad obi. 1.
105. Ibid., q. i, art. i, ad obi. 2.
106. Ibid., art. i, ad obi. 3.
107. Ibid., art. ii, respondeo.
108. Ibid., art. iv, respondeo.
109. Ibid., q. iii, art. i, sed contra 2.
110. Ibid., q. iii, art. i, respondeo.
111. Ibid., q. iii, art. ii, respondeo.
112. Ibid., q. iii, art. ii, ad obi. 4.
113. Ibid., q. iii, art. iii, respondeo.
114. Ibid., q. iii, art. iv, respondeo.
115. Ibid., q. iii, art. v, respondeo.
116. On John Peckham's teaching on the will, and its development by later Franciscans like Richard of Middleton and Duns Scotus, see D. E. Sharp, *Franciscan Philosophy in the Thirteenth Century* (Oxford, 1930), and infra, Ch. 6.
117. Annibald d'Annibald, *Scriptum*, dist. iii, quaest. i, art. i, ad 1.
118. Ibid., q. i, art. i, respondeo.
119. Ibid., art. ii, 1-2.
120. Ibid., art. ii, 3.
121. Ibid., art. ii, respondeo.
122. Ibid., art. ii, ad obi. 1.
123. Ibid., art. ii, ad obi. 2.
124. Ibid., art. ii, ad obi. 3.
125. Ibid., q. ii, art. i, respondeo.
126. See Frederick Stegmueller, *Repertorium Commentariorum In Sententias Petri Lombardi* (Wurzburg, 1937), p. 108, and T. Kaeppeli, *Scriptores Ordinis Praedicatorum Medii Aevi* (Rome, 1970-1993), I, 246-247. According to both

Stegmueller and Kaeppeli, Bombolognous composed his commentary on the sentences sometime between 1256 and 1265.

127. F. J. Roensch, *Early Thomistic School* (Iowa, 1964), does not consider Peter, Annibald or Bombolognous although the first two preceded and the third of these was – at latest – contemporaneous with Bernard of Trilla whom Roensch considers to be the first 'Thomist' at Paris. For Bernard of Trilla, see infra, ch. 6.
128. Glorieux, I, n. 1.
129. Bologna Universitaria MS. 753 (1506), fol. 5v: prologue, q. 5, 'Ad aliud de perfectione dicundum (est) quod humanus ad altiorem finem ordinatur quam aliis creaturis quamuis pluribus auxiliis indigerat ad ipsum. Consequenter... physica sola non sufficiatur humano tangere perfectionem.'
130. Ibid., fol. 6r: prologue, q. 6, 'Sed contra. Laudabile est fidem defendere contra adversarios quod non potest fieri auctoribus quia non recipiuntur. Ergo ordinata quod fiat rationibus.'
131. Ibid., fol. 13r., lib. I, dist. iii, art. i, i. 'Sed Deus nec sensibilis est nec sua species potest intellectu informari. Nec de deo est potest iudicium haberi quia vero dicitur Augustinus in "de vera religione" non est iudicium nisi est iudicium de inferiori… ergo. etc.'
132. Ibid., d. iii, art. i, ii. 'Finita non transeat super infinitum. Sed divina est infinita et omnis ait cognitio creaturae est finita... ergo etc.'
133. Ibid., d. iii, art. i, iii. 'Plus distat intelligibilis increatus ab intellectu nostro quam intelligibile quamquam creatu ab sensu [nostro]. Sed nullus intelligibilis creatus potest cognosci a sensu.. ergo etc.'
134. Ibid., d. iii, art. i, sed contra.
135. Ibid., fol. 13r., dist. iii, art. ii.
136. Ibid., d. iii, art. ii, 1. 'Ad secunda sic procedetur. Videtur quod deus esse per se notum quia secundum Boethium omnia desiderant summum bonum. Summum bonum solum deus est. Ergo omnia desiderant deum. Sed non potest desiderari quod non cognitum. Ergo etc.'
137. Ibid., fol. 13v, d. iii, art. ii, 2. 'Nobis per se nota quorum cognitio est nobis [quod] naturaliter inditat. Sed cognitio existendi deum omnibus naturaliter est inserta ut dicit damascenus. Ergo etc.'
138. Ibid., d. iii, art. ii, 3. 'Deum est ipsum esse suum. Sed non potest cogitari contravenire id [quod] de se ponatur ut quidam homo non sit homo. Ergo etc.'
139. Ibid., d. iii, art. ii, sed contra. 'Conclusio demonstrationis non est per se notum. Sed deum esse vero dicit Avicenna metaphysica id est probatio demonstrationis.'
140. Ibid., d. iii, art. ii, respondeo. 'Secundum Avicennam Deum esse non per se notum sed per demonstrationem scitum [est]. Sed ait Anselmus deum esse per se notum est... quia nullus possit intellectus interiori cogitare deum non esse quamuis hoc possit exteriori praetextiri.'
141. Ibid., d. iii, art. ii, respondeo. '...quia in deo id est quod est et sit ut dicit Boethius et idem talis Anselmus et quidem talis dicit vero avicenna esse enim divinitum nec additione sit quiditate... Sed quia quiditas dei non est nobis per se nota propter eius elongacionem ab sensu nostro, divinitas est sensibile non et non perciperi vero dicitur

potest... Ideo deum esse quo ad nos non est per se nota sed indiget demonstrationem. In autem Patria... deum esse videbitur multo amplius et nobis notum quam nunc sit per se notum quod affirmatio et negatio non sint similis.'

142. Ibid., d. iii, art. ii, ad obj. 2. 'Ad id ergo quod positio objicitur quod omnia desiderant deum didicitur quia summum bonum distincte desiderant uno modo in sui esse et sic non omnia desiderant deum sed sola rationalia.'
143. Ibid., d. iii, art. ii, ad obi. 3. 'Ad quod dicamus quod cognitio existendi deum dicitur naturaliter omnibus inserta... unum possit pervenire ad cognitione deum esse per naturalia ratio quia excogitatio ratione potest cognoscere ipsum esse; demonstratio enim demonstrat deum esse et demonstro quod per effectibus...'
144. Ibid., d. iii, art. ii, ad obi. 4. 'Ad quod positio respondeo quia est et si quiditas dei sit summum esse talis quiditas nobis ignota est.'
145. Ibid., d. iii, art. iiì, sed contra.
146. Ibid., d. iii, art. iii, respondeo. 'Quia ergo omnis cognitio est per assimilationem modo talis quod ex consideratione creaturarum aliqualiter possumus conscendire in dei cognitionem... Cognitio quod dei ex creaturis est tractatu secundam dionysionem, per eminationem, per causalitem, et per remissionem...'
147. Ibid., d. iii, art. iii, ad obj. 3. 'Ad sic didicitur quod ratio procedit quia intellectus noster se ipsum per se cognoscet non, enim se per se dum est in corpore non cognoscet nisi per accidentibus, videlicet per obiectibus acti sui. Philosophus de anima dicit quia intellectus est intelligibile sicut alia intelligibilia quia expositio communis dicit quod intellectus se intellegit per intentionem sicut alia intelligibilia...'
148. Thomas Aquinas, *Liber de Veritate Catholicae Fidei Contra Errores Infidelium Qui Dicitur Summa Contra Gentiles*, ed. by P. Marc, C. Pera and P. Caramello, 3 vols (Turin-Paris, 1967), I, lib. 1, c. 1.
149. Ibid.
150. Ibid.
151. Ibid.
152. Ibid., c. 2.
153. Ibid., c. 2 (1).
154. Ibid., c. 2 (2).
155. This point is made by John Clayton, 'Religions, Reasons and Gods', in *Religious Studies*, 23, n. 1 (1987), 1-17 (p. 12).
156. Thomas Aquinas, *Liber... Qui Dicitur Summa Contra Gentiles*, I, lib. I c. 2 (3): 'Thus, against the Jews we are able to argue by means of the Old Testament, while against heretics we are able to argue by means of the New Testament. But the Mohammedans and the pagans accept neither the one nor the other.'
157. Ibid.
158. An argument in favour of the view that Thomas wrote the work at the direct request of Raymond d' Pennyafort for missionary activity in Spain, is found in the introduction to the Paris-Turin, 1967 edition of the *Summa contra gentiles* used here, and usefully summarised in T. Murphy, 'The Date and Purpose of the *Contra Gentiles*,' *Heythrop Journal*, 10 (1969), 405-415. The authenticity of the legend upon which the argument

depends, is conclusively undermined by René-Antoine Gauthier O.P., *Saint Thomas d'Aquin, 'Somme contre Les Gentils': Introduction* (Editions Universitaires, 1993).

159. Gauthier, pp. 109ff.
160. Gauthier, pp. 109-115.
161. Gauthier, pp. 118-119.
162. Gauthier, pp. 119-130. This view is already widely accepted, and is defended, for example, by M. M. Gorce, 'La Lutte Contra Gentiles â Paris au XIIIe siècle', in *Mélanges Mandonnet* 2 vols, in *Bibliothéque Thomiste*, 13-14 (Paris, 1930), pp. 223-243.
163. Gauthier, pp. 130-142.
164. N. Kretzmann, *The Metaphysics of Theism: Aquinas's Natural Theology in "Summa contra gentiles I"* (Oxford, 1997), p. 50.
165. See Gauthier, pp. 109-142 and Kretzmann, *Metaphysics of Theism*, pp. 43-51.
166. See for example, N. Kedar, *Crusade and Mission: European Approaches to the Muslims* (Princeton, 1984), R. Chazan, *Daggers of Faith: Thirteenth-Century Christian Missionising and Jewish Response* (Berkeley, 1989), Idem, *Barcelona and Beyond: The Disputation of 1263 and Its Aftermath* (Berkeley, 1992), and J. Cohen, *The Friars and The Jews* (Cornell, 1982).
167. Clayton, 'Religions, Reasons and Gods', p. 12.
168. Ibid., p. 3.
169. The unity of God or Tawhid, expressed as 'God is one, there is no God but God,' is central to the Islamic tradition and to the social consciousness of Islamic culture. The root of the word Islam, *slm* in Arabic means 'to be in peace, to be an integral whole', just as God is one. The root of all error according to Islam is *shirk* – the sin of polytheism broadly interpreted as the association of anything with the Divine: 'God forgives not that anything should associated with him' (Quran, 4.116). See for example, Fazlur Rahman, 'Islam: An Overview', in *Encyclopaedia of Religion*, ed. by M. Eliade, 16 vols (New York; London 1987), VII, 303-322; Dominique Sordel, *Medieval Islam* (London; New York, 1979).
170. Thomas Aquinas, *Liber... Qui Didicitur Summa Contra Gentiles*, I, cc. 3-4.
171. Ibid., I, cc. 5-6.
172. Ibid., I, c. 7.
173. Ibid., I, c. 7.
174. Compare ibid., lib. II, 30.
175. Ibid., lib. I, c. 13: 'Impossibile est aliqua contraria et dissonantia in unum ordinem concordare semper vel pluries nisi alicuius gubernatione, ex qua omnibus et singulis tribuitur ut ad certum finem tendant. Sed in mundo videmus res diversarum naturarum in unum ordinem concordare, non ut raro et a casu, sed ut semper vel in maiori parte. Oportet ergo esse aliquem cuius providentia mundus gubernetur.' See also Albertus Magnus, *In sententiarum*, lib. I, dist. iii, art. ii: 'Nec est simile de fabro lignorum et domo, et Deo: quia faber lignorum separatur a domo, et opus eius similiter, et transit. Unde etiam sequitur: si domus est, faber lignarius est, vel fuit. Sed in Deo opus universaliter non separatur a creatura: quia postquam creata est, adhuc in nihilum caderet nisi contineretur ab ipso: et ordo eius in universo

corrumperetur, nisi ab ipso gubernaretur. Non tamen dico, quod sequatur, quod Deus fuit: sed sequatur, quod ipse est propter rationem aeternitatis quae est tota simul et perfecta.'

176. Ibid., lib. III, c. 21: 'Unde Dionysius dicit III Cap. *Caelestis Hierarchiae*, quod *omnium divinius est Dei cooperatorem fieri:* secundum quod Apostolus dicit, I Corinth. 3, 9: *Dei adiutores sumus.*'

177. See Humbert of Romans' 'The Formation of a Preacher', in S. Tugwell, *Early Dominicans* (New York, 1982), pp. 181-325.

## Chapter 6

# Contested Traditions

To assume that the issues at stake in the debate over Anselm's argument were to do with justifying faith on rational grounds, is to impose modern philosophical concerns upon the thirteenth century. Faith was never at stake in this period as it came to be in modern philosophy of religion. Anselm, Thomas and Bonaventure all thought that it was possible to find reasons which could establish the existence of God without the aid of faith. Nonetheless, they were not engaged in the project of providing rational foundations for belief. No one required such foundations, and if they had required them, it is likely that they would have been considered heretics. Although reason was thought to function separately from faith, it is a mistake to assume that it must therefore have functioned to justify faith. To understand the role of theistic arguments in the context of the broader doctrinal schemes and forms of life of the thirteenth century is to understand a different kind of relationship between reason and belief.

In the work of Thomas, Bonaventure and their contemporaries, theistic arguments – and philosophy generally – served to open up the space within shared doctrines where differences of interpretation could be articulated and contested. Towards the last quarter of the thirteenth century, differences of interpretation were becoming apparent over a number of philosophical positions – concerning in particular, the nature of the soul, the creation of the world in time, and the relationship between reason and faith. The Franciscan William de la Mare's *Correctorium Fratris Thomae*, published in 1279, sparked a pamphlet war between the orders in which the rivalry between them finally became explicit. The *Correctorium* attacked, in particular, Thomas's teachings on the unity of form within the soul: a position incompatible with Franciscan assumptions about the soul's immediate awareness of itself. Adopted officially by the Franciscan order at the General Chapter of Strasbourg in 1282, Franciscan lectors were instructed not to read the works of Friar Thomas without a copy of the *Correctorium*.[1] With respect to the natural knowledge of God, however, the Franciscans were themselves forced to fight a defensive campaign.

### I

The concern to defend the Franciscan treatment of the natural knowledge of God against Dominican criticism is already reflected in the sentence commentary of Walter of Bruges (d. 1307). Walter was regent in the Franciscan school from 1267 to 1269, contemporary with the second regency of the Dominican, Peter of Tarentaise.[2] First of all, in response to the Dominican arguments, Walter argued that the denial of God's existence followed from the deprivation of human reason by sin. Evil causes a person to think of God as less than what God is, i.e. less than something than which no greater can be thought. It is possible to think that God does not exist only if God is misunderstood. It may also be possible to deny that a specific god is God. Walter goes on to say, however, that it is not possible to deny a first being or a highest truth since being and truth both presuppose that there is a first being and truth.[3] For Walter of Bruges, like his fellow Franciscans, the proper understanding of God (and therefore of theology more generally) depends upon the spiritual state of the soul. Faith teaches that God is something than which no greater can be thought – only the corruption of the soul can cause it to mistake God for something less.

Walter attempts to present a version of the Franciscan teaching which both avoids the difficulties pointed out by the Dominicans and which confirms the Franciscan view that all forms of knowledge – including arguments for God's existence derived from the senses – are ultimately dependent upon God's illumination. In effect, the Thomistic objections had placed the Franciscans on the horns of a dilemma: either the teaching that the mind knows God when it knows truth is heretical or it means only that the mind knows a created reflection of God. Walter states that in God's own nature, God is the truth illuminating everyone. God is thus really present to the individual soul. In this sense God is not demonstrable, but is, as Augustine says, the source of our knowledge of all other things, so that, whatever our mind understands, it understands in the light of the first truth.[4]

Does this mean that the mind knows God in this life? Walter avoids the heretical implications of the doctrine of divine illumination by separating the illumination of God from the naturally inserted knowledge of God. This latter knowledge is not a knowledge of God's own nature, but rather a created reflection, an image of the first truth. This is the self-evident knowledge of God in the truth, goodness and being that are found in all things. In this way the knowledge of God is self-evident, naturally inserted, and cannot be demonstrated – except to those whose reason has been obscured by malice and cannot see what is self-evident to others.[5]

Walter of Bruges therefore accepted the interpretation of Thomas Aquinas of the Franciscan position namely, that God's existence is self-evident to the soul. In doing so he was accepting that the knowledge of God's existence is derived from a knowledge of what God is. By doing this, however, he unwittingly conceded the other side of Thomas's challenge: since the inserted knowledge of God is only a created image of the first truth, how can it lead the soul beyond itself? In conceding this, he was jeopardising a central assumption of the Franciscan academic tradition: that the soul was immediately joined to God in its intellective operations. The idea of God's existence being self-evident to the soul did not do justice to the subtlety of the Franciscan position. It was left to Walter of

Bruges' successor and Thomas Aquinas's most redoubtable Franciscan opponent, John Peckham, to clear up the mess.[6]

John Peckham (c. 1235-1292) entered the Friars Minor in around 1257 and was later sent to Paris to complete his theological training. He occupied the Franciscan chair there between 1269 and 1271, before becoming Regent Master at Oxford (1271-1275). In 1275 he became provincial of the Franciscan order in England, before becoming in 1279 archbishop of Canterbury, in which position he continued to intervene in doctrinal matters at Oxford against followers of Thomas Aquinas's teachings.[7] In the sentence commentary dating from his period as successor to Walter of Bruges at Paris, Peckham re-affirms the traditional Franciscan arguments, that God is the immediate source of truth in human understanding, but avoids the problematic solution of Walter of Bruges. In effect, he offers a more sophisticated rebuttal of Aquinas's charge and yet one that succeeds in preserving the previous Franciscan position. Though Peckham affirms that the knowledge of truth within the human mind has its source in the infallible light of God, he agrees with Aquinas, that the eternal principles *by* which we know things should not be confused with *what* we know by those principles.[8] Hence, to say that God is the light of the understanding is not to say that the understanding sees God when it understands.

Peckham says that there are three ways in which God is known, through natural impression, through the vestiges of creatures, and through scriptures.[9] Unlike Walter, Peckham does not distinguish the natural impression from the supernatural light of God. Rather the natural impression is the reflection of the divine light. Anselm's argument brings to light the inserted knowledge of God, and reveals that it is apophatic or negative knowledge. Neither Anselm nor the Franciscans claim an argument for God's existence from a definition of God or from a vision of what God is. The inserted knowledge is not a knowledge of what God is, but of what God is not: God is not that than which a greater can be thought; God cannot, therefore, be thought not to exist. Hence, it is not that God's existence is self-evident to us, but that God's non-being cannot be thought. It is for that reason that the soul can rise above itself to that which is the source of its knowing, yet without knowing God in God's self. (This in fact, was the meaning of the final stage of Bonaventure's *Journey of the Soul*, in which all intellectual activities would cease before passing over into God.)

It is in the knowledge of truth that the presence of God within nature and within the soul is to be found. It is that presence which is thereby the source of our knowledge rather than an inference from it. Nonetheless, it is precisely because we do not possess quidditive knowledge of God (a knowledge of *what* God is) that we deny God's existence by thinking that God is something less than God.[10] Peckham says that this is the source of error in the Fool who says in his heart 'there is no God'.[11] It is precisely by trying to define God, in other words, that the mind is led into error. In this sense, God truly is, as Gerard de Prato says, 'incircumscibable'.[12] Peckham clarifies the implications of the Franciscan doctrine: it is contrary neither to reason nor to the teaching of Christian faith.

John Peckham's successors in the Franciscan chair at Paris, William de la Mare (d. 1285) and Matthew of Acquasparta, maintain the Franciscan positions, and in the *Correctiorium Fratris Thomae* go on the offensive. The third distinction of Matthew's *Commentary on the Sentences* presents a detailed re-statement of the Franciscan approach to the natural knowledge of God. Whereas for the Dominicans the natural state of the human mind with respect to the knowledge of God is one of ignorance, for Matthew of Acquasparta, ignorance of God's existence lies in a defect of the intellect's natural powers. The difference between Franciscans and Dominicans over this issue embodies the wider contrasts between the religious orders with respect to the apostolic life itself.

Matthew of Acquasparta (1240-1302), who was later elected Minister General of the Franciscan order and reigned for the period 1287-1289, was acting Regent Master at Paris between 1275 and 1277. In his teaching it was once again the conclusion of Anselm's argument – that God cannot be thought not to exist – together with the teachings of John of Damascus and of Augustine concerning truth, that supply the continuity of the Franciscan position.[13] The indubitable knowledge of God's existence is integral to the Franciscan position, because God is the light of the intellect by which it can know anything at all.[14] Matthew clarifies how God's presence to the intellect leads the mind to truth. He begins by explaining what indubitable means in this case by investigating the causes of doubt and in what sense they are absent with respect to God.

Doubt arises in two ways, Matthew says, either on account of the operation of reason itself, or on account of a defect of reason. In terms of the natural operation of reason doubt arises through a lack of evidence in the object of knowledge, in the medium of its proof, or in the apprehension of the mind. In none of these ways, however, does the knowledge of God involve doubt. In terms of the apprehension of the intellect the knowledge that God exists is inserted within the rational mind in as much as the desire, knowledge and memory of the mind is made in the image of God and naturally tends toward the operation and renewal of itself.[15] Thus the insertion of the knowledge of God is a moving object of the mind rather than an object of the mind's knowledge.[16] The very operations of the soul, in its knowledge and in its will, presuppose a knowledge of God: the image of God within the soul is the very dynamic of the soul rather than a static object of knowledge.

In terms of the proof of God, the medium of creatures, 'whether they be considered according to their perfections, or according to their dependency, cry out, in voices loud and clear, that God exists'.[17] In itself, the first truth is most immediately known, since when it is said that God exists the truth of the predicate is included in the subject. Just as the union of opposites and the division of a unity are repugnant to our intellects, so the division of existence from that which is, and the identity of the highest being and non-being are most evident in their falsehood.[18]

If the existence of God is dubitable at all, therefore, it is not because of a lack of evidence, but because of a triple defect on the part of the knower. The knower may be deficient in the acts of apprehending, comparing and resolving. The intellect may fall into doubt if the significance of the word 'God' is not fully apprehended, and some idol is taken for God. The intellect also acts defectively when it compares the apparent prosperity of the impious and concludes that there must be no government in the universe. Similarly, the intellect falls into doubt if it fails to resolve its knowledge of corporeal things to that which is the first principle of things. In these different ways the mind does not apprehend the significance of this name 'God' as that than which no greater can be thought, and it comes to think what cannot be thought.[19]

Whereas for the Dominicans the mind is naturally ignorant of God, for the Franciscans the natural state of the mind is to know indubitably that God exists. For Matthew it is a truth that is presupposed in the working of the mind itself. The Fool who says in his heart 'there is no God' is in error not merely because he lacks a knowledge provided by faith or demonstration, but because his mind is blinded. Moreover, the blindness arises from the will rather than from reason. Hence, for Matthew, knowledge is grounded in the ordering of the soul towards the first light. The Franciscan and Dominican approaches to the natural knowledge of God imply different accounts of the soul – one in which reason follows the will, and the other whereby the will submits to reason. It is no coincidence that Matthew completes the third distinction by consideration of the question of whether something believed by faith can be, at the same time, also known by reason.[20]

This question was to become a central component of the controversy sparked by William de la Mare's *Correctorium Fratris Thomae.*[21] Those different attitudes to reason and the will, reason and faith, underpin in turn the greatest controversies between the Franciscan and Dominican masters of the late thirteenth century because they directly impinge upon their strategies with respect to the unbeliever. For the Franciscans, the proper operation of reason depended upon the orientation of the soul. Faith elevated reason above its natural limits and truth was outwardly recognised by the unbeliever only because it was already inwardly hidden within his/her soul. Rational apprehension of truth was ultimately a gift of faith itself – the product of the purification of the soul wrought by faith. This was a concept of faith inherent within the Franciscan conception of mission – a conception of preaching by deeds rather than by arguments. For the Dominicans, however, reason was useful to the preacher only to the extent that its sources were completely independent of faith and shared by believer and unbeliever alike. For the Dominicans, to make reason dependent upon faith or faith upon reason served only to undermine both in the eyes of the unbeliever, and to rob faith of its merit for the believer. Once something was understood by reason it ceased to be a matter of faith. The Franciscan and Dominican accounts of reason were in conflict not merely because they were different: they were in conflict because they were mutually exclusive. Their differences with respect to the role of reason were embedded in, and constitutive of, two different accounts of the '(un)natural ignorance' and natural knowledge of God.

## II

It is wrong, of course, to suggest that Thomas Aquinas and Bonaventure represented the last word in Dominican and Franciscan teaching. By the 1280s most Dominican masters appear to have sided with Thomas, encouraged no doubt, by the very process of debate itself, and the criticism to which Thomas was subjected. Nonetheless, there were always critics who envisaged a different relationship with God, even within the order. The most prominent of these was to be Robert Kilwardby (d. 1279).[22] As Archbishop of Canterbury in 1277 he condemned teachings concerning the unity of form in the soul. The sources for that condemnation are already found in the sentence commentary that Kilwardby produced as successor to Richard Fishacre at the Dominican school in Oxford in the 1250s. What was at stake in the later condemnation was an account of the soul so intimately related to the body that it was capable of knowing nothing apart from the bodily senses. That Kilwardby should have gone on to challenge this teaching is indicated by passages within his commentary on the *Sentences*. Here Kilwardby already taught that incorporeal substances like God and the soul are the object of 'pure intellectual vision' and are present to the mind through themselves:

> Augustine called 'intellectual vision' only those things which are present to the mind through themselves, and such things are faith, will, the soul, understanding and things of this kind; and God is among their number.[23]

Notably, in the same work, Kilwardby argued that reason was useful to the Church not only because it may be used to refute infidels, but also because faith could be augmented by understanding what was believed.[24] Although his treatment of the natural knowledge of God does include passing references to the *Proslogion*, and to the Augustinian arguments from truth, there is not enough discussion to warrant a firm conclusion about a contrast with Thomas in Paris.[25] A clearer example of differences within the order on the issue of the natural knowledge of God is found not among the Oxford Dominicans, but among Thomas's former classmates in Cologne.

Ulrich of Strasbourg's *Summa de Bono* was completed later than Thomas Aquinas's sentence commentary, sometime between 1260 and 1272. Under the influence of Albertus Magnus, and like Thomas, Ulrich adapted the Pseudo-Dionysian scheme of causation, negation and eminence and elements from Aristotle's account of the mind's acquisition of knowledge through the senses.[26] Working in a different context, however, Ulrich wove those themes according to a different pattern. That he does so is an indication that Thomas was arguing as much against theses brought forward within the Dominican order as against those championed by the Franciscans. Thomas's sentence commentary represents the teaching of a bachelor in a central Dominican school responsible for the training of lectors and preachers throughout the order. Ulrich, on the other hand, belonged to a province distinguished from the rest of the order not by a particular vocation toward heretics, Jews or Muslims, but by its pastoral responsibility for religious women: a responsibility formalised by Pope Clement IV in 1267.[27] Though taken from the same sources, Ulrich's account of the natural knowledge of God differs significantly from that of Thomas, and articulates a different relationship between God and the soul. Although he does not cite Anselm's argument, he argues for an account of God that is self-evident to the soul.

The first point that Ulrich makes is that besides the supernatural knowledge we have from grace, God is also knowable to us by the light of natural reason. Though we can know God, however, our knowledge leaves more unknown than known. The knowledge which we have is that God exists, but we cannot have a natural knowledge of God as Trinity.[28] Ulrich states that there are five ways which can come to a knowledge of God.[29] In contrast to Thomas, he argues not only that the knowledge of God is naturally inserted within the soul, but that the existence of God is self-evident to us.[30] Furthermore, Ulrich argues, just as first principles are not able to be denied in the heart, though they may be denied by the mouth, God is not able to be thought not to exist. In effect, God's existence does not actually require proof. Just as there are uncultivated minds who in ignorance deny first principles, however, so there are those who deny that God exists. It is against such people that proofs are worthwhile to show them their error.[31]

The knowledge of self-evident principles is held in a confused 'habitus' that is naturally inserted within the intellect and which experience, without need for proof, is sufficient to bring to actual and determinate knowledge. There is a similitude of God naturally inserted within the possible intellect that is brought to determinacy by experience of God's effects. Hence, Aristotle says that if there were a people who always lived under the earth and who one day came to the surface, they would see the land and the sea, the heavens, the night and the stars, and observe their movement, and they would conclude that there must be gods, and that what they had seen was the operation of their works. It is self-evident to us, therefore, that God exists.[32]

Despite his emphasis on the role of sensible experience in bringing the knowledge of first principles to determinacy, Ulrich states that the cause of error is the darkening of the mind through its involvement in sensible and material images and by the carnal passions through which the eye of the mind is unable to turn to the cause of created effects.[33] Whoever turns, by the light of reason, to the divine effects themselves will see that God's existence is self-evident, that it cannot be denied, and that it is not in need of proof.[34]

With Thomas Aquinas, Ulrich affirms the need for experience of divine effects. Unlike Thomas, however, Ulrich affirms that the knowledge that is brought about through experience is actually self-evident. Ulrich states that the knowledge is derived from an image of God within the soul, and that God's existence cannot be denied. Unlike the Franciscan masters, however, Ulrich mentions neither Anselm nor John of Damascus, ascribing his doctrines instead to the Epicurean philosophers and Aristotle.[35] Ulrich's apparent ignorance of the sources known to the Franciscans suggests that he formed his doctrine independently of the Franciscan tradition at Paris. He was articulating a separate Dominican tradition that existed in the German schools whose sensitivity toward an interior spirituality reflected its responsibility for contemplative nuns.

In the final chapter, summarising what can be known concerning God by the natural intellect, Ulrich employs the language of ascent and overcoming. When the intellect is not proportioned to the divine object it knows mathematics and physics more certainly than it does God. Nevertheless, when our intellect is elevated through the grades of its perfection and is assimilated to the divine object, then it knows God more certainly. For the same reason, the more the mind is submerged in material things the more it is ignorant of God. This is why the Fool says in his heart 'there is no God'.[36] For Ulrich, the enquirer must be purified if he or she is to savour the truth.[37]

Ulrich of Strasbourg reveals the same concerns with the Pseudo-Dionysius, with Aristotelian philosophy, with the separation between Faith and natural reason, grace and nature, and with the distinction between God and the similitude of God that are found in Thomas. He is also concerned with the self-sufficiency of the mind that does not require a superadded light but is instead brought to completion through its sensory experience of the created world. Yet he takes those elements in a very different direction and one which is illustrated by his emphasis upon the inserted knowledge of God's existence.[38] In any case, from Cologne, it was Thomas whom Albertus Magnus sent to Paris, and Ulrich whom he later appointed as provincial in his archbishopric of Ratisbon.[39]

Albert's own *Summa Theologiae* composed in the 1270s is also akin to the Franciscan tradition to which his early sentence commentary stood in sharp contrast. The thought expressed in this work is certainly embedded in the Dominican east, not in the Parisian school. That Albert travelled to Paris in 1277 to defend the memory of Thomas against the suspicions created by the condemnations of the 1270s, however, may provide a clue to the purpose of the *Summa* composed during this period.[40] The inclusion of Anselm's argument in his extended treatment of the natural knowledge of God suggests that his late *Summa* represents an attempt to reconcile the Aristotelian approach to natural knowledge with that of its critics. In any case, unlike Thomas, Albert affirms that God's existence cannot be thought not to be, and that this is a peculiar character of God's existence.[41] At the same time, however, and like Thomas, he also wants to maintain that God's existence is not self-evident. God's existence requires demonstration.[42] Anselm's argument is employed *after* the self-subsistent character of God's existence has been established, using the same route that lies at the heart of Thomas's proofs. The self-subsistent existence of God is established from the experience of contingent, created existence: 'being is the effect of the first cause in all those things that are.'[43]

Albert tries to make sense of Anselm's argument as a consummation of the natural knowledge of God, rather than as the route to a first principle. He affirms that the mind has a confused habitual knowledge of God as the principle of the intellect, but this is to affirm no more than Thomas. From this habitual knowledge the mind is able to arrive at a knowledge of God's existence, it does not already possesses that knowledge.[44] Anselm's argument is brought in after the nature of God's existence is known by other means. If some form of reconciliation was the goal of Albert's *Summa*, however, then it was to be undermined by the fact that several Dominican masters were to defend and to propagate Thomas's teachings in thoroughly Thomistic terms.

Thomas Sutton, a master in Oxford in the 1280s, was one of several Thomists to arise in England despite – perhaps because of – the opposition of Richard Kilwardby. The first of his *Ordinary Questions* considers Anselm's argument in terms of the question of whether God's existence is self-evident.[45] His extensive treatment, which runs to no less than thirty three pages in the printed edition, does not consider the issues that surround the question – namely the role of God in human knowledge – but rather focuses directly on what it means to say that something is a self-evident proposition (*per se notum*). His treatment of the issue nonetheless seems to clarify an advantage of the Dominican over the Franciscan position.

Like Aquinas, Sutton accepts that when Anselm says that God cannot be thought not to exist, he is talking about a self-evident proposition. A self-evident proposition, says Sutton, is one in which the predicate is already included in the meaning of the subject, and is manifest when the proposition cannot be denied without contradiction. Sutton acknowledges that the proposition 'God is' fulfils that criteria but, like Aquinas, distinguishes between propositions that are self-evident in themselves, and those which are self-evident to us.[46] Moreover, the reason for this distinction is weakness on our part, not on the part of the things themselves that, in the case of separate substances, are 'most manifest according to themselves and maximally intelligible'.[47] Yet for such things to be self-evident also to us it is necessary that the meaning of the subject is not shown by means of something more evident to our intellects.[48]

The meaning of the subject, says Sutton, is acquired by our intellects in three ways. The first, and easiest way, is when the meaning of terms is seen immediately by the senses encountering sensible things: namely, the meaning of whole, part, greater, smaller, equal, or unequal.[49] Such things are self-evident to us as well as in themselves. A less immediate form of self-evident proposition is acquired when the meaning of its terms requires memory and several experiences. This is the case with experimental knowledge, and such knowledge is self-evident only to those who are learned – not to those without learning. A third way by which the meaning of a subject is acquired involves a form of proposition that is self-evident in itself, but never in relation to us – regardless of the extent of our learning.

The proposition that is self-evident in itself but never in relation to us, is one in which the meaning of the subject is known only as the result of a demonstration. No amount of experience or memory can make the meaning of such a subject clear to us. Hence, to know that the soul is the act of the body, is a proposition that is self-evident in itself, but our recognition of its truth depends upon knowledge that we have already acquired and that is more evident to us than the proposition itself. In other words, it is the conclusion of a demonstration, and not the result of experience.[50] When Anselm talks about not being able to think that God does not exist he makes it clear that he is talking about anyone who already knows the meaning of the word 'God'. Such meaning is available only through faith or through demonstration: it is not self-evident in itself. Hence, in a sense, Sutton claims that the Franciscan interpretation of Anselm's argument is mistaken – Anselm does not claim that God's existence is known in experience.[51] Moreover, he is able to account for the special character of God's existence without committing himself to the claim that God is available to experience. One arrives at a knowledge of God by faith or by argument: since 'through the effects of God that are manifest to us we can prove the cause of their being'.[52]

In a shorter compass, another English Dominican, Robert d'Orford expresses the same position as his contemporary, Thomas Sutton: God's existence is self-evident in itself, but not to us. The knowledge that God's existence is included within the definition of God's nature is a knowledge dependent upon faith or demonstration.[53] God's existence is not an object of, or an ineliminable aspect of, experience: rather, it is the conclusion of a demonstration based upon experience. For the same reason, the argument that truth cannot be denied without contradiction is not an argument for the knowledge of God. Rather, it is an argument that shows that God is not the only thing that cannot be denied without contradiction: for the knowledge of truth is not the knowledge of God.[54] Robert can therefore agree with Anselm that God's existence is that than which no greater can be conceived, and that God's existence cannot be denied directly by someone who knows the meaning of the terms. The Dominican position is thus able to encompass the Franciscan position but without the problematic and dangerous idea that God is somehow available to direct experience.[55]

Bernard of Trilla, another contemporary of Thomas Sutton, and Regent in the Dominican school in Paris between 1284 and 1287, directed the recently published eighth distinction of his disputed questions, *On the knowledge of the soul joined to the body*, against the Franciscan position on natural knowledge.[56] The question does not concern itself with Anselm's argument or with the issue of whether God's existence is a self-evident truth (*per se notum*). Nonetheless, it provides a clear account of the epistemological issues that underpinned that debate, and why it was he followed Thomas in rejecting the Franciscan perspective. Bernard puts the question in this way – 'is the first truth the first thing which is known by the soul joined to the body in this life?' Bernard says that there are four opinions on this issue – three of which represent the variety of ways in which Franciscans and now also the secular master, Henry of Ghent, present the role of God in natural knowledge.[57] The fourth position, and the one Bernard endorses, is the position of Thomas Aquinas.

The first truth is the first thing known to the human mind in this state, according to some, says Bernard, not as the object and end of knowledge, but as the reason and medium of knowing.[58] However, either the media or reasons of knowing (that is, the eternal reasons of things) are identical with God or they are separate from God. Both positions, however, are heretical. One suggests that the human mind knows God as the blessed in heaven; the other suggests that God depends upon eternal reasons separate from the divine being, by which all things are created.[59] What the authorities drawn to support this position (i.e. Augustine) really teach, is that the eternal principles of things are a similitude of the first truth, and not the first truth itself.

The second opinion among those who claim that the first truth is the first thing known to the mind in this life is that the first truth illumines the mind in its knowledge of all things. Just as the sun illumines the eye for the sight of material things, so the first truth illumines the mind for material things. Although the eye does not look directly at the sun when it sees material things, it cannot see those things without first seeing the light of the sun. Similarly, the mind cannot see the transcendentals in terms of which it understands intellectual things, being, truth and goodness, without first apprehending uncreated being, truth and goodness.[60] Yet, since the mind cannot see itself except through its objects, Bernard argues, the intellectual light, whether created or uncreated, cannot be the first thing seen by the mind. Moreover, if the natural light of the intellect is not the first thing known, how much less the spiritual light. When Augustine was talking about God as the light of the intellect, Bernard explains, he was talking about its effective cause, not about the object of intellectual knowledge.[61]

The third opinion of those who think that the first object of human thought is the first truth is that the first truth is the last thing known to the mind through investigation of creatures. Nonetheless, they argue, it is the first thing known by means of the simple apprehension of things, since whatever the mind knows it knows through the most simple conceptions: namely, the concepts of being, truth goodness, unity and such like. The more simple a conception is, the more prior it is in the order of knowing. Although this position is more reasonable than the other two, Bernard argues, it is still mistaken. The first conceptions of the mind – the transcendentals – are received from the similitudes of created things, and later predicated of the uncreated being. The order of our knowledge is the reverse of the order of things – which is why we come into a knowledge of God from God's effects.[62]

Finally, Bernard endorses the position of Thomas Aquinas, that in this life the first truth is not the first thing known by human understanding. Rather, the first thing known in this life are the things abstracted from their individuating conditions by the material senses. The first things that are known by the intellect are the universal forms – or transcendentals: the more universal they are, the more prior they are. Yet these are abstracted from the phantasms or images of sensible things. Hence, when we know a particular person we know first that there is a body before we know there is an animal; an animal before we know there is a human being; a human being before we know there is Socrates or Plato. In this way, the transcendentals of being, goodness and truth are the first objects of the mind, but they are derived from experience. When Aristotle teaches that we know all doctrines and disciplines from pre-existent knowledge, he means that all our knowledge, intellective as much as sensitive, comes about by means of abstraction from material things. Therefore, since God is in every way immaterial, God is not the first thing known in this life, but that which is known through other things. That is why St Paul writes in Romans 1: 20: 'The invisible things of God are clearly understood from the things which are made, namely his eternal power and divinity.'[63]

Bernard, along with his colleagues in Paris, such as Romaine de Rome, illustrate the extent to which Thomas's teachings were accepted in the face not just of Franciscan criticisms, but even against alternatives presented within the order itself. What vindicated Thomas's position was not that it would have had a wider following than the alternatives on offer, but simply because it articulated assumptions that were implicit within specifically Dominican practices.

## III

The subsequent academic history of the Middle Ages shows that Bonaventure in particular was not to monopolise the allegiance of the Franciscan movement in the way that Thomas did among the Dominicans. This was in part, no doubt, because the criticisms of contemporary Dominicans such as Thomas Sutton, Robert d'Orford, Bernard of Trilla and others had shown that the Franciscan position was fraught with difficulties. Thus, although the Franciscan acceptance of Anselm's argument is indicative of rational standards that were internal to their community – standards reflective of Franciscan spiritual commitments – it was nonetheless possible for Dominicans to challenge those standards.

The Franciscans were committed to the view that without faith no rival account of reality, potential or actual, would be in a position to vindicate its claims. The Dominican rejection of this position in itself illustrated a weakness of the Franciscan tradition: Christians themselves rejected the claim that faith was necessary to attain true knowledge about nature. Moreover, with respect to the internal problematic of Franciscan enquiry, the Dominicans were able to explain a central difficulty of the Franciscan position in terms that were available to anyone, and not merely in terms that were limited to a particular tradition of Christian thought. They argued that it is possible to be ignorant or to deny God's existence not because of an inexplicable defect on the part of the mind, but simply because God's existence is not self-evident to us. Thus, the Dominicans were thereby better able to explain one of the problems involved in the Franciscan position than the Franciscans were themselves – at least in terms of the resources which the Franciscan tradition provided until that point.

A more serious problem yet was presented in the Franciscan commitment to the view that the source of the natural knowledge of truth is the divine light. This was the exemplarist/illuminationist approach to the first principles of natural knowledge expressed through the Franciscan application of Anselm's argument. The Franciscans masters who defended some version of the exemplarist/illuminationist account, were faced with the difficulty of explaining how the mind knows truth through God without knowing God. John Peckham's response to this issue was clever, but unsatisfying: if God is not known directly in this life, and the image of God inserted in the soul is only a created reflection, how does this really differ from the position favoured by the Dominicans? Either it was heretical or it was simply wrong to interpret this doctrine in the way Franciscans suggested. The knowledge of truth is not the same as a knowledge of God: one is created and derived, the other is not. Bernard of Trilla illustrates the potentially heretical implications of trying to identify the knowledge of truth with the knowledge of God. Surely it is more economic, and certainly less hazardous theologically, to abandon it?

For the most part, the leadership of the Franciscan order, including the Ministers General Matthew of Acquasparta and Alexander of Alexandria (d. 1314) continued to defend Bonaventurean positions. Nonetheless, to ignore those criticisms would have been incompatible with the medieval Christian conception of truth shared by Franciscans and Dominicans alike, and would also have served to remove the Franciscans effectively from rational debate. Others within the order recognised the need for another strategy.[64] Among the most radical revisionists, Richard of Middleton (d. c. 1305), an English Franciscan who was Regent Master at Paris (1284-1287), abandoned divine illumination as it had been defended until now within the Franciscan school, and along with that, rejected the argument of Anselm's *Proslogion*, for the following reason. That which cannot be thought not to be is not necessarily greater than something that can be thought of as not being. Something may be capable of being thought not to be not on account of its deficiency, but on account of its very supremacy.[65] Like Thomas Aquinas, Richard insists that the sources of the mind's knowledge lie in the senses. The inserted knowledge of God's existence taught by John of Damascus refers only to the mind's knowledge of the transcendentals, being, unity, goodness and truth which refer to both God and creatures analogically. Hence, they are not to be identified with God in God's self. Like Thomas Aquinas, Richard interprets John of Damascus as referring to an innate power to seek God through creatures, not that the knowledge of God is already inserted within the soul like a self-evident proposition.[66] In direct contrast to Bonaventure and to John Peckham, Richard of Middleton also denies that the soul is able to have any direct knowledge of itself. Like Thomas, he argues that the soul arrives at a knowledge of itself only through its acts and objects.[67] Again like Thomas, Richard argues that the existence of God is shown from a consideration of creatures that, as effects, bear a likeness to their cause. The arguments in the sentences conclude that God is the first mover, the governor of the universe and the ultimate end of all things.[68]

It would be wrong to think, however, that Richard had simply capitulated to the teachings of his Dominican contemporaries. Unlike Thomas Aquinas, Richard is interested in arguing from the soul's awareness of the natural law and from the soul's appetites to the existence of the immutable law giver and an ultimate good and end of all things. The operator in these arguments is not, as it would have been in Bonaventure, that the knowledge of God is somehow implied by the awareness of natural law or the appetites of the soul. The operator in these arguments is rather the Aristotelian principle that nature makes nothing in vain. From our experience of the immutable natural law, the unquenchable appetite of the soul, and the tendency of the will, it must follow that there is an immutable law giver,[69] an ultimate uncreated good in which our appetites are fully satisfied,[70] and an ultimate end to which the will tends.[71] The arguments are inferences from experience rather than claims about something implicit within experience. Nonetheless, they provide a significant contrast with the inferential arguments of Thomas Aquinas partly because they anticipate an account of the priority of the will over the intellect in the ordering of the soul's faculties. In pursuing this point, Richard follows and develops a position that only begins to be given explicit statement in the work of John Peckham.[72] What Richard concedes to the Dominicans on the doctrines of natural knowledge of God and the soul, he regains through his account of the will.

The arguments he puts forward for this position at various points in his sentence commentary are listed by D. E. Sharp, but are worth recounting here partly because they illustrate his use of Dominican principles to derive a distinctively Franciscan perspective. The dependency of the intellect upon the will was implicit in the exemplarist/illuminationist route to God favoured by Richard's Franciscan predecessors. Richard discovered that precisely by eliminating the teachings on natural knowledge most vulnerable to Dominican critique he was able to establish a key assumption of Franciscan anthropology, and one which is embedded in a religious life that is focused on doing rather than on knowing. Precisely because the intellect cannot grasp the reason of truth or exemplar cause in the divine mind, its object is not being as truth, but being as being. However, the object of the will is being under a more noble nature, namely being as goodness. If the object of the will is nobler than that of the intellect, the will itself must be nobler since, as Aristotle says, we come to a knowledge of potencies through a knowledge of their acts and objects. In the second place, the primacy of the will deducible from the facts that charity is the noblest virtue, that the love of God is our ultimate end, and from the general opinion that it is nobler to love God than to know Him. In the third place, and in marked contrast to Thomas's teaching in the *Summa contra gentiles*, Richard teaches that it is more possible to become like God in our wills than in our intellects. Finally, he argues, the will must be nobler than the intellect because the cognitive act can never satisfy the rational creature unless it culminates in an act of the appetitive potency.[73]

On the primacy of the will the Franciscans were to find themselves on more robust ground, and for that reason it was this teaching, and not the exemplarist approach to the natural knowledge of God that was to become the main focus of Franciscan attention in the fourteenth century. Nonetheless, even within this context of re-arranged priorities, Franciscans continued to work on the problem of the natural knowledge of God in ways that responded to Dominican criticism. Among the Franciscans who attempted to maintain a distinctively Franciscan position on the question of the natural knowledge of God was yet another English Franciscan, William of Ware (d. c. 1300), teacher of Duns Scotus. By introducing degrees of self-evidence, William argued that God's existence was not as self-evident as other propositions. Propositions like 'man is an animal' or 'the whole is greater than the part' are self-evident because they are knowable by the senses. Other propositions, like God's existence, are not known to the senses, and so can be attained 'only with great labour'. Yet God's existence is a self-evident proposition in the sense that when the meaning of the terms are known, the proposition cannot be denied.[74] In this way, William can accept Anselm's argument, although in doing so he already concedes the main ground. Nonetheless, the most significant part of William of Ware's treatment of the natural knowledge of God is his introduction of a pre-requisite for any proof of God's existence. To prove the existence of God, he argues that it is necessary to arrive at a being infinite in power and in essence.[75]

The atmosphere in which this new approach to the concept of God emerges was created by the final and most significant of ecclesiastical condemnations of philosophical developments in the thirteenth century. Once again, it was prompted by the teaching of Aristotelian and Arabic sciences in the Faculty of Arts. At the heart of Bishop Stephen Tempier's condemnation was one particular doctrine: the Aristotelian account of God as the final cause in a necessary system.[76] The implication of Greek and Arabic natural philosophy, according to the condemnation, was to deprive God of freedom to create immediately and freely without the intervention of secondary causes. Roland Hissette has undermined the thesis that the condemnation of 1277 was directly inspired by anti-Thomistic Franciscans.[77] Regardless of the inspiration for the condemnation itself, however, the attack on Greek determinism takes central place within the proof for God's existence in William of Ware, Duns Scotus and among his followers. The original Franciscan position had concentrated on displacing the distant final cause that did not know particulars by an account of God that was intimately present within all being through exemplarism. William of Ware, and more intensively, his pupil, Duns Scotus, attack the Aristotelian doctrine by emphasising God's freedom of action through the absence of restriction on God's power: an emphasis that begins in the proof for God's existence itself.

Once again, the nature of such a proof involved a particular account of God and, therefore, of reality. William of Ware insisted that if the mind is to arrive at a natural knowledge of God, it must show that God is infinite both in power and in essence and not merely that there must exist a first cause. Aristotle's causal arguments can help us understand the meaning of the term 'God', but they do not show that God exists.[78] Similarly, Duns Scotus argued that proofs that argue from movement to a first mover do not take the mind beyond the system of the universe. Thus, the God whose existence physics can demonstrate is bound to act as a necessary physical cause. In that sense, the Anselmian proof has a distinct advantage over its Thomistic rival: 'that than which no greater can be thought' cannot be subscribed within the limits of physical necessity. For Scotus, as for William of Ware, the proof of God is therefore incomplete until it demonstrates the necessity of God's existence with the infinity of power that means that God acts freely.

Like Richard of Middleton, Duns Scotus accepts that all human knowledge is sourced in the senses, but argues that the very possibility of metaphysics depends upon the concept of being – derived from the senses, but univocally applied to both God and creatures. Instead of beginning in the contingencies of movement and causation, Duns Scotus' proof begins in the concept of being itself – the first object of the mind. In doing so, Scotus was able to combine the strengths of both the Thomistic and the Anselmian proofs in one. Having accepted that the concept of being is itself derived from the senses, Scotus turns to the concept itself and discovers that two primary modes intrinsic to it, are the finite and the infinite. To prove that God exists is to prove that the 'infinite being' exists. This is done in two stages. First it must be shown that a primary in the order of being exists, and secondly that this primary is infinite.

After showing the conceptual necessity of the primary being that is without cause, in a move very similar to that of Richard Rufus, Duns Scotus argues that if such a being is possible it necessarily exists. As Gilson explains, the possibility of that whose being is causable does not bring with it its actual existence. That which excludes all cause with regard to its own being, however, cannot not exist, since that which has no cause cannot have a cause of its non-existence. The only conceivable cause of the possibility of such a being is the existence of the being itself.[79]

The infinity of this Primary is established in several ways. Duns Scotus concentrates on arguments deriving from the pre-eminence of the primary being in the order of perfection. The first in the order of perfection must be the supreme intelligence. It must therefore be capable of embracing all that can be known simultaneously. It must therefore be infinite. The infinity of the First is also proved by the natural inclination of our will and by our intelligence. Once again, if such a being is possible it must exist. Our will would not incline toward an infinite good as toward its real object if this infinite good were contradictory and could not exist – the possibility of such an attraction in the will implies that its centre of attraction is at least possible. It is the same with regard to intelligence. 'Why does the intellect, whose object is being, not find the notion of something infinite repugnant? Rather, the infinite seems to be the most perfect thing it can know.'[80]

Once again, the point of these arguments is not to show, as in Bonaventure's case, that the knowledge of the existence of the infinite being is inserted in the will or in the mind, but that the objects of will and of mind imply that such a being is possible. For if it is possible, it necessarily exists. Nonetheless, Duns Scotus's elaborate proof of the infinity of the primary being incorporates a distinctively Franciscan psychology: one in which the primary object of the will and of the intellect is the infinite being.

It is in the context of the two-stage argument, concerning the necessity of a first in the order of being and the infinity of that primary being, whose barest outlines are traced above, that Duns Scotus re-employs Anselm's argument. This time the argument is not used to show that God is such that God cannot be thought not to be or that doubt arises because of a defect of the soul. Rather, the point of the argument is that it encapsulates the two stages of the proof showing the necessary existence of an infinite being. Duns Scotus adapts only from the second chapter of the *Proslogion.* God is a being 'conceived without contradiction, who is so great that it would be a contradiction if a greater being could be conceived'.[81] It follows, Duns Scotus argues, 'that the greatest object conceivable without contradiction can actually exist in reality'. Moreover, from this, it follows that the highest being exists not just in the intellect of the thinker, but also in reality:

> Otherwise it both could exist, because as something possible it is conceivable, and yet could not exist, because the idea of existing in virtue of some cause [i.e. The mind that thinks it] is repugnant to its very nature... Therefore, what exists in reality is conceivably greater than what exists only in the intellect.[82]

Duns Scotus's integration of Anselm's argument into his much larger proof for the existence of God illustrates the extent to which the meaning of the argument could be altered to suit new agenda. Duns Scotus's proof for God's existence represents an extension of the Franciscan critique of Aristotelian/Arab philosophy. Like Richard of Middleton, Duns Scotus abandons the illuminationist/exemplarist account of natural knowledge. His account of the natural knowledge of God provides instead the conceptual account of God that is counterpart to the primacy of the will in the human creature. In doing so, Scotus traces this Franciscan priority back to the source of reality itself. As Gilson writes:

> The role played in Thomism by the existential purity of the divine act of being is played in Scotism by the divine will... In Scotism, the will of God intervenes to bridge the ontological gap there is between the necessary existence of Infinite Being and the possible existence of finite beings. In the universe of Avicenna, because the First was necessary, all the rest enjoyed a conditional necessity; in the universe of Duns Scotus, because

> the First is infinite, all the rest is contingent. Between the necessary and the contingent the only conceivable link is will.[83]

The place of Anselm's argument in Duns Scotus is quite different and far less significant from what it had been among his Franciscan predecessors. It holds the status of a 'persuasive consideration' rather than a demonstrative argument. Nonetheless, the continuity with the Franciscan tradition is more than just a weak textual link. As well as reviving the thought of an earlier Franciscan master, Duns Scotus's proof represents an attack on the necessitarian account of God implied by Aristotle's First Cause, just as earlier masters used Anselm's argument to highlight God's intimate relationship with the soul and with creation as a whole. Moreover, because his proof of God's existence placed God's freedom and will at the centre, it expressed the metaphysical counterpart of the Franciscan emphasis upon the priority of will in obeying God's law, and imitating God through love.

The point of adding this all too brief account of Duns Scotus to the history of the reception of Anselm's argument is not to suggest for a minute that one community finally triumphed over the other.[84] It is rather to illustrate how far rational contestability was important to the representatives of the traditions. The Franciscans were not content to leave unanswered the doubts raised by Thomas Aquinas: the authenticity of their religious experience was at stake. The rivalry between the orders was bitter precisely because while both claimed the authenticity of their religious experience, the theoretical articulations of their practices indicated that their positions were incompatible: in such a situation, only one, if either, could be vindicated. When, before the age of Duns Scotus, John Peckham wrote to the bishop of Lincoln in 1285 expressing his views about the doctrines of Thomas Aquinas, he made clear to which order he believed the perception of Christian truth really belonged:

> I do not in any way disapprove of philosophical studies insofar as they serve theological mysteries, but I do disapprove of irreverent innovations in language, introduced within the last twenty years into the depths of Theology against philosophical truth, and to the detriment of the Fathers, whose positions are disdained and openly held in contempt. Which doctrine is more sound, the doctrine of the sons of St Francis, that is, of holy memory, brother Alexander and brother Bonaventure and others who depended in their writings upon the philosophers and the saints against all adversaries; or the very recent and almost entirely contrary doctrine, which fills the entire world with wordy quarrels, weakening and destroying with all its strength what Augustine teaches concerning the eternal rules and the unchangeable light, the faculties of the soul, the seminal reasons included in matter, and innumerable questions of the same kind?[85]

The doctrine of Thomas seemed novel to John Peckham, but as far as the Dominicans were concerned, Thomas only articulated assumptions that they already held, but which Thomas brought to clearest expression. For that reason, the Franciscan commitment to the doctrines of Bonaventure, was more than matched by the Dominican commitment to the teaching of Thomas. By the time of Peckham's appointment as Archbishop of Canterbury, the authorities within the Dominican order had already thrown their weight behind Thomas. As the declaration of the Dominican general chapter of 1309 shows, by the beginning of the fourteenth century, Thomas's authority within the order was second only to that of the Bible itself:

> We desire and determine that all lectors and sub-lectors lecture from the works of our venerable doctor, Friar Thomas Aquinas, and solve questions according to his doctrine; that they instruct their students in the same and bind them to study these works with diligence. Should any be found acting contrariwise and unwilling to revoke what they have done after being warned, they are to be punished severely and at once by the provincial priors or Master of the Order that their punishment may serve as a warning to others.
>
> We grant to students living outside their provinces the right to sell their books, with the exception of the Bible and the works of Friar Thomas, to provide for themselves the necessities of life in case recourse cannot be had to their provincial for permission, and in case no other means can be found. They are to obtain the advice or consent of the prior, the masters, the bachelors or lectors, or a greater part of the community.[86]

The differences between Franciscan and Dominican philosophies were not, therefore, the result of arbitrary commitments to traditions of thought only incidentally related to their religious interests. Reason was not separate from religious commitments, it was the means by which those commitments were articulated, contested and defended. In both cases, philosophy served tradition as a craft within the community.

Long after their particular preoccupations had ceased to dominate the academy, the Franciscans and Dominicans continued to adhere to, and to defend, thinkers of their own canon – especially Bonaventure, Duns Scotus and Thomas Aquinas.[87] Texts that were expressive of the wider interests of the communities went on to shape the communities themselves. As Krailsheimer has written of the Franciscans, 'in terms of actual books read and hours spent in study by Friars of the sixteenth century, the Fathers must fall far behind the medieval writers from Peter Lombard onwards'.[88] At the twilight of medieval scholasticism, as late as the seventeenth century, one historian has written of the place of Bonaventure, along with Duns Scotus, and Thomas Aquinas within the orders' curricula: 'As a rule, regular professors loyally championed the position of the philosophical school to which their order was pledged'.[89] However, the intellectual projects of the orders were constituted by, and constitutive of, their religious traditions, and not merely incidental to them.

## IV

The fact that it was a religious issue that was at stake in the philosophical conflicts between the Friars regularly goes unnoticed. Part of the reason for this lies with the origins of the study of medieval philosophy itself. When Leo XIII (1878-1903) summoned Catholic teachers to apply the thought of Thomas Aquinas to the concerns of the modern world, he instigated an agenda that is reflected in the writing of the history of the subject.[90] The image of scholasticism that grew from the agenda of the papal encyclical *Aeternis Patris*, was very much the product of post-Enlightenment concerns. Scholasticism was constructed in the image of modern philosophy.[91] Above all else, it was depicted as a system of philosophical debate that stood by itself: Christian orthodoxy may have framed the parameters of discussion, and entailed a concern with natural theology, but medieval thought was nonetheless depicted as containing a large proportion of 'pure' philosophical material.

What did this mean? Scholastic historians agreed that the object of their enquiry was to retrieve the 'philosophies' of medieval thinkers. This set the agenda for the kinds of questions they asked, and for the kind of picture that they would eventually create. The central question that divided them was the extent to which medieval philosophy could be understood apart from its theological context. Despite their differences, however, they agreed that the influence of Christianity was homogenous. Gilson, for example, talked of all medieval 'philosophies' having 'a common Christian spirit', whilst De Wulf and Van Steenberghen agreed that the unity of scholastic philosophy was to be explained by the 'unified civilisation of medieval Christendom', and that medieval Christendom provided a common foundation for different philosophical outgrowths.[92]

Moreover, with the exception of Gilson, scholastic historians regularly consider the influence of Christianity upon philosophical speculation merely in terms of the promotion or restriction of debate. Van Steenberghen argues, for example, that the significance of Christianity for philosophy during this period 'was both positive and negative'.[93] Hence, while few scholastic historians have failed to note the coincidence of Franciscan and Dominican rivalry in philosophical debates, the religious significance of those debates is rarely explored. The tendency to 'externalise' the role of religious considerations is typified by the view that philosophical tensions between Franciscans and Dominicans were *exacerbated* by the separate matter of their rivalry as religious orders. The possibility that philosophical debate was in fact the expression and embodiment of religious rivalry itself is thereby avoided.[94]

The admission of Thomas and Bonaventure to the canon of great books and to the canon of great thinkers has also affected the ways they have been understood by historians. Van Steenberghen, for example, thought that Thomas assumed a 'personal' mission – to supply Christendom with a 'philosophy expressing its particular culture and peculiar needs'.[95] Historians who wanted to break the mould of the Augustinian versus Aristotelian view of medieval philosophy also capitalised on this individualising perspective. John Francis Quinn, for example, characterised the work of Bonaventure and Thomas as 'personal' syntheses, 'distinctively Bonaventurean' and 'distinctively Thomistic' rather than Augustinian or Aristotelian.[96]

By contrast with such emphases, the preceding chapters aimed to show that the thinking of such figures as Bonaventure and Thomas was essentially Franciscan and Dominican: their arguments were validated dialogically, and rationality was the expression of the thought of communities rather than of lone individuals. The reception of Anselm's *Proslogion* illustrates the extent to which Bonaventure and Thomas Aquinas were important to their contemporaries more because they expressed the interests of their wider communities – less because of an originality that might have set them apart. If not all Franciscans and Dominicans were to side with Bonaventure and Thomas – in fact, there were always exceptions – it was because the nature of the religious life was a site of contest within the communities as well as between them.[97] The role of philosophical argument in this context was not one of providing common foundations for belief. Instead it was one of providing a public language for contesting and defending beliefs and assumptions whose expression might otherwise be limited to uncontested and incontestable readings of Scriptures and authorities.

The debates between masters within Christendom was, however, ultimately part of a wider debate within monotheism more generally. The absorption of Aristotelian thought within monotheism was, in one sense, a joint project of the Muslim, Jewish and Christian communities. Aquinas for example, learned from his Jewish and Muslim predecessors, Maimonides, Avicenna and Averroës. In another sense, however, the absorption of Aristotle within monotheism was a competitive enterprise. Aquinas was as committed to contesting the Aristotelianism of his Jewish and Muslim predecessors as he was to showing the compatibility of Christian and Aristotelian reason. The Aristotelian texts provided for the possibility of inter-religious dialogue which both orders of Friars embraced – though, as we have seen, they did so in different ways.

Among the Friars themselves there emerged a more pressing issue: that of 'which Christianity?' The Franciscans and the Dominicans were both orthodox Christians by the standards of their day, but they held different, even competing, insights into the nature of the Christian life. In the course of debate, reason did not express, in the deist mould, a shared rational core to their religion. Nor did philosophical reason leave behind a common Christian backdrop in favour of disinterested enquiry. Rather, for a time at least, the debate over Anselm's argument came to embody the religious differences between the two orders – which means that it embodied their different approaches to the encounters with God, with nature and with the unbeliever.

In the teaching of the Franciscan order, Anselm's argument helped articulate a sense of God's immanence in nature and in the human soul. It also helped articulate an approach to truth that emphasised the importance of humility and faith. Only the soul that was inwardly pure could achieve the knowledge of God. Moreover, such a soul owed its knowledge to God and not to its own powers. For such a soul, Christ was both the example to be imitated, as well as the interior teacher. The apostle of God in this case persuaded the unbeliever not by verbal argument, but rather by the outward imitation of truth/humility which reminded the unbeliever of the truth shining within: Christ the one master of all. By contrast, the Dominican downplayed an interior awareness of God in favour of the exterior human teacher, appointed by the Church as God's co-worker. His approach to God was grounded in exterior sources and remained there. The contemplation of natural and revealed truth did not lead the preacher upon an interior journey, but rather enabled him to help the souls of others. It was precisely by doing this that the preacher imitated and came closest to God incarnate. The debate over Anselm's argument, and over the other arguments with which it was regularly joined in the discussion of the natural knowledge of God, was therefore central to the validation and self-discovery of two rival forms of religious life within Christian orthodoxy.

## Notes

1. See Maur Burbach, 'Early Dominican and Franciscan Legislation Regarding St Thomas', in *Medieval Studies*, 4 (1942), 139-158.
2. P. Glorieux, *Répertoire des Maîtres en Théologie de Paris au XIIIe siècle*, 2 vols (Paris, 1933), II, n. 315.
3. E. Longpré, 'Questions Inédites du Commentaire sur les Sentences du Gauthier de Bruges', *Archivum d'Histoire Doctrinale et Littéraire du Moyen Age*, 7 (1932), 251-282: Walter of Bruges, *Com. in I lib. sent.* 2, i, respondeo, 3: 'Ad tertium dic secundum Damascenum, I libro, c. 3 quod ratio recta non potest cogitare non esse aliquid quo maius nequit cogitari, it est Deum, sed ratio per malitiam depravata potest; sed ex hoc non efficitur hoc quo maius nequit cogitari minus bonum, quia cum aestimatio recta nihil addit Deo, multo minus nec aestimatio falsa aliquid tollit. Vel dic quod cum dicitur: Deus quo maius nequit cogitari, aut cogitatur omnino hic signans aut res signata et hoc dupliciter: aut in speciali, secundum quod est quid optimum, aut in generali secundum conditiones generales, quia sunt veritas, bonitas et huiusmodi. Primis duobus modis potest perversus cogitare Deum non esse, tertio modo non potest: si enim cogitat, cogitat ens, verum et huiusmodi quae omnia supponunt primum ens et verum, quod Deum dicimus...'
4. Longpré, p. 263. Walter of Bruges, *Com. in I lib. sent.*, 2, ii, respondeo: 'Primo modo

Deus est veritas *illuminans omnem hominem*, Joan. 1, 9, et sic Deum esse non est demonstrabile, sed ipse est ratio demonstrandi et cognoscendi quodam modo omnia secundum Augustinum, qui dicit quod quidquid videmus, in prima luce videmus.'

5. Longpré, pp. 263-264. Walter of Bruges, *Com. in I lib. sent.*, 2, ii, respondeo: 'Secundo modo Deum esse est per se notum, eo quod verum, bonum et huiusmodi proprietates in omnibus rebus evidenter Deum, licet non distincte, notificant; et sic intellexit Damascenus qui dixit quod cognitio existendi Deum omnibus est inserta; et sic etiam non est demonstrabile, sicut nec principium per se notum, licet illi in quo malitia corrumpit et destruit humanae cognitionis insertionem possit demonstrari.'
6. John Peckham's treatment of God's existence is included among the texts collected in P. Daniels, *Quellenbeiträge und Untersuchungen zur Geschichte der Gottesbeweise im Dreizehenten Jahrhundert* (Munster, 1909), pp. 41-50. References will be to this and to John Peckham, *Com. in I lib. sent.*, d. ii.
7. Glorieux, II, n. 316.
8. Daniels, p. 44. John Peckham, *Com.in I lib. sent..*, d. ii, q. i, contra 4: 'Nec secundum valere videtur quia enuntiabile est in anima ut in subiecto; ergo si anima est mutabilis, omne scitum ab anima est mutabile: vel si est simpliciter immutabile erit Deus: Ergo et duo et tria esse quinque est Deus.' In his response, John Peckham combines a doctrine of illumination with Aristotelian abstraction. See ibid., pp. 47-48, John Peckham, *Com. in I sent.* d. ii q. i, primum, solutio oppositorum 4: 'Ad quartum dicendum, quod propositiones necessariae videntur in luce aeterna. Unde Augustinus in *Soliloq.* I omnia quae in disciplinis creduntur nisi ab alio quodam quasi suo sole illustrentur, videri atque intelligi non possunt. Dicendum ergo secundum Augustinum, quod quamuis extrema talium propositionum sint in phantasmate, ut species totius et partis, vel ad minus in memoria intellectuali, ut ternarii et quaternarii, quando dicitur tria et quatuor sunt septem, ista tamen ad veritatis infallibilis evidentiam non sufficiunt, nisi eorum rationes aeternae et incommutabiles visu aliqualiter attingantur. Igitur de enuntiabilibus verbis est dupliciter considerare: vel secundum quod repraesentantur in speciebus abstractis, vel secundum quod ostenduntur in rationibus sempiternis. Primo modo sunt commutabilia et ab anima per oblivionem delebilia et in singulis animabus numerata, et inceperunt quando ab intellectu formata. Secundo modo sunt aeterna, secundo modo sunt incommutabilia, in rationibus aeternis lucentia.'
9. Daniels, p. 45. John Peckham, *Com. in I sent.*, d. ii, q. i, Ad primum quaesitum, respondeo: 'Deum esse est verum et verorum evidentissimum, quantum est de se. Est quidem generaliter cognitum; sed naturalia imperfecta sunt nec sufficiunt nisi arte vel gratia promoveantur. Unde Damascenus Libro I, cap. I: "Cognitio existendi Deum ab ipso naturaliter nobis inserta est, et providentia et gubernatio creature magnitudinem divinae praedicant naturae et per legem et prophetas deinde per unigenitum filium secundum, quod possibile est nobis, sui ipsius manifestavit cognitionem." Ex his verbis colligitur, quod Deus a nobis tripliciter cognoscitur, scilicet per naturalem impressionem, per investigationem quae ex creaturis colligitur, et per revelationem quae in scripturis invenitur...'
10. Daniels, pp. 49-50. Peckham, *Com. in I lib. sent.*, d. ii q. ii, Ad secundo quaesitum

respondeo: 'Dicendum quod Deum cogitare non esse potest intelligi dupliciter: vel sola terminorum apprehensione et dissensione intellectus et sic cogitatur omne falsum... Sed quamuis sit naturaliter notum Deum esse, non tamen quid sit Deus est notum: et ideo plures existimantes de Dei quidditate intra concludunt Deum non esse.'

11. Daniels, p. 50. Peckham, *Com. I lib. sent.*, d. ii, q. ii, 2, solutio oppositorum, 1: 'Ad primum obiectum patet, quod insipiens non cogitat quid sit Deus, et credo quod cum pleno mentis assensu impossibile est hoc cogitari. 2. Ad secundum quod non potest cogitari non esse, quia nec secundum possibilitatem nec secundum veritatem potest cum assensu cogitari non esse: quod non contingit in aliqua creatura. Deus ergo, quia habet esse in identitate plena et in plenitudine, non habet esse circumscriptibile. Quod autem insipiens dicit Deum assumptionem adiungit, vel ponendo idolum esse Deum, vel providentiam quam erroneam putat Deo ascribendo.'
12. See supra, ch. 4, sec. iv.
13. Matthew of Aquasparta's treatment of God's existence is included among the texts collected in Daniels, pp. 59ff. References will be to this and to Matthew of Aquasparta, *Com. in I lib. Sent.*, dist. II.
14. See Matthew of Aquasparta, *Quaestiones de cognitione*, q. ii, in Matthew of Aquasparta (*Mathaei ab Aquasparta*) *Quaestiones disputatae de fide et de cognitione*, ed. by Collegium S. Bonaventurae ad Claras Aquas, 2nd ed. (Quaracchi, Florentiae, 1957).
15. Daniels, p. 60. Matthew of Aquasparta, *Com. in I lib. sent.*, dist. ii, q. iii, resp.: 'Est enim evidens ipsi... vel comprehendenti, quia cognitio existendi Deum insita est et facta menti rationali, in quantum tenet rationem imaginis, ratione cuius insertus est sibi naturalis appetitus et notitia et memoria illius ad cuius imaginem facta est in quem naturaliter tendit ut ipso possit beatificari.'
16. Cf. Matthew, *Quaestiones de cognitione*, q. ii, Ad argumenta in contrarium, 29.
17. Daniels, pp. 59-61. Matthew of Aquasparta, *Com. in I lib. sent.*, dist. ii, q. iii, resp.
18. Daniels, p. 60. Matthew of Aquasparta, *Com. in I lib. sent.*, dist. ii, q. iii, resp.
19. Daniels, p. 61. Matthew, ibid.
20. See Daniels, p. 52.
21. See M. D. Jordan, 'The Controversy of the *Correctoria* and the Limits of Metaphysics', in *Speculum*, 57, 2 (1982), 292-314.
22. See D. A. Callus, *The Condemnation of St Thomas Aquinas at Oxford* (Oxford, 1964) and J. Roensch, *Early Thomistic School* (Iowa, 1964).
23. Robert Kilwardby '*De Natura Theologiae*', ed. by F. Stegmueller in *Opuscula et Textus*, Series Scholastica, ed. by M. Grabmann et Fr. Pelster, Fasc. 17 (Aschendorf, 1935), pp. 19-22, p. 20: 'Augustinus enim vocat intellectualem visionem eorum solummodo cognitionem quae per semetipsam menti praesentia sunt, cuiusmodi sunt propria fides, voluntas, mens, cognitio et huiusmodi; et de eorum numero Deus est... Et ita Deus cognosci potest visione pure intellectuali, non obstante dicta propositione Aristotelis.'
24. Robert Kilwardby, *Quaestiones in librum primum sententiarum*, ed. by J. Schneider (Munchen, 1986), quaestio 6.
25. Ibid., quaestio 31.

26. For the parallels between Ulrich's *Summa de Bono* and Albert's later *Summa Theologiae*, see Alain de Libera, 'Ulrich de Strasbourg, lecteur d'Albert le Grand', in *Freiburger Zeitschrift für Philosophie und Theologie*, 32 (1985), 105-136.
27. See for example, O. Davis, *Meister Eckhart: Mystical Theologian* (London, 1991), p. 70.
28. Ulrich of Strassbourg, 'Summa de Bono', ed. by J. Daguillon in *Bibliothèque Thomiste* 12 (1930), pp. 6-10, lib. I, cap. ii.
29. Ibid. pp. 10-13, lib. I, cap. iii.
30. Ibid.
31. Ibid.: 'Notandum quoque est quod cum primi generis principia quisque probet audita nullus potest ea negare corde, licet neget ea ore, et ideo non potest cogitari non esse, quia hoc esset ea negare corde, nec indigent aliqua probatione, sed discentem oportet credere. Sed secundi generis principia inexperti negant etiam corde et cogitant ea non esse, et ideo interdum contra tales oportet ea probare...'
32. Ibid.: 'Sed Dei notitia in habitu lucis intellectus agentis que est Dei similitudo naturaliter inserta est in intellectu possibili, et hec confusa cognitio, ut ad actum determinatum producatur, non exigit nisi experimentum tale quale sumitur de causa; hoc enim est experimentum effectus illius cause, in tantum quod etiam ipse Aristoteles, in *Libro de natura deorum* [secundum Ciceronem, *Libro de natura deorum*, lib. ii, xxxvii], dicit, quod si essent homines qui semper sub terra habitassent, accepissent ante sola fama esse quoddam numen, deinde contigisset eos exire in hec loca que nos habitamus, cum repente terram et maria celumque vidissent et nubes et solem et stellas et motum eorum, profecto et esse deos et hec omnia esse opera eorum arbitrarentur; ergo patet propositum, scilicet per se notum nobis esse quod Deus est.'
33. Ibid.: 'Unde multo fortius est hoc possibile contingere in altissimo et nobis maxime inproportionato principio, precipue cum non solum ad experimenta suorum effectuum non convertimus oculos mentis, sed insuper ipsum oculum pene totum obtenebramus fantasiis errorum, et conversatione circa sensibilia et materialia per studium et sollicitudinem, et carnalibus passionibus.'
34. Ibid.: 'Et contra tales etiam in philosophia inquiritur Deus et divina, et ipse Dominus probat se esse multis rationibus, Isaiah xl, usque ad xlv capitulum. Qui vero lumine rationis convertunt ad experientiam divinorum effectuum ipsis, ut probatum est per se notum est, Deum esse nec possunt hoc negare corde, nec possunt cogitare eum non esse, nec requirunt de sua existentia probationem...'
35. Ibid.
36. Ibid., cap. viii.
37. Ibid., cap. vii.
38. See, for example, J. A. Weisheipl, *Thomas d'Aquino and Albert His Teacher* (Toronto, 1980), p. 11.
39. Ibid.
40. Glorieux, I, n. 6.
41. Albert Magnus, *Summa Theologiae*, ed. by Dionysius, W. Kübel et H. Georgio Vogels in *Opera Omnia*, 34, 1 (Aschendorff, 1978- ), lib. I, tract. 4, q. 19, cc. 2 and 4.
42. Ibid., lib. I, tract. 3, q. 17.

43. Ibid., lib. I, tract. 3, q. 18, cap. 1.
44. Ibid., lib. I, tract. 3, q. 17, ad ob. 6-8: 'Sed ex hoc non sequitur, quin posit haberi via per rationem ad ostendum ipsum.'
45. Thomas Sutton, *Quaestiones Ordinariae*, ed. by J. Shneider (Munich, 1977), q. 1.
46. Ibid. pp. 14-15: 'Habemus igitur istam distinctionem a philosopho, quod quaedam sunt magis nota secundum se, id est secundum naturam suam, et quaedam sunt magis nota quoad nos.'
47. Ibid., p. 15: 'Sed difficultas cognoscendi substantias separatas non est ex parte ipsarum rerum, quia ipsae sunt manifestissimae et secundum se maxime intelligibiles, sed difficultas est ex parte nostra, scilicet propter defectum intellectus nostri.'
48. Ibid., p. 18: 'Et ideo non sufficit ad hoc, quod propsoitio sit per se nota quoad nos, quod subiectum includat praedicatum, sed cum hoc requiritur quod nihil aliud sit magis notum intellectui nostro, per quod possit ostendi nobis ratio subiecti, secundum quam subiectum includit praedicatum.'
49. Ibid., p. 18.
50. This example is used in ibid., p. 22.
51. Ibid., pp. 31-32: Resp. 3-4: 'Ad tertium dicendum quod, quamuis nos sciamus quod subiectum includit praedictum, et per hoc sciamus quod propositio est per se nota secundum se, tamen quia rationem subiecti acquirimus de subiecto per syllogismum vel per fidem, non est per se nota quoad nos. Ad quartum dicendum quod bene conludit responsionem, quia non fuit responsio secundum mentem Anselmi, quia intentio eius est quod quicumque intelligit deum esse id, quo maius cogitari non potest, non potest cogitare deum non esse, sive fuerit fidelis sive sine fide. Et ideo dicit Anselmus ad deum: "Si te esse nolim credere, non possum non intelligere." Vult igitur quod non credens per fidem non potest non intelligere. Vult igitur quod non credens per fidem non potest non intelligere deum esse, quando intelligit ipsi convenire hanc rationem *quo maius intelligi vel cogitari non potest*.'
52. Ibid., p. 33: 'Ad duodecimum dicendum quod deum esse fit nobis notum per aliud quod est posterius, quia per effectus dei manifestos nobis probamus causam eorum esse...'
53. Robert d'Orford, *Reprobationes Dictorum A Fratre Egidio In Primum Senentiarum*, ed. by A. P. Vella (Paris, 1968), p. 66, distinctio iii: 'Adhuc quod Deus non potest cogitari non esse, hoc non est verum quia nobis innotescit quidditas Dei in cuius ratione includitur esse Dei. Sed quia cum non sit procedere in infinitum, cogitare quamcumque creaturam est standum ad eius altissimam causam, que est Deus. Hoc autem postquam intelligimus Deum esse non potest intelligi, quia non fit hoc quod intelligimus, Deum esse habetur vel per fidem vel per demonstrationem.'
54. Ibid., p. 66: 'Quod postea dicit, solus Deus non potest cogitari non esse, dicendum quod falsum est, quia veritas etiam non potest cogitari non esse, quia si veritas est, verum est veritatem non esse, et ita hoc cogitare est verum.'
55. Ibid., p. 67: 'Sic etiam intelligitur quod dicit Anselmus, quia supposito quod Deus sit, non potest directe negari non esse, secundum quod sic habetur per fidem vel demonstrationem, sicut Philosophi demonstrarabant Deum esse, et Magister similiter demonstrat in *Littera*.'

56. See W. Goris, 'Die Kritik des Bernard von Tillia An Der Lehre Von Gott als Ersterkanntem. Einleitung Und Textausgabe', in *Recherches de Théologie et Philosophie Médiévales*, 65, 2 (1998), 248-282.
57. The secular master in question is Henry of Ghent.
58. Goris, p. 288: 'Prima opinio: Quidam enim dixerunt quod primum quod a mente humana in statu viae cognoscitur seu intelligitur est veritas prima, non quidem ut obiectum et terminus congitionis – sic enim videtur a beatis in patria – sed ut ratio et medium cognoscendi, quia in ea et per eam omnis alia veritas cognoscitur ab intellectu.'
59. Goris, p. 289: 'Quare impossibile est quod videatur deus ut ratio cognoscendi et non videatur ut obiectum cognitionis... Si autem nos poneremus rationes ideales extra mentem divinam per se existentes quas intuens deus ut ad exemplar mundum condidit, ut Platonici imponunt... nam hoc opinari sacrilegum est.'
60. Goris, p. 296: 'Et ita secundum istos in conceptione entis, veri, boni et huiusmodi, prius apprehenditur ab anima bonum, ens verum increatum quam creatum.'
61. Goris, pp. 294-295: 'Non intendit Augustinus dicere quod quidquid anima cognoverit in statu viae cognoscat in lumine divino obiective, ut dictum est, sed solum effective, in quantum quidquid cognoscimus, cognoscimus per participationem divinea lucis in nobis.'
62. Goris, p. 298: 'Et ita patet quod intellectus noster informatus similitudinibus rerum corporalium sucipiens rationem entis vel boni vel unius et huiusmodi non prius in eis intelligit ens vel bonum vel verum increatum quam creaturm, sed potius et contrario.'
63. Goris, p. 303: 'Cum igitur utraque nostra cognitio, tam sensitiva quam intellectiva, fit per abstractionem a rebus materialibus sensibilibus, deus autem sit omnino immaterialis, patet quod deus, qui est veritas prima, non est primo cognitum a nobis in statu viae, sed aliquid aliud per quod devenimus in cognitionem eius.'
64. Alexander of Alexandria follows Matthew of Acquasparta and Bonaventure on the natural knowledge of God in his sentence commentary, Rome, Vat. Ross. Lat. MSS. 252 fols 9r, 15r-16r. For evidence of revisionist thought within the Franciscan community, see for example, J. Marshall, 'The Causation of Knowledge in the Philosophy of Peter John Olivi, O.F.M.', in *Franciscan Studies*, 16 (1956), 313-318. See also C. Bérubé, 'Olivi, Interprète de Saint Anselme', in *Analecta Anselmiana*, 4, I (1975), 147-58.
65. Richard of Middleton's treatment of God's existence is included among the texts collected by Daniels, and printed on pp. 84-88: Richard of Middleton, *Scriptum super primum sententiarum*, dist. iii, q. ii, 'Utrum Deum esse sit nobis per se notum'.
66. Daniels, pp. 84ff. Richard of Middleton, lib. I, dist. iii, q. ii 'Utrum Deum esse sit nobis per se notum'.
67. See D. E. Sharp, *Franciscan Philosophy at Oxford in the Thirteenth Century* (Oxford, 1930), pp. 256-257.
68. Daniels, pp. 84ff. Richard of Middleton, lib. I, d. iii, q. iii, respondeo 3 and 4.
69. Ibid., Richard of Middleton, lib. I, d. iii, q. iii, respondeo 1: 'Item, experimur legem naturalem quae immutabilis est. Nobis autem per se notum est legem immutabilem

non posse nobis imprimi nisi ab aliquo qui simpliciter immutabilis est: ergo ex his per se notis concluditur aliquem esse qui simpliciter immutabilis est, et hic est Deus.'

70. Ibid., Richard of Middleton, lib. I, d. iii, q. iii, respondeo 2: 'Item, experimur appetitum nostrum non posses plenarie quietari in quocunque bono creato; sed nobis per se notum est omnem naturalem appetitum rationalis creaturae quietari posse ab aliquo nisi impedimentum apponatur accidentale: ergo ex his tanquam ex per se notis concluditur esse aliquod increatum bonum quod nostrum appetitum potest plenarie quietare, et hoc Deus est.'
71. Ibid., Richard of Middleton, lib. I, d. iii, q. iii, respondeo 5: 'Item, omnia entia tam sensibilia quam intellectualia tendunt in finem, haec est per se nota; sed si esset finis ultra finem infinitum, appetitus naturalis voluntatis nostrae non tenderet ad quiescendum in fine, quia hic appetitus vanus esset cum esset ad aliquid quod nullo modo haberi posset: ergo restat quod omnium entium est finis ultimus, et hic est Deus.'
72. Sharp, pp. 202-203.
73. Ibid., pp. 258-259. Sharp also notes that in criticising the opponents of the primacy of the will Richard points out that the will is the principal mover of all other potencies. In fact, the intellect, in its complete action, the production of the mental word, depends on a previous act of the will. Like John Peckham, Richard argues that Augustine only suggests that the intellect is the noblest faculty when, as including the will, it is opposed to the sensitive and vegetative powers. According to Richard, to hold a primacy of the intellect is to confuse a temporal priority with one of nature, for although the intellect like a servant with a lamp, points out the way, the will, like the master is not bound to follow its guidance.
74. William of Ware's treatment of God's existence is included among the texts collected in Daniels, pp. 89-103. William of Ware, *Questiones super libros Sententiarum*, 21, in Daniels, *Quellenbeitrage*, pp. 98ff.
75. Daniels, pp. 89ff: William of Ware, *Questiones*, 14.
76. E. Grant, 'The effect of the Condemnation of 1277', in *The Cambridge History of Later Medieval Philosophy*, ed. by N. Kretzmann, et al. (Cambridge, 1982), pp. 537-539.
77. R. Hissette, *Enquête sur les 219 Articles condamnés á Paris Le 7 Mars 1277* (Louvain, Paris, 1977).
78. Daniels, p. 103, William of Ware, *Questiones*, 21: Solutio Oppositorum, 2, 'Ad aliud dicunt quidam quod VIII Phys. non probat Deum esse, sed probat significatum huius termini Deus.'
79. É. Gilson, *History of Christian Philosophy in the Middle Ages* (London, 1978), p. 458.
80. Duns Scotus, *Philosophical Writings* (Hackett, 1987), p. 72: 'Item, quare intellectus, cujus objectum est ens, nullam invenit repugnantiam intelligendo aliquod infinitum; immo videtur perfectissimum intelligibile.'
81. Duns Scotus, *Philosophical Writings*, p. 72: 'Deus est quo cognito sine contradictione majus cogitari non potest sine contradictione.'
82. Ibid. pp. 73-74: 'Et tunc arguitur ultra, quod illud sit loquendo de esse existentiae. Summe cogitabile non est tantum in intellectu cogitante, quia tunc posset esse, quia

cogitable possibile, et non posset esse, quia repugnat rationi eius esse ab aliqua causa, sicut patet prius in secunda conclusione de via efficientiae. Majus ergo cogitabile est quod est in re quam quod est tantum in intellectu.'

83. Gilson, *History*, p. 460.
84. For an account of the continuation of the debate on the Dominican side into the fourteenth century, see E. Weber, 'La Démonstration de l'Existence de Dieu chez Hervé de Nedellec et Ses Confrères Prêcheurs de Paris', *Preuve et Raisons a l'Université de Paris: Logique, Ontologie et Théologie au XIV$^{e}$Siècle*, ed. by Z. Kaluza and P. Vignaux (Paris, 1984), pp. 25-41.
85. John Peckham, (*Ioannis Peckham*) *Registrum epistolarum*, 3 vols, ed. by C. T. Martin, *in Rerum Britannicarum Medii Aevi Scriptores* [n. 77] (London, 1882-5), III, 896-902.
86. *Cit. in* Burbach, p. 149. The 1313 Chapter of Metz confirmed that the Dominican order was especially bound to abide by the doctrine of Thomas Aquinas, and forbade any friar 'to be sent to Paris for study until he has for three years carefully studied the doctrine of Friar Thomas' (Burbach, p. 150).
87. C. Bérubé, 'La Première École Scotiste', in *Preuve et Raisons*, op. cit. pp. 9-24 notes that later Franciscans emphasised continuity between Duns Scotus and the older Franciscan tradition as represented by Bonaventure.
88. A. J. Krailsheimer, *Rabelais and the Franciscans* (Oxford, 1963), p. 293.
89. L. W. B. Brockliss, *French Higher Education in the Seventeenth and Eighteenth Centuries: A Cultural History* (Oxford, 1987), p. 196.
90. See B. McSweeney, *Roman Catholicism: The Search for Relevance* (Oxford, 1980), pp. 62ff: 'The elements of Thomist writings which attracted the attention of the Pope and his consultants were St Thomas's theory of knowledge and his political writings' (p. 71). 'By 1892 no one could hold a chair at any Catholic institution who did not subscribe fully to the doctrine of St Thomas as interpreted by the Vatican authorities' (p. 74).
91. T. F. O'Meara, 'Thomas Aquinas and German Intellectuals, Neoscholasticism and Modernity in the Late 19$^{th}$ Century', in *Gregorianum* vol. 68, 3-4 (1987), 719-736 (735): 'From its inception in the nineteenth century neo-Thomism was occasionally fashioned by nineteeenth century interests in epistemology and apologetics... it spent increasing energy on the epistemology of knowing reality and believing revelation...'
92. Compare Étienne Gilson, *The Spirit of Mediaeval Philosophy* (New York-London, 1936), and *History of Christian Philosophy in the Middle Ages*, 3$^{rd}$ ed. (London, 1978); Maurice De Wulf, *History of Medieval Philosophy* (London, 1926); Frederick Van Steenberghen, *The Philosophical Movement in the Thirteenth Century* (Edinurgh, 1955).
93. Van Steenberghen, *The Philosophical Movement in the Thirteenth Century*, pp. 94-106.
94. See for example, C. S. R. Harris, *Duns Scotus*, 2 vols (New York, 1959), I, 82: 'Moreover, the rivalry between the Dominican and Franciscan Orders served to intensify the struggle.'
95. Van Steenberghen, The Philosophical Movement, pp. 106-114.

96. J. F. Quinn, *The Historical Constitution of St Bonaventure's Philosophy* (Toronto, 1973), *passim*.
97. This of course goes for such Dominican theologians as Meister Eckhart and Durandus of St Pourçain. On the position of such figures within the order see the illuminating remarks in Alasdair MacIntyre, *Three Rival Versions of Moral Inquiry, Encyclopaedia, Genealogy, and Tradition* (London, 1990), pp. 162ff.

# Conclusion

The history of theistic arguments generally, and of Anselm's argument in particular, illustrate that many of the issues of modern philosophy of religion are culturally-specific. That this is only grudgingly acknowledged, if at all, among professional philosophers of religion, is due in part to the self-image of philosophy as a timeless and spaceless discourse, whose questions are and always have been equally relevant to all human beings. It is ironic, then, that the culturally-specific character of such questions is illustrated by the history of one of the central texts of the philosophy of religion itself.

The case of Anselm's argument serves to illustrate that one can only understand philosophical issues by looking at them in their historical contexts. This is because the same form of argument – even the same argument – can be used for different ends. The forms of argument that were used in the seventeenth century to articulate an idea of God allegedly common to all traditions, for example, were used in the thirteenth century to contest and defend competing accounts of God within the same broad tradition of Christianity. What was taken to be representative of 'universal' and 'independent' reason in the seventeenth century served to express rationalities that were embedded within specific communities in the thirteenth.

To understand 'reason' and 'rationality' in the context of religion is to look beyond the text-book approach to the rationality of religious belief, and to enquire how reason operates within living contexts: both of present, as well as of past cultures. It is also to recognise that reasoning is essentially dialogical. It is the essentially dialogical character of the human condition, as Charles Taylor has written, that has been 'rendered almost invisible by the overwhelmingly monological bent of mainstream modern philosophy'.[1] The same can also be said about the nature of rational enquiry. As MacIntyre has written:

> Rational enquiry about my practical beliefs, relationships, and commitments is... not something that *I* undertake by attempting to separate myself from the whole set of my beliefs, relationships, and commitments and to view them from some external standpoint. It is something that *we* undertake from within *our* shared mode of practice by asking, when we have good reason to do so, what the strongest and soundest objections are to this or that particular belief or concept that we have up to this point taken for granted.[2]

Practical beliefs, relationships and commitments within a religious context are formed in dialogue not only with the authorities of the religious tradition, but also within a community of interpreters. For this reason, to understand 'reason' and 'rationality' in the contexts of religion is to recognise that what counts as a reason for one community may not do so for others. The New Testament as Thomas Aquinas pointed out, provides reasons for Christians and heretics, but not for Jews and Muslims. However, as the competing intellectual perspectives of the Franciscans and Dominicans show, the same can also be said for communities that belong to the same tradition. In that case, the reasons brought forward in favour of a community's experience of God are derived from within the community itself, and may only be fully recognised by those who belong to that community.

A religious tradition flourishes, however, only to the extent that it is capable of making its central commitments available for public examination both within and beyond its boundaries. That is the condition for the public communication of those commitments, and therefore also for their very survival. The importance of a community maintaining its public contestability is illustrated by the position of the Friars within Christendom. Had the Franciscans or the Dominicans been unable to rebut the charges of irrationality or worse, heresy, they would not have survived the Middle Ages. The charge of heresy would have crippled them as religious orders within Christendom – as it did to many others during the period – while the charge of irrationality would have removed their whole raison d'être: to convince and convict the unbeliever.

Thomas Aquinas's appeal, in the *Summa contra gentiles* to a notion of natural reason 'to which all men are forced to give their assent', is an example of an attempt to render those commitments available for public encounter beyond Christendom. Nonetheless, given that in Thomas's account, as in those of his contemporaries, rational argument must always submit to the judgement of revelation, even here he was appealing to rational standards that were embedded within his own community. There is no sense in which Thomas suggests that one finds truth by divorcing oneself from prior commitments, relationships and beliefs. It is rather that those commitments, relationships and beliefs themselves provide the account of truth that is put to the question. In the course of debate, reason is allowed to construct itself, sometimes employing arguments from nature, sometimes arguments from authority, even where the opponents in a debate stand outside the tradition to which the authority pertains.

What the history of Anselm's argument shows is that reason is not always doing the same thing, and not always employing its tools in the same way. It is, so to speak, context-constituted. Within the work of the Friars it came to be used to contest rival accounts of intellectual knowledge, and ultimately, rival accounts of the religious life. In that debate the argument was used in ways quite unlike its use in modern philosophy of religion. Furthermore, neither scholastic nor modern analytic philosophy read Anselm's argument in quite the same terms as it would have been read by the devotional audience for whom it was composed.

While reason is context-constituted, however, it is also context-constituting. In the case of the Franciscans and the Dominicans, reason served not to replace the religious traditions in question, but to construct them. When the Franciscans, for example, were faced with criticisms levelled against them, both by seculars outside the community and by anti-scholastic radicals who threatened division from within, they addressed themselves – via Anselm's argument – to the first principles of their religious life. Academic Franciscans thereby attempted to show that their own practices were not opposed to those principles, but represented a necessary development of them. The development of rational enquiry in this case was also therefore, a development of the Franciscan tradition.

The history of Anselm's argument shows that it is precisely by looking at those features of an argument which are most particular, most tied to time and place that we gain a greater understanding of what an argument is being used for. In the case of the Franciscans and the Dominicans, it was precisely those concerns most particular to them that were at stake in their enquiries. Reason was thus used to articulate claims at once particular, in that they belonged to specific communities during a specific period, and at the same time universal, in that they were taken to be universal truths by the communities by which they were held.

At stake were two different and incompatible accounts of the human encounter with God, which underpinned in turn two different and incompatible accounts of the authentic religious life. One of those encountered God primarily within the soul; the other primarily beyond it. In this case, the differences between the Franciscans and the Dominicans over the natural knowledge of God embodied their religious differences more generally. Natural theology represented the metaphysical counterpart of the religious life.

Once again, none of this could be understood by looking at the Friars' treatment of Anselm's argument in isolation from a wider context in which there was always an implicit debate about what the authentic religious life should look like. In this context, Anselm's argument contributed to an enquiry not so much about the foundations of religious belief, but about the aims or ends of religious life – what form the authentic imitation of the original Christians should take. What made the question so insidious was that the Friars' accounts were incompatible with one another.

What Roger Scruton would perhaps call 'time-bound' and 'parochial' concerns therefore, were the very issues that occupied the thought of Thomas Aquinas and Bonaventure along with their contemporaries: even when they did treat the 'perennial' and 'timeless' issues of God's existence. This form of philosophical history may not have the significance for contemporary questions that Scruton has suggested. This does not mean that it has no relevance for contemporary philosophical enquiry, however.

Recognising the context-constituted and context-constituting character of rational enquiry raises important issues about the nature of validation and the possibility of meaningful debate between communities from different contexts. The case of the Friars illustrates that the beginning of enquiry does not depend upon the prior removal of difference and particularity. Rather, it proceeds upon, and creates, an awareness of difference and particularity.

The Franciscans and Dominicans found each other in their encounters with Aristotle, and 'found themselves' in their encounters with each other. Their incompatible approaches to the challenge represented by the unbeliever generally and by Aristotle in particular meant that conflict between the orders was inevitable. The traditions of the Friars each represent, in MacIntyre's words, a 'historically extended, socially embodied argument', and the arguments which their traditions embodied concerned the goods or goals constitutive of their traditions.[3] What the Friars debates also illustrate, however, and what MacIntyre tends not to consider, is that such enquiries may be, in fact may essentially be, concerned with religious goods rather than only moral or political goods. Both orders embodied internal conflicts, but together with these, their encounter with the unbeliever and latterly with each other, led to the articulation and development of differences that had existed between them at a non-rational level since their origins. In giving voice to those differences, however, they made those differences, in a sense, more real.

It does not follow from the fact that the Friars were never to attain a final consensus that their enquiries somehow ended in failure. Rational consensus is not the only successful outcome of encounter. Progress may also be measured by greater understanding of the nature of difference.[4] Such awareness is critical for the survival and development of cultural identities and, arguably, such an awareness was attained at Paris in the thirteenth century. At the very least, it might be suggested that the debate about ends and the clarification of difference represents a more viable form of discourse than one that demands separation from commitments and beliefs at the outset, and that can only conclude with the eradication of difference.

By looking at the operations of rationality rather than by attempting to define 'reason' in the abstract, it is possible to understand more about the functions it can serve within communities and between them. The kinds of rational engagement practised in medieval Paris illustrate the ways in which reason constructs itself in the course of its operations, according to the ends for which it is used: in this case, the defence and construction of two subtly different Christian traditions.

## Notes

1. Alasdair MacIntyre, *Dependent Rational Animals: Why Human Beings Need The Virtues* (London, 1999), p. 157.
2. Charles Taylor, *Multiculturalism*, ed. by A. Gutmann (Princeton, 1994), p. 32.
3. Alasdair MacIntyre, *After Virtue: a Study in Moral Theory*, 2nd ed. (London, 1985), p. 222.
4. See John Clayton, *Thomas Jefferson and the Study of Religion* (Lancaster, 1992).

# Bibliography

## Manuscripts


Assisi, MS. Lat. 131.

Bologna Universitaria, MS. 753 (1506).

Oxford, Bodleian, MS. Laud. misc. 363.

Oxford, Merton College, MS. 131, 8r-9r.

Paris, Bibliothèque Nationale, MS. Lat. 3073.
Paris, Bibliothèque Nationale, MS. Lat. 3423.
Paris, Bibliothèque Nationale, MS. Lat. 3424.
Paris, Bibliothèque Nationale, MS. Lat. 3436.
Paris, Bibliothèque Nationale, MS. Lat. 10640.
Paris, Bibliothèque Nationale, MS. Lat. 14910.
Paris, Bibliothèque Nationale, MS. Lat. 15652.

Paris, Mazarine, MS. Lat. 331.
Paris, Mazarine, MS. Lat. 862.

Rome, Vatican MS. Lat. 1187.
Rome, Vatican MS. Lat. 4301.
Rome, Vatican MS. Lat. 6771.
Rome, Vatican MS. Lat. 12993.
Rome, Vatican MS. Barb. Lat. 729.

Troyes, MS. Lat. 1245 (Clairvaux).


## Published Primary Sources


Abelard, *Sic et Non*, ed. by B. B. Boyer and R. McKeon (Chicago, 1976-197).

Abulafia, A. S. and Evans, G. R., *The Works of Gilbert Crispin, Abbot of Westminster* (London, 1986).

Albertus Magnus, St, *Opera Omnia*, ed. by A. Borgnet, et al., 38 vols (Paris, 1890-1895).

Albertus Magnus, St, *Summa Theologiae*, ed. by Dionysius, W. Kübel et H. Georgio Vogels in *Opera Omnia* (Aschendorff, 1978- ), v. XXXIV.

Alexander Nequam, *Speculum Speculationum*, ed. by R. Thomson (Oxford, 1988).

Alexander of Hales, *Summa Theologica*, ed. by V. Doucet, 5 vols (Quaracchi 1924-1948).

Alexander of Hales, *Glossa in Quatuor libros Sententiarum Petri Lombardi* (Quaracchi, 1951-1957).

Annibald' d'Annibald, *Scriptum super libris magistri sententiarum*, in Thomas Aquinas, *Opera Omnia*, ed. by T. P. Fiaccodori (Parma, 1852-1873; reprinted in Musurgia 1948-1950), v. XXII.

Anselm of Canterbury, St, *Anselmi Opera Omnia*, ed. by F. S. Schmitt, 6 vols (Rome and Edinburgh, 1938-1961).

Armstrong, R. J. and Brady, I. C., *Francis and Claire: The Complete Works* (London, 1982).

Augustine, St, *De Tractatu Johanini*, in *Patrologia Latina*, ed. by J. P. Migne, et al., 217 vols (Paris, 1844-1879), vol. XXXV, cols 1375-1970.

Augustine, St, *De Trinitate*, in *Corpus Christianorum Series Latina*, ed. by W. J. Mountain (Turnholt, 1968), vol. L.

Augustine, St, *Augustini Confessionum*, Lib. XIII, *Corpus Christianorum Series Latina*, ed. by L. Verheijen (Turnholt, 1981), vol. XXVII.

Benedict, St, *The Rule of St Benedict*, ed. and trans. by J. T. McCann (London, 1951).

Bérubé, C. and Gieben, S., 'Gilbert de Tournai and Robert Grosseteste Sources Inconnues de Saint Bonaventure, Suivi de L'Édition Critique de Trois Chapitres du *Rudimentum Doctrinae* de Guibert de Tournai', in *S. Bonaventura 1274-1974*, ed. by J. G. Bougerol, 5 vols (Rome, 1973-1974), III, 627-654.

Bonaventure, St, *Opera Omnia*, 10 vols (Quaracchi, 1882-1902).

Bonaventure, St, *The Works of Bonaventure*, tr. by J. de Vinck (Patterson, 1960-1970).

Daniels, P. A., *Quellenbeiträge und Untersuchungen zur Geschichte der Gottesbeweise im Dreizehenten Jarhundert* (Münster, 1909).

Denifle, H., *Auctarium Chartularii Universitatis*, ed. by A. Chatelain (Paris, 1894-1964).

Duns Scotus, *Philosophical Writings*, ed. and trans. by A. Wolter (Cambridge M. A., 1987).

Eadmer, *The Life of St Anselm*, ed. and trans. by R. W. Southern (Oxford, 1962).

Foster, K., *The Life of Saint Thomas Aquinas: Biographical Documents* (London, 1959).

Gál, G., 'Viae ad Exsistentiam Dei Probandam in Doctrina Richardi Rufi OFM', *Franziskanische Studien*, 38 (1956), 177-202.

Gerard de Frachet, *Lives of the Brethren of the Order of Preachers, 1206-1259*, ed. B. Jarrett and trans. by J. Conway (London, 1924).

Gerard de Prato, *Il Breviloquium super Libros Sententiarum di Frate Gherardo da Prato Dell' ordine de' Minori*, Pubblicato per la prima volta e corredato di Alcuni Studi dal Padre Marcellino da Civezza O.F.M. (Prato, 1882).

Gibson, S., *Statuta Antiqua Universitatis Oxoniensis* (Oxford, 1931).

Goris, W., 'Die Kritik des Bernard von Tillia An Der Lehre Von Gott als Ersterkanntem. Einleitung Und Textausgabe', in *Recherches de Théologie et Philosophie Médiévales*, 65, 2 (1998), 248-282.

Gremacoli, G., 'La Summa di Rolando da Cremona, Il Testo del Prologo', *Studi Medievali*, 16 (1975), 825-876.

Habig, M. A. (ed. and trans.), *St Francis of Assisi, Writings And Early Biographies: English Omnibus of The Sources for The Life of St Francis* (Chicago, 1973).

Hilary, St., *De Trinitate*, in *Patrologia Latina*, ed. by J. P. Migne, et al., 217 vols (Paris, 1844-1879), v. X, cols 9-472.

Hugh of St Victor, *De Sacramentis*, in *Patrologia Latina*, ed. by J. P. Migne, 217 vols (Paris, 1844-1879), t. CLXXVI.

Hugh of St Victor, *Eruditionis Didascalicae*, in *Patrologia Latina*, ed. by J. P. Migne, 217 vols (Paris, 1844-1879), t. CLXXVI, cols 749-838.

John Peckham (*Ioannis Peckham*) *Registrum epistolarum*, 3 vols, ed. by C. T. Martin in *Rerum Britannicarum Medii Aevi Scriptores*, LXXVII (London, 1885).

John Quidort, *Le Correctorium Corruptorii 'Circa' de Jean Quidort de Paris*, ed. by J. P. Muller (Rome, 1941).

Lanfranc, *The Monastic Constitutions of Lanfranc*, ed. and. trans. by D. Knowles (Edinburgh, 1951).

Longpré, É., 'Questions Inédites du Commentaire Sur Les Sentences de Gauthier de Bruges', in *Archives d'Histoire Doctrinale et Littéraire du Moyen Age*, 7 (1932), 251-275.

Matthew of Aquasparta, *Questiones Disputatae Selectae: i. Questiones de Fide et de Cognitione*, ed. by Collegium S. Bonaventurae ad Claras Aquas, 2nd ed. (Quaracchi, 1903).

Moore, P. S., *The Works of Peter of Poitiers, Master in Theology and Chancellor of Paris 1193-1205* (Notre Dame, 1936).

Pergamo, B., 'De Quaestionibus Ineditis Fr. Odonis Rigaldi, Fr. Gulielmi de Melitona et Codicis Vat Lat. 782 circa Naturam Theologiae deque earum Relatione ad Summam Theologicam Fr. Alexandri Halensis', in *Archivum Franciscanum Historicum*, 29 (1936), 3-54, 308-364.

Peter John Olivi, *Petrus Johannis Olivi O.F.M., Quaestiones in Secundum Librum Sententiarum*, ed. by B. Jansen (Quaracchi, 1922-1926).

Peter Lombard, *Sententiae in IV libris distinctae*, ed. by Collegium S. Bonaventurae ad Claras Aquas (Grottaferrata, 1971).

Peter of Tarentaise, *Innocentii Quiniti In IV Libros Sententiarum Commentaria*, ed. by T. Turci and J. B. de Marinis (Toulouse, 1652).

Reichert, B. M. et al. (ed.), *Monumenta Ordinis Fratrum Praedicatorum Historica* (Rome and Louvain, 1896-1966), 25 vols.

Richard of St Victor, *De Trinitate*, in *Patrologia Latina*, ed. by J. P. Migne, et al., 217 vols (Paris, 1844-1879), v. CXCVI, cols. 887-994.

Robert d'Orford, *Les Premières Polémiques Thomistes: Robert d'Oxford, Reprobationes Dictorum a Fratre Egidio in Primum Sententiarum*, ed. by A. P. Vella (Paris, 1968).

Robert Grosseteste, *Hexaëmeron*, ed. by R. C. Dales and S. Gieben (Oxford, 1982).

Robert Kilwardby, '*De Natura Theologiae*', ed. by F. Stegmueller in *Opuscula et Textus*, Series Scholastica, ed. by M. Grabmann et Fr. Pelster, Fasc. 17 (Aschendorf, 1935).

Robert Kilwardby, *De Ortu Scientorum*, ed. Judy, A. G., in *Auctores Britannici Medii Aevi*, iv (Toronto, 1976).

Robert Kilwardby, *Quaestiones in librum primum sententiarum*, ed. by J. Schneider (Munchen, 1986).

Roger Bacon, *Opera Quaedam Hactenus Inedita*, ed. by J. S. Brewer (London, 1859).

Roger Bacon, *Compendium of the Study of Theology*, ed. and trans. by T. S. Maloney (Leiden, 1988).

Roland of Cremona, *Summa Theologiae, Liber Tercius*, ed. by A. Cortesi in *Monumenta Bergomensia*, t. vii (Bergamo, 1962).

Stegmueller, F., 'Les Questions du Commentaire des Sentences de Robert Kilwardby', in *Recherches de Théologie Ancienne et Médiévale*, 6 (1934), 55-80.

Tanner, N. P. ed. and trans. *Decrees of the Ecumentical Councils* (Georgetown, 1990).

Thomas Aquinas, St, *Opera Omnia*, ed. by T. P. Fiaccodori et al. (Parma, 1852-1873; reprinted in Musurgia 1948-1950).

Thomas Aquinas, St, *On Being and Essence*, trans. by A. Maurer (Toronto, 1949).

Thomas Aquinas, St, *Expositio in Librum Boethii de Trinitate*, ed. by B. Decker (Leiden, 1955).

Thomas Aquinas, St, *Summa Contra Gentiles*, trans. by A. G. Pegis (New York, 1955).

Thomas Aquinas, St, *Quaestiones Disputatae*, ed. R. Spiazzi, 2 vols (Turin 1964, 1965).

Thomas Aquinas, St, *Liber de Veritate Catholicae Fidei contra Errores Infidelium qui dicitur Summa Contra Gentiles*, Cura et Studio P. Marc, C. Pera, P. Caramello (Turin-Paris, 1967).

Thomas of Eccleston, *Tractatus De Adventu Fratrum Minorum in Angliam*, ed. A. G. Little (Manchester, 1951).

Thomas Sutton, *Quaestiones Ordinariae*, ed. by J. Shneider (Munich, 1977).

Tugwell, S. (trans.), *Early Dominicans* (London, 1982).

Ulrich of Strassbourg, 'Summa de Bono', ed. by J. Daguillon in *Bibliothèque Thomiste*, 12 (1930).

William of Auxerre, *Magistri Guillelmi Altissiodorensis, Summa Aurea*, ed. J. Ribaillier, 5 vols (Paris; Rome, 1980-1987).

## Secondary Sources

Aertsen, J., *Medieval Philosophy and the Transcendentals: The Case of Thomas Aquinas* (Brill, 1996).

Alverny, M. Th. d', 'Achard de Saint Victor, Eveque d'Avranches – Disciple de Saint Anselme', in *Analecta Anselmiana*, 2 (1970), 217-222.

Aron, M., *Saint Dominic's Successor* (London; St Louis, 1955).

Asad, T., *Genealogies of Religion: Discipline and Reasons of Power in Christianity and Islam* (Baltimore; London, 1993).

Barth, K., *Anselm: Fides Quarens Intellectum*, trans. by I. W. Robertson (Cleveland and New York, 1962; 1st pub. in 1931).

Bennett, R. F., *The Early Dominicans: Studies In Thirteenth-Century Dominican History* (Cambridge, 1937).

Benson, R. L. et al., *Renaissance and Renewal in The Twelfth Century* (Oxford, 1982).

Berger, D., 'Mission to the Jews and Jewish-Christian Contacts in the Polemical Literature of the High Middle Ages', *American Historical Review*, 91 (1986), 576-591.

Bérubé, C., 'Le "Dialogue" de S. Bonaventure et Roger Bacon', *Collectanea Fransciscana*, 39 (1969), 59-103.

Bérubé, C., 'Olivi, Interprète de Saint Anselme', *Analecta Anselmiana*, 4, 1 (1975), 147-158.

Bérubé, C., 'La Première École Scotiste', in *Preuve et Raisons a l'Université de Paris: Logique, Ontologie et Théologie au XIV$^{e}$ Siècle*, ed. by Z. Kaluza and P. Vignaux (Paris, 1984), pp. 9-24.

Bettoni, E., *Il Problema Della Conoscibilità di Dio Nella Scuola Francescana* (Padua, 1950).

Bettoni, E., *Duns Scotus: The Basic Principles of His Philosophy*, trans. by B. Bonansea (Washington D. C., 1961).

Blumenkranz, B., *Juifs et Chrétiens, Patristique et Moyen Age* (London, 1977).

Boehner, P., 'The Spirit of Franciscan Philosophy', *Franciscan Studies*, 2 (1942), 217-237.

Boehner, P., 'The System of Metaphysics of Alexander of Hales', *Franciscan Studies*, 5 (1945), 366-414.

Bolton, B., 'Tradition and Temerity: Papal Attitudes to Deviants, 1159-1216', in *Schism, Heresy and Religious Protest*, ed. by D. Baker, Studies in Church History, ix (Cambridge, 1972), pp. 79-91.

Bolton, B., *The Medieval Reformation* (London, 1983).

Bonansea, B. M., *God and Atheism* (Washington, 1979).

Bonansea, B. M., 'The Human Mind and The Knowedge of God – Reflections On A Scholastic Controversy', *Franciscan Studies*, 40: 18 (1980), 5-17.

Bougerol, J. G., *Introduction To The Works of Bonaventure*, trans. by J. de Vinck (New Jersey, 1963).

Bougerol, J. G., 'Saint Bonaventure et Saint Guillaume de Saint-Thierry', *Antonianum*, 46 (1971), 189-231.

Bougerol, J. G., 'Saint Bonaventure et Saint Bernard', *Antonianum*, 46 (1971), 3-79.

Bougerol, J. G., 'Saint Bonaventure et Saint Anselm', *Antonianum*, 47 (1972), 333-361.

Bougerol, J. G. (ed.), *S. Bonaventura 1274-1974*, 5 vols (Grottaferrata, 1973-1974).

Brady, I., 'The Distinctions of Lombard's Book of Sentences and Alexander of Hales', *Franciscan Studies*, 25 (1965), 90-116.

Brady, I., 'The Writings of Saint Bonaventure Regarding the Franciscan Order', *Miscellanea Francescana*, 75: 1-4 (1975), 129-135.

Brady, I., 'St Bonaventure's Sermons On Saint Francis', *Franziskanishe Studien*, 58: 1-2 (1976), 129-141.

Brockliss, L. W. B., *French Higher Education in The Seventeenth and Eighteenth Centuries: A Cultural History* (Oxford, 1987).

Brooke, C. N. L., 'St Dominic and His First Biographer', *Transactions of the Royal Historical Society*, 17 (1967), 23-40.

Brooke, R. B., *Early Franciscan Government* (Cambridge, 1959).

Brooke, R. B., *The Coming of the Friars* (London, 1975).

Buckley, J. M., *At The Origins of Modern Atheism* (New Haven, 1987).

Burbach, M., 'Early Dominican and Franciscan Legislation Regarding St Thomas', *Medieval Studies*, 4 (1942), 139-158.

Burns, R. I., 'Christian-Islamic Confrontation in the West: The Thirteenth-Century Dream of Conversion', *American Historical Review*, 76: 4-5 (1976), 1386-1434.

Burr, D., 'The "Correctorium" Controversy and the Origins of the "Usus Pauper" Controversy', *Speculum*, 40: 2 (1985), 331-342.

Burrell, D. B., *Knowing The Unknowable God: Ibn-Sina, Maimonides, Aquinas* (Indiana, 1986).

Burrell, D. B., 'Aquinas and Islamic and Jewish Thinkers', in *The Cambridge Companion to Aquinas*, ed. by N. Kretzmann and E. Stump (Cambridge, 1994), pp. 60-84.

Bynum, C. W., 'Did the Twelfth Century Discover the Individual?', in *Journal of Ecclesiastical History*, 31, 1 (1980), 1-18.

Cahill, B., *Dominic the Preacher* (London, 1988).

Callebaut, A., 'Essai Sur L'Origine du Premier Couvent des Mineurs à Paris, Et Sur L'Influence De Fr. Grégoire de Naples', *France Franciscaine*, 11 (1928), 5-30, 179-209.

Callus, D. A., 'Two Early Oxford Masters On The Problem of The Plurality of Forms: Adam of Buckfield, Richard Rufus of Cornwall', *Revue Néoscolastique de Philosophie*, 42 (1939), 411-445.

Callus, D. A., 'The Philosophy of St Bonaventure and St Thomas', *Blackfriars*, 21 (1940), 151-164, 249-267.

Callus, D. A., 'The Introduction of Aristotelian Learning to Oxford', *Proceedings of the British Academy*, 29 (1943), 229-281.

Callus, D. A., *The Condemnation of St Thomas at Oxford* (Oxford, 1948).

Callus, D. A. (ed.), *Robert Grosseteste: Scholar and Bishop* (Oxford, 1955).

Callus, D. A., 'Correctoria', in *New Catholic Encyclopedia* (Washington, 1957), iv, 349-352.

Campbell, R., *From Belief to Understanding* (Canberra, 1976).

Campbell, R., 'Anselm's Theological Method', *Scottish Journal of Theology*, 32: 6 (1979), 541-562.

Campbell, R., 'Anselm's Background Metaphysics', *Scottish Journal of Theology*, 33: 4 (1980), 317-344.

Catto, J. I. (ed.), *The History of The University of Oxford* (Oxford, 1984), vol. I.

Catto, J. I., 'Theology and Theologians, 1220-1320', in ibid., I, pp. 471-517.

Charlesworth, M. J., *St Anselm's Proslogion* (Oxford, 1965).

Châtillon, J., 'De Guillaume d'Auxerre à Saint Thomas d'Aquin: L'Argument de Saint Anselme Chez Les Premiers Scolastiques du XIIe Siècle', *Spicilegium Beccense*, 1 (1959), 209-230.

Chazan, R., 'Confrontation in the Synagogue of Narbonne: A Christian Sermon and a Jewish Reply', *Harvard Theological Review*, 67 (1974), 437-457.

Chazan, R., 'The Barcelona 'Disputation' of 1263: Christian Missionising and Jewish Response', *Speculum*, 52 (1977), 824-842.

Chazan, R., 'From Friar Paul to Friar Raymond: Development of Innovative Missionising Arguments', *Harvard Theological Review*, 73: 3 (1985), 289-306.

Chazan, R., *European Jewry and the First Crusade* (Berkeley, 1987).

Chazan, R., *Daggers of Faith: Thirteenth-Century Christian Missionising and Jewish Response* (Berkeley, 1989).

Chazan, R., *Barcelona and Beyond: The Disputation of 1263 and its Aftermath* (Berkeley, 1992).

Chenu, M.-D., *La Théologie au Douzième Siècle* (Paris, 1957).

Chenu, M.-D., *Toward Understanding St Thomas*, trans. by A. M. Landry and D. Hughes (Chicago, 1964).

Chenu, M.-D., *Nature, Man and Society in the Twelfth Century: Essays On New Theological Perspectives in the Latin West* (Chicago, 1968).

Clanchy, M. T., 'Abelard's Mochary of St Anselm', *Journal of Ecclesiastical History*, 41: 1 (1990), 1-23.

Clanchy, M. T., *From Memory to Written Record: England, 1066-1307*, 2nd ed. (Oxford, 1993).

Clayton, J. P., 'Religions, Reasons and Gods', *Religious Studies*, 23 (1987), 1-17.

Clayton, J. P., 'Piety and the Proofs', *Religious Studies*, 26 (1990), 19-42.

Clayton, J. P., *Thomas Jefferson and the Study of Religion* (Lancaster, 1992).

Clayton, J. P., 'The Otherness of Anselm', in *Neue Zeitschrift Für Systematische Theologie und Religionsphilosophie*, 37 (1995), 125-143.

Cobban, A. B., *The Medieval Universities: Their Development and Organisation* (New York; 1975).

Cobban, A. B., *The Medieval English Universities: Oxford and Cambridge to 1500* (Aldershot, 1991).

Cohen, J., *The Friars and The Jews* (Cornell, 1982).

Cohn, N., *The Pursuit of the Millennium* (London, 1957).

Colish, M. L., *Peter Lombard*, 2 vols (Leiden, 1994).

Collinge, W., 'Monastic life as a Context For a Religious Understanding in St Anselm', *American Benedictine Review*, 35: 4 (1984), 378-388.

Copleston, F. C., *Aquinas* (New York, 1955).

Copleston, F. C., *A History of Medieval Philosophy* (London, 1972).

Cousins, E. H., 'The Coincidence of Opposites In the Christology of Saint Bonaventure', *Franciscan Studies*, 28 (1968), 27-45.

Cousins, E. H., *Bonaventure* (New York, 1978).

Cousins, E. H., 'Francis of Assisi: Christian Mysticism at the Crossroads', in S. T. Katz, *Mysticism and Religious Traditions* (Oxford, 1983), pp. 163-190.

Crowe, M. B., 'St Thomas Against The Gentiles', *Irish Theological Quarterly*, 29 (1962), 93-120.

Crowe, M. B., 'Peter of Ireland: Aquinas's Teacher of the Artes Liberales', in *Arts Libéraux et Philosophie au Moyen Age, Actes du Quatrième Congrès international de philosophie Médiévale* (Montréal; Paris, 1969), pp. 617-626.

Cutler, A. H. and Cutler, H. E., *The Jew as Ally of the Muslim: The Medieval Roots of Anti-Semitism* (Notre Dame, 1986).

Dales, R. C., 'The Influence of Grosseteste's *Hexaëmeron* on the Sentence commentaries of Richard Fishacre, O.P., and Richard Rufus of Cornwall O.F.M.', *Viator*, 2 (1971), 271-300.

Dales, R. C., 'A Twelfth-Century Concept of Natural Order', *Viator*, 9 (1978), 179-192.

Dales, R. C., *Medieval Discussions of the Eternity of the World* (New York, 1990).

Daly, L. J., *The Medieval University, 1200-1400* (New York, 1961).

Daniel, E. R., *The Franciscan Concept of Mission in The High Middle Ages* (Kentucky, 1975).

Daniel, N., *Islam and the West: the Making of an Image* (Edinburgh, 1960).

Daniel, N., *Islam, Europe and Empire* (Edinburgh, 1966).

Daniels, P. A., *Quellenbeiträge und Untersuchungen zur Geschichte der Gottesbeweise im Dreizehenten Jarhundert* (Münster, 1909).

Davies, B., *The Thought of St Thomas Aquinas* (Oxford, 1992).

Davies, O., *Meister Eckhart: Mystical Theologian* (London, 1991).

Dawson, C., *The Mongol Mission: Narratives and Letters of the Franciscan Missionaries in Mongolia and China in the Thirteenth and Fourteenth Centuries* (London, 1955).

De Wulf, M., *History of Mediaeval Philosophy*, trans. by E. C. Messenger (London-New York, 1926).

Dod, B. G. 'Aristoteles Latinus', in *The Cambridge History of Later Medieval Philosophy*, ed. by N. Kretzmann et al. (Cambridge, 1982), pp. 45-79.

Doucet, V., 'The History of the Problem of The Authenticity of the Summa', *Franciscan Studies*, 7 (1947), 26-41, 274-312.

Doucet, V., 'A Travers Le Manuscrit 434 de Douai', *Antonianum*, 27 (1952), 531-580.

Doucet, V., 'Commentaires sur les Sentences. Supplément au Répertoire de M. Frédéric Stegmueller', *Archivum Franciscanum Historicum*, 47 (1954), 88-170; 400-427.

Douie, D. L., *Archbishop Pecham* (Oxford, 1952).

Douie, D. L., *The Conflict Between The Seculars and the Mendicants at The University of Paris in the Thirteenth Century* (London, 1954).

Dovais, C., *Essai Sur l'Organisation des Études dans l'Ordre des Frères Prêcheurs au XIIIe et au XIVe Siècle (1216-1342)* (Paris, 1884).

Dronke, P. (ed.), *A History of Twelfth-Century Western Philosophy* (Cambridge, 1988).

Dunphy, W. B., 'The Five Ways and Some Parisian Professors of Philosophy', in *St Thomas Aquinas 1274-1974, Commemorative Studies*, ed. by É. Gilson (Toronto, 1974), pp. 73-104.

Edwards, J., 'Mission and Inquisition Among "Conversos" and "Moriscos" in Spain, 1250-1550', in *Persecution and Toleration*, ed. by W. J. Sheils in Studies in Church History, xxi (Oxford, 1984), pp. 139-151.

Edwards, J., 'Religious Faith and Doubt in Late Medieval Spain: Soria c. 1450-1500', *Past and Present*, 120 (1988), 3-25.

Ehrle, F., 'S. Dominico, Le Origini del Primo Studio Generale del suo Ordine a Parigi e La Somma Teologia del Primo Maestro, Rolando da Cremona', *Miscellanea Dominicana*, 1 (1924), 85-134.

Elder, E. R. (ed.), *From Cloister to Classroom: Monastic and Scholastic Approaches to Truth. The Spirituality of Western Christendom* (Michigan, 1986), III.

Emden, A. B., *A Biographical Register of the University of Oxford to A.D. 1500*, 3 vols (Oxford, 1957-1959).

Emden, A. B., *A Biographical Register of the University of Cambridge to 1500* (Cambridge, 1963).

Evans, G. R., 'St Anselm and Knowing God', *Journal of Theological Studies*, n.s., 28: 2 (1977), 430-444.

Evans, G. R., *Anselm and Talking About God* (Oxford, 1978).

Evans, G. R., *Anselm and a New Generation* (Oxford, 1980).

Evans, G. R., *Old Arts and New Theology: The Beginnings of Theology as an Academic Discipline* (Oxford, 1980).

Febvre, L., *Le Problème de L'Incroyance au XVIe Siècle* (Paris, 1949).

Felder, H., *Histoire des Études dans L'Ordre de S. Francois*, trans. into French by E. de Bar-Le-Duc (Paris, 1908; 1st pub. in 1904).

Fisher, J., 'Hugh of St Cher and The Development of Medieval Theology', *Speculum*, 31 (1956), 57-69.

Gabriel, A. L., *Garlandia; Studies in the History of the Mediaeval University* (Notre Dame, 1969).

Gál, G., 'Viae ad Exsistentiam Dei Probandam in Doctrina Richardi Rufi, O.F.M.', *Franziskanische Studien*, 38 (1970), 177-202.

Gál, G., 'Opiniones Richard Rufi Cornubiensis a Censore Reprobatae', *Franciscan Studies*, 35: 13 (1975), 136-193.

Galbraith, G. R., *The Constitutions of the Dominican Order 1216-1360* (Manchester, 1925).

Gaskin, J. C. A., *Varieties of Unbelief* (London, 1989).

Gauthier, R.-A., O.P., *Saint Thomas d'Aquin, 'Somme contre Les Gentils': Introduction* (Editions Universitaires, 1993).

Gayyba, B. P., *Aspects of the Mediaeval History of Theology* (Pretoria, 1988).

Ghellinck, J. de, *Le Mouvement Théologique du XIIe Siécle* (Paris, 1914).

Giddens, A., *The Consequences of Modernity* (Stanford, 1990).

Gieben, S. 'Traces of God in Nature according to Robert Grosseteste: with the text of the Dictum "Omnis creatura speculum est"', *Franciscan Studies*, 24 (1964), 144-158.

Gilson, É., 'Saint Bonaventure et L'Évidence de L'Existence de Dieu', *Revue Néoscholastique de Philosophie*, 25 (1923), 237-262.

Gilson, É., *The Philosophy of St Thomas Aquinas*, trans. by E. Bullough (Cambridge, 1929).

Gilson, É., *The Spirit of Mediaeval Philosophy* (New York; London, 1936).

Gilson, É., *The Philosophy of St Bonaventure* (London, 1940).

Gilson, É., *Elements of Christian Philosophy* (New York, 1960).

Gilson, É. (ed.), *St Thomas Aquinas 1274-1974, Commemorative Studies* (Toronto, 1974).

Gilson, É., *History of Christian Philosophy in the Middle Ages*, 3rd edition (London, 1978).

Glorieux, P., *Répertoire Des Maîtres en Théologie de Paris au XIIIe siècle*, 2 vols (Paris, 1933).

Glorieux, P., *La Littérature Quodlibétique de 1260 à 1320*, 2 vols (Paris, 1935).

Glorieux, P., 'Les 572 Questions du manuscrit de Dovai 434', *Recherches de Théologie Ancienne et Médiévale*, 10 (1938), 123-152; 225-267.

Glorieux, P., 'L'Enseignment en Usage a La Faculté de Theologie de Paris au XIIIe Siècle', *Archives d' Histoire Doctrinale et Litteraire du Moyen Âge*, 35 (1969), 65-186.

Gollnick, J. I., 'The Monastic-Devotional Context of Anselm of Canterbury's Theology', *Monastic Studies*, 12 (1976), 239-248.

Gorce, M. M., 'La Lutte Contra Gentiles â Paris au XIIIe siècle', in *Mélanges Mandonnet*, 2 vols, in *Bibliothéque Thomiste*, 13-14 (Paris, 1930), pp. 223-243.

Grabmann, M., 'Der *Liber de Exemplis Naturalibus* des Franziskanertehologen Servasanctus', *Franziskanische Studien*, 7 (1920), 85-117.

Graham, W., *Beyond the Written Word* (Cambridge, 1987).

Grant, E., 'The effect of the condemnation of 1277', in *The Cambridge History of Later Medieval Philosophy*, ed. by N. Kretzmann, et al. (Cambridge, 1982), pp. 537-539.

Gratien, B., *Histoire de la Fondation et de l'Evolution de l'Ordre des Frères Mineurs au XIII Siècle* (Paris, 1928).

Grunwald, G., *Geschichte der Gottesbeweise im Mittelalter bis zum Ausgang der Hochscholastic* (Münster, 1907).

Hackett, J. M. G., 'The Attitude of Roger Bacon to the *Scientia* of Albertus Magnus', in *Albertus Magnus and The Sciences*, ed. by J. A. Weisheipl (Toronto, 1980), pp. 53-71.

Hankey, W. J., *God in Himself: Aquinas' Doctrine of God as Expounded in the Summa Theologiae* (Oxford, 1987).

Harris, C. S. R., *Duns Scotus*, 2 vols (New York, 1959).

Hartshorne, C., *Anselm's Discovery* (La Salle, 1965).

Haskins, C. H., 'Science at the Court of Emperor Frederick II', in idem, *History of Mediaeval Science* (Cambridge MA, 1924), pp. 242-271.

Henquinet, F. M., 'Les Manuscrits et l'Influence des Écrits Théologiques d'Eudes Rigaud O.F.M.', *Recherches de Théogie Ancienne et Médiévale*, 11 (1940), 324-350.

Henquinet, F. M., 'Eudes de Rosny O.F.M., Eudes Rigaud et la Somme d' Alexandre de Halès', *Archivum Franciscanum Historicum*, 33 (1940), 3-54.

Henry, D. P., *The Logic of Saint Anselm* (Oxford, 1967).

Henry, D. P., *Medieval Logic and Metaphysics: A Modern Introduction* (London, 1972).

Hess, C. R., 'Roland of Cremona's Place in the Current of Thought', *Angelicum*, 45 (1968), 429-477.

Hick, J. and McGill, A. C., *The Many-Faced Argument* (London, 1968).

Highfield, R., 'Christians, Jews and Muslims in The Same Society: the Fall of "Convivencia" in Mediaeval Spain', *Studies in Church History*, 15 (1978), 121-146.

Hinnebusch, W. A., *A History of the Dominican Order I: Origins and Growth to 1500* (New York, 1966).

Hissette, R., *Enquête sur les 219 Articles condamnés á Paris Le 7 Mars 1277* (Louvain, Paris, 1977).

Hopkins, J., *A Companion to the Study of St Anselm* (Minneapolis, 1972).

Huber, R. M., 'Alexander of Hales, O.F.M.; His Life and Influence on Medieval Scholasticism', *Franciscan Studies*, 5 (1945), 353-365.

Humphreys, K. W., *The Book Provisions of The Medieval Friars, 1215-1400* (Amsterdam, 1964).

Hunt, R. W. et al., *Studies in Medieval History Presented to F. M. Powicke* (Oxford).

Hunt, R. W., *The Schools and the Cloister: The Life and Writings of Alexander Nequam (1157-1217)*, ed. and rev. by M. T. Gibson (Oxford, 1984).

Jarrett, B. (ed.), *Lives of the Brethren of the Order of Preachers 1206-1259*, trans. by J. P. Conway (London, 1956).

Johnson, H. J., '"Contra Anselmum" But "Contra Gentiles": Aquinas's Rejection of the Ontological Argument', *Schede Medievali*, 13 (1986), pp. 18-27.

Jones, C. et al. (eds), *The Study of Spirituality* (Cambridge, 1986).

Jones, W. R., 'Franciscan Education and Monastic Libraries; Some Documents', *Traditio*, 30 (1974), 435-445.

Jordan, M. D., 'The Controversy of the *Correctoria* and the Limits of Metaphysics', in *Speculum*, 57, 2 (1982), 292-314.

Kaeppelli, T., *Scriptores Ordinis Praedicatorum Medii Aevi*, 4 vols (Rome, 1970-1993).

Katz, S. T., *Mysticism and Religious Traditions* (Oxford, 1983).

Keane, K. P., 'The Logic of Self-Diffusive Goodness in the Trinitarian Theory of the Summa Fratris Alexandri' (unpublished doctoral thesis, Fordham University, 1978).

Kedar, N., *Crusade and Mission: European Approaches to the Muslims* (Princeton, 1984).

Kelly, J. N. D., *The Oxford Dictionary of Popes* (Oxford, 1986).

Kenny, A., *The Five Ways: St Thomas Aquinas' Proofs of God's Existence* (New York, 1969).

Klocker, H. R., 'Bonaventure's Refinement of the Ontological Argument', *Mediaevalia*, 4 (1978), 209-223.

Knowles, D., *The Religious Orders in England*, 3 vols (Cambridge, 1948-1959).

Knowles, D., *The Monastic Orders in England 940-1216* (Cambridge, 1963).

Kors, A. C., *Atheism in France, 1650-1729* (Princeton, 1990).

Krailsheimer, A. J., *Rabelais and the Franciscans* (Oxford, 1963).

Kretzmann, N. et al. (eds), *The Cambridge History of Later Medieval Philosophy* (Cambridge, 1982).

Kretzmann, N., *The Metaphysics of Theism: Aquinas's Natural Theology in "Summa contra gentiles I"* (Oxford, 1997).

Kretzmann, N. and Stump, E. (eds), *The Cambridge Companion to Aquinas* (Cambridge, 1994).

Lambert, M. D., *Franciscan Poverty* (London, 1961).

Landgraf, A. M., 'The first Sentence Commentary of Early Scholasticism', *New Scholasticism*, 13 (1939), 101-132.

Landgraf, A. M., *Introduction à l'Histoire de la Littérature Théologique de la Scholastique Naissante* (Montreal; Paris, 1973).

Langmuir, G., *History, Religion, and Anti-Semitism* (Berkeley, 1990).

Langmuir, G., *Toward a Definition of Anti-Semitism* (Berkeley, 1990).

Lawn, B., *The Rise and Decline of The Scholastic 'Quaestio Disputata'* (Brill, 1993).

Lawrence, C. H., 'Stephen Lexington and Cistercian University Studies in The Thirteenth Century', *Journal of Ecclesiastical History*, 11 (1960), 163-178.

Lawrence, C. H., 'The Letters of Adam Marsh and the Franciscan school at Oxford', *Journal of Ecclesiastical History*, 42, 2 (1991), 218-238.

Lawrence, C. H., *The Friars* (New York, 1994).

Le Goff, J., *Intellectuals in the Middle Ages* (Blackwell, 1993).

Le Patourel, J., *The Norman Empire* (London, 1976).

Leclercq, J., *The Love of Learning and the Desire For God* (New York, 1960).

Leclercq, J. 'The Renewal of Theology', in Benson, R. L. et al., *Renaissance and Renewal in The Twelfth Century* (Oxford, 1982), pp. 68-87.

Leff, G., *Heresy in the Later Middle Ages*, 2 vols (Manchester, 1967).

Leff, G., *Paris and Oxford Universities in the Thirteenth and Fourteenth Centuries. An Institutional and Intellectual History* (New York, 1968).

Lewicki, J., 'Saint Anselme et les Doctrines des Cisterciens Du XIIe Siècle', in *Analecta Anselmiana*, 2 (1970), 209-216.

Libera, A. de, 'Logic et Existence Selon Saint Albert le Grand', *Archives de Philosophie*, 43, 4 (1980), 529-558.

Libera, A. de, 'Ulrich de Strasbourg, Lecteur d'Albert le Grand', *Freiburger Zeitschrift für Philosophie und Theologie*, 32 (1985), 105-136.

Little, A. G., *The Grey Friars in Oxford* (Oxford, 1892).

Little, A. G., 'Educational Organisation of the Mendicant Friars in England', *Transactions of the Royal Historical Society*, n.s. 8 (1917), 49-70.

Little, A. G., *Studies in English Franciscan History* (Manchester, 1917).

Little, A. G., 'Theological schools in Medieval England', *English Historical Review*, 55 (1940), 624-630.

Little, A. G., *Franciscan Papers, Lists and Documents* (Manchester, 1943).

Little, A. G., 'Roger Bacon', in Idem, *Franciscans Papers*, pp. 72-93.

Little, A. G., 'The Franciscan School at Oxford', in Idem, *Franciscan Papers*, pp. 55-71.

Little, A. G., 'Thomas Docking', in Idem, *Franciscan Papers*, pp. 98-121.

Little, A. G., 'The Friars and the Foundation of the Faculty of Theology in the University of Cambridge', in Idem, *Franciscan Papers*, pp. 122-143.

Little, A. G., and Pelster, F., *Oxford Theology and Theologians, 1282-1302* (Oxford, 1934).

Long, R. J., 'The Science of Theology According to Richard Fishacre', *Medieval Studies*, 34 (1972), 71-98.

Long, R. J., 'Richard Fishacre's Way to God', in *A Straight Path, Studies in Medieval Philosophy and Culture*, ed. by R. Link-Salinger (Washington, 1988) 174-182.

Longpré, E., 'Fr. Thomas d' York, O.F.M.: La Première Somme Métaphysique du XIIIe Siècle', *Archivum Franciscanum Historicum*, 19 (1926), 875-930.

Lottin, D. O., 'Roland de Crémone et Hugues de Saint-Cher', *Recherches de Théologie Ancienne et Médiévale*, 12 (1940), 136-144.

Louth, A., *The Origins of the Christian Mystical Tradition, from Plato to Denys* (Oxford, 1981).

Luscombe, D. E., *The School of Peter Abelard* (Cambridge, 1969).

Lynch, K. F., 'Some Fontes of the Commentary of Hugh de Saint Cher: William of Auxerre, Guy d'Orchelles, Alexander of Hales', *Franciscan Studies*, 13, 2-3 (1953), 119-146.

Lynch, L. E., 'The Doctrine of Divine Ideas and Illumination in Robert Grosseteste, Bishop of Lincoln', in *Medieval Studies*, 3 (1941), 161-173.

MacIntyre, A., *After Virtue: a Study in Moral Theory* (London, 1981).

MacIntyre, A., 'The Relationship of Philosophy to its Past', in *Philosophy in History*, ed. by R. Rorty, et al. (Cambridge, 1984), pp. 31-48.

MacIntyre, A., *Whose Justice? Which Rationality?* (London, 1988).

MacIntyre, A., *Three Rival Versions of Moral Inquiry: Encyclopaedia, Genealogy, and Tradition* (London, 1990).

MacIntyre, A., *Dependent Rational Animals: Why Human Beings Need the Virtues* (London, 1999).

Makdisi, G., 'The Scholastic Method in Medieval Education: An Inquiry into its Origins in Law and Theology', *Speculum*, 49 (1974), 640-661.

Mandonnet, P. F., *St Dominic and His Work* (St Louis; London, 1944).

Marenbon, J., *Later Medieval Philosophy 1150-1350* (London; New York, 1991).

Martin, C. J. F., *An Introduction to Medieval Philosophy* (Edinburgh, 1996).

Mathias, T. R., 'Bonaventurean Ways to God Through Reason', *Franciscan Studies*, 36: 14 (1976), 192-232.

Maurer, A., *On Being and Essence* (Toronto, 1949).

McEvoy, J., *The Philosophy of Robert Grosseteste* (Oxford, 1982).

McGill, A., 'Recent discussions of Anselm's argument', in *The Many-Faced Argument*, ed. by J. Hick and A. C. McGill (MacMillan, 1968).

McIntyre, J., *St Anselm and His Critics* (Edinburgh, 1954).

McKeon, P. R., 'The Status of the University of Paris as Parens Scientiarum: an Episode in the Development of its Autonomy', *Speculum*, 39 (1964), 651-675.

McLean, G. E. (ed.), *Thomas and Bonaventure. A Septicentenary Commemoration.* Proceedings of the American Catholic Philosophical Association, 48 (Washington, 1974).

McSweeney, B., *Roman Catholicism: The Search for Relevance* (Oxford, 1989).

Melani, G., 'Servasanto da Faenza', in *Enciclopedia Cattolica* (Vaticano, 1953), xi, col. 403-404.

Moore, R. I., *The Birth of Popular Heresy* (London, 1975).

Moore, R. I., *The Origins of European Dissent* (Toronto, 1994, 1st pub. in 1977).

Moore, R. I., *The Formation of a Persecuting Society: Power and Deviance in Western Europe, 950-1250* (Oxford, 1987).

Moorman, J. R. H., *The Sources for the Life of St Francis of Assisi* (Manchester, 1940).

Moorman, J. R. H., 'The Foreign Element Among the English Franciscans', *English Historical Review*, 62 (1947), 289-303.

Moorman, J. R. H., *A History of the Franciscan Order from its Origins to the Year 1517* (Oxford, 1968).

Moorman, J. R. H., *Richest of Poor Men: The Spirituality of St Francis of Assisi* (London, 1982).

Morris, C. *The Discovery of the Individual, 1050-1200* (London, 1972).

Morris, C. 'Individualism in Twelfth Century Religion: Some Further Reflections', in *Journal of Ecclesiastical History*, vol. 31, no. 2. (1980), 195-206.

Muldoon, J., *Popes, Lawyers, and Infidels: The Church and the Non-Christian World 1250-1550* (Philadelphia, 1979).

Muldoon, J. 'The Nature of the Infidel: The Anthropology of the Canon Lawyers', in *Discovering New Worlds: Essays on Medieval Exploration and Imagination*, ed. by S. D. Westrem (New York; London, 1991), pp. 115-124.

Muller, J. P., *Le Correctorium Corruptorii "Quaestione": Texte Anonyme du Ms Merton 267* (Rome, 1954).

Murphy, T., 'The Date and Purpose of The *Contra Gentiles*', *Heythrop Journal*, 10 (1969), 405-415.

Murray, A., 'Piety and Impiety in Thirteenth-Century Italy', *Studies in Church History*, VIII (1962), pp. 83-106.

Murray, A., 'Confession as a Historical Source in the Thirteenth Century', in *The Writings of History in the Middle Ages* ed. by R. H. C. Davis and J. M. Wallce-Hadrill (Oxford, 1981), pp. 275-322.

Murray, A., 'The Epicureans', in *Intellectuals and Writiers in Fourteenth-Century Europe*, ed. P. Boitani (Cambridge, 1986), pp. 138-163.

Nelson, J., 'Society, Theodicy and the origins of heresy: towards a reassessment of the medieval evidence', in D. Baker (ed.), *Schism, Heresy and Religious Protest*, ed. by D. Baker, Studies in Church History, IX (Cambridge, 1972), pp. 65-77.

Newell, J., 'Rationalism at the School of Chartres', *Vivarium*, 21, 2 (1983), 108-126.

Nimmo, D., *Reform and Division in the Franciscan Order* (Rome, 1987).

Nozick, R., *The Nature of Rationality* (Princeton, 1993).

O'Meara, T. F., 'Thomas Aquinas and German Intellectuals: Neoscholasticism and Modernity in the Late Nineteenth Century', *Gregorianum*, 68: 3-4 (1987), 719-736.

Oliger, P. L., 'Servasanto da Faenza O.F.M. e il suo *Liber de Virtutibus et Vitiis*', in *Miscellanea Dominicana*, ed. by F. Ehrle (Roma, 1924), I, pp. 148-189.

Owens, J., *St Thomas Aquinas on the Existence of God: Collected Papers of Joseph Owens, C.Ss.R.*, ed. by J. R. Catan (Albany, 1980).

Owens, J., 'Aquinas on Knowing Existence', in Idem, *St Thomas Aquinas*, pp. 20-33.

Owens, J., 'Aquinas on the Five Ways', in Idem, *St Thomas Aquinas*, pp. 132-141.

Owens, 'J., 'Faith, ideas, illumination, and experience', in *The Cambridge History of Later Medieval Philosophy*, ed. by N. Kretzmann, et al. (Cambridge, 1982), pp. 440-459, 448.

Owens, J. 'Aristotle and Aquinas', in *The Cambridge Companion to Aquinas*, ed. by N. Kretzmann and E. Stump (Cambridge, 1993), pp. 38-59.

Pegis, A. C., 'St Bonaventure, St Francis and Philosophy', *Medieval Studies*, 15 (1959), 1-13.

Pegis, A. C., 'St Anselm and the Argument of the *Proslogion*', *Medieval Studies*, 28 (1966), 228-267.

Pegis, A. C., 'The Bonaventurean Way to God', *Medieval Studies*, 29 (1967), 206-242.

Pegis, A. C., 'Toward a New Way to God: Henry of Ghent', *Medieval Studies*, 30 (1968), 226-247.

Pegis, A. C., 'Toward a New Way to God: Henry of Ghent (II)', *Medieval Studies*, 31 (1969), 67-117.

Pegis, A. C., 'Four Medieval Ways to God', in *The Monist*, 54 (1970), 317-358.

Pegis, A. C., 'Toward a New Way to God: Henry of Ghent (III)', in *Medieval Studies*, 33 (1971), 158-179.

Pegis, A. C., 'St Thomas and the Coherence of the Aristotelian Theology', in *Medieval Studies*, 35 (1973), 67-117.

Pegis, A. C., *St Thomas and the Problem of The Soul in the Thirteenth Century* (Toronto, 1976).

Pergamo, B., 'De Quaestionibus Ineditis Fr. Odonis Rigaldi, Fr: Gulielmi de Melitona et Codicis Vat Lat. 782 circa Naturam Theologiae deque earum Relatione ad Summam Theologicam Fr. Alexandri Halensis', in *Archivum Franciscanum Historicum*, 29 (1936), 3-54, 308-364.

Post, G., 'Alexander III, the Licentia Docendi and the Rise of the Universities', in *Anniversary Essays in Medieval History by Students of Charles Homer Haskins* (Boston, 1929), pp. 255-277.

Post, G., 'Parisian Masters as a Corporation, 1200-1246', *Speculum*, 9 (1934), 421-445.

Powicke, F. M., *Ways of Medieval Life and Thought* (London, 1949).

Powicke, F. M., 'Oxford', in Idem, *Ways of Medieval Life*, pp. 213-229.

Powicke, F. M., 'Bologna, Paris, Oxford: Three Studia Generalia', in Idem, *Ways of Medieval Life*, pp. 149-179.

Powicke, F. M., 'The Medieval University in Church and Society', in Idem, *Ways of Medieval Life*, pp. 198-212.

Pride, E.P., 'Ecclesiastical legislation on Education, A.D. 300-1200', *Church History*, 12:4 (1943), 235-254.

Principe, W. H., *The Theology of the Hypostatic Union in the Early Thirteenth Century*, 3 vols (Toronto, 1963, 1967, 1970).

Principe, W. H., 'Odo Rigaldus, a Precursor of St Bonaventure on the Holy Spirit as "Effectus Formalis" in the Mutual Love of the Father and the Son', *Medieval Studies*, 39 (1977), 498-505.

Quinn, J. F., 'Chronology of St Bonaventure (1217-74)', *Franciscan Studies*, 22 (1972), 168-186.

Quinn, J. F., *The Historical Constitution of St Bonaventure's Philosophy* (Toronto, 1973).

Quinn, J. F., 'Certitude of Reason and Faith in St Bonaventure and St Thomas', in *St Thomas Aquinas 1274-1974, Commemorative Studies*, ed. by É. Gilson (Toronto, 1974), pp. 105-140.

Raedts, P., *Richard Rufus of Cornwall and the Tradition of Oxford Theology* (Oxford, 1987).

Rahman, F., 'Islam: An Overview', in *Encyclopaedia of Religion*, ed. by M. Eliade, 16 vols (New York; London 1987), VII, 303-322.

Raitt, J., et al. (eds), *Christian Spirituality; The High Middle Ages and Reformation* (London, 1987).

Rashdall, H., *The Universities of Europe in the Middle Ages*, rev. and ed. by F. M. Powicke and A. B. Emden, 3 vols (Oxford, 1987, 1st pub. in 1936).

Reeves, M., *The Influence of Prophecy in the Later Middle Ages. A study in Joachimism* (Oxford, 1969).

Reidl, J. O., 'Bonaventure's Commentary on Dionysius' "Mystical Theology"', in *Thomas and Bonaventure: A Septicentenary Commemoration*, ed. by G. E. McLean, Proceedings of the American Catholic Philosophical Association, 48 (Washington, 1974), pp. 266-276.

Reynolds, S., 'Social Mentalities and the Case of Medieval Scepticism', *Transactions of the Royal Historical Society*, 6th ser., 1 (1991), 21-41.

Robson, M. J. P., 'Saint Anselm's Influence Upon Saint Bonaventure's Theology of Redemption' (unpublished Ph.D. thesis, University of Cambridge, 1988).

Roensch, F. J., *Early Thomistic School* (Dubuque, 1964).

Roggen, H., 'Saint Bonaventure Comme "le Second Fondateur" de l'Ordre des Frères Mineurs?', *Franziskanische Studien*, 49 (1967), 259-271.

Rorty, R., *Philosophy and the Mirror of Nature* (Oxford, 1980).

Rorty, R., et al. (eds), *Philosophy in History: Essays on the Historiography of Philosophy* (Cambridge, 1984).

Rouse R. H. and Rouse, M. A., '*Statim invenire*: Schools, Preachers, and New Attitudes to the Page', in *Renaissance and Renewal in the Twelfth Century*, ed. by R. L. Benson, et al. (Harvard, 1982), pp. 201-228.

Salman, D., 'Sur la Lutte "Contra Gentiles" de Saint Thomas', *Divus Thomas*, 40 (1937), 489-509.

Schufrieder, G., *An Introduction to Anselm's Argument* (Philadelphia, 1978).

Schufrieder, G., *Confessions of a Rational Mystic: Anselm's Early Writings* (Indiana, 1994).

Scruton, R., *A Short History of Modern Philosophy*, 2nd ed. (London; New York, 1995).

Sharp, D. E., *Franciscan Philosophy at Oxford in the Thirteenth Century* (Oxford, 1930).

Sheehan, M. W., 'The Religious Orders 1220-1370', in *The History of The University of Oxford*, ed. by J. I. Catto (Oxford, 1984), I, pp. 193-221.

Sighart, J., *Albert the Great, O.P.: His Life and Scholastic Labours* (New York, 1932).

Smalley, B., 'Robert Bacon and the Early Dominican School at Oxford', *Transactions of the Royal Historical Society*, 4th Ser., 30 (1948), 1-19.

Smalley, B., 'The Questiones of Simon Hinton', in *Studies in Medieval History Presented to F. M. Powicke*, ed. by R. W. Hunt et al. (Oxford, 1948), pp. 209-222.

Smalley, B., *The Study of the Bible in the Middle Ages* (Oxford, 1952).

Smart, N., *World Religions: A Dialogue* (Pelican, 1966).

Smith, C. E., *The University of Toulouse in The Middle Ages: Its Origins and Growth to 1500 A.D.* (Milwaukee, 1958).

Sordel, D., *Medieval Islam* (London and New York, 1979).

Southern, R. W., 'St Anselm and his English Pupils', *Medieval and Renaissance Studies*, 1 (1941), 14-17.

Southern, R. W., *Western Views of Islam in the Middle Ages* (Cambridge, 1962).

Southern, R. W., *Saint Anselm and His Biographer: a Study in Monastic Life and Thought* (Cambridge, 1963).

Southern, R. W., *Medieval Humanism and Other Studies* (Oxford, 1970).

Southern, R. W., *Western Society and the Church in the Middle Ages* (London, 1970).

Southern, R. W., 'The Schools of Paris and the School of Chartres', in *Renaissance and Renewal in the Twelfth Century*, ed. by R. L. Benson et al. (Toronto, 1982), pp. 113-137.

Southern, R. W., *St Anselm: A Portrait in a Landscape* (Oxford, 1990).

Southern, R. W., *Robert Grosseteste: The Growth of An English Mind in Medieval Europe*, 2nd ed. (Oxford, 1992).

Southern, R. W., *Scholastic Humanism and the Unification of Europe* (Oxford, 1995).

Stegmüller, F., *Repertorium Commentariorum in Sententias Petri Lombardi*, 2 vols (Würzburg, 1947).

Stolz, A., 'Anselm's Theology in the Proslogion', in *The Many-Faced Argument*, ed. by J. Hick and A. C. McGill (London, 1968), pp. 183-206.

Synan, E. A., 'Brother Thomas, the Master and the Masters', in *St Thomas Aquinas 1274-1974, Commemorative Studies*, ed. by É. Gilson (Toronto, 1974), pp. 219-242.

Synan, E. A., 'Albertus Magnus and the Sciences', in *Albertus Magnus and the Sciences*, ed. by J. A. Weisheipl (Toronto, 1980), pp. 1-12.

Taylor, C., 'Philosophy and its History', in *Philosophy in History*, ed. by R. Rorty, et al. (Cambridge, 1984), pp. 17-30.

Taylor, C., *Sources of the Self* (Cambridge, 1989).

Taylor, C., *Multiculturalism*, ed. by A. Gutmann (Princeton, 1994).

Thorndike, L., *University Records and Life in the Middle Ages*, 2nd ed. (New York, 1949).

Tracy, D. (ed.), *Celebrating the Medieval Heritage: a Colloquy on the Thought of Aquinas and Bonaventure*, Journal of Religion, 58: supplement (Chicago, 1978).

Tugwell, S., *Early Dominicans* (London, 1982).

Tugwell, S., *Ways of Imperfection: An Exploration of Christian Spirituality* (London, 1984).

Tugwell, S., 'The Dominicans', in *The Study of Spirituality*, ed. by C. Jones, et al. (Cambridge, 1986), pp. 296-300.

Van Steenberghen, F., 'L'Organisation des Études au Moyen Age et ses Répercussions sur le Mouvement Philosophique', *Revue Philosophique de Louvain*, 52 (1954), 572-592.

Van Steenberghen, F., *The Philosophical Movement in The Thirteenth Century* (Edinburgh, 1955).

Van Steenberghen, F., *Introduction à L'Étude de la Philosophie Médiévale* (Louvain; Paris, 1974).

Vicaire, M.-H., *Saint Dominic and His Times*, trans. by K. Pond (New York; London, 1964).

Waddell, H., *The Wandering Scholars* (London, 1953; 1st pub. 1927).

Wakefield, W. L. and Evans, A. P. (ed. and trans.), *Heresies of the High Middle Ages* (New York, 1969).

Wakefield, W. L., 'Some Unorthodox Popular Ideas of the Thirteenth Century', *Medievalia et Humanistica*, n.s. 4 (1973), 25-35.

Ward, B., *The Prayers and Meditations of St Anselm* (London, 1973).

Weber, E., 'La Démonstration de l'Existence de Dieu chez Hervé de Nedellec et Ses Confrères Prêcheurs de Paris', *Preuve et Raisons a l'Université de Paris: Logique, Ontologie et Théologie au XIVe Siècle*, ed. by Z. Kaluza and P. Vignaux (Paris, 1984), pp. 25-41.

Weisheipl, J. A., 'Albertus Magnus and the Oxford Platonists', *American Catholic Philosophical Association*, 31 (1958), 124-139.

Weisheipl, J. A., *Thomas d'Aquino and Albert his Teacher* (Toronto, 1980).

Weisheipl, J. A. (ed.), *Albertus Magnus and the Sciences* (Toronto, 1980).

Weisheipl, J. A., 'The Life and Works of St Albert the Great', in ibid., 13-52.

Weisheipl, J. A., *Friar Thomas d' Aquino* (Washington, D. C., 1983).

Westrem, S. B., *Discovering New Worlds* (New York; London, 1991).

Wheeler, P. M., 'The Twelfth-Century School of St Victor' (Unpublished Ph.D. Thesis, University of Southern California, 1970).

Wieruszowski, H., *The Medieval University: Masters, Students, Learning* (Princeton, 1966).

Williams, R., *The Wound of Knowledge* (London, 1979).

Wippel, J. F., 'Thomas Aquinas and Participation', in *Studies in Medieval Philosophy*, ed. by J. F. Wippel (Washington, D. C., 1987), pp. 117-158.

Wolterstorff, N., 'The Migration of the Theistic Arguments: From Natural Theology to Evidentialist Apologetics', in *Rationality, Religious Belief and Moral Commitment: New Essays in the Philosophy of Religion*, ed. by R. Audi, and W. J. Wainwright (Cornell UP, 1986), pp. 38-81.

Zinn, G. A., 'Book and Word: The Victorine Background of Bonaventure's Use of Symbols', in *S. Bonaventura 1274-1974*, ed. by J. G. Bougerol, 5 vols (Grottaferrata, 1973-1974), II, 143-169.

# Index